A Future
with a History

**The Wesleyan Witness
of the
Free Methodist Church**

**1960 to 1995
and Forward**

David L. McKenna

A Future with a History
by David L. McKenna

All scripture quotations, unless otherwise indicated, are taken from the HOLY BIBLE, NEW INTERNATIONAL VERSION®. NIV®. © 1973, 1978, 1984 by International Bible Society. Used by permission of Zondervan Publishing House. All rights reserved.

ISBN 0-89367-220-3

© 1997
Light and Life Communications
Indianapolis, IN 46253-5002
Printed in the U.S.A.

Contents

Prologue
A REDEMPTIVE STORY

Part I
OUT OF THE FIRST CENTURY
Pre-1860 to 1960

Part II
INTO THE SECOND CENTURY
A Church on the Threshold

Part III
A MISSION ON THE MOVE
1960 to 1995 and Forward

Part IV
INTO THE 21ST CENTURY
The Years Ahead

Epilogue
SERVANT LEADERS OF OUR GENERATION

A Future with a History

Dedicated to:

Hugh A. and Edna C. White

Outstanding Lay Leaders
of our generation whose
vision never faded

Faithful Lovers
of their Lord, their family, and each other whose
model is exemplary

Unswerving Loyalists
to their church, from local congregation to
distant mission field, whose
imprint is indelible
and

Humble Stewards
of all their resources whose
investment is eternal

A Tribute To

Hugh A. and Edna C. White

Partners in Ministry

God gave Edna and Hugh White the gifts of creativity and generosity, which they used to serve Him in many different parts of the Free Methodist Church. Before she was married, Edna teamed up with Esther Young to teach school and pioneer Sunday schools in the Kentucky mountains. Hugh's father's ill health had caused Hugh to leave school after the eighth grade to run the family farm.

Seven years later, his father, then recovered, asked Hugh, "Would you like to go to Spring Arbor for high school?"

"I couldn't have been happier if he had said, 'Would you like to go to heaven?'" Hugh remembered.

After they were married and had two children, Edna always kept their bags packed to be ready to go wherever Hugh's job as a bank auditor took him. Edna was just as quick to respond to the Lord's call, visiting every family from the Ferndale (Michigan) Sunday school through two generations, taking food and clothes to them, along with Jesus' love. Hugh also taught in the Sunday school during all those years, leading a variety of classes from third grade boys to high school seniors.

During the Depression, the church's school at Spring Arbor ran out of money, the creditors foreclosed, and the sheriff chained the doors shut. Hugh felt the Lord telling him not to let the school go under, so he went to the bank and bought the mortgage, promising to pay it himself. Under his leadership, Spring Arbor survived the Depression and, in the '60s, became a four-year college.

Another creative idea the Lord gave Hugh was the Free Methodist World Fellowship. In the late '50s, independence movements were brewing across Africa. Hugh served for many years on the Commission on Missions, and he and Edna visited our missionaries all over the world. He developed the World Fellowship, which energized and freed the church overseas to grow so that now it is more than triple the size of its parent in America.

Hugh devised the Division of Planned Giving to help people in our church dedicate more of their resources to the Lord. He then planned for it to become the independent Free Methodist Foundation which now manages more than $110 million, channeling its funds into various Free Methodist ministries. Tracking down Edna and Hugh's giving is difficult, because they usually kept it hidden. Following the Whites' visits to mission stations and needy Free Methodist churches, money would often appear for special projects. Their gifts included the youth building and gymnasium at the Ferndale, Free Methodist church and Beta Hall, a three-story dormitory at Spring Arbor College.

Their two children and seven grandchildren have followed the example of Edna and Hugh in serving the Lord by entering the ranks of Sunday school teachers, missionaries, delegates, pastors, professors and trustees. They are trying to pass Edna and Hugh's creativity and generosity on to the 15 great-grandchildren.

— *Dr. Charles E. White,*
for the White family

Foreword

Perhaps as at no other time in its 135 years of existence, the Free Methodist Church stands at a crossroad. Stability, tradition, order, reliability and comfortable forms mark one path. In contrast, a spirit of innovation, cultural change, lowered interest in history, growth orientation and creative energy beckon for radical change. No longer will shibboleths or stories of past days satisfy the cravings of younger Christians. Nor will they satisfy the curious of the contemporary culture that question the meaning of our existence and the purpose of our mission.

In brief, the Free Methodist Church again seeks to define its soul, articulate its mission, respond to its origin and seek a fresh understanding of God's purpose for this day. At Hebron, David enjoyed the luxury of the men of Issachar who "understood the times and knew what Israel should do." We, too, look for those who understand the issues, clearly comprehend the alternatives and offer sound insight and advice.

If leadership is defined as understanding the issues and consequences better than those around them, the author of this work, Dr. David L. McKenna, comes with pristine leadership credentials. His skills of analysis coupled with his understanding of the church commend him to this task.

Ordained in the Michigan Conference (now Southern Michigan Conference) in 1952, McKenna felt the call of God to complete doctoral studies. With his academic background, serving on the faculties of Ohio State University and the University of Michigan, and burgeoning leadership skills, he became president of Spring Arbor College in 1961, where he served for seven years. Following that, he served Seattle Pacific University as president for 14 years.

In 1982 McKenna's theological ability and leadership skills resulted in his selection as the fourth president of Asbury Theological Seminary. On his watch and under his leadership occurred the most outstanding growth in the institution's history. His further contributions include scores of articles and books produced by a variety of publishers.

Seldom do unusual wisdom, superior intellect and a passionate love for the church reside in one person. All three flourish in David McKenna. His devotion to the task of "getting his hands around the amoeba of the Free Methodist Church" has provided a challenge worthy of his finest effort.

Undaunted by unexpected physical difficulties and encouraged by his jubilant and faith-filled wife, Janet, McKenna has rendered a service to his church that will inform both its loyalists and critics for decades to come.

A Future with a History: The Wesleyan Witness of the Free Methodist Church will inspire your heart, inform your mind and bring you to a clearer understanding of the exciting challenges at hand.

— *John E. Van Valin,*
Publisher

Appreciation

Publishing denominational histories requires substantial financial support. The value of such writing, however, can never be measured in currency. The effect on individuals, pastors, church workers, institutions of higher learning and the reservoir of ministerial knowledge continues for generations. An undertaking of this magnitude would have proved impossible without the generous support of many friends of the Free Methodist Church and the author Dr. David L. McKenna.

Profound gratitude is extended to:

The White Foundation
Glenn E. and Ruth Evelyn White
Charles Edward and Carol White
David Bruce and Nancy White
Nancy Elizabeth and Stuart Bergsma
for their generous, major funding of this project,

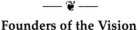

Founders of the Vision
for their significant gifts,

Marty and Bob Briner
William J. Dowley
Seattle Pacific University
Oliver J. and Leah Van Wagoner
Vera Walls

— ❧ —

Patrons of the History
for their faithful support,

Author's Preface

Bishops of the Free Methodist Church have a keen sense of history. Shortly after the turn of the century, Bishop Wilson T. Hogue chronicled the first 40 or so years of the church in two volumes entitled *History of the Free Methodist Church*. Bishop Leslie R. Marston followed in 1960 with the centennial history under the title *From Age to Age A Living Witness*. Both works are recognized for their scholarship and spirit.

Consistent with the sensitivity of their predecessors, the bishops of the church — Gerald E. Bates, David M. Foster and Richard D. Snyder — called for the writing of an updated history from 1960 to the present with a view to completion on or before the year 2000.

Knowing of my pending retirement from the presidency of Asbury Theological Seminary, the bishops invited me to be the author. As a person whose life and career in the church spans the period under study, I responded with interest in the project, but withheld a final decision until I had time for prayer, reflection and counsel. When my wife, Janet, and I talked over our priorities for retirement, we remembered how much we owe the church, love its people and care about its future. All other projects of retirement fell into second place, and we were ready to accept the bishops' invitation with a joyous "Yes."

But first we had to be assured of the resources to write a history that deserved to stand on the shelf next to the works of Hogue and Marston. Graciously and generously the family of the White Foundation provided the seed grant to initiate the project. Expertise was gained when distinguished research historians and representative church leaders responded affirmatively to an invitation for membership on the steering committee for the history. Those members are:

Gerald Bates — Bishop of the Free Methodist Church
David Bundy — Professor of Church History and Director of the
  Library at Christian Theological Seminary

Melvin Dieter — Professor Emeritus of Church History, Asbury Theological Seminary

Dwight Gregory — Superintendent of the New York Conference of the Free Methodist Church

Frances Haslam — Director of the Marston Memorial Historical Center of the Free Methodist Church

Evelyn Mottweiler — Retired Director of the Marston Memorial Historical Center of the Free Methodist Church

Richard Stephens — President Emeritus of Greenville College

Florence Taylor — Retired Administrative Assistant to the Board of Bishops of the Free Methodist Church

John Van Valin — Publisher of Light and Life Communications of the Free Methodist Church, Chairman

Robert Wood — Retired Editor of the Francis Asbury Press of Zondervan Publishing Company

To complete the team for the writing of the history, Carolyn Dock followed by Jeanne Acheson-Munos served as administrative assistants to the author and Robert Haslam and Robert Wood served as editors.

No word is adequate to express my personal gratitude to Miss Florence Taylor for her countless hours of work researching primary sources, compiling information on computer, and cross-checking the historical accuracy of the manuscript. Her encyclopedic mind is uncanny and her ability to put the flesh of firsthand experience on the skeleton of historical facts is amazing.

Publisher John Van Valin is a rarity in his field. While he must keep one eye on the marketplace and the other eye on the budget, he never lost focus of the purpose of the project nor compromised on its quality. He took risks of leadership to launch the project, remained flexible during my unexpected illness, yet kept up the "inspiration" of the publisher's deadline.

In the wisdom of Ecclesiastes 4:9 we read, "Two are better than one, because they have a good reward for their labor." In the writing of this history, "many" have proved better than one and with each of them I share the "good reward of their labor."

— *David L. McKenna*

A
Redemptive
Story

HISTORICAL PERSPECTIVE

Free Methodists are people with a story. Whenever they hear the inevitable question, "What is a *Free* Methodist?" their best answer is, "Let me tell you a story." Simply and straightforwardly, then, they can unfold the drama of Free Methodist history beginning more than 150 years ago. It is a story of epic proportions, complete with political intrigue, personal sacrifice, spiritual conflict and far-reaching social consequences. Once the story is heard, the listener will know why Free Methodists find their mission for the future in the meaning of their history.

A Story of Community

A sense of history has been lost in our secular society. Robert Bellah, in his book *Habits of the Heart*, notes that one of the greatest losses of a secular age is the richness of a "community of memory" through which people remember their past and find the foundation for a "community of hope" in the future. In their place, a secular society offers only a "community of interest" as temporary therapy for the loneliness of radical self-interest.[1]

A COMMUNITY OF INTEREST — Bellah's primary thesis in *Habits of the Heart* is that the American character is being shaped by radical individualism in a secular society. Self-interest is the motivational force that leads individuals to "be what they want to be for their own good" and "do what they want to do for their own pleasure." The reward is self-gratification, but the penalty is loneliness. Consequently, the search for community becomes therapy for isolation. Bellah writes, "In a 'community of interest,' self-interested individuals join together to maximize individual good."[2]

While adopting the language of a caring climate with such code words as "love," "intimacy," "belonging" and "identity," the fact is that the "community of interest" still perpetuates individual good in the pursuit of self-actualization. "Personal support networks" are a favored synonym for the community of interest. At best, the community of interest is a stopgap measure that may temporarily alleviate loneliness, but its memory is narrow and its hope is short.

A COMMUNITY OF MEMORY — According to Bellah, "community" is loosely used in popular language today. He sees community, however, as a strong word that means "a group of people who are socially interdependent, who participate together in discussion and decision-making and who share certain practices that both define the community and are nurtured by it."[3] As a community, they tell stories of its past, share practices of commitment to its purposes and speak a "second language" that only community members can understand. Bellah adds, "It almost always has a history and so is also a *community of memory*, defined in part by its past and its memory of its past."[4]

Because secularism literally means "this Age-ism," history becomes a handicap. All meaning is wrapped up in the present moment. Current events are celebrated as "happenings" that come and go, suffering is reported by "sound bites," and heroes rise and fall in their "fifteen minutes of fame." A "community of memory" in a secular society is a contradiction in terms.

A COMMUNITY OF HOPE — By definition, a secular society that finds all meaning in the present moment has no promise for the future. Some baby boomers, for instance, hold little hope for society but anticipate great promise for themselves. In contrast, when aspirations for the future are added to the memory bank of stories in the community of memory, Robert Bellah sees the group transformed into a "community of hope." Optimism for the future is not limited to individual aspirations. As visions for the future are collectively shared and mutually developed, a sense of contributing to the "common good" adds qualitative meaning to life. Bellah sees religion as the primary example of a community of hope. He writes,

> Religious communities, for example, do not experience time in the way the mass media presents it — as a continuous flow of qualitatively meaningless sensations. The day, the week, the season, and the year are punctuated by an alternation of the sacred and the profane. Prayer breaks into the daily life at the beginning of a meal, at the end of the day, at common worship reminding us that our utilitarian pursuits are not the whole of life, that a fulfilled life is one in which God and neighbor are remembered first.[5]

Religion, then, is the natural vehicle for a community of memory and a community of hope. With a sense of history, there is a line of continuity from the past to the present and from the present into the future.

A Story of Redemption

A secular perspective of time is a direct contradiction to the biblical time line of redemption. God's perspective in history can be understood only as a continuous thread through the glory of the past, the reality of the present and the promise of the future.

REMEMBERING THE GLORY OF THE PAST — The theme for the book of Deuteronomy is "Remember." With God's miraculous act of deliverance from slavery in Egypt, a community of memory was created for the children of Israel (Deuteronomy 5:15). Throughout their history in the wilderness of Sinai, the establishment of the kingdom, and even into their days of suffering in Babylonian exile, their guiding hope was to remember what God had done in the Exodus from Egypt.

CONFRONTING THE REALITY OF THE PRESENT — The reality of the present requires the acceptance of what William Bridges calls "old endings" and "new beginnings."[6] Some old things need to end and some new things need to begin for transformation to take place. Because the Jews became a people "stuck in place" while needs changed and revelation moved on, they missed the Messiah. During the long years of their Babylonian exile, for instance, some Jews remembered the Exodus and bewailed the silence of God in their plight. Others forgot the miracles of the past, exploited the commercial opportunities of Babylon and succumbed to the idolatry of the pagan culture. Only those who remembered the miracles of the past and repented of the sins that brought them into exile became the remnant through whom God could work again.

ANTICIPATING THE PROMISE OF THE FUTURE — To the Jews in Babylonian exile who remembered the glory of the past and confronted the reality of the present, God spoke again. He tells His people, "Forget the former things. Do not dwell upon the past. See, I am doing a new thing! Now it springs up; do you not perceive it? I am making a way in the desert and streams in the wasteland" (Isaiah 43:19).

In this revelation is our biblical perspective for history. Remembering the glory of the past, we can confront the reality of the present and anticipate the future with the promise of hope.

Free Methodism and Redemptive History

Free Methodists represent a counterculture in a secular society. They are not a church created out of a community of interest, but a company of the committed who belong to a community of memory and share a community of hope. More than that, they align themselves with the biblical time line of redemptive history. Remembering the glory of their past, they know who they are. At the same time, they know that it would be fatal to put the Free Methodist Church into a time warp in which the past cannot be distinguished from the present or the future. It would be equally fatal to succumb to the secular temptation to find all meaning in the reality of the present.

For these reasons, the movement of Free Methodism cannot be interpreted with dominance in any one era. To be biblically redemptive and historically sound, our updated history of the Free Methodist Church from 1960-1995 and forward must begin not with 1960, but with a search for roots in history that even predates the founding of the church in 1860.

Once the community of memory is established, our study can proceed to confront the reality of the present from 1960-1995. Memory and reality will not bring us to despair. Because Free Methodism has a chosen role in the biblical time line of redemption, its future can be anticipated with God's promise for a community of hope. This is the story of the people called Free Methodists.

Part I

OUT OF THE
FIRST CENTURY

Pre-1860-1960

The story of the Free Methodist Church from 1960-1995 and forward does not stand alone. To understand the church of this generation, one must pull the long thread of history that predates the founding of the Free Methodist Church in 1860 and reaches back to its roots in biblical, Christian and Wesleyan church history.

Part I searches out these historical roots as they come into focus in 1860 to define the character and mission of the Free Methodist Church. The story of the fledgling church then unfolds as naturally as the development of an individual in the life-cycle of human growth. From its birth in the trauma of severance from the mother church, Free Methodism experienced the exuberance of aggressive evangelism in its childhood years, the storm and stress of conflicting motives in its adolescence and the mixed values of a maturing denomination in its early adulthood.

Not unlike the development of the human personality, we will learn that the heredity of Wesleyan theology and the environment of Methodist organization are the dominant forces shaping the character of the Free Methodist Church in its first century. To know the story in the past is to understand Free Methodism in the present.

C H A P T E R 1

From Birth Through Childhood

Pre-1860-1893

A church, though ordained of God, is a human institution with a life cycle not unlike other living organisms. It is born to change and grow but also is subject to aging and death. Like other living organisms, the church goes through the stages of conception, birth, infancy, childhood, adolescence and early and mature adulthood in a predictable pattern of development. Between each of these stages is a transition period that usually involves some stress and strain as the living organism, or the church organization, leaves one stage and advances to another. At this crucial time, the way in which the stress of transition is handled determines whether the result is growth, stagnation or decline. Even more critically, transition is the time when the living organism, or the church organization, can become sick and possibly die. In such cases, external and drastic intervention may be required as therapy for renewal.

The difference between a healthy and an unhealthy church can also be read in the analogy of the living organism. Healthy organisms, or church organizations, direct the bulk of their energy outwardly and proactively to accomplish a task or achieve a goal. Unhealthy organisms or church organizations, in contrast, expend their energy inwardly on self-preservation or dysfunctional conflict.

Yet, there is hope. While neither living organisms nor church organizations are immortal, they can be renewed by redirecting the energy toward the external mission, particularly during a time of transition. Furthermore, health can be maintained in the living organism, or the church organization, by preventive measures to keep the direction of energy flowing outwardly.[1]

As a new perspective on the Free Methodist Church, a synopsis of its history during the first century is well-suited to the life cycle of a living organism. Through this analogy, the church can be described at each stage in its development, seen in its times of transition, analyzed for the direction of its energy and evaluated for the results of its performance. Because the Free Methodist Church is not a perfect human institution, an overview of its life cycle during the first century of its history will not only personalize its successes and its struggles, but more importantly, it will reveal its readiness in 1960 to be the Spirit-guided and mission-driven ministry envisioned by its founders.

A Reluctant Birth
Pre-1860

CONCEIVING SPIRITUAL LEADERSHIP — While the Free Methodist Church was formally born on August 23, 1860, its conception predates that event by many years. In the 1840s, a student at Wesleyan College in Connecticut named Benjamin Titus "B.T." Roberts heard the evangelist Dr. John Wesley Redfield preach during a campus revival. Although Roberts had been converted earlier and changed his career plans from law to ministry, the ministry of Redfield stirred his soul with a passion for revival that he never lost. In one sense, when the intellectually gifted and socially sensitive Roberts confessed Jesus Christ as his Lord and Savior and responded to the call to ministry, the first seeds of Free Methodism were sown.

B.T. Roberts became an aggressive witness to his faith and a fearless advocate for his convictions. Whether he knew it or not, he also embodied the principle believed by John Wesley and articulated by Charles Wesley when he prayed, "Let us unite these two, so long divided, learning and vital piety." To understand this principle of integration between learning and piety is not only to understand Wesleyan theology, it is to understand the mission and meaning of the Free Methodist Church.

B.T. Roberts met another crisis on his spiritual journey at a camp meeting in 1850, the year of his ordination, where Phoebe Palmer and her husband propounded the work of holiness. Charles E. White, who gave Palmer the title of "Grandmother of Free Methodism," described her ministry, "Mrs. Palmer's message at that camp meeting was simple: one could be endued with power from on high if he laid his all on the altar, trusted God to make him holy and then bore witness that God had kept His word. She taught that this was the entire sanctification that Wesley preached, the holiness that the Bible promised."[2]

In response to the call, B.T. Roberts testified:

Two paths were distinctly marked out for me. I saw that I might be a popular preacher, gain applause, do but a little good in reality and at last lose my soul; or I might take the narrow way, declare the whole truth as it is in Jesus, meet with persecution and opposition but see a thorough work of grace go on and gain heaven. Grace was given me to make the better choice. I deliberately gave myself anew to the Lord, to declare the whole truth as it is in Jesus and to take the narrow way. The blessing came. The Spirit fell on me in an overwhelming degree. I received a power to labor such as I had never felt before. This consecration has never been taken back.[3]

Thus inflamed by the fire of Pentecost and empowered by the filling of the Holy Spirit, B.T. Roberts took revival with him wherever he went, whether to dying congregations as a pastor or to new fields of harvest as an evangelist.

True to his Wesleyan experience, he also brought with him the moral fervor of his biblical convictions about human slavery and compassion for the poor. As Elton Smith has pointed out, Roberts was a risk taker who declared at the time of his sanctification, "Yet the determination is fixed, to obey the Lord and take the narrow way, come what will."[4] When his spiritual fervor and his moral fire combined with his pointed pen, trouble inevitably brewed in the established hierarchy of the Methodist Episcopal Church, where he served as a parish minister.

CARRYING BIBLICAL CONVICTIONS — B.T. Roberts did not intentionally incite a division in the church and among the clergy. A breech already existed between those who espoused spiritual revival in the church and those who protected the status quo of a church accommodated to the culture. But now, the fuel of name-calling flashfired the coals of controversy into open flame.

In the Genesee Conference, in New York, where B.T. Roberts served as a pastor, the ministerial ranks were already divided into factions labeled "The Buffalo Regency" (the entrenched establishment of the Genesee Conference) and "The Nazarites" (the contenders for reform in personal and social holiness). Rather than confronting the fundamental issues of doctrine, ethics, spirituality and seeking a biblical path to reconciliation, however, politics and personalities took over.

The line in the sand was drawn when B.T. Roberts wrote a paper entitled "New School Methodism," a sardonic twist on the fact that the revivalistic Nazarites had been accused of abandoning the faith of "Old School Methodism." Roberts showed his paper to George Estes, a prominent layperson, who published and circulated the article throughout the conference without the author's approval. Once the word was out, however, the point of his pen became a barb as he accused The Buffalo Regency — the ecclesiastical power brokers of the Genesee Conference — with charges of:

— subordinating devotion to beneficence in doctrine;
— combining regeneration and sanctification into one experience;
— distrusting the profession of deep Christian experience;

— displacing the class meeting, love feast and prayer meeting with social parties;
— building elaborate churches with rented pews and professional musicians to attract a fashionable audience;
— encouraging by silence, the adornment of gold and costly apparel; and
— selling pews and holding bazaars as the substitute for biblical stewardship.[5]

While these charges are necessarily stated in the negative, they contain the essence of the biblical and Wesleyan affirmations from which the Free Methodist Church was conceived.

LABORING WITH PAIN — The political conflict that raged over the next three years in the Genesee Conference illustrates how vicious ecclesiastical politics can be. Charges of "immoral and unchristian conduct unbecoming a minister" were brought against Roberts in 1857, yet he was returned to his Pekin charge with an appeal pending with the General Conference of 1860.

Although B.T. Roberts might have launched a counteroffensive of political support for his position, he chose not to follow a course that would split the church. Instead, he appealed through the established ecclesiastical process from the district to the Genesee Annual Conference. Meanwhile, suspended from the ministry and under the compulsion to preach, he made the procedural error of joining the church as a layperson and then reapplying for probationary ministerial status before the issue of his ministerial credentials was settled in the higher court.

Later, this decision would become the legal noose that would hang him, but the action itself probably reflects Roberts' naiveté in dealing with the subterfuge of a kangaroo court. His political savvy fared no better. By continuing to preach with revival results and opening himself to the charge of circulating the inflammatory article, "New School Methodism," the outcome of appeal became inevitable. At the Perry, New York, session of the Annual Conference in 1858, Roberts was expelled from ministry in the Methodist Episcopal Church along with other clergy and laity who shared his views.

The die was cast. Although Roberts, like John Wesley, never set out to found another church, the momentum of spiritual revival and social conscience could not be stopped. Church history records a fundamental fact. When the enthusiasm generated by the movement of God's Spirit is stifled within the established church, new forms for its expression will be found. Laymen's Conventions became those new forms of expression throughout New York State during the time of Roberts' appeal and after his expulsion from the Methodist Episcopal Church.

Laymen's Conventions in the East and West protested against the injustices of the Methodist clergy and particularly against the expulsions of B.T. Roberts and Joseph McCreery, clergymen whose holy lives and spiritual ministries condemned the charges as concocted and absurd. A denomination was in the making, but not by intent.

The resolution for the first Laymen's Convention in Albany, New York, in 1858 read: "We trust that none will think of leaving the church, but let us all stand by and apply the proper and legitimate remedy for the shameless outrages that have been perpetrated under the forms of justice ... We recommend Rev. B.T. Roberts and Rev. J. McCreery to travel at large and labor as opportunity presents, for promoting the work of God and the salvation of souls."[6]

In the midst of these tumultuous days, the 1860 General Conference of the Methodist Episcopal Church convened at Buffalo, stronghold of The Buffalo Regency faction.

Injustice was compounded as the General Conference:
- united in tacit support of human slavery and against the Nazarite faction;
- refused to investigate the Genesee Conference problem involving B.T. Roberts and other expelled clergypersons; and
- sustained the Genesee Conference action against Roberts by a tie vote and refused to entertain further appeals.

With all legal avenues closed and the breech irreparable, there was no recourse but the formation of a new church. Therefore, in August 1860 the invitation went out:

A Convention will be held at Pekin, for the purpose of adopting a Discipline for the Free Methodist Church, to commence at the close of the camp meeting, August 23rd. All societies and bands that find it necessary, in order to promote the prosperity and permanency of the work of holiness, to organize a Free Church on the following basis, are invited to send delegates:

1. Doctrines and usages of primitive Methodism, such as the Witness of the Spirit, Entire Sanctification as a state of grace distinct from justification, attainable instantaneously by faith. Free seats, and congregational singing, without instrumental music in all cases; plainness of dress.
2. An equal representation of ministers and members in all the councils of the Church.
3. No slaveholding, and no connection with secret and oath bound societies.

   Each society or band will be entitled to send one delegate at least; and an additional one for every forty members.[7]

BIRTHING A FREE CHURCH — In response to the call, 15 preachers and 45 laymen gathered at Pekin, New York, and vigorously debated the issue of whether or not a new church should be organized at this time. Roberts himself had been in doubt until moments before the convention opened. While sitting under an apple tree with other leaders just prior to the opening of the convention, he conceded that years of "hoping against hope" for the reform of the Methodist Episcopal Church had run their course and no alternative remained. So when Dr. John Wesley Redfield closed the debate by saying, "We are ready, and the West and East should move in this matter simultaneously," B.T. Roberts, along with two-thirds of the clergy and 40 members of the laity, voted the Free Methodist Church into being.

Was the timing right? Was the decision inevitable? Was the action schismatic? These are questions for judgment that are specifically addressed in Roberts' book *Why Another Sect* and Bowen's *Origin of the Free Methodist Church*. It is certain that B.T. Roberts never intended to found a church, and it is equally certain that justice suffered in the ecclesiastical power plays that led to his expulsion.

Small relief though it may be, in 1910 the Genesee Conference of the Methodist Episcopal Church rescinded its action and posthumously restored the credentials of B.T. Roberts. His son attended the service, graciously and honestly addressed the conference and received his father's ordination papers as the symbol of full restoration.

Like a newborn child, the Free Methodist Church entered its infancy with fervor and freedom to grow under the parenting of its first general superintendent, B.T. Roberts, who had proposed a standing committee of three to administer the new organization. Instead, the convention overruled his recommendation and elected him as their leader, to which Roberts responded, "To my surprise the choice fell on me. Lord, give me heavenly wisdom to guide me ... Let me have Thy presence and help, O God of powers!"[8]

Roberts' election symbolized the balanced spirit that prevailed at the founding of the church. His educational stature, theological understanding, journalistic discipline and ecclesiastical statesmanship served as the check and balance upon his evangelistic fervor, his experiential emphasis, his expressive preaching and his entrepreneurial vision. From its very beginning, the genius of Free Methodism has depended upon this balance.

A Prodigious Childhood
1860-1893

In the life cycle of organizations, the line from birth through childhood rises rapidly as the vision of its founder engages the commitment and mobilizes the energies of its members. Free Methodism is no exception. From the time of its founding in 1860 and through the next 30 or more years of its development, the church flourished as the B.T. Roberts' agenda for reform was implemented. Without exaggeration, it may be said that the first generation of the Free Methodist Church from 1860-1893 reflects the spirit, style and strategy of Roberts' leadership vision. In the major events of this era, we see the norms upon which Free Methodism is built.

THE MISSION OF THE CHURCH — In the 1862 *Discipline* of the church, the twofold mission of Free Methodism is declared "to maintain the biblical standard of Christianity, and to preach the gospel to the poor." In the simplicity and the clarity of this mission statement, we feel the engaging and mobilizing power that accounts for the rapid spread of early Free Methodism. Directly reflecting B.T. Roberts' convictions, the statement defines holiness in both its personal and social dimensions.

John Wesley's words can be heard again as he propounded the position, "'Holy solitaries' is a phrase no more consistent with the gospel than holy adulterers. The gospel of Christ knows of no religion but social; no holiness but social holiness."[9] Furthermore, in these words we hear again the mandate for American Methodism as given in the organizing conference of 1784, "To spread scriptural holiness across the land and reform the nation."

THE DOCTRINE OF HOLINESS — When the "Articles of Religion" for the Free Methodist Church were written, two additions were made to the doctrines of the parent church. One was the doctrine of eternal rewards and punishments, a creedal point that had been missed in the Articles but clearly taught in Methodist theology. The other addition, on the doctrine of entire sanctification, set Free Methodism apart on belief, experience and practice.

With biblical holiness specifically defined as the doctrine of entire sanctification, Free Methodism found the place to stand from which it could move its world in the growth era of its first third of a century. Leslie R. Marston sums up the significance of the doctrine when he writes, "From the event of its founding, the touchstone of Free Methodism's doctrinal integrity has been its faithfulness to the Wesleyan witness to entire sanctification as a distinct work of grace."[10]

Again, B.T. Roberts led the way with his writings on holiness which were later compiled by his son Benson H. Roberts under the title *Holiness Teachings*.[11] In sum, Roberts defined the doctrine in these principles:

1. Holiness begins in regeneration and is consummated in entire sanctification.
2. Entire sanctification is the full cleansing of man's nature and his complete surrender of every power and passion to the Spirit's control, so that all his motives are promptings of perfect love toward

27

God and all men.

3. The holiness of the entirely sanctified may be replaced by corrupting tendencies to sin again invading the nature, and these inner propensities may lead to the outward transgressions of a backslidden state.
4. The process of sanctification, either initial or entire, does not make a man less than human.
5. The core principle of holiness is perfect love to God and man.
6. "Christian perfection" is a broader term than "entire sanctification" or "perfect love," applicable to any stage of a sincere Christian's development toward full maturity.

As the "core within the core" of its founding convictions, the doctrine of holiness cannot be shunted from the center of belief and experience for Free Methodists without changing the essential character of the church.

THE EXPRESSION OF WORSHIP — Free Methodists inherited the charge of "enthusiasm" in their worship through the heritage of the Wesleys and early Methodism. When Roberts' protagonists in the Genesee Conference resorted to name-calling, they dubbed the reformers "Nazarites."

Later, at the Pekin Convention in 1860, one third of the clergy delegates, who also called themselves Nazarites or the "Nazarite Band," voted against a new organization and separated themselves from the Free Methodist Church, primarily because of their demand for fanatical freedom in worship. Rather than remaining separate, however, they set out to disrupt the worship of the new Free Methodist churches until Roberts, in his role as general superintendent, found it necessary to repudiate them publicly.[12]

Although the issue of fanaticism resurfaces time and time again throughout the early history of Free Methodism, Roberts framed a policy that guided his attitude toward freedom in worship, "We do not fear any of the spiritual manifestations of the Spirit of God ... What we want is not noisy meetings, not still meetings — but the SPIRIT OF THE LIVING GOD in all our worshipping assemblies."[13]

Balancing the freedom of expression was the formality of the sacraments, the restriction against instrumental music and professional choirs and the stability of the hymnody.

In sacraments, the Lord's Supper held first position in balancing freedom and formality. Early on, the ritual of infant baptism was also adopted along with adult baptism as a sacrament of the church. The difference is the adult's public declaration of faith while the infant, whose parents declare their faith on behalf of the child, must confirm that faith in a public declaration after conversion.

Freedom of expression in worship was further balanced by the restriction against instrumental music and professional choirs. Free Methodism's strong stance against instrumental music and professional choirs continued through the growth era from 1860-1893. At the same time, the hymnody, with the sound theological texts and singable tunes of Charles Wesley, lent order to the freedom of joyous praise.

THE EFFECTIVENESS OF EVANGELISM — Reflecting the convictions of its founder, B.T. Roberts, the Free Methodist Church declared a worldwide commitment to evangelism in the *Discipline* of 1862, "The provisions of the gospel are for all. The 'glad tidings' must be proclaimed to every individual of the human race. God sent the true light to illuminate and melt every heart. To savage and civilized, bond and free, black and white, the ignorant and learned, is freely offered this great salvation."[14]

Under the inspiration of this declaration and with the mandate of its mission statement, Free Methodism marched across North America during the period from 1860-1893. From the founding base in New York, Free Methodist churches and conferences moved west into Illinois and Michigan in the 1860s, south and west into Ohio, Minnesota, Iowa, Wisconsin and Missouri during the 1870s, north into Canada and west into South Dakota, Kansas, Colorado, Texas, Oklahoma and California during the 1880s, south into Kentucky-Tennessee and far west into Arizona-California during the early 1890s.

Whether by limited perspective or strategic priority, no distinction is made between domestic evangelism and world missions in the first *Discipline* of the Free Methodist Church. Neither professional evangelists nor professional missionaries were designated by title and function. Rather, the *Discipline* charges each annual conference to employ missionaries whose task is "to establish new churches, where the interests of the cause of God require."[15]

Church planting is not new! Every preacher appointed to a circuit carried the portfolio of a planter. Moreover, no one in the Free Methodist Church carried the official title of "evangelist" until the category was added to the 1874 *Discipline* for lay workers. Support for these missionary planters, clergy and laity, came from the voluntary gifts of local church members. As simple as it may seem, the march across America proved that it worked.

The General Conference of 1882 marked a turning point in early Free Methodist history when delegates passed legislation to create a General Missionary Board with a view toward separating "foreign missions" from "home missions." At the next General Conference in 1886, funding for foreign missions was separated from general missions. Four years later the division was complete when the General Conference ordered the General Missionary Board to "have charge of all the General and Foreign Missions of the Church established by the Board."[16]

Most significantly, at the same time that specific offerings for foreign missions were introduced, the apportionment for home evangelism was reduced from 25 to 15 cents per member. The action symbolized more than a new emphasis upon foreign missions. Aggressive evangelism at home had led to the emergence of Pentecost Bands whose enthusiasm, particularly among young people, pushed against the boundaries of church control. When the General Conference of 1890 enacted legislation regulating these Pentecost Bands, the stage was set for more than their eventual separation from the church. The fires of aggressive evangelism that characterized Free Methodism during the first 30 years of its history were banked, if not snuffed out.

THE EMERGENCE OF WORLD MISSIONS — At the same time that home evangelism began to wane, foreign missions came into its own. In fact, the first Free Methodist missionaries to India, the Rev. and Mrs. Ernest F. Ward, went to the field in 1881 as independents with only the support of the Illinois Annual Conference, because the church had no official body for overseas appointments.

Not until the General Missionary Board was incorporated in 1885 did the Free Methodist Church send out missionaries to overseas fields. Once the tide began to flow, however, foreign missions rose to represent the new field of outreach for aggressive evangelism.

Missionary appointments to Africa in 1885, the Dominican Republic in 1889 and South Africa in 1891, as well as confirmation of the Wards in 1885, led the way in this new ministry of the church. To record the names of the missionaries and tell the story of their sacrificial achievements is a history in itself which is best told in such volumes as Byron S. Lamson's book, *Lights In the World*, published by the General Missionary Board in Winona Lake, Indiana in 1951.

REFORMATION OF GOVERNANCE —As would be expected, the leaders of the new church wrote a *Discipline* that redressed the abuses that B.T. Roberts, Joseph McCreery, Loren Stiles and others had suffered under Methodist Episcopal jurisdiction. First and foremost, the new Free Methodist Church provided equal representation of lay and ministerial delegates in all annual and general conferences. This provision balanced Free Methodism between an episcopal system, dominated by clergy, and a congregational system, ruled by laity.

In a companion move, the founding fathers rejected the title of "bishop" for the leadership of the church and in its place chose the term "general superintendent" as a further check upon episcopal dominance. Still further, three Restrictive Rules were established as legal protection for (1) general rules of conduct and the Articles of Religion; (2) laws requiring lay representation, an itinerant ministry and free seats in all churches; and (3) provisions for clergy and laity to the right of an impartial trial and the right of appeal. From the very beginning, then, the nonnegotiables of governance were set for the Free Methodist Church.

MEMBERSHIP DISCIPLINE — In seeking a balance between Christian doctrine and conduct, the newly organized Free Methodist Church sought to define how its members should live as well as what they should believe. Following closely after Wesley's General Rules for Christian Conduct, the original *Discipline* of the Free Methodist Church was an adoption of the General Rules of the parent body with the addition of the prohibition against "... buying, selling or holding of a human being as a slave."

Except for minor refinements of the General Rules, they have remained intact throughout the history of the church. Applied specifically to members of the church: "Free Methodists are to abstain from all use, processing or merchandising of tobacco, opiates, and alcoholic beverages; dress plainly and inexpensively; carefully observe the Lord's Day; avoid worldly amusements; refrain from membership in the oath-bound lodge; avoid profane language and evil speaking; maintain business integrity; and follow other regulations based upon the General Rules."[17]

Through the early history of the church (1860-1893), these Rules not only regulated the conduct of the membership, but also determined the qualifications for both entry and exclusion in the membership ranks.

CHRISTIAN EDUCATION — While the Free Methodist Church was born out of revival and identified as an "evangelistic" church, the complementary ministry of Christian education was not neglected.

B.T. Roberts, a well-educated man of intellect, undoubtedly influenced the direction when he personally purchased a tavern in North Chili, New York, and founded Chili Seminary only six years after the birth of the church. Notably, the chartered purpose of the seminary was for general education defined as "mental and moral culture" and taught in a classical curriculum of humanities, sciences and religion.

Not unlike the pioneers who ventured out on the fast-moving Western frontier, Free Methodists built their homes, their churches and a school in their march across America. In Michigan it was Spring Arbor Junior College (1873), in Nebraska, Orleans Seminary (1884), in the Dakotas, Wessington Springs Seminary (1887), in Washington state, Seattle Seminary (1891) and in Illinois, Greenville College (1892). In addition, there were the short-lived educational ventures of Evansville Seminary in Wisconsin (1880) and Neosho Rapids Seminary in Kansas (1887).

Observers of other revivalistic churches are surprised to learn that none of these schools, despite the name "seminary," was established as a Bible college, none had the primary purpose of ministerial training and none was put under the control of the general church. The length and shadow of B.T. Roberts' educational background and Wesleyan theology are clearly seen in the nature and philosophy of these schools.

While Christian higher education held high priority in the early development of the church, the spiritual nurture of children and youth was largely neglected because so much time and energy went into aggressive evangelistic efforts. Not until the General Conference of 1878 did a report of a Committee on the Sunday school awaken the church with this word of alarm: "It is a lamentable fact that many children of Free Methodist parents are being lost to the church. Even when converted many of them go to other denominations for their church homes. Is not the reason for this found in the lack of careful instruction in the Word of God? If our principles are unscriptural, let us throw them away; but if they are not, let us teach them to our children."[18]

Out of this General Conference came an action plan that required preachers to report on the results of their Sunday school work and the general superintendents to promote Sunday school conventions and teachers' meetings throughout the conferences under their jurisdiction. At the 1890 General Conference, the general superintendents were instructed to develop a catechism as an instructional aid for Sunday schools, educational institutions and home study.

CONNECTIONALISM THROUGH PRINT — As Nathan Hatch observed in his book *The Democratization of American Christianity*, the Holiness and Pentecostal Movements took the lead in utilizing the emerging communication systems in 19th-century America.[19] B.T. Roberts, with his gift for writing, took full advantage of the rapidly developing print media.

Prior to 1860, he had already published *The Earnest Christian*, a journal through which he could communicate the convictions that led to the founding of the Free Methodist Church. The value of a regular journal, as a communication link with the members of the new church, was readily recognized, but finances prohibited its development within the denomination until 1886.

Meanwhile, private publishers kept the idea of *The Earnest Christian* alive and even published the first *Free Methodist* magazine in 1868. After several abortive attempts at purchasing these publishing interests for the denomination, the General Conference of 1886 voted to establish a denominational paper, purchase the privately held *Free Methodist*, plan and fund a denominational publishing house and employ a manager and elect an editor. In 1886, then, T.B. Arnold was elected editor and a publishing house was established in rented quarters in Chicago.

COMPASSION FOR THE POOR — B.T. Roberts' passion for social holiness expressed itself in two convictions that he preached and practiced. One was freedom from slavery. With equal conviction and more immediate action, the Free Methodist Church captured B.T. Roberts' social passion for the poor.

Roberts did not come late to these convictions. Immediately after his conversion, he took the risk of social censure by teaching a Sunday school class for young black women. Even more significant, Roberts' genuine love for the poor was demonstrated when he established a "free" church without rented pews in Buffalo, New York, between a bar and a brothel. He and his wife opened their home to young women who were outcasts from society but converted under their ministry. As Roberts wrote in an article entitled "Mission Field": "To the young women who become converted we furnish a home in our family until the way is opened for them to take care of themselves in a respectable manner."[20]

When slavery was abolished at the national level and free churches were established throughout the denomination, the concerns for social holiness among Free Methodists passed to other issues. Roberts himself courageously led the way into controversy by addressing the plight of the disenfranchised farmer (1874) and the need for economic reform (1876). More unanimity prevailed on legislation enacted by General Conference against secret societies (1866), the use and commerce of alcohol (1882), endorsement of political parties (1886), covetousness (1886) and, especially, racial discrimination (1866).

No mistake can ever be made about the crowning character of the Free Methodist Church. The foundational doctrine of entire sanctification and the denominational discipline of simplicity cannot be ends in themselves. Rather, they are the spiritual means to the social end of Christlike compassion for the poor.

The *Discipline* makes this purpose clear and unequivocal in the words, "But for whose benefit are special efforts to be put forth? Who must be particularly cared for? Jesus settles this question. 'The blind receive their sight, and the lame walk, the lepers are cleansed, and the deaf hear, the dead are raised up.'" As if all this would be insufficient to satisfy John of the validity of His claims, He adds, "the poor have the gospel preached to them."[21]

From Adolescence to Early Adulthood

1894-1960

In the life cycle of human organisms and church organizations, a major crisis comes in the transition between childhood and adolescence. For the human, adolescence comes with puberty around the ages of 12 to 14 years. Churches, however, come to adolescence when the life cycle turns from the first to the second generation of leaders and congregations, or 30-some years after its founding. Especially as the founding leader or leaders retire from the scene and second generation leaders take over, a crisis of vision, energy and commitment is not uncommon.

The difficulty of transfer is compounded by the necessary development of an administrative structure to preserve the spectacular successes and coordinate the multiple ministries of a growing church. Form can take over function, and when it does the church will prematurely begin the aging process. But if the church can free itself of its founder's dominant role, without the loss of its founding mission and with the commitment of a new leadership team that can articulate the mission, the stress of adolescence can lead to the strength of adulthood.

Would the church continue to grow to adulthood, as B.T. Roberts envisioned in his evangelistic thrust, or would it become prematurely old in its drive for organizational stability? By looking at the history of the church from 1894-1960, in the stages of its life cycle from adolescence to adulthood, the question will be answered.

A Stressful Adolescence
1894-1930

Institutions in their adolescence are caught between the "push" of agitation from the past and the "pull" of administration in the future. Temporarily, at least, growth is stalled between these two worlds. Relief comes through accommodation to the reality of the present. Without repudiating the past, institutions resolve the tension by developing formal programs that channel and control the original vision. Administrative efficiency is gained but not without some loss of energy in the vision.

The Free Methodist Church developmentally entered adolescence in its life cycle at the General Conference of 1894. Although the early signs of adolescence began to show themselves at the General Conference in 1890, the tension between the prodigious growth of childhood and the stressful demands of adolescence became most evident at the next quadrennial session.

REPUDIATION OF B.T. ROBERTS — A sad but inevitable note sounded at the General Conference of 1890. For the first time in the history of the church, the leadership of B.T. Roberts was repudiated by three actions that were personal blows for the founder of the church. One was the defeat of his efforts to secure the ordination of women, despite the fact that he built his case on biblical and historical grounds.

Also, a majority of the 1890 General Conference voted to uphold a recommendation condemning the Rev. R.W. Hawkins' book on redemption as "unsound and unscriptural" because of what Roberts felt was a technical error in his position on the redemption of the body. As remarkable as it seems, this was the only major theological controversy in the early history of the church. Roberts, with his irenic spirit, took the modifying course of trying to resolve the issue without destroying Hawkins, a gifted man of good intent and faithful ministry. Roberts also argued that ecclesiastical censure could not be justified because the church itself had not yet established its own doctrine on the issue. Still, the majority prevailed to censure R.W. Hawkins who soon left the church and died.

Perhaps the final blow came with the decision of the 1890 General Conference to regulate the aggressive evangelism of the Pentecost Bands. Not unlike the controversy that brought Free Methodism into being in the first place, history tended to repeat itself as Free Methodism in 1890 had to deal with the issue of "enthusiasm" from "a church within the church." Roberts must have had history in mind as he tried to save the Pentecost Bands for the church rather than regulating them with the threat of expulsion. Although Roberts lost his case and the General Conference set rigorous rules for the Pentecost Bands, the issue did not go away.

For the next four years, under the leadership of V.A. Dake, the Pentecost Bands continued to strain the lines of relationship with the church until separation became inevitable. Roberts, however, may have seen the handwriting on the wall. Despite the excesses of the Pentecost Bands and the recalcitrance of their leaders, the action of General Conference symbolized the shift of the church away from the risks that must be taken and the creativity that must be exercised to sustain the energy of aggressive evangelism.

B.T. Roberts left the 1890 General Conference as a disappointed man, if not a disillusioned leader. In the biography written by his son B.H. Roberts, the founder spoke to his wife, "I do not know that I want to attend another General Conference."[1] And he never did.

REVERSAL OF GROWTH — If B.T. Roberts had a premonition that the Free Methodist Church had peaked in its growth, he was right. He died in 1893, without hearing the report of the Committee on the State of the Work at the General Conference in 1894. The committee reported soberly, "There are too many preachers who, instead of devoting themselves to earnest, faithful pastoral work, and to feeding the flock of God, want to be running hither and thither as evangelists."[2]

Four years later, at the General Conference of 1898, the same committee said, "We are compelled to admit that our work does not grow internally as fast as we desire. ... We often enter new fields to the loss of old ones; thus we expand rather than grow."[3] More conclusively, when the Committee on the State of the Work reported to the next General Conference in 1903, the word was given that "foreign missions had far outstripped home evangelism along all lines."[4]

If the history of the Free Methodist Church has a turning point, this is it. As Marston notes, "In Free Methodism's turning from the conflict to an increasing introversion lay the major cause of the church's lower rate of growth, beginning in the nineties and becoming painfully apparent by 1903. This introversion of interest and energy was to continue for many years."[5]

Not until 1915 did the General Conference set up evangelistic boards in each annual conference "to carry on aggressive evangelistic work within its bounds."[6] From this small start, the 1919 General Conference established the General Board of Aggressive Evangelism and gave it a separate identity from the General Missionary Board, under which home evangelism had continued since the board was founded in 1882. These actions illustrate a telling point. Without undue exaggeration, the rest of the history of the Free Methodist Church can be written in the multiplication of strategies and systems to jumpstart aggressive evangelism and get the church going again.

RELIANCE UPON PROGRAMS — With the waning of church growth, attention shifted toward the institutionalization of ministries within a denominational structure. Symbolic of the shift was the restoration of the title "bishop" for the leaders of the church who had been designated "general superintendents" since the time of the founding. While still maintaining the historic balance between clergy and laity in the governing units of the church, the leaning back toward the episcopacy signaled the settling into an established denomination with more emphasis upon maintenance than on growth.

Missions, as already noted, became the growth edge of the church. Not only was foreign missions outstripping home evangelism at every point, but the motive for missions led to the organization of the Women's Missionary Society in 1894 for the chartered purpose of (1) the promotion of missionary intelligence, (2) the deepening of interest in world evangelism and (3) securing sympathetic contributions for missions. Fulfilling her husband, B.T.'s legacy, Ellen Roberts, was elected the organization's first president.

As further evidence of the shift of energy and creativity from home evangelism to world missions, the Women's Missionary Society parented the Junior Missionary Society in 1898 and the Young People's Missionary Society in 1919. Laudable goals for these organizations included winning the young to Christ, teaching them about the church and its ministries and guiding them into the service of the church, whether clergy or laity, at home and abroad.

Although expansion and growth in the North American church may have been stalled, aggressive evangelism continued to take overseas missions into new fields. Missionaries were appointed to Japan and Transvaal in 1895, China in 1903 and Brazil in 1928.

Christian education continued to grow as well during the 1894-1931 era. Los Angeles Free Methodist Seminary (Los Angeles Pacific College and High School) was founded in 1903 and Lorne Park Seminary (Lorne Park College) in 1924. There were, however, losses in the sector. Neosho Rapids Seminary was closed in 1895, Evansville Junior College discontinued operations in 1926, and Campbell Free Methodist Seminary at Campbell, Texas, closed in 1921. In each case, the decision turned on the lack of financial support.

Alarms sounded early in the era for Christian education of children and youth. At the General Conference in 1894, the same Committee on the State of the Work that lamented the decline in growth added the warning that the church was not winning, discipling and holding its own children and youth. In 1903 the warning became a screaming siren when the committee reported, "The greatest problem before us, next to the maintenance of the experience and practice of holiness, perhaps, is the salvation of our children and young people."[7]

As part of the corrective, the 1907 General Conference elected the Rev. W.B. Olmstead as the first full-time general Sunday school secretary. The pastoral address of the bishops in that General Conference set the tone for years to come when they said, "If, in our early history, the 'struggle for existence' made necessary by almost universal opposition, and by our limited numbers, resources and equipments, made us less attentive to the children and the Sunday-school work than we should have been, we are now largely redeeming ourselves as a denomination from that neglect and its unfavorable results."[8]

The social compassion that prompted the Free Methodist Church to take its strong stand on behalf of freedom from slavery and free seats for the poor in worship also became more institutionalized in this era. Benevolent institutions were founded for the care of needy children and the aged. Following the lead of the Gerry Homes, New York, and Woodstock Homes, Illinois, which were founded in the late 1880s, the Deaconess Hospital, Oklahoma, was organized in 1900, and the Life Line Children's Home, Kansas, was chartered in 1908.

Significance is attached to the development of these institutions because, while they were officially recognized by the general church, they represented social compassion for the needy arising out of local, conference and regional church settings. As Marston notes, "But to this day the general church has provided to these area institutions little more than an inspecting and accrediting service and the allotment of 'patronizing territory' to each from which it may solicit support."[9]

By and large, then, introversion characterized the Free Methodist Church during the era from 1894-1930. One cannot help but note the absence of affirmative events during the era, while negative actions stand out. In 1911, for instance, the Committee on Reforms got the General Conference to adopt resolutions of protest against worldliness, tobacco, liquor, moving pictures, trusts, divorce, secrecy, covetousness, light conversation, social evils and even longish sermons! At the same time, the church passed legislation that permitted women to be ordained as deacons, but categorically denied them elder's orders.

The General Conference of 1915 added sanctions prohibiting entertainment in church buildings. In 1923 legislation was passed to counter the concern that Free Methodist doctrine was not being adequately taught in the educational institutions of the church. As backup to that legislation, the General Conference also required that two-thirds of the trustees and faculties of the schools be members of the Free Methodist Church.

So, like any adolescent, during the period from 1894-1930, the Free Methodist Church survived the trauma of growing up between the tensions of the glorious past and the realistic present. As the church entered the 1930s, the fragments of many programs that had developed over the years lay scattered on the landscape, organizationally uncoordinated and financially underfunded. Furthermore, the outlook of the church needed to be turned from a defensive mentality to a proactive outlook.

An Expectant Early Childhood
1931-1959

In the life cycle of organizations, a church comes to maturity when there is a balance between effectiveness in ministry and efficiency in administration. This is a delicate balance, because the temptation is to err on the side of one extreme or the other. During the early years of the Free Methodist Church, we have seen that effectiveness in evangelism took precedence over efficiency in administration as a natural reaction against the heavy-handed hierarchy that had forced Free Methodism into existence. But by the turn of the century, the growth of the church had outstripped the support systems for consolidating the gains. Therefore, the process of institutionalization took over.

REORGANIZING THE CHURCH — "How should the Free Methodist Church be organized for increased efficiency in administration and greater effectiveness in ministry?" In response to this question, the General Conference of 1931 undertook a complete reorganization of the denomination. Up to that time, separate boards administered the multiple departments of the church. In the reorganization plan, a central Board of Administration was created with "general supervision of all the activities of the church during the intervals between General Conference sessions."[10]

From the membership of the Board of Administration, four commissions were created with responsibilities defined by their names: the Executive Commission, the Commission on Missions, the Commission on Christian Education and the Commission on Evangelism, Charities and Church Extension. Later, at the General Conference in 1939, a Board of Bishops was authorized for "counsel, general church planning and tasks assigned to it by the General Conference and the Board of Administration."[11]

The process toward centralization of authority and coordination of ministries continued through the era of 1931-1959. In 1935, the Publishing House relocated from Chicago to Winona Lake, Indiana, and in 1955, the General Conference ordered all denominational departments moved to the same campus under the identity as "Free Methodist World Headquarters." Organizationally, Free Methodism seemed ready for a new era.

At the same time that the denomination moved to centralize functions, minuscule moves were forming a countertrend toward decentralization. In 1947, a long-standing struggle ended when the time limit on pastoral tenure was removed, and in 1955 local congregations were authorized to take a confidential vote on the return of a pastor as part of the decision-making process of the stationing committee. Long-term consequences would follow these trendsetting actions.

REDIRECTING THE FOCUS — After years of an introverted attitude and a defensive mentality, Free Methodism followed reorganization of ministries with redirection of focus. Evangelism, in particular, returned as the centerpiece for denominational priorities. Internally, the church needed to look to the future rather than the past.

In 1947 Dr. C. Hoyt Watson, president of Seattle Pacific College, led in launching the Forward Movement with the "clear conviction that Free Methodism must be more than a witness for the defense — its message and program must be employed in a great spiritual and evangelistic outreach."[12]

Externally, then, the church needed a symbol of its outreach. "The Light and Life Hour," a radio ministry begun in 1944 with Dr. LeRoy M. Lowell in the Ferndale, Michigan church, served as that symbol when the denomination initiated the broadcast. Under the direction of Dr. Myron F. Boyd, the program gained national and international stature in the rapidly developing field of religious broadcasting.

By 1955, the bishops could recommend in their Pastoral Address to the General Conference that "evangelism and church extension be the major program of all agencies and departments of the church, and that our entire membership plan its stewardship of finances, time and talent in line with this emphasis."[13]

RETHINKING THE *DISCIPLINE* — Perhaps as a companion of introversion, the Free Methodist Church also tended toward a legalism of discipline for its churches and its members. History played a part in setting definitive rules that governed corporate worship and individual conduct of its members. As a protection against formality of worship and laxity of conduct in the Methodist Episcopal Church of the mid-1800s, Free Methodists developed a *Discipline* that specifically addressed these issues. In the *Discipline* of 1860, for instance, instrumental music and choirs in public worship were strictly forbidden.

Contrary to later interpretation, legalism did not motivate this emphasis upon the conduct of Free Methodists. Simplicity of life was a principle that arose naturally out of the doctrine of holiness. As noted earlier, an inseparable connection existed between personal and social holiness in Wesleyan theology. Within that context, another connection existed between the simplicity of life and compassion for the poor. Biblical stewardship called for simplicity in the style of life, worship and church architecture in order to provide both the witness and resources for the ministry to the poor.

Pressure to change the prohibition against instrumental music surfaced as early as the General Conference of 1898, but the church held firm through a succession of proposals in almost every quadrennial conference until 1943. At that time, provision was made for a local church to bring in one instrument, but without a choir, if two-thirds of the congregation favored the decision and the annual conference had already voted to approve music. At the 1955 General Conference, the remaining restrictions against instruments and choirs were removed with the decision solely in the hands of the local church.

Paralleling the release from this restriction was the equally volatile issue of the wedding ring, considered a symbol of worldliness. As far back as the General Conference of 1874, the prohibition against the wearing of gold included the wedding band. In 1939 the prohibition was expanded to include any finger rings, and as late as 1943 the rule was reinforced. But after due discussion, the 1951 General Conference deleted all references to the wedding ring in the Special Rules.

In the midst of these controversies, the General Conference of 1951 received a committee report distinguishing between principles and prudentials in the Discipline of Membership. "Principles of conduct ... are clearly taught in Scripture, or are directly implied by the Word ... Prudentials are those rules formulated by the church and required of its members as aids to godliness."[14] According to this definition, prudentials, not principles, were at stake in lifting the prohibitions against instrumental music and the wedding ring.

RECOGNIZING THE GLOBAL COMMUNITY — Enlightened leadership foresaw the opening of the world as a "global village" in the years after World War II. Free Methodist overseas missions had continued to grow through the first half of the century as missionary statesmen and stateswomen put into practice the biblical principles of evangelism, church planting, discipling and leadership training implied in the Great Commission.

Even more important, missionaries communicated an affirmative vision for the future of the church that engaged the imagination and mobilized the energies of the people whom they served. Perhaps most important, Free Methodist missionaries took with them in their portfolios the indigenous principle, which respects the culture of nationals and esteems their potential for self-governance.

On the threshold of the centennial year, the Commission on Missions made this request of the Board of Administration in 1958:

> The Free Methodist Church of N[orth] A[merica] is approaching the time when it must think in terms of a world church of related national churches, and plan with representatives of national Free Methodist groups looking toward the organization of largely autonomous national churches within the various countries now controlled in large measure by mission extensions of the home church.
>
> Therefore, the Board of Administration is requested to take steps toward setting up a World Planning Council for Free Methodism.[15]

The request was accepted and Free Methodism symbolically broke from the shell of its introversion, opened the door to the future and modeled the spirit of the founders of the church, not just overseas, but at home as well.

On this high note, the Free Methodist Church came of age. In 1960, with an eye to the future and a hand reaching out to the world, the church stood ready for its second century.

Part II

INTO THE SECOND CENTURY

A Church on the Threshold

A ll history is written with benchmarks in mind. Against these benchmarks, the direction and speed of change can be read. For the Free Methodist Church in 1960, three benchmarks are chosen. One is the benchmark of *biblical convictions and denominational distinctives* which define the character of the church. The second is the benchmark of *denominational development* which aligns Free Methodism with all human organizations in which natural momentum takes them from a visionary movement to an established institution. The third is the benchmark of *cultural change* to which the church responds as a divine-human institution "in the world" and sometimes "of the world."

So, like a snapshot of a subject at a given point in time, Part II stops the action of history long enough to set these benchmarks in place. The stage is then set to assess both continuity and change in the Free Methodist Church between 1960-1995 and forward.

A Calling
to Fulfill

Founding Principles

Free Methodists are people with strong and deep roots in history. The taproot is theological; the entwining root is organizational. Biblical convictions serve as the source of life for the theological taproot, and denominational distinctives feed its entwining companion. Both roots go deeply into the past — long before the Free Methodist Church was founded in 1860. Bishop Leslie Marston, in *From Age to Age A Living Witness*, shows the importance of these roots by devoting half of the pages of his book to a story that begins in the late 17th century and continues into the 20th century. If time and space had permitted, Marston might well have written chapters that covered events prior to this period:

— Beginning with a grounding in the Scriptures for the doctrines of the church;
— Proceeding through to the church fathers who framed the canon and the creeds in which Free Methodists believe;
— Including the patristic fathers of catholic (universal church) tradition who profoundly influenced John Wesley with their clarity concerning the doctrine of Christian perfection and holiness;
— Adding Jacobus Arminius who countered Calvin's predestination with human freedom of choice in matters of salvation, made possible by God's grace;
— Identifying the Free Methodist Church as an heir of the Protestant Reformation through the doctrine of justification by faith; and
— Tracing the line from the Thirty-Nine Articles of Religion of the Anglican Church through to John Wesley's Twenty-Four Articles that he sent to the developing Methodist Episcopal Church in America.

As a historian, however, Marston had to make the difficult choice of the historical time line that he would develop as background for the founding of the Free Methodist Church. He chose to begin with the 17th century genesis of the Wesleyan Revival in England and its missionary outreach to the American colonies through the Methodist Episcopal Church. The defection, then, of that church from the biblical conviction that characterized the spiritual vitality and social witness of historic Methodism became the immediate setting from which Free Methodism arose.

Marston made another choice as a historian. He chose to write the story of Free Methodism in its first century as an institutional response to the defection of the Methodist Episcopal Church from its biblical moorings. He might have chosen to write the history from the perspective of the personal biographies of its leaders, the characteristics of its people as a community, the relationship between the developing church and the changing culture or the parallels between Free Methodism and the holiness movement, which waxed and waned as a major religious force during the first century of Free Methodism. Instead, exercising the discipline of a scholar, Marston focused upon the roots of founding principles for the Free Methodist Church that justified its existence as a denomination and defined its mission as a movement, ordained of God and guided by His Spirit. Those founding principles are:

1. *Doctrine*: The Scriptural doctrine of entire sanctification according to the Wesleyan interpretation;
2. *Experience*: A corresponding experience of cleansing and power;
3. *Worship*: Spirituality and simplicity of worship in the freedom of the Spirit;
4. *Piety*: A way of holy living that separates the Christian from the world; and
5. *Stewardship*: Full consecration for service to God and man.[1]

Marston concluded his centennial history with the statement, "The founding principles of Free Methodism, still maintained by the denomination after a century, are still vital Christian issues, and therefore Free Methodism has a continuing mission."[2]

While accepting Marston's conclusion, the perspective of changing times suggests the need to refine and expand the founding principles of the Free Methodist Church. Precedence for this perspective came at the General Conference of 1951, when principles were separated from prudentials in church governance as a response to the reality of changing times. In like manner, there is merit in dividing the "biblical convictions" of the church from the "denominational distinctives."

Biblical convictions, of course, serve as core values, or nonnegotiable principles, for the church. Timing, wording and procedures related to these biblical convictions may change without the loss of principle, but if they are sacrificed in content rather than changed in context, the essential character of the Free

46

Methodist Church would be radically changed. Denominational distinctives, on the other hand, may be altered in response to changing times to increase the effectiveness of the church and its potential for growth. As the 1993 *Book of Discipline of the Free Methodist Church in Canada* notes with wisdom,

> In certain aspects, denominations change with the passing of the decades. They change because they are set in the pulsation of history which, like time itself, is an ever-flowing stream. They change because they stand vis-à-vis with culture and must interact with culture in order to be relevant. They change because change is the only alternative to death.
>
> Nevertheless, stable denominations have benchmarks from which they take their sightings. Such benchmarks give stability in the midst of change.[3]

The benchmarks for the Free Methodist Church in 1960 are best stated as complementary principles. As such, they represent the genius of Wesleyan theology and Methodist tradition by a Spirit-guided balance between principles which may appear to be competitive, but in actuality are complementary. These biblical convictions and denominational distinctives are:

BIBLICAL CONVICTIONS
1. *Faith* is both doctrine and experience.
2. *Worship* is both freedom and order.
3. *Holiness* is both personal and social.
4. *Growth* is both educational and evangelistic.

DENOMINATIONAL DISTINCTIVES
1. *Governance* is both episcopal and congregational.
2. *Stewardship* is both unified and diverse.
3. *Mission* is both local and global.
4. *Direction* is both connectional and ecumenical.

The tendency, where complementary principles such as these are involved, is to tip the scale toward one side or the other. For instance, the faith position of Wesleyan theology views doctrine and experience as complementary, not conflicting or competitive, principles. Even with Wesley's heavy emphasis upon the Aldersgate experience as foundational to faith, his ready acceptance of the Thirty-Nine Articles of the Anglican Church, as the creedal base for Methodism, leaves no doubt about his position. Doctrine and experience are never independent. They confirm each other in a dynamic faith.

Therefore, one of the tests of the viability of the Free Methodist Church during its first century is to determine how the complementary components within the biblical convictions and denominational distinctives are balanced and integrated over time. Of necessity, the assessment of these founding principles in the period 1860-1960 requires some repetition of historical actions and events — especially those that may have tipped the balance toward one complementary principle or another.

Biblical Convictions

Four sets of biblical convictions, based upon the theological position of the Free Methodist Church, can be discerned in the history of the first century of the denomination.

1. FAITH IS BOTH DOCTRINE AND EXPERIENCE — Marston identified doctrine and experience as two separate founding principles, probably because of their importance to the movement. Doctrine and experience, however, are not separate or conflicting principles. They represent two ends of the continuum defining a faith position. Depending upon the primacy given to doctrine or experience, denominations are identified as creedal or confessional. Free Methodism is neither. Rather, it is a balance between the two.

As with John Wesley, who wrote no systematic theology, Free Methodist leaders were practical theologians who worked out their faith in experience. The doctrine of assurance is an example. Rather than relying upon the development of a systematic theology to explain the security of the believer, as Calvin did with the doctrine of predestination, Wesley and his followers found their assurance through the confirming witness of the Holy Spirit that they were forgiven of sin and accepted as children of God. Whether in justification or sanctification, experience confirmed the doctrine.

If anything, Free Methodists have tipped the scale toward experience. In both the doctrines of justification and sanctification, the confirmation of a crisis experience was proclaimed and professed. Especially for the cardinal doctrine of entire sanctification, the Articles of Religion specify, "Entire sanctification is that work of the Holy Spirit, subsequent to regeneration, by which the fully consecrated believer, upon exercise of faith in the atoning blood of Christ, is cleansed in that moment from all inward sin and empowered for service. The resulting relationship is attested by the witness of the Holy Spirit and is maintained by faith and obedience."[4]

Still, with the counterbalance of sound doctrine, Free Methodists were checked against making the nature of the crisis a litmus test for the evidence of the indwelling Spirit. When Pentecostals, for instance, elevated the gift of tongues to evidence of the sanctifying experience, Free Methodists tended to repudiate this new movement, even though they shared a common holiness heritage.

Bishops, in their pastoral addresses, took the lead in preserving the balance between doctrine and experience. For the 1907 General Conference, the general superintendents wrote that the church had, "unfalteringly borne faithful witness through all the land to the great fundamental truths of Christianity, and particularly regarding the privilege and obligation of believers to be sanctified wholly in the present life."

Only once did the General Conference take on the role as a monitor of orthodoxy. In 1923, the section of the *Discipline* on the schools of the church was changed to require all teaching to be in harmony with the Scriptures "as generally interpreted by the Free Methodist Church and set forth in her *Discipline*."[5] Later, in 1943, the General Conference added the stipulation that all instructors in the religion departments of the schools must sign a statement agreeing with the church's position on the doctrine and experience of entire sanctification. In that action, the scale tipped toward doctrine. But without the legal mechanisms of church control over the schools or without the sanction of withdrawing financial support, the church had to count upon the loyalty of the schools to maintain the standard.

2. WORSHIP IS BOTH FREEDOM AND ORDER — When B.T. Roberts published his paper on "New School Methodism" in 1857, the nature and meaning of worship became one of the most volatile points of contention. Without regard for personal risk, he issued a stinging rebuke against statements published in the *Buffalo Advocate* that denied Christianity as a system of devotion, demeaned worship as an affront to God and taught that emotional expression in worship is a detriment to the "development of genial and humane dispositions and the formation of habits of active, vigorous goodness."[6] Not only did Roberts denounce these statements as "a sneer ... not unworthy of Thomas Paine himself,"[7] but he charged the New School Methodists with an agenda in which "The Lodge must supersede the class-meeting and the love-feast; and the old-fashioned prayer-meeting must give way to the social party."[8]

Against this background of controversy, it is no surprise to find that the founding principle of Free Methodism regarding freedom and order in worship tips the balance toward freedom. In his rebuke against formal and fashionable worship as promoted by the New School Methodists, Roberts called for "... free churches, congregational singing, and spirituality, simplicity and fervency in worship."[9]

Early on, however, Roberts had to face the challenge of the Nazarites who exploited freedom and indulged themselves in excesses in worship. According to Roberts' diary, they twisted the purpose of worship from the "salvation of sinners and the sanctification of believers" to having a "free time" without restraint, placed the Spirit's leadership above the Bible, gloried in reproach and resented reproof as persecution.[10]

The issue of imbalance toward "enthusiasm" persisted from the beginning of the church to the end of Roberts' life. Just a year before his death in 1893, he wrote an article entitled "Fanaticism" in which he repeated his warning against the dangers of freedom without the restraints of reason, and, at the same time, pleaded for spiritual worship against the deadness of formalism. "We must never forget that the essence of our Christianity is not doctrinal beliefs, nor observance of forms, but the indwelling Spirit."[11]

As a check and balance upon excessive freedom in worship, Roberts called for the primacy of the Scriptures, the steadying influence of reason and the guiding wisdom of the Holy Spirit. The principle of spirituality and simplicity with freedom in the Spirit should then prevail. More specifically, the prohibition against instrumental music and choirs was intended as a guard against formality and an encouragement to spontaneous expressions of praise, conviction or burden among the worshipers. But more important than the prohibition were the affirmations of ritual, especially the Lord's Supper, as a regular part of Free Methodist worship.

The hymnody that Free Methodists inherited from the Wesleys and Methodism served as another check upon excesses of freedom in worship. The doctrinal soundness and the praise-filled tunes of the Methodist hymnal were attested by the decision to use the hymnbook until 1883, when Roberts led the development of the *Hymnbook of the Free Methodist Church*. Metrical tune books during the 1880s and the revisions of the hymnal, in 1910 and 1951 during its first century, indicated the continuing value of hymns tested by time and experience as a means of expressing freedom through order in the worship services.

3. HOLINESS IS BOTH PERSONAL AND SOCIAL — In the beginning, the founding principles of personal and social holiness were almost inseparable in B.T. Roberts' call for reform. He proclaimed and practiced compassion for the poor in his call for a "free" church as vigorously as he advocated the discipline of personal holiness among his people.

Affirmatively, this meant demonstrating the Wesleyan motive of "faith working through love." Negatively, it also meant rules of discipline upon a member that prohibited "... wasteful personal habits, the extravagant or immodest fashion of one's dress and the types of worldly amusements in which he indulges."[12]

Compassion for the poor motivated Roberts' unequivocal stand for free seats in the churches and freedom from human slavery in the nation. He won his case for free seats with the founding of the Free Methodist Church in 1860, and the nation abolished slavery as the outcome of the Civil War a few years later. Perhaps these successes proved to be Pyrrhic victories (winning at great loss) for the agenda of social holiness in the Free Methodist Church for years to come. Denominational focus shifted from social issues in the culture toward the discipline of membership on matters of personal conduct.

John Wesley's General Rules, which were adopted in 1860 with the addition of the rule prohibiting the "buying, selling or holding of a human being as a slave," remained intact throughout the century. Special rules adopted by General Conferences from 1866 to 1951 regarding alcohol, tobacco, marriage and divorce, dress and secret societies better defined the church during this era than its social witness. Yet resolutions of social conscience, relating to such matters as racial discrimination, militarism and war and stewardship of wealth and prohibition, continued to be filed and adopted.

The imbalance toward personal morality is evident in Marston's confession which he wrote in 1960, "Conservative in matters of doctrine and firm in the discipline of conduct, the church may have lagged for a time behind the socially progressive pace of its reforming pioneers, but whatever degree of social indifference may have affected the Free Methodist Church in its mid-period or earlier, evidence points to a present effort to maintain the outward, social reach of the gospel, along with the upward reach of a personal faith."[13]

Whatever the reason, the Free Methodist Church after the 1860s became better identified with the discipline of personal holiness than the compassion of social holiness.

4. GROWTH IS BOTH EDUCATIONAL AND EVANGELISTIC — Churches grow primarily by one of two means: conserving the young through education or converting the lost through evangelism. Among all of the founding principles, the balance between education and evangelism is the most precarious, particularly for the Free Methodist Church.

Although the colleges founded under the auspices of the Free Methodist Church were expected to be vital centers for the promulgation of the founding principles, Roberts and other ecclesiastical leaders who followed him carefully protected the educational integrity of the institutions. The expectations did not include heavy-handed church control, a camp meeting climate, a Bible school curriculum or the dominance of a ministerial training program. In the early years of the church, education and evangelism were neither competitive nor fully integrated into the mission of the church. Each had its own integrity; each pursued its own course without highly specific theological or legal restrictions; and each made its unique contribution to the church.

A defining moment came for Free Methodism in 1947 when John Wesley Seminary Foundation was established at Asbury Theological Seminary, a free-standing institution in the Wesleyan and holiness tradition. After the Board of Administration authorized the launching of a denominational seminary in 1945, Dr. George Turner, a Free Methodist professor at Asbury, suggested the alternative of affiliation with a well-established institution. Negotiations moved rapidly and in the fall of 1947, the new relationship with an accredited graduate school of theology began.

By 1960, 179 Free Methodists had completed graduate degrees in theology at Asbury with almost all of them entering the pastoral ministry of the church. Leadership for the church across the spectrum, from the local parish to the mission fields, began to flow from the Foundation.

The affiliation with Asbury and the promotion of seminary education accent the importance of the role of education in the church as it stood on the threshold of its second century. It is a phenomenon, indeed, for an evangelistic church to give priority to graduate theological education. Although there were still other tracks to the ordained ministry, the expectations were raised and the seminary graduate became a prime candidate for leadership.

The concern for the loss of the church's children continued into the doldrum days of the 20th century. As long as the conversion and transfer of adults covered the losses of the children of the church, Christian education did not seem necessary. But when evangelism waned and the losses appeared, the strategy shifted to Christian education of children and youth as the compensating hope. As Bishop Marston, a nationally noted educator as well as theologian and churchman, pressed home the point when he wrote his centennial history in 1960, "Free Methodism's growth increasingly depends upon its bringing its own children and youth into established church membership."[14]

This is not to say that evangelism was neglected during the first half of the 20th century when Free Methodism was in the midst of finding itself. Some weight shifted to the side of evangelism, but Christian education had momentum in its favor. When the church celebrated its centennial in 1960, the jury was still out.

Denominational Distinctives

A second set of founding principles adds insight into our understanding of the development of the Free Methodist Church during its first century. Organizational characteristics, rather than theological convictions, define these founding principles. The critical difference between the two sets of founding principles is the flexibility for substantive change in organizational emphasis without necessarily sacrificing the fundamental mission of the church. Free Methodism, therefore, may be identified by these organizational characteristics, but not defined by them. For this reason, "denominational distinctives" is chosen to designate these founding principles.

As with the biblical convictions, denominational distinctives come in four sets of organizational characteristics which may appear to be opposites, but in reality are complementary characteristics that are balanced in the healthiest of organizations. In other words, they are characteristics that can be described as "both/and," not "either/or." Once understood, they become benchmarks from which we can follow the changing nature of the denomination throughout its history and into its future.

1. GOVERNANCE IS BOTH EPISCOPAL AND CONGREGATIONAL — As a natural reaction against the abuses suffered at the hands of the leaders

and governing bodies of the Methodist Episcopal Church, the founders of Free Methodism built into the new organization three specific protections designed to assure the balance between clergy and laity in church governance. First, in protest against the potential of injustice at the hands of all-clergy governance, equal representation of laity and clergy was guaranteed in the annual and quadrennial legislative bodies of the new church. Second, the title of bishop (a lifetime appointment in the Methodist Episcopal Church) was replaced by the four-year-term election of a general superintendent who, in turn, was responsible to an executive committee elected by the General Conference.

Third, restrictive rules limited the legislative power of the General Conference by the requirement of a two-thirds majority vote ratified by a three-quarters vote by members of the annual conferences in order to change certain church laws. In another tip of the scale toward the congregation, class leaders in the local societies were elected by the membership rather than appointed by the pastor, as was the case in the parent body.

Because Free Methodism had no formal constitution until 1915, the aforementioned legislation served as the law of the church during its first half century. In practice, however, the leadership of the clergy, and especially the general superintendents, beginning with B.T. Roberts, took the initiative to see the vision, state the mission and set the tone for the denomination. Roberts' visionary agenda of reform has already been noted.

As the church grew, E.P. Hart was elected as the second general superintendent in 1874. Twelve years later, G.W. Coleman became the third general superintendent, and in 1890 the need to coordinate the work of the three resulted in the organization of a Board of General Superintendents. The history of the Free Methodist Church in its first century can be written as a biography of its clergy leaders, and particularly those who served as general superintendents or bishops.

R.R. Blews' book *Master Workmen*, written in 1939 and updated as a companion to Marston's centennial history in 1960, represents that biographical history through the life and ministry of the esteemed leaders Roberts, Hart, Coleman, Jones, Hogue, Sellew, MacGeary, Warner, Clark, Zahniser, Griffith, Vincent, Warren and Pearce. As an addendum to the book, the bishops of 1960 could be included: Marston, Ormston, Fairbairn, Taylor and Kendall. Likewise, the biographies of departmental executives, educators, evangelists and missionaries — almost all of whom were clergy — could also be written as major influences in the direction of the church.

Complementing the strength of clergy leadership, the church made organizational moves that tipped the balance toward episcopal governance. In 1894 the motion was put to restore the title of "bishop" to the general superintendency. It failed, only to be resurrected and rejected again in 1898 and

1903. Finally on the fourth attempt in 1907, the majority was reversed and the title of "bishop" was restored.

One cannot forget that during this same period from 1890 to 1907, the ordination of women was rejected as a nod toward the centralized power in the hands of male leadership. The hold was partially broken in 1911 when legislation was passed permitting women to be ordained as deacons but without the right of proceeding to full ordination as elders. Women were thus blocked from leadership at the level of the superintendency in district, annual or general conferences. This position on the ordination of women prevailed throughout the first century of the church and well into its second.

Reorganization in 1931 confirmed the role of episcopal leadership for the church. Bishops presided over the four commissions as well as the Board of Administration and the General Conference. Although equal clergy and lay representation on each of these governing units prevented ministerial tyranny and provided full voice and vote on policies and programs, the strategic position held by the bishops gave them a "bully pulpit" to influence the direction of the church.

Still another move toward episcopal governance took place with the order of the 1955 General Conference to centralize executive and departmental functions at Winona Lake, Indiana. The designation of "Headquarters" followed the earlier move of the Publishing House to Winona Lake in 1935, and symbolized the continued flow of power upward toward centralization and episcopal leadership.

Not that this direction was inevitable. In addition to the constant check of equal representation between clergy and laity in the legislative bodies of the church, small but significant actions that leaned toward congregational governance were taken throughout the first century. As early as 1923, the three-year term for the itinerant ministry was unsuccessfully challenged, but in the next quadrennial session the term was increased to four years.

In 1947 the General Conference lifted the time limit on pastoral appointments and, in the most significant move of the era, the 1955 General Conference authorized congregations to take a confidential vote on the return of the pastor. Although the results of the vote were kept in confidence and served only to advise the stationing committee on its appointments, the action moved governance away from the episcopacy and toward the congregation, a harbinger of the future.

2. STEWARDSHIP IS BOTH UNIFIED AND DIVERSE — When Marston cites stewardship as a founding principle for the Free Methodist Church, he is biblically correct to identify the principle with "full consecration for service to God and man" and true to Wesley's conviction that Christian stewardship evidenced itself in compassion for the poor. This principle was consistent with

Free Methodism's emphasis upon simplicity of lifestyle, plainness of dress and economy of church architecture. Not unlike John Wesley, B.T. Roberts took strong stands on economic matters, ranging from such national issues as money, banking and tax reform to the personal stewardship of possessions and earning abilities.[15] The *Discipline,* as well, makes clear the link between the stewardship of possessions and compassion for the poor:

> The Scriptures teach the privilege and responsibility of private ownership. Christians hold title to possessions under civil law, but regard all they have as the property of God entrusted to them as stewards. Although they may accumulate goods they lay not up for themselves treasures on earth (Matthew 6:19-20; Luke 12:16-21), but give liberally for the needs of others and the ministry of the church (2 Corinthians 8:1-5; 9:6-13).[16]

Stewardship for the support of the ministries of the church reveals another balance point for the denominational distinctives of Free Methodism. As the church grew and denominational programs increased to solidify the growth, actions were taken to assure unified support from the tithes and offerings of the membership at the local level. In 1860, "missions" meant home missions with the establishment of new churches and the extension into new areas. To support this work, class leaders encouraged their members to give, voluntarily, 1 cent a week for home missions and to contribute to a public missionary offering taken by the local church. The funds were sent to the annual conference for discretionary distribution within the scope of home evangelism.

When the General Conference of 1882 divided "missions" into "home missions" and "foreign missions," a mandatory fee of not less than 20 cents per member was in place, along with required offerings for missions within the annual conference. Not until 1890 did the General Conference divide the fees and offerings for missions into "foreign missions" and "home evangelism."

Years later, when the scope of denominational programs began to outstrip available resources, proposals were advanced for a denominational budget under the name General Service Fund. The General Conference of 1923 rejected the proposal and 24 years passed before the concept was accepted in 1947. With this action, the balance tipped toward mandatory support for denominational ministries through apportionments to local churches and annual conferences in the General Service Fund. The stage was set for a continuing contest between the stewardship responsibility for world missions and home evangelism. It was framed in the context of complementary principles. Will the general church budget be supported by mandatory assessments or diversified funding through voluntary gifts?

3. MISSION IS BOTH LOCAL AND GLOBAL — The issue of funding

for home evangelism and world missions prompts a look at another denominational distinctive for the Free Methodist Church. When the church was organized in 1860, it was preoccupied with home evangelism. The unreached communities of the East and the rapidly expanding Western frontier served as its mission field. Not by accident, each annual conference had "charge of all missions within its bounds" with full authority "to employ missionaries to labor within its bounds."[17]

Perhaps it is only coincidence, but when Free Methodism reached the Western seaboard, the General Missionary Board sent its first missionary. The California Conference was established in 1883, and the Oregon-Washington Conference in 1885, the latter date coinciding with the appointment of M. Louisa Ranf to India. From then on, the balance between home and foreign missions began to tip in favor of a global outlook.

At the same time that the North American church became introverted and parochial, world missions provided the relief valve for the thwarted energies of aggressive evangelism. Dr. Byron S. Lamson, elected as Missionary Secretary for the General Missionary Board in 1944, spoke the vision that kept the Free Methodist Church from a choking parochialism when he said, "If we give ourselves to save the lost world, God will take care of His church."

In 1860 "missions" embraced only home evangelism; in 1960 the term meant world evangelism. As the balance tipped, Bishop Marston turned prophet with the centennial observation, "At present rates of growth, within ten years the overseas churches will overtake the American church in membership and perhaps in enterprise for the Kingdom."[18]

Would Lamson's self-correcting vision of world evangelism prove true? If so, when the Free Methodist Church closed its first century in 1960, the North American church could anticipate rejuvenation from the energy of world missions as it entered its second century.

4. DIRECTION IS BOTH CONNECTIONAL AND ECUMENICAL — The Free Methodist Church, from the time of its founding, enjoyed the advantage of its connectional relationship. Cohesion characterized a community of believers who were brought together, not just by disillusionment with a denomination that had lost its moorings, but especially by the commitment to biblical convictions. Structural support for these convictions identified Free Methodism as a "connectional" church.

Beginning with the class meeting — "a church within a church" — the mutuality of believers, seeking spiritual growth and accepting corporate discipline, prepared the way for the "love feast" where confession and forgiveness bonded the participants in a deeply moving community of faith. Societies, then, formalized the relationship in corporate worship, centered around the Word of God with freedom of the Spirit and the order of the Sacrament.

Spiritual and structural connectionalism received further reinforcement through the organization of district, annual and general conferences that did business in a climate of communal celebration. No wonder that Free Methodists gained a sense of "home" when the denominational headquarters moved to a gracious campus and conference setting in Winona Lake.

Paralleling its connectional strength, Roberts brought an ecumenical spirit with him to the leadership of the Free Methodist Church. As early as 1862, the General Conference appointed a committee to reach out to a group known as Bible Christians in the spirit of fellowship and with the prospect of union. But the tone for cooperation with other Christians was set in the policy adopted by the General Conference of 1882:

> We have Christian fellowship and love, for all persons of whatever denomination, who show by their lives that they 'Follow peace with all men, and holiness without which no man shall see the Lord.'

> We will unite with all well disposed persons, in an open, Christian manner, in promoting social and civil reforms.

> But we cannot unite, where we are required to compromise our principles, in holding union meetings with any person, or denomination, whose practical standard of Christian character and church fellowship, is obviously below that plainly set forth in the New Testament.[19]

It is no surprise, then, to learn that in 1883 Roberts represented the Free Methodist Church as a charter member of the newly formed World Methodist Council. Joining even with those who expelled him from the Methodist Episcopal Church, Roberts had the confidence of his convictions that permitted him to participate in the larger Methodist ecumenical community. In 1886 as the National Holiness Association gained momentum as a movement, the General Conference adopted the resolution that read:

> Whereas entire sanctification gives the unity of the Spirit without regard to denominational preference, and Whereas we recognize that God has greatly blessed the holiness movement both within and without the Free Methodist Church: Therefore, Resolved, that we extend hearty fellowship and cooperation to all churches, associations, or other agencies that are in harmony with the Word of God in teaching and practice.[20]

Understandably, the Free Methodist Church became a stalwart member and leader in the National Holiness Association (later, the Christian Holiness Association).

The ecumenical spirit was further extended when the National Association of Evangelicals was formed in 1943. Although not a Wesleyan, Arminian or holiness organization, its advocacy of a united voice and cooperative action on behalf of evangelical Christianity against both a soft liberalism and a hard fundamentalism prompted the Free Methodist Church to join and take a leadership role.

But ecumenicity has it limits. When the National Council of Churches was formed, Free Methodists were invited to join and refused. In fact, a major controversy developed in the 1950s when the Free Methodist Church was listed as a prospective member, though the church had already taken a position against membership. The church balked at the Council's syncretistic approach to doctrine, its liberal agenda and its goal of organic union.

Still, the Free Methodist Church was caught up in the trend toward organic unity in the optimistic days of the mid-20th century. The Wesleyan Methodist and Free Methodist denominations reopened their earlier conversations about merger, and in 1959 the Holiness Movement Church of Canada, including 5,000 members in Egypt, officially united with Free Methodists as one body.

So as the Free Methodist Church closed its first century, renewed confidence in its biblical convictions and denominational distinctives not only strengthened its connectional relationships, but also permitted it to contribute affirmatively to the larger holiness, evangelical and Wesleyan communities. The stranglehold of introversion seemed to be broken, and the restored balance between the cohesive strength of denominational connectionalism and the confident spirit of ecumenical cooperation gave promise of a new outlook for the second century.

Through this overview of biblical convictions and denominational distinctives, we see the roots that shaped the Free Methodist Church in the first century. Changes in theology were minimal, but adjustments in structure and governance were significant. The shifting and reshifting balance between complementary principles is particularly valuable for understanding the movement of the church as a dynamic organization.

According to the relative weight of emphasis upon one side or the other of these founding principles, how would the Free Methodist Church be described at the turn of its first century in 1960? Its faith would be defined by *experience*, its worship represented by *freedom*, its discipline by *personal holiness* and its strategy by an emphasis upon *Christian education*. Likewise, among its denominational distinctives, the scale would tend to be tipped toward the *episcopacy* in governance, a *unified budget* in stewardship, *global missions* in scope and an emerging *ecumenism* in outlook.

Although this interpretation is open for debate, it does give us a benchmark against which to study trends in the church throughout the period of 1960-1995 and forward. History serves us well when we view Free Methodism as a dynamic movement rather than a static organization.

C H A P T E R 4

A World
Turned
Upside Down

1960-1995

With renewed optimism, the Free Methodist Church celebrated its 100th anniversary in 1960. The social and religious setting of North American culture reinforced this optimism.

John F. Kennedy set an idealistic tone for his presidency and captured the imagination of Americans when he promised to put a man on the moon and wipe out hunger in the nation by the end of the decade. In parallel vision and spirit, Bishop Walter S. Kendall keynoted the Centennial General Conference with the vision for Free Methodism to "Double in a Decade."

Beginning in the early 1960s the world, and particularly the United States, went through a revolution whose reverberations are still rocking the globe. No one can either chronicle or critique the events of history from 1960-1995 in one volume. Yet, as noted earlier, the history of Free Methodism cannot be written independently of the social and religious culture of which it is a part. True, its biblical mandate and its spiritual mission transcend the culture. But this is not to deny the impact of cultural change upon the church.

The Sobering Sixties

The heady optimism with which the 1960s began died with the gunshot that killed John F. Kennedy. Americans who boasted, "It can't happen here," lost their case as the national ego suffered a puncture of immeasurable proportions. As if triggering a revolution, the ripple effect of the assassination unearthed issues that smoldered under the gloss of the 1950s. Like soldiers marching in single file, the tragedies and tensions of the decade originally dubbed as "The Soaring Sixties" can be remembered by the names of places:

DALLAS	1963	The assassination of President Kennedy
SELMA	1965	The beating of blacks marching for civil rights
DETROIT	1967	The race riot that charred a city
MEMPHIS	1968	The assassination of Martin Luther King, Jr.
LOS ANGELES	1968	The assassination of Robert Kennedy
CHICAGO	1968	The violent disruption of the Democratic National Convention
BERKELEY	1969	Student takeover of the campus at the University of California
WOODSTOCK	1969	The glorification of illegal drugs, free sex and rock music
MY LAI	1969	The massacre of innocent Vietnamese villagers by U.S. troops[1]

With such tragic events on its record, the "Soaring Sixties" became better known as the "Sobering Sixties." Beginning with the highest of idealistic hopes, the dreamers were mugged by reality. Young people born and reared during the decade suffered the most and became identified as baby boomers who turned inward for self-protection and thus earned the added title in the 1970s of the "Me Generation."

In his book *A Generation of Seekers*, Wade Clark Roof astutely describes the 1960s as "a time when mountains were moving."[2] Baby boomers grew up in the upheaval of moral values, the dilemmas of affluence, the issues of gender and racial equality, the offerings of entitlement, the rising expectations of higher education and the moral impact of the media. At the very least, the turmoil of the 1960s created a shell-shocked generation whose mission of spiritual search and discovery helps define the changing nature of religion throughout the remaining decades of the 20th century.

MORAL REVOLUTION — Under the eruptions on the social landscape, deep moving shifts were taking place along a moral fault line. A sound society depends upon (a) a moral consensus among its people, (b) an acceptance of legitimate leadership and (c) effectiveness in the primary institutions of the home, the church and the school. In the 1960s, each of these foundational premises came under attack and either lost ground or succumbed to the onslaught. Woodstock symbolized the breakdown of the moral consensus, particularly regarding drugs, sexuality and music, but reaching deeper into the moral reservoir to reject absolute truth and traditional standards of right and wrong.

Close behind came the denial of legitimate authority. Leaders who had been heroes became traitors. Whether in government, education, business or religion, leaders received a vote of no confidence, found their credibility questioned and their competence denied. Completing the breakdown, the authority and legitimacy of the home, the church and the school as nurturing institutions came under fire.

With sexual freedom came a challenge to traditional marriage and family relationships. With the loss of authority came doubts about the validity and value of the teachings of the church. With the breakdown in moral consensus, schools had no core values upon which to build a curriculum.

Out of the 1960s came an attitude of entitlement — "You owe it to me" — which government fostered, education nursed and society embraced.

RELIGIOUS ACCOMMODATION — In this sobering climate, religion responded weakly. Nero-like, most churches fiddled while Rome burned. Liberals tended to espouse the social and moral agenda of the radicals, and conservatives kept an arm's length from the conflict but enjoyed the abundant fodder for preaching and prophecy. Just as if nothing were happening, liberals charged full speed ahead on the ecumenical agenda for organic union, theological syncretism and religious pluralism.

Conservative churches tended to pull within themselves, create their own counterculture and let parachurch groups do the evangelizing of rebels and youth. Meanwhile, symptomatic of a culture turning inward for self-protection, a host of new psychologies took over the role of the church and its clergy for confession, healing and growth. Evangelicals in particular bought into the new psychology and the "relational theology" that it introduced.

THE COLD WAR — Meanwhile, the Cold War raged between the superpowers of the USSR and the United States. Evil at home may have been dehorned, but on the international scene the devil had a face. Except for "better-red-than-dead" activists, Americans had one rallying point: The "domino effect" of communism across the world and especially in the developing nations had to be stopped at all costs. Presumably, whoever won the two-thirds world won the whole world.

The Surprising Seventies

When the dawn broke upon the decade of the 1970s, campus revolt preoccupied the national agenda. Both sides were stalemated until troops of the National Guard gunned down student protesters at Kent State University (Ohio). A numbed nation caught a glimpse of its soul and saw evil at work. Whether by common sense or fatigue, a truce was drawn and preoccupation shifted to the resolution of the stalemate in Vietnam.

ONE DIVINE MOMENT — Hidden in our national history, however, is a defining moment whose impact upon culture, at home and abroad, radiates through the 1970s and on through the century.

Appropriately entitled "One Divine Moment,"[3] the Spirit of God moved upon the students of evangelical Christian colleges, notably beginning at Asbury College, but almost simultaneously at the Free Methodist schools, Greenville College, Seattle Pacific College, Roberts Wesleyan College, Spring Arbor College and Central College. Marathon chapels for orderly confession, repentance, regeneration and sanctification led to witness teams spreading across the nation and carrying the spirit of revival to students, not just in Christian colleges, but in public and private secular schools as well. Because genuine spiritual awakenings take at least one full generation to reveal their impact upon society, the results of revival are still coming to fruition in the 1990s.

NATIONAL REPENTANCE — Approaching the middle of the decade, the soul-searching that began with the Kent State University killing became wrenching pain with the Watergate revelations. Whatever shreds of confidence remained in established leadership after the revolt of the 1960s were lost in Richard Nixon's betrayal of his presidential trust. With his resignation and exile, he became a symbolic scapegoat for the sins of the nation. The only evidence of a call for national repentance is lost in the Congressional Record when Senator Mark Hatfield received a courtesy voice vote for his Proclamation for a National Day of Humiliation, Fasting and Prayer on April 30, 1974, following the same form used by Abraham Lincoln in the crisis of 1863 and based upon 2 Chronicles 7:14.

EVANGELICAL RESURGENCE — Without knowing the full impact of his proclamation upon history, Senator Hatfield must have sensed the national need for repentance. Just a year or so later, George Gallup discovered a phenomenon called "The Born Again Movement" in which 45 percent of Americans identified themselves as "born again, Bible-believing and witnessing Christians." *Time* magazine's recognition of 1976 as "The Year of the Evangelical" did not come by accident. But the attitude of repentance did not last long. When President Jimmy Carter dared to bare his soul by calling attention to a "national malaise," he learned that Americans still wanted leaders to tell them what they wanted to hear.

A MAJORITY MENTALITY — Regrettably, the "Born Again Movement" turned political. Led by such media personalities as Jerry Falwell, Pat Robertson and Jim Bakker, evangelical Christianity became identified with either Fundamentalism, Pentecostalism or arch-Republicanism in the minds of the public.

With a touch of genius, Jerry Falwell organized the Moral Majority around a mingling of social and political issues that constituted a right-wing agenda. Many evangelicals did not agree with the apparent contradiction between Falwell's rigid theology and his flexible politics, but none can deny his foresight in seeing the future of transdenominational networking around a single cause.

A CULTURAL CHASM — Morally, the stage was being set for a clash of subcultures. Daniel Yankelovich, in his studies of American character, found a major shift, especially among younger and better educated people, from what he called the "ethic of self-denial" to the "ethic of self-fulfillment."[4] Adopting the analogy of the earthquake, he, too, talked about "giant plates" of the culture moving against each other with pressure building for an eruption. The young and educated lived on the fault line.

So while Gallup identified millions who were "born again" to the Christian ethic of self-denial, Yankelovich uncovered millions more whose interest centered in self-fulfillment and whose morality reversed the standards of consensus regarding such matters as marriage, family, work and sexuality that had prevailed in the minds of the general public in the 1950s.

While evangelicals categorically denounced the moral reversal and the radical self-interest of the rising generation, they too became victims of its pervasive cultural influence. At the same time that evangelicals attested absolute truth and unbending moral standards for themselves, they became more tolerant of diversity compelled by a changing culture. The changing attitude toward divorce and remarriage is a prime example.

The Enigmatic Eighties

Not by surprise, Ronald Reagan won election as President of the United States in 1980 on a conservative agenda that echoed the platform of the Moral Majority. With his election, evangelicals entered the center of political power and basked in the limelight of public visibility. Evangelical leaders enjoyed ready access to the Oval Office and vaulted to the top of religious television, book publishing and media attention. Politicians who had long ignored the evangelical sector now knew that they could not be reelected without their support. In consequence, evangelicals skirted the dangerous edges of "civil religion" and eventually paid the price. When President Reagan used the platform of the National Association of Evangelicals to denounce the USSR as the "evil empire," it became clear that evangelicals had attached themselves to a political agenda at the risk of their redemptive mission.

What happened to the Born Again Movement? By and large, it succumbed to the wiles of conservative politics. Losing its prophetic stance, which would include an honest critique of the Reagan policy and program, those who professed to be born again fell victim to the intoxication of political power. Before the decade was out, however, evangelicals learned how fickle the winds of politics can be. After 80 percent of evangelical Christians voted George Bush into office, he pushed them from the center to the margins of power and did not realize what he had done until it was too late.

A MORAL CHASM — The chasm between the subculture of the "new morality" and the subculture of "traditional values" widened during the decade of the 1980s. Studs Terkel, after interviewing scores of people across America, summed up his findings in the title of his book *The Great Divide*. He described the scene by the analogy of right and left wing forces confronting each other at a distance and lofting accusations like missiles over a widening moral chasm, but overshooting the needs of the masses in the middle.[5] Yankelovich, in his continuing survey of public attitudes, discerned a shift among the baby boomers away from the "ethic of self-fulfillment" and toward an "ethic of commitment."[6]

RELIGIOUS REVERSAL — Religiously, the 1980s brought shock to mainline denominations. Assuming a 1950s mentality for their members and espousing a bankrupt liberal agenda, the people marched with their feet, leaving those denominations in droves.

Roman Catholics confronted the reality of a papal regime that was not in touch with the people on such crucial matters as birth control, abortion, marriage of priests and the role of nuns. To add to their dismay, Roman Catholic seminaries and convents emptied under the stigma of sex scandals, a discredited priesthood or sisterhood and entry into marriage.

In one sense, only evangelicals prospered. Counteracting the trends of decline in most mainline denominations, evangelicals grew in number and influence, but not primarily in established denominations. Adopting the market strategies of the secular world to church growth, independent churches grew like topsy to attract those who were disillusioned with mainline denominations or turned off by traditional worship. Along with this movement, wave after wave of new religions appeared on the scene, products of a consumer's search for spirituality.

In this climate, one would expect churches specifically identified with the Holiness Movement to flourish. Instead, they continued to struggle as a beleaguered minority, even within the evangelical sector. A sad fact underscores the struggle of the Holiness Movement. In an unpublished study reported at the 1984 annual convention of the Christian Holiness Association, the survey results showed that a high percentage of people in holiness churches did not understand or experience the flagship doctrine of entire sanctifica-

64

tion. Another high percentage of colleges in the holiness tradition did not teach the doctrine and a still higher percentage of the young did not understand, experience or accept the doctrine.

GLOBAL AWAKENING — Amidst the conflicting forces in North America, however, unmistakable signs of spiritual awakening appeared in the two-thirds world south of the equator and among young and poor but aspiring peoples. Walbert Buhlmann, in his book *The Coming of the Third Church*, predicted that spiritual awakening would come, in order, first to the Third Church in the two-thirds world, second to the First Church of Eastern Europe and third to the Second Church of North America.[7] His first prediction came true in the 1980s as spiritual awakening swept through the nations and tribes of Africa, South America, Asia, India and the islands of the South Seas. His second and third predictions awaited the advent of the 1990s.

The Negotiable Nineties

A TUMBLING WALL — In the 1990s, the turning point came, not in North America, but in West Germany when the Berlin Wall came down. Students danced on top of the wall, chipped at its concrete and sang, "This Is the Day That the Lord Hath Made," celebrating not just the end of the Cold War and the opening of Eastern Europe, but the promise of spiritual awakening in what Buhlmann calls the First Church.[8]

Evangelicals raced through that open door with all of the sophisticated evangelistic techniques of their Western culture only to encounter people of simple and sacrificial faith who put them to shame. Thus, the burden shifted to affluent America and evangelical Christians who had the resources to underwrite the world revival for which they prayed, but they did not realize the cost.

A CASE OF AFFLUENZA — Affluent Americans, however, seemed to be going in the opposite direction. With the close of the Cold War, the driving force of what President Eisenhower called "The Military-Industrial Complex" began to lose its obsessive hold upon the economic priorities of the nation. Rather than redirecting the available resources to such domestic issues as poverty, crime and health care, another set of forces flowed into the vacuum created by the end of the Cold War. The new priority for the American dollar is "The Sports-Entertainment Complex" whose expenditures exceed the total budgets of most of the nations of the world.

Spiritual awakening in the two-thirds world continued in the New Testament pattern of "adding to the church daily those who were being saved." Although the unprecedented pace of expansion introduced the new problems of discipling converts and training leaders for the masses, many of the young and poor churches demonstrated their maturity in parenting new congregations and sending missionaries to other nations, including the Western world.

A NEW PARADIGM — Global connectedness was further enhanced by humankind's entry into "The Information Age." With information becoming wealth and access to information the source of power, another revolution was in the making. As television impacted the values of the culture in the 1960s, computers, fax machines and modems upset all of the ways in which people think, communicate and behave. The buzzword for the decade represents the revolutionary nature of "The Information Age." The call is for a "new paradigm" or "... a set of rules and regulations (written or unwritten) that does two things: (1) it establishes and defines boundaries and (2) it tells you how to behave inside the boundaries in order to be successful."[9]

BEYOND DENOMINATIONALISM — In the United States, the church continued to undergo unprecedented change. Mainline denominations continued to suffer significant losses and move toward the margins of influence. The National and World Council of Churches, struggling with internal controversy and liberal theology, faced the reality of fighting a rear-guard action to maintain a semblance of credibility. Issues of gender, race and sexuality led the way. Moreover, in order to survive, traditional denominations made such radical adjustments that students of church organizations have chosen the term "Post-denominational Confessionalism" to describe the magnitude of the shift.[10]

Driving the forces of change was the fact that the old bonds that held denominations together became loose and frayed in the short span of three decades. Without these bonds, denominations lost social cohesion and members' loyalty. Hierarchies within the denominations showed the strain first and fought vigorously to maintain their bureaucratic structure. Further threat came from the special-purpose groups and trans-denominational networks that competed for members' loyalty and usually won because they responded to changing needs and offered a choice.

Mainline denominations lost the most, namely, their credible "adhesive and dynamic principles."[11] Evangelical denominations and organizations, however, gained the most as they inherited the adhesive and dynamic principles of a moral and spiritual campaign to Christianize the nation.

Most visibly, Post-denominational Confessionalism "emerges in the megachurches and family life centers, mall-like congregations offering both superstore and boutique religion."[12] The critical discernment of biblical exegesis and hermeneutics goes begging so that theology becomes a matter of individual interpretation based upon consumer preference. Watching this trend, Leith Anderson has warned that, unless the foundation of sound biblical theology is built under these new movements, we will see a "tidal wave of heterodoxy in the next generation."[13]

HUNGER FOR HOLINESS — A major theological shift is also evident in the opening years of the 1990s. Counteracting the fruitless years of organizational tinkering, ecumenical fantasies, therapeutic theology and copycat strategies, the hidden hunger for genuine spirituality, which most churches ignored or neglected, became a desperate search. Now it was clear that the church had forfeited the field to the mysticism of Eastern religions and the half-truths of the New Age Movement. As a quick corrective, seminaries put "Spiritual Formation" at the center of their curriculum, clergy and laity flocked to workshops on spiritual disciplines, classical devotionals regained popularity and publishing houses unabashedly advertised books on "holiness" and "spirituality."

Holiness churches might well have been first to respond to this newly awakened hunger for genuine spirituality and wholeness. Despite more than a century of preaching and teaching the doctrine, they were left on the sideline. Why? Whether they carried the old stigma of "Christian perfection," insisted upon a narrow definition of sanctification, tripped over their own language or found themselves bypassed as non-consequential, the answer is still not known.

Keith Drury, Director of Local Church Education for the Wesleyan Church, bearded the lion in his den at the 1994 Annual Convention of the Christian Holiness Association when he dared to take the title for his luncheon address, "The Holiness Movement Is Dead."[14]

Defining a movement by its momentum, Drury backed up his thesis with the question, "Why did we die?" Answering his own question, he said:

(1) We wanted to be respectable; (2) We have plunged into the evangelical mainstream; (3) We have failed to convince the younger generation; (4) We quit making holiness the main issue; (5) We lost the lay people; (6) We overreacted against the abuses of the past; (7) We adopted church-growth thinking without theological thinking; and (8) We did not notice when the battle line moved.

"But here is the irony," Drury said. "There has perhaps never been a time in history when the church more needs a holiness movement." Recognizing the search for holiness in the 1990s, Drury asked in conclusion, "Will the old holiness be *in* the new holiness movement?" He left the question open.

Whatever the reason, holiness churches contributed little to the ongoing search for spirituality. But for their people, the doctrine of holiness took on the new language of the "Spirit-filled life" and the new experience of "Spiritual Formation" as a developmental process.

Free Methodism's Challenge

Gleanings from this overview of the period reveal 10 specific trends that challenged the Free Methodist Church from 1960-1995. These trends are neither absolute nor complete. Their beginning may well precede 1960, and their ending may well be far in the future. As further caution, these trends should not be interpreted in "either/or" categories. Historical trends must be read as a moving picture in content as well as time. For this reason, the trends are traced on the "from/to" line of time and content.

I. FROM NATIONAL ISOLATION TO GLOBAL INTERDE-PENDENCE — The "global village," predicted in the 1960s by Kenneth Boulding, is reality in 1995.[15] Whatever shreds of isolationist or protectionist attitudes remain in the minds of people in any corner of the world, they are short-lived. On earth as well as in the universe, "everything is connected to everything else."

Now, as Buhlmann wrote so prophetically, the spiritual connections among the First, Second and Third Churches shift the old patriarchal and non-contextual patterns of world missions to a new interdependence in which all peoples are partners in the global body of Christ. World revival may well turn on the pivot of the church accepting this new relationship.

II. FROM CULTURAL HOMOGENEITY TO DEMOGRAPHIC DIVERSITY — As a companion to global interdependence, demographic diversity is making every city and country a microcosm of the changing world. Most notable is the coloring of the United States. Along with the multiplying numbers of African-American and Hispanic peoples are the migrants of color from Asia, India, South America, Central America, the Caribbean and Africa who will soon outnumber Caucasians in the national population.

With them come spiritual needs and expectations that cannot be met by the traditional patterns of the white, Anglo-Saxon, middle-class religious subculture. Further complicating the coloring of the culture is urban migration. With the development of world class cities, whose populations number in the millions, and the reality that a majority of persons live in or near these cities, the structure and style of the small, rural church cannot be transferred to the new setting.

The changing role of women adds another ingredient to the salad bowl of diversity. Wade Clark Roof saw the status of women changing in the 1960s as a natural result of World War II when men went to war and women went to work. Three decades later, women have won recognition as persons, acceptance in careers at home or away, participation in governance and positions of leadership. As with ethnics, the goal of full and equal status for women may be still in the future, but the momentum for change cannot be denied.

III. FROM WRITTEN TEXT TO VISUAL IMAGE — Despite the protest of librarians, the written text is all but dead. In its place is the visual image of electronic communication with all of the power of "cool" media. Whoever controls the image has the wealth and power that was reserved for the economically rich just a generation ago. At the same time, communication by image releases new discretionary power into the hands of the people who have more information with which to make more choices.

   Theology, in particular, is at stake. How will the Word of God be accurately translated by picture as well as print? How will the good news of the gospel be communicated through images? Can Christianity compete with "The Sports-Entertainment Complex," a creation of the image industry?

IV. FROM ETHICAL CONSENSUS TO MORAL TOLERANCE — The influence of the moral revolution of the 1960s is pervasive. Not even those who were repelled by the rejection of legitimate leadership, the breakdown of primary institutions and the undermining of moral consensus could escape its influence. With the adoption of the term "lifestyle" to describe a person's moral as well as social behavior, sin lost its stigma. Also, "relative values" took the place of "moral standards," and "preferences" became the alternative for "convictions."

   Not only are evangelical Christians more tolerant of behavior euphemistically known as the "Five Fundy Sins" of drinking, smoking, card-playing, movie-going and dancing, but their tolerance extends to theological ambiguity in regeneration and sanctification, relational breakdown in marriage and divorce and spiritual stewardship in sports, entertainment and Sabbath observance.

   For such difficult moral judgments as the attitude toward premarital sex and homosexuality, evangelical Christians are impaled on the horns of a dilemma between the pronouncement of sin and the provision for grace. Even on the issue of abortion, the house is divided between the extremes of jus-

69

tice and mercy. Easy tolerance rather than costly grace is often the middle ground chosen between extremes.

V.   FROM COMMUNAL RULES TO PERSONAL OPTIONS — Some social analysts of the era draw a dividing line between the limited choices for citizens in the pre-1960 society and the multiple options in the 1990s. The ad showing the availability of 31 flavors of ice cream today versus vanilla, chocolate and strawberry just a generation ago illustrates the point that consumer options characterize the nature of a market-driven, affluent society. In the period from 1960-1995, the church continued to struggle with the clarity of its mission and message as it faced the competitive threat of a market mentality.

VI.   FROM COLD WAR TO CULTURAL WARFARE — The chasm between the absolutes of revealed truth and the ambiguities of relative truth is not new. But the coalition of evangelicals, conservative Roman Catholics and Orthodox Jews is a complete turnaround in attitude within the period 1960-1995.

In 1960 evangelicals strenuously opposed the election of a Roman Catholic president and had no communication with Jews. Now in the life and death struggle of cultural warfare, the "cobelligerents" are not only talking, but uniting under the single banner of revealed truth against such issues as abortion-on-demand and sexual permissiveness. A common commitment to absolute truth as revealed in the Word of God, whether Old or New Testament, makes partners of old enemies.

VII.   FROM CORPORATE ORGANIZATION TO POST-DENOMINATIONAL CONFESSIONALISM — As the baby boomers born or reared in the 1960s come to their mid-30s and early 40s, they are taking the lead in creating the spiritual climate within which the church must minister. If, as Wade Clark Roof writes, they are a generation of seekers and the church must be "seeker sensitive," profound changes will have to take place in traditional denominations. As noted earlier, the nature of this change has been described as Post-denominational Confessionalism.[16]

In 1960, established denominations were identified with corporate denominationalism in structure and governance and policy and programs. But by the mid-1990s, the denominations were either stagnated or showing signs of serious decline. Whether or not established denominations can make the adjustment to the flex and flow of Post-denominational

Confessionalism and still maintain their core values is a point upon which the future turns.

VIII. FROM SYSTEMATIC THEOLOGY TO RELATIONAL THE-OLOGY — Prior to World War II, faith and psychotherapy eyed each other either with suspicion or downright antagonism. But out of the war came the counseling and testing movement that made psychotherapy more acceptable. Evangelical Christians bought into the movement under the umbrella of "relational theology" defined as affirming in others what Christ affirms in us.

Since then, evangelical Christianity has been profoundly influenced by the behavioral sciences of psychology as applied to personal relationships and sociology as applied to family systems and church growth. Particularly among the baby boomers and the "X" generation, their theology is driven by the relational questions focused upon issues of self-fulfillment, personal growth and interpersonal development. Even their understanding and acceptance of regeneration and sanctification is defined, not by the rational theology of the past, but the relational theology of the present.

A century ago, the church struggled with the integration of revelation and reason. At the end of the 20th century, the struggle continues, but with "revealed truth" and "relational theology" as the key players in the contest.

IX. FROM PARACHURCH ORGANIZATIONS TO TRANS- DE-NOMINATIONAL NETWORKS — As needs change and established institutions fail to meet those needs, God raises up new, need-responsive institutions. In the 1960s, the parachurch movement swept over the religious landscape with visionary leadership, flexible organizations and free-flowing style in response to changing spiritual needs, especially among the young.

In the 1970s and 1980s, when the phenomenon of single-purpose networking became a new force in society, trans-denominational networking replaced parachurch organizations as the front edge of the evangelical movement.

By the mid-1990s, such trans-denominational networks as Marriage Encounter, Promise Keepers, Concerts of Prayer, Emmaus Walk, SonLife and the Flagpole movement among high schoolers enlisted the loyalty of hundreds of thousands of evangelical Christians and took over the function of established denominations of resourcing the ministry of the local

71

church. Initially, at least, denominations are not viewing the new networks as competitive, but if the loyalty and financial support of its members continue to develop as a threat to the denomination, strained relationships can be predicted.

X. FROM WESLEYAN HOLINESS TO EVANGELICAL SPIRI-TUALITY — With the social issues, slavery and free seats, upon which Free Methodism was founded, no longer defining the denomination, the burden of distinction falls upon the doctrine of entire sanctification. Reality, however, reminds us that internally the doctrine is neither proclaimed, experienced or practiced in its traditional context. Externally, the threat is increased by generic spirituality rising out of relational theology.

Literally, a new paradigm is being created for holiness. The boundaries are broad, the principles are developmental and the rules are flexible. Language is a part of the problem but not the whole issue. As an inclusive term, the "Spirit-filled life" can embrace Wesleyan or Reformed theology, provide for crisis or gradualism in experience, accept a Pentecostal or Holiness witness and permit the practice of faith working through sin or through perfect love. Among all of the challenges to Free Methodism during the period from 1960-1995, none is more fundamental to its future.

To say the least, Free Methodism in the first generation of its second century knew the meaning of Dickens' opening line in *The Tale of Two Cities*, "It was the best of times; it was the worst of times." Both danger and opportunity walked through the era hand in hand. How did Free Methodism respond? The answers are in the history of the church and its people from 1960-1995.

Part III
A MISSION
ON THE MOVE

1960 to 1995
and
Forward

In 1960, the Free Methodist Church entered its second century with a spirit of optimism grounded in its historic mission and expressed in far-ranging denominational ministries. Within less than three years, however, a stable society was shaken by a moral and spiritual earthquake of global proportions with aftershocks reverberating throughout the remaining years of the century. *How did the Free Methodist Church fare in these turbulent times?*

Part III answers this question with the story of the Free Methodist Church at work in its mission and ministry. Beginning with the foundation of its faith position, the structure, governance and stewardship provide the framework for its ministries of aggressive evangelism, Christian education, world missions, social compassion and ecumenical action. Through the record of the church at work between 1960 and 1995 and forward, the strength of its mission and the effectiveness of its ministries can be read as Free Methodism's response to a world turned upside down.

C H A P T E R 5

Defining
Our
Faith

Quaker pioneers, who met after a long period of separation, greeted each other with the question, "How does the truth fare in thy parts?" The question is one that Free Methodists should ask about their faith in each generation. "How does the truth fare in thy parts?" is the question that leads directly to the theology of the church in its Articles of Religion and their application in the experience and conduct of its membership.

In the first century of Free Methodism, the truth fared well. Wesley's Twenty-Four Articles of Religion (with the addition of articles on Entire Sanctification and Last Things), his *Notes Upon the New Testament* and his 52 sermons formed the standards of Methodist doctrine that the Free Methodist Church adopted as its own. From this strong base, the Free Methodist Church aligned itself theologically with biblical revelation, the church fathers, the Protestant Reformation and especially Anglican-Arminian belief and teaching.

To the credit of Free Methodism, no significant theological contention divided the church during its first century, and no major changes were made in the Articles of Religion as written in the *Discipline*. Both the strength and weakness of the Free Methodist Church may be revealed in this non-contentious theological climate. As a strength, it means that the energies of the church could be directed outwardly in evangelism rather than inwardly on debate. The lack of continuing theological dialogue may be its weakness.

Yet it cannot be forgotten that Wesley's Articles of Religion, *Notes Upon the New Testament*, and 52 sermons, which he sent with Thomas Coke as standards for the church in America, came out of vigorous debate between Wesley and his colleagues, Charles Wesley, John Fletcher, Adam Clarke and others in the second-story quarters of New Room in Bristol, England. Free Methodism needed that continuing theological dialogue in its first century. Except for the continuing clarification of the doctrine of entire sanctification through the books and editorials of B.T. Roberts and his bishop colleagues, debate over major theological issues was limited.

Among the new generations of Free Methodists, an appreciation for putting deep roots of the church into biblical revelation, the church fathers, Arminian theology, Anglican tradition and Methodist history may seem to have been neglected. Still, the strengths outweigh the weaknesses. The Free Methodist Church began its second century in 1960 with unanimous affirmation of its founding principles in belief, experience and practice. With this benchmark as a guide, the Quaker's question can be asked, "How then does the truth fare in the second century?" Let the record of the church speak for itself.

Clarifying the Meaning of Scriptural Holiness

As the Free Methodist Church stood on the threshold of its second century, Bishop Marston's warning could be heard, "If there is a doctrinal weakness, it is not decline in acceptance of the doctrine so much as lack of clarity in defining it and lack of forcefulness in proclaiming it."[1]

The warning did not go unheeded. In the pastoral address for 1960, Bishop Walter Kendall, speaking on behalf of the Board of Bishops, intentionally chose to reaffirm the founding principle of scriptural holiness. Drawing first on the leadership of B.T. Roberts, he quoted his words to Free Methodist ministers: "Our preachers, if they would succeed in their work, must preach entire sanctification. They must preach it clearly, distinctly and definitely. On this subject the gospel trumpeter must give no uncertain sound."[2]

Bishop Kendall exhorted, "Today, at the close of our first century, we may well feel the gravity of the trust that is ours. *Is the banner of holiness still flying at the top of the mast?*"

Still, change was in the making. Anticipating the prospect of organic union with other holiness churches, the bishops recommended "that we maintain the ideal of a sanctified church as the unity of true believers, and promote union with other holiness churches where such can be effected, in harmony with Wesleyan doctrines and Wesleyan standards of holy living."[3] Accordingly, a constitutional amendment was proposed for Article XIII to make "Entire Sanctification" more relevant for communication and more effective for application without compromising the essence of the doctrine.

The proposed amendment of 1960 came, not as the result of a theological study commission on the doctrine of entire sanctification, but as part of the proposed *Book of Discipline* developed in 1954 by a joint committee for the merger of the Free Methodist Church and the Wesleyan Methodist Church into the United Wesleyan Methodist Church. Although the merger itself was

76

rejected, the constitutional amendment passed with the support of Free Methodist theologians and church leaders. Ratification by the annual conferences followed, and the revised Article XIII became the doctrine of the church. No other changes have been made in this statement except for an action of the 1974 General Conference to reword the article in the form of a confession of faith rather than a declaration of faith. That wording remained until the 1989 General Conference returned the Articles to declarative form. Accordingly, it reads as follows:

ARTICLE XIII — Entire Sanctification

> Entire sanctification is that work of the Holy Spirit, subsequent to regeneration, by which the fully consecrated believer, upon exercise of faith in the atoning blood of Christ, is cleansed in that moment from all inward sin and empowered for service. The resulting relationship is attested by the witness of the Holy Spirit and is maintained by faith and obedience. Entire sanctification enables the believer to love God with all his heart, soul, strength and mind, and his neighbor as himself, and it prepares him for greater growth in grace.[4]

Consistent with the leadership role of their predecessors, bishops of the Free Methodist Church since 1960 have continued to speak and write about the doctrine of entire sanctification through pastoral addresses to general conferences, bishops' columns in the *Free Methodist* or *Light and Life* magazine and through books on the subject. Bishop J. Paul Taylor, for instance, wrote his book, *The Finished Foundation,* on the subject of holiness, utilizing the 1960 revision of Article XIII as his primary source.

The Pastoral Address of the 1989 General Conference, given by Bishop Gerald E. Bates, further affirms the faithfulness of church leadership to the doctrine in the words, "Thoughtful Christians of every tradition are talking about holiness, searching the Scriptures, seeking a theology ... Centuries ago, God, in His all-wise providence, spoke this redeeming message again through the Wesley brothers. We have inherited this cherished message as our unique assignment under God. We, in the footsteps of the early Methodists, are called to proclaim holiness across these lands."

Other than pastoral addresses at General Conferences, the major instrument for communicating the message of holiness, however, has been the *Free Methodist* or later, the *Light and Life* magazine in which the bishops rotate on regular bishops' columns. Through these articles, every bishop has affirmed the doctrine of entire sanctification. An abbreviated bibliography from the denominational magazine underscores their leadership on the subject:

Walter S. Kendall, "Holiness: A Charitable Spirit," February 1960
J. Paul Taylor, "Holiness: The Finished Foundation," February 1963

Charles V. Fairbairn, "A Prayer For a Clean Heart," March 1964
E.C. John, "Living at Our Best," June 1964
Leslie R. Marston, "The Mind of Christ," June 1964
Paul N. Ellis,
   I. "The Beginning of Holiness," May 1980
   II. "Hunger for Holiness," June 1980
   III. "Christians Who Are Christians," July 1980
W. Dale Cryderman, "Holiness," May 1983
Elmer E. Parsons, "Seek God's Best," December 1983
Clyde E. Van Valin, "Resolve to be Holy," January 1988
Robert F. Andrews, "Pursuit of the Perfect," February 1988
Gerald E. Bates, "The Path of Holiness," July 1992
David M. Foster, "Humpty Dumpty, Stay on the Wall," February 1989
Richard D. Snyder, "Obeying God With a Smile," January 1993

Moreover, as a complement to the more formal documents of pastoral addresses, state-of-the-work reports and the occasional newsletter, *Confidentially Yours*, the *Light and Life* magazine has been the major instrument for communicating to the church constituency other biblical convictions and denominational distinctives as well as entire sanctification. An overview of these bishops' columns and articles from 1960-1995 shows the bishops giving special attention to the issues of tongues in Christian experience, music in worship, prayer in piety, tithing in stewardship, the New Day vision in evangelism and global growth in missions.

Social concerns of the bishops centered on the position of the church regarding marriage, divorce and sexual behavior. Major themes of the conservative agenda in the 1980s also included articles on abortion, abstinence, substance abuse, pornography, gambling, citizenship and Sabbath observance. Selective attention was given to education, ministry to the poor, scriptural authority, ecclesiology, authority of Scripture, membership discipline, the pastoral ministry, church governance and the spiritual disciplines of prayer, fasting and Bible study. Fewer articles, however, should not be interpreted as the lack of interest in the issues.

A timeliness can be detected in the publication of the articles. Bishops spoke to the position of the church on the authority of Scripture, for instance, during the inerrancy debates of the 1970s and 1980s. A readers' poll for *Light and Life* magazine attests the influence of the bishops' writings. In fact, on the basis of the poll, the editor moved their columns from the back to the front of the magazine. Available evidence, then, shows that the bishops have taken seriously the leadership charge to keep the banner of holiness flying at the top of the mast.

Studying Theological Issues

Beginning in 1969, the General Conference recognized the need for in-depth study of the theological issues that were emerging from the changing society and from merger talks with the Wesleyan Church. Out of that conference, instructions were given to the Board of Bishops to form an advisory committee of theologically astute clergy for the purpose of consulting with them on theological issues. Their initial assignment was to study the question of infant baptism and dedication.

In 1972 the Board of Administration formalized the role of the advisory committee as the Study Commission on Doctrine (SCOD) with infant baptism and divorce as part of its initial assignment. The first full report of SCOD came at the 1974 General Conference with the recommendation for a disciplinary statement on "Speaking in Tongues," which was adopted as the official position of the church.

In that same General Conference, the theological issues underlying the merger talks enlarged the agenda of SCOD and vaulted the commission into a position of power in the church. At the 1979 General Conference, the adoption of SCOD recommendations on disciplinary changes regarding "Simplicity of Life" and the "Ordination of Ministry" along with "A Manifesto on Evangelism" reflected the priorities of the church at that time.

By 1981 the SCOD agenda had been further expanded to include studies on entire sanctification, ordination of ministers, marriage and divorce, the Lord's Supper and children, an article of religion on "The Father" and development of a Membership Covenant. Out of this substantial agenda came the SCOD report to the 1985 General Conference. Bishop Clyde Van Valin, chair of the commission, presented papers and recommendations on "Ordination and Leadership," "Marriage and Divorce," "Membership Covenant," "Lectionary" and "Entire Sanctification." SCOD had been advanced to the role of the theological "think tank" for the church with a vote of confidence that it could address the most crucial issues of the day. Further evidence of its importance came in 1985 when the General Conference appointed four lay persons, two of whom were women, as members of the committee.

By the General Conference of 1989, SCOD had moved to the center of action on doctrine and polity. A formal printed report with recommendations had now expanded into the: (a) *theological* issues of the authority of Scripture, holiness, tongues and the return of Christ; (b) the *sacramental* issue of the Lord's Supper; (c) the *relational* issues of marriage, divorce and remarriage; (d) the *social* issue of dancing; (e) the *governance* issues of judicial administration and the role of superintendents and bishops; and (f) the *moral* issue of bioethics.

As for the present and future, the SCOD report on the controversial issue of the rewritten Membership Covenant became the centerpiece for General Conference debate and action in 1995. If the first century of the Free Methodist Church lacked theological dialogue, the last two decades of the second century have reactivated both the vitality of debate and the potential for controversy over matters of faith.

Rewriting the *Discipline*

Among the multiple issues related to doctrine that occupied the church during the period 1960-1995 and forward, three stand out. First, merger talks with the Wesleyan Church produced a major rewriting of the *Discipline* in order to accommodate the integration of the two traditions. Second, the church's position on marriage, divorce and remarriage went through change after change in response to the new reality of cultural impact upon the lives of both members and ministers. Third, the shift in the discipline of membership from general and specific rules to a Membership Covenant, which grew out of the Proposed Articles of Agreement and Constitution for merger in 1974, continued to escalate through the next two decades until it stands alongside worship style as one of the most critical issues of the 1990s.

I. MERGER AGREEMENT — In anticipation of merger of the Free Methodist and Wesleyan churches, the Articles of Religion were rewritten in 1974 along with the constitution for the organization of the new church. More contemporary language was adopted for the revision than in the historic creeds upon which the earlier articles were based. Prepared by a joint Committee on Merger Exploration (COME), the agreement received the approval of the general boards of administration of both denominations as recommendations to their respective general conferences, and to their annual/district conferences for ratification. The Free Methodist Church, meeting at the General Conference of 1974, added an article on "The Father" and revised the format for the Membership Covenant into a confessional style. Chapters on the Principles of Christian Conduct, Christian Experience and Christian Worship were also revised to accommodate the new union.

Not everyone agreed. Some sharp theological minds felt as if the precision of centuries of scholarship had been sacrificed in the revision, particularly in regard to such cardinal doctrines as the Trinity and Original Sin. In fact Article II on "The Father" became an item of theological debate from the time it was added to the merger report of 1974 where it remained until 1985 when the General Conference voted to delete it as potentially a doctrinal heresy. Contention centered around the phrase, "We believe that God the Father, *with the Son and Holy Spirit*, is the cause of all that exists."

Opponents of the italicized phrase argued that (1) Article II did not appear in any Free Methodist Discipline before 1974; (2) an article on the Father does not appear in any of the historic creeds; (3) the article adds nothing to affirmations that are said elsewhere and more appropriately; and (4) the statement may lead to tritheism and a rerun of the Arian heresy, which Free Methodists categorically reject. In 1979 an amendment to Article II was referred to SCOD for study. In 1985 the General Conference voted to delete the article.

When the annual and general conferences failed to ratify the deletion, the matter came up before the 1989 General Conference once again for a final decision. The required majority upheld the previous action, and Article II was deleted from the Articles of Faith. Then, as if to put a final period upon the lost merger agreement, the General Conference voted to restore the Articles of Faith to their original declarative form prior to the revision of 1974, which put the Articles into confessional form. For example, in confessional form, the opening sentence of Article I reads, "We believe in the one living and true God ... ," while the declarative form reads, "There is but one living and true God. ..."

II. MARRIAGE, DIVORCE AND REMARRIAGE — No theological issue of practical import for Free Methodists spans the era from 1960-1995 so pervasively as the position of the church on marriage, divorce and remarriage. It began in 1960 with an amendment to the paragraph in the *Discipline* on divorce, which read:
- If divorce is granted on grounds of adultery, the innocent spouse may remarry and be a member of the Free Methodist Church;
- Persons divorced prior to Christian conversion and application for membership shall not for that reason be barred from membership;
- If divorce was granted on other grounds than adultery, the individual may be a member if a statement was signed stating that adultery did exist on the part of the divorced partner.

Although the General Conference of 1960 adopted the amendment, its implementation was delayed pending further study and report by the Board of Bishops. In 1964 the bishops reported that the amendment required a constitutional change and therefore ratification by the annual conferences. Their opinion was referred to the Judiciary Committee, which met during the General Conference and ruled in favor of its constitutionality. At that moment, the amendment of 1960 took effect.

Questions of divorce and remarriage did not go away. As a reflection of the social and moral revolution of the 1960s, pastors in the field had to deal with the sticky issue of members and converts who came through divorce and remarriage. In the 1974 conference, the statement on divorce was revised to provide for marital separation: Members may separate when an otherwise impossible situation is destroying the peace of the home: neither may remarry; and the way to reconciliation must be kept open.

Further stipulations were placed in the disciplinary section on Marriage, Divorce and Remarriage at the General Conference of 1979. Guidelines were drawn prohibiting divorce because of an unchristian mate, permitting remarriage after desertion that leads to divorce, and pronouncing a member of the church guilty of adultery if he or she remarries after divorce on other than biblical grounds.

When the dilemmas of divorce and remarriage reached into ministerial ranks, the General Conference of 1979 set up the Board of Bishops as the screening committee for approval of ministerial candidates who were divorced prior to consideration for conference membership. Also, if a ministerial member or a supply pastor were to be divorced, remarriage was prohibited unless the Board of Bishops ruled that the divorce involved biblical grounds.

At the General Conference of 1985, the church took a major step toward a more redemptive stance for members who were divorced. Ministries of reconciliation were recommended for troubled marriages, and if divorced members sought to remarry, the local pastor's cabinet was designated to serve as a resource for guidance.

Still another step toward redemption was taken in the recommendations of SCOD to the General Conference of 1989. The disciplinary statement was enlarged to include: defining the nature of marriage, nurturing healthy marriages, healing troubled marriages, separation, divorce, recovery after divorce, remarriage, refusal of counsel and exceptional cases.

Scriptural grounds for divorce, e.g., adultery, were also expanded into the following principles:

(1) "When one marriage partner is a Christian and the other a nonbeliever, the Christian may not for that reason divorce the unchristian mate, because Christian love may redeem the unbeliever and unite the home in Christ; (2) A person denies the faith who deserts a spouse deliberately and for an extended period of time. When the desertion leads subsequently to divorce, the deserted partner is no longer bound by the marriage; (3) Even when a marriage is violated by sexual infidelity, the partners are encouraged to work for the restoration of the union. Where reconciliation is impossible, divorce may be unavoidable."

The latter sentence adopted in 1989 must be compared with the position of the church in 1960. While still holding to biblical grounds for divorce, there is a definitive shift toward reconciliation as the guiding principle. If reconciliation fails, however, divorce is recognized as a permissible option only in cases of sexual infidelity. Not yet included are cases where reconciliation has failed for other moral reasons, such as domestic violence or spousal abuse.

Even more complicated, the knotty issue of "irreconcilable differences"

— a legal provision for divorce in the secular society — may well come into play in future deliberations.

III. REDEFINING THE MEANING OF MEMBERSHIP —A prelude to change in the rules for membership in the Free Methodist Church can be read in the action of the 1951 General Conference when the body voted to exclude the wedding ring from the prohibition against "gold, pearls and costly array." Paralleling that action, the conference also unanimously adopted a paper distinguishing the difference between principles and prudentials. According to the paper, "Principles of conduct are clearly taught in Scripture, or are directly implied in the Word"; but "Prudentials are those rules formulated by the church and required of its members as aids to godliness."[5] Further stimulated by merger talks in the 1970s, the modification of membership rules set in motion a series of studies and reports throughout the 1980s and into the 1990s that are now leading to a defining moment in the history of Free Methodism as it turns toward the 21st century.

Out of the 1979 General Conference came a petition calling for "principles" rather than "rules" in the Membership Covenant. The body did not act upon the petition, but instead referred it to the Study Commission on Doctrine, which was rapidly becoming the source for referral when issues were either in doubt or too explosive to handle. The commission reported its findings at the General Conference of 1985 with the bold recommendation to limit the Membership Covenant to basic principles and to expand the relevant chapters of the *Discipline* that detail the application of those principles in practice.

Although the General Conference adopted the recommendation, it failed to be ratified in a referendum of the annual and general conferences. To no one's surprise, petition after petition flooded the General Conference of 1989 with the continuing concern for the legalism of the rules contained within the Membership Covenant. Theological questions relating to the meaning of salvation and ecclesiastical questions relating to the nature of church were asked. But lurking beneath these more theoretical questions was the reality of a changing culture. Growing congregations and church plants had converts and transfers desiring membership in the church before demonstrating the spiritual maturity that the rules implied.

A key to understanding the issue at stake is the sentence in a paper presented to the General Conference of 1989 that read, "Members of the Free Methodist Church are required to assent to making the membership covenant and the guidelines for Christian conduct the *goals* [emphasis added] of their maturing Christian lives." Recognizing the potential impact of the sentence upon the character and ministry of the church, the General Conference referred the paper to SCOD with instructions to bring back a report and recommendations to the General Conference of 1995.

The four areas of study that SCOD outlined for its work affirm the seriousness with which the members took their assignment. Those areas of exploration were: (1) The theology of conversion and biblical standards for church membership; (2) Methodist practice vis-à-vis rules and their rationale; (3) The role of membership in the ethical development of persons; and (4) Church-growth insights bearing upon membership requirements and standards.

Volumes of papers were completed by the SCOD committee and its subcommittees as they sought to address these areas with such far-reaching implications. As they interpreted their charge, they accepted the awesome responsibility to maintain the moral vision of the church as a body of believers who pursues holiness and love as a way of life. At the same time, they sought to rescue the church from the legalism of rules by rewriting the Membership Covenant on sound theological and ecclesiastical grounds.

At the risk of oversimplifying the volumes of papers prepared by SCOD members in preparation for the General Conference of 1995, an interpretative summary of their responses to the four areas of study that they outlined may be helpful:

1. Biblically and theologically, the prerequisites for membership are conversion, faith and baptism with New Testament imperatives placed upon believers for faithful living that will lead to spiritual maturity.

2. Methodists, under the leadership of John Wesley, adopted the General Rules to (1) do no harm; (2) do good; and (3) observe all of the ordinances of God. These are the qualifications for membership in a society that is backed by a support system of classes and bands for progressive spiritual development toward the goal of "perfectness in the fear of God."

3. Free Methodists, to correct the theological and ecclesiastical laxity of the Methodist Episcopal Church, adopted general and special rules for membership not primarily as a "means" to spiritual maturity, but as an "end" to preserve the purity of the church.

4. Church growth evidenced by the entry of new members along with character development within the body of Christ, especially where new churches are involved, is hindered when spiritual maturity is an entrance requirement and ethical conformity is made a condition of "belonging."

With these findings as their guide, the SCOD report for the 1995 General Conference recommended major modifications in the Membership Covenant to emphasize entry principles backed by separate sections on maturity goals. Notable also was the recommendation to shift from the first person "I" to the third person "we" in the vows for membership. This shift assumed that the local church congregation as a body of believers accepted mutual responsibility for the spiritual maturity of its members.

Rather than reciting completely the revision of the new Membership Covenant and comparing it with the 1989 *Discipline* version, the difference can be detected in the commitment regarding alcohol, tobacco and harmful drugs. In the 1989 *Discipline*, under the section "As Regards Myself and All Men," a candidate for membership vows to abide by the specific rule: "I will abstain from the manufacture, sale and use of alcoholic beverages and harmful drugs and from the cultivation, manufacture, sale and use of tobacco." For contrast, with the affirmative action of the General Conference of 1995 and the SCOD recommendations, the *Discipline* will now present the broader principled commitment, "We seek to be free from habits and attitudes that defile the mind and harm the body." A backup section on the "Misuse of Drugs" would then cite the special rules of the earlier Membership Covenant.

Opponents of the proposed Membership Covenant were quick to point out that Free Methodism would be recycling the history of defection in the Methodist Episcopal Church, which led to the formation of the Free Methodist Church in the first place. Theological advocates of the traditional holiness position saw the crisis experience of entire sanctification co-opted within the theory of developmental psychology. Students of pastoral care asked for the assurance of supporting structures to assume mutual accountability for the spiritual maturity of members. And, of course, an older generation rued the loss of distinction for holy living as the unique witness of church membership.

Dr. Paul Livermore, professor of theology at Roberts Wesleyan College and a Free Methodist pastor, countered these concerns in a scholarly paper entitled, "The Form and the Power of Godliness: Historical Uses of the General Rules for the United Societies." First, he contended that John Wesley envisioned sequences of salvation (*ordo salutis*) that (1) began with the *natural state* of sin prior to the time when the Spirit of God works secretively by prevenient grace; (2) moved on to the *legal state* when God "awakens" the soul to sin, to the provisions of forgiving grace, and to the act of repentance; (3) advanced to the *justified* or *initially sanctified state* in which atoning grace confirms the believer's trust in Christ; and (4) came to a level of spiritual maturity in the *entirely sanctified state* of cleansing and empowerment in perfect love, with the promise of continuing growth.

Livermore further contended that Wesley matched the legal state with societies and classes, the justified state with bands and the entirely sanctified state with select bands as the essential support system for growth in grace. Livermore asserted that Free Methodism, to correct the abuses of the Methodist Episcopal Church, short-circuited the sequences of salvation by collapsing the awakened or legal state into the natural or sinful state, combining the function of the bands with the classes and putting membership criteria for the classes and bands upon the societies at large as entry prerequisites. Livermore saw the theological sequences of salvation and the ecclesial structure of support as inseparable.

If, according to Livermore, the Free Methodist Church were to return to its biblical and Wesleyan roots, the legal state of the awakened soul would be recognized for membership in the church. Then supporting structures akin to classes and bands would be restored to assist with the discipling for Christian growth in attitudes and behavior, along with nurturing toward Christian perfection, as evidenced through the experience of entire sanctification.

Dr. Robert Wall, professor of religion at Seattle Pacific University, brought yet another perspective to the debate by building upon Free Methodist history and a theology of the church. Wall contended that Free Methodism finds the reason for its existence in the spiritual demonstration of self-renunciation and the social witness of abolition. Simply put, the integration of personal and social holiness defines the past, present and future of Free Methodism. Therefore, according to Wall, the sections of the *Discipline* on "Christian Experience," "Christian Conduct" and "Christian Community" must be theologically consistent with the spiritual distinctives of renunciation and abolition.

These distinctives, according to Wall, should also run like dual threads through the life of the church and its membership. Without these threads of distinction, he concluded, the Free Methodist Church would become the victim of a middle-class mentality, losing its prophetic edge and becoming "the very denomination against which it once reacted and sought to revive."[6] Wall's paper indicated the depth and intensity of the theological and ecclesiastical debate that was provoked by the shift from codified rules to covenant principles as the basis for entry into membership.

The General Conference of 1995 — A Defining Moment

When the 1995 General Conference convened at Anderson, Indiana, on July 1, one issue stood out above all others in the minds of the delegates. Early on, a survey of the delegates confirmed the fact that the SCOD resolutions on membership criteria and procedures held first place in their priorities for action on the conference agenda. The issues simmered in committees for the first two and one-half days of the meetings while rumors circulated about a standoff between proponents and opponents of the SCOD recommendations.

Yet as the delegates labored over matters of lesser import, it became evident that the most crucial issue might be pushed into the last day of conference sittings and shortchanged on debate because of the pressure of time.

The presiding Board of Bishops, therefore, utilized the findings of the survey on delegates' priorities and recommended that the resolutions on membership, already processed by ministry committees, be made the order of the day.

Initial debate revealed the depth of the division between the contending factions on the principal points of preparatory membership, the Membership Covenant, nurture of believers and transfers, and requirements for leadership in the local church. The third sitting closed on July 5 without resolution but with referral back to committee for possible revision to reconcile the differences.

Late-night and early-morning work brought unexpected results. When the General Conference convened for its final day on July 6, representatives from both sides enthusiastically voiced support for a revision of the SCOD proposal that addressed the concerns of its opponents, while confirming the essence of the original recommendation.

In sum, both parties accepted the four premises upon which the SCOD recommendation was based:

1. That we call the church to pursue holiness;
2. That we call the Free Methodist Church to renewed evangelism and disciple-making;
3. That we reaffirm our vision of the Christian life as described in Chapter III of the *Book of Discipline,* as the conduct descriptive of our mature Christian lives; and
4. That we change the entry level in our church by focusing on repentance, faith and baptism as the primary requirements for membership.

To put these premises into practice for admission to adult membership in the Free Methodist Church, three major proposals followed. First, the original SCOD recommendation remained unchanged with the instruction to "all leadership of the Free Methodist Church to promote and participate in a church-wide emphasis upon evangelism, holy living, and discipleship training as part of the New Day emphasis." Second, major revisions were made in the conditions for membership. Paragraph A/360 of the *Book of Discipline* was revised to read as follows (with the revisions of the original SCOD recommendation italicized):

The following are the conditions for membership. *The numbering of the steps is a* suggested order; individual situations may vary. The purpose of this process is to allow new believers and transfers to identify life issues and receive assistance; identify theological/doctrinal questions and answers; and learn the mission of the church and express ownership (steps 4-8 of the membership process may be designated by a local church or annual con-

ference as "preparatory membership" and the "preparatory *ritual*" *in paragraph A/351 may be used):*
1. *Awakening to God, a desire to seek God (Par. A/301).*
2. *Assent to participate in the maturing opportunities offered by the church,* such as classes, Bible studies, and small groups (Par. A/307).
3. Evidence of genuine conversion (Par. A/302).
4. *Receive the catechism of baptism and receive the sacrament of baptism,* or if baptized in infancy, public assent to the baptismal covenant (Par. A/124).
5. *Completion of the approved course of instruction for prospective members where the history, theological distinctives and mission of the Free Methodist Church are clearly taught.*
6. Commitment to the Membership Covenant (Par. A/154-160) and Christian Conduct section (Par. A/315-342).
7. Interview by the pastor and/or Membership Care Committee, who will verify the person's conversion, baptism and willingness to commit to a holy Christian life (Par. A/306-307).
8. Approval by the Official Board of the church upon recommendation of the Membership Care Committee (Par. A/404.4 [4.d]).
9. Affirmative response to the questions for membership before a public meeting of the church (Par. A/360).

In overview, the changes show the four concerns of the opponents to the SCOD recommendation that were resolved in the final recommendation adopted by the General Conference. One concern related to the *consistency of membership criteria with the Wesleyan doctrine of salvation.* By adding as the first condition "Awakening to God, a desire to seek God," the full scope of the Wesleyan doctrine of salvation was given to Free Methodist membership.

Another concern involved the *process of new believers to Christian maturity.* By including in the membership conditions the "assent to participate in the maturing opportunities offered by the church … ," giving greater emphasis to the catechism of baptism, and requiring the completion of an approved course of instruction on the "history, theological distinctives and mission of the Free Methodist Church … ," the implied commitment to the spiritual growth of believers was made specific.

Concern about the *elimination of preparatory membership* was met by the provision for a local option exercised by individual churches or annual conferences. At their discretion, "preparatory membership" and the "preparatory ritual" in Paragraph A/351 of the *Book of Discipline* may still be used.

Finally, concern continued to be expressed that the SCOD recommendation involving the *level of spiritual maturity required for leadership positions* in the local church, annual conference and church-at-large needed to be reinforced. In prior years, preparatory members were not eligible for leadership position. But with the elimination of the category, the specific criteria of "spiritual depth, vital in faith, faithful in church attendance, and in agreement with the doctrine, conduct and mission of the Free Methodist Church" were added as qualifications for leadership. Further reinforcement came with the unequivocal expectation that nominating committees and societies elect to leadership only those persons "whose lifestyles are in harmony with the level of maturity on the issues defined in the Scripture portions above (Exodus 18:21; Acts 6:3; 1 Timothy 3:1-13; and Titus 1:5-9) and in the *Book of Discipline*, Chapters 1 and 3."

When the vote was taken, Free Methodists witnessed another defining moment in the history of their church. As the overhead screen in the auditorium flashed the vote of 292 yes and 17 no, the whole conference body spontaneously began to sing, "We Are One in the Bond of Love." Fears of a split church or a divided body were dispelled with the recognition that only the Holy Spirit could have been the reconciling agent.

Once enacted, the new membership procedures required supportive action. For example, with the upgraded emphasis upon baptism, the Board of Bishops was instructed to prepare pre-baptism/membership courses to be used in the churches according to a suggested outline from Ephesians as a model for the catechism. Also, recognizing that the particulars of church membership are influenced by cultural factors, the General Conference adopted a resolution that stated, "Each full conference of mission origin may establish its own membership requirements and expectations to best interpret our Wesleyan-Arminian faith to its culture. Nothing shall be contrary to our Articles of Religion or "Christian Experience" and "Christian Conduct" sections (Par. A/300-342) of the *Discipline*."

Nor was the work of SCOD done. The General Conference instructed the committee to follow up the work on adult membership with a similar study of the process for children and youth in time for the 1999 General Conference. In addition, unresolved issues from past general conferences were also referred to the committee, such as clarity of theological language in the Articles of Religion relating to the "co-eternality of Christ" and "inclusion of Jesus in human sinfulness." Equally intriguing was the assignment for the committee to explain why Free Methodists both baptize and dedicate infants. As someone quipped, "General Conference may work from sun to sun, but SCOD's work is never done."

Does the action of the 1995 General Conference echo the moment in history when B.T. Roberts failed to head off action against the Pentecost Bands in 1890? The press for change in the conditions for membership in the church came primarily from churches on the growing edge of Free Methodism who might also be considered the "irregulars" of the 1990s. To the credit of the church, rather than disciplining or dispelling them for pushing on the boundaries of denominational control, the issue was referred to the Study Commission on Doctrine for search into the theological roots of biblical doctrine and Wesleyan interpretation.

Quite in contrast with the divisive and reactionary decision of the 1890 General Conference, Free Methodism in 1995 came to one of its finest moments, not just in the demonstration of spiritual unity on the conference floor, but in the keen theological thought that informed the decision. If the contrast continues, Free Methodism may well have reversed an error of history with a return to the spirit of aggressive evangelism with which the church was born and for which it had been searching for more than 100 years.

Bishop Emeritus Elmer Parsons found another historic moment through which to see the action of the 1995 General Conference. In an article written for *Light and Life* magazine (January 1996), he compared the change in the conditions of membership in 1995 to the establishment of the Free Methodist World Fellowship in 1962. He adopted the analogy from Isaiah 54:2, in which the prophet sees the lengthened cords of vision and the strengthened stakes of faith as the future hope for Israel.

Perspective on Faith
1960-1995 and Forward

In 1960 the Free Methodist Church celebrated its centennial in a time of theological calm. The fundamentals of faith were accepted essentially without contest in both the church and the culture. But with the social upheavals of the 1960s and 1970s, orthodox theology based upon divine revelation came into question along with all sources of authority. While the Free Methodist Church did not compromise on its faith position, it got a theological wake-up call from both liberal scholarship and a secular mindset that subtly influenced the Christian community. The establishment of the Study Commission on Doctrine in 1972 and its rise to prominence in 1995 illustrates the shift in theological awareness, especially for the clarification of biblical and Wesleyan doctrine in the midst of social revolution.

While the banner of entire sanctification continued to fly at the top of the masthead in bishops' writings and in the affirmations of General Conferences between 1960 and 1995, fundamental questions were being asked by pastors and people who struggled with the pain and potential of ministering in an increasingly secular age. Reflected in such dilemmas as divorce and remarriage and especially in the requirements for membership, the Free Methodist Church came to a theological crossroads. On the signposts at the intersection were such questions as these:

- Will the position of the Free Methodist Church on the doctrine of holiness be specifically Wesleyan or generically evangelical?

- Will its requirements for membership be centered in a connectional code or a relational covenant?
- Will it balance spiritual crisis and character development in Christian experience?
- Will it provide the structure and systems of support in pastoral care and congregational commitment to bring believers to spiritual maturity?
- Will it be primarily a "spiritual hospital" for wounded souls as Wesley envisioned or a "spiritual wellness center" for perfected saints?
- Will its membership be identified as persons "having the form and *seeking* the power of godliness" or persons who "have the form and *have* the power of godliness" (2 Timothy 3:5)?
- Will its standards of Christian experience, conduct and community be informed by its distinctives of personal and social holiness?

The 1995 General Conference took the initiative to address these questions, set a Wesleyan theological framework for their answers, and provided a procedure for their implementation. Now, as one delegate noted, the issues rest with the effectiveness of leadership in modeling, communicating and activating these principles and procedures in the life of the local congregation. No guarantees can be given other than the evidence of the guiding presence of the Holy Spirit in the 1995 General Conference.

The history of an era comes down to one question, "Will the distinctive Wesleyan faith position become the conscious identity of its members?" If the answer is "yes," Bishop Parsons' vision of the Free Methodist Church as a tent with lengthened cords and strengthened stakes can become a reality at home as it has abroad.

91

Structuring
Our
Fellowship

The Free Methodist Church spoke in 1860 as a prophetic voice in a denominational wilderness. Prophetic voices, whether individual or corporate, are usually organizational mavericks. Prophetic strategy dictates a focused but free-flowing organizational structure.

Free Methodism is a variation on the rule. Although it spoke prophetically on behalf of free seats for the poor, abolition for the slaves and perfect love for the justified, it only corrected the abuses of the organizational structure of the Methodist Episcopal Church from which it came. After guaranteeing equal representation between clergy and laity, changing the title of "bishop" to "general superintendent" and guaranteeing the right of due process for all its members, the founders of Free Methodism adopted *en toto* the structural pattern of Methodism as conceived by John Wesley and modified for America. The decision further confirms the fact that B.T. Roberts, like John Wesley before him, was a loyal churchman who did not intend to start a new denomination. With this decision came advantage and disadvantage.

As an advantage, the Free Methodist Church did not have to go through a trial and error experiment with organizational models. Rather, its creative energy could go directly into the evangelistic application of its missional distinctives, personal and social holiness. But as a disadvantage, the Free Methodist Church put itself on a track toward a lumbering denominationalism that absorbed energy and stifled creativity.

By 1960 the Free Methodist Church displayed the characteristics of full-fledged denominationalism — a headquarters in Winona Lake, a policy-making body of stakeholders in the General Conference, visible stature in the executive branch, commissions to oversee departments, program specialists in middle management and close coordination with units in the field. Did the Free Methodist Church rise to its crest by the turn of the century and then subside for the next 40 or more years? The rising and falling wave is not inevitable. If, during the period from 1960 to 1995, its strategy dictated its structure rather than structure dictating strategy, Free Methodism can be pronounced alive and well.

Structure of the Church 1960

If the organizational charts for the Free Methodist Church of 1960 and 1994 are compared, the essential structure remains intact. A general conference sets policy, a board of bishops supplies the vision, a board of administration executes policy, commissions on administration, evangelism, education and missions oversee programs, and denominational executives administer the ministries.

Within this basic structure, significant changes were made between 1960 and 1994. Reorganizations are noted in the General Conferences of 1964, 1969, 1974 and 1989. To detail these changes would be onerous and unproductive, because many are minor and many others are changed again at a later time. A comparative snapshot of the structure of the Free Methodist Church in 1960 and 1994 is more instructive.

Chart 1   Organizational Structure
Free Methodist Church of North America, 1960

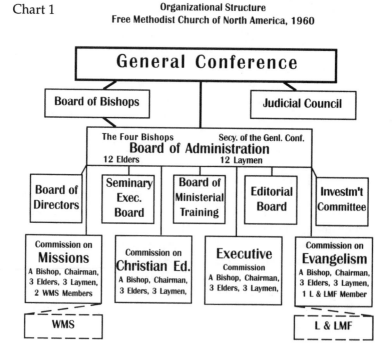

As the organizational model for the church in 1960,[1] Chart 1 provides a baseline against which to follow the changes in structure during the next 35 years. Three major features may be highlighted.

1. THE DIFFUSION OF LEADERSHIP — Although it is not immediately evident from Chart 1, the structure of the church in 1960 resulted in a diffused alignment of executive authority. Without a designated chief executive who would implement the policy of the general conference and administer the programs of the Board of Administration, the structure placed the primary responsibility for administration in the Board of Bishops. While their task description focused upon counsel and church planning, each bishop carried the functional responsibility for administration by virtue of his chairmanship of one of the four commissions.

Equally important, but not self-evident from the chart, was the role of the "senior bishop" as chairman of the Executive Commission, which functioned as the Board of Administration during the interim between the board's regular meetings and served as the budget committee for the general church and its departments.

Not that the structure failed. With the cohesion of the denominational mission, an affirming sense of direction set by the general conference, the guiding presence of the senior bishop and the good will of the denominational executives, overt conflict was minimized and creative freedom was allowed within rather wide boundaries for a denomination whose organization far outdistanced its size.

2. THE COORDINATION OF FUNCTIONS — After the reorganization of the church in 1931 into the four commissions, other units of governance were added between that time and 1960 that significantly changed the structure of the church. The Board of Bishops was added in 1939 and the Judicial Council in 1951. By their positioning on Chart 1, it appears as if they represent a balance among the legislative (General Conference), executive (Board of Bishops) and judicial (Judicial Council) functions of governance.

The addition of numerous boards and committees, which are between the Board of Administration and the commissions on Chart 1, reveals a strength and a weakness of the structure of the church in 1960. Its strength is in the evidence of the church responding to changing needs. Each of these governing units came into being after the reorganization of 1931: Seminary Executive Board (1947), Board of Directors (1951), Editorial Board (1951) and the Board of Ministerial Training (1955).

The validity of these functions cannot be denied, but the failure to place them under the coordination of the basic structure exposes a weakness in the organization. As "floating functions," they tend to become self-contained units that further diffuse the clarity of the organization, create a politicized climate and accent the need for executive leadership.

The fact that none of these boards or committees was absorbed into one of the commissions and that each of them reported directly to the Board of Administration, in effect, either limited the commissional model as a comprehensive structure for the coordination of functions or represented again the need for chief executive leadership.

3. THE MANAGEMENT OF MINISTRY — Further compounding the diffusion of executive leadership in the organization of 1960, most of the secretaries, directors or executives of the commissions or boards were elected directly to their positions by the General Conference. The general missionary secretary, general evangelistic secretary and editor of the *Free Methodist* magazine, for instance, all served by election through the General Conference. Awkward in the best of circumstances and almost impossible in conflict, it is a credit to the cohesion of the church and the commitment of its denominational executives that the system worked for denominational effectiveness rather than perpetual managerial wrangling.

With accountability to the General Conference, a denominational executive in one of these positions served as an independent manager for the period between elections. In such situations, informal structures for authority and responsibility take over the system, and internal politics become the mode of operation. Both for the sake of the church and its denominational executives, in the organization of 1960, the commissions and boards needed clarification, and the denominational executives needed coordination.

Reengineering the Structure 1960-1995

The structural history of the Free Methodist Church from 1960-1995 can be written in the efforts of each General Conference and the Board of Administration to resolve the organizational issues that were present in 1960. A detailed recitation of all of the starts and stops of these reorganization efforts would be unduly laborious and basically unproductive because many of those changes are no longer in effect. A review of actions that bear directly upon the issues identified in the organizational chart of 1960 is most relevant:

1960 General Conference — Generally elected one or more bishops and a general conference secretary; and selectively elected the editor of the *Free Methodist,* general superintendent of Free Methodist Youth, general secretary of evangelism and Sunday school secretary with other denominational executives, including the general missionary secretary.

96

1964 General Conference — (1) Generally elected two or more bishops, general conference secretary and editor of the *Free Methodist*; all others were employed by the Board of Administration, including publisher, general church treasurer, secretaries of commissions and directors of departmental ministries, e.g., Light and Life Hour; (2) Stipulated that the president of the Board of Administration was to be the chairman of the Board of Bishops, not the "senior bishop" as previously designated; (3) Instructed general church officers to form a General Church Council to coordinate the work of their departments; (4) Made all officers elected by the General Conference or employed by the Board of Administration responsible to the Board of Administration as to the performance of their official duties with supervision by their respective commission, board or committee; and (5) Ordered an executive secretary of the denomination to be employed by the Board of Administration upon nomination by the Board of Bishops with duties including general conference secretary and executive secretary to the Board of Bishops.

(1967 Board of Administration — Formed the Department of Christian Education by combining the Intermediate Youth, Free Methodist Youth, Sunday school, Servicemen and Service Training. The Executive Secretary to the Board of Bishops was made a part-time position.)

1969 General Conference — (1) Generally elected two or more bishops; all other officers were to be employed by the Board of Administration; and (2) Authorized a study of bishops' duties in order to relieve administrative overload.

1974 General Conference — (1) Elected two or more bishops; (2) Ordered bishops to live in Winona Lake; (3) Authorized the employment of a general church secretary to assist bishops in administrative duties; and (4) Authorized employment of a director of information and stewardship to secure financial support for denominational ministries.

(In 1976 the Board of Administration also authorized employment of an administrative assistant to the Board of Bishops at the level of departmental executive.)

1979 General Conference — (1) Elected two or more bishops; (2) In lieu of the proposal for a bishop with executive responsibilities, authorized employment of a headquarters administrator to implement Board Of Administration policies, manage staff policies, prepare budgets, coordinate programs, purchasing, mailing, travel, etc.; and (3) To relieve bishops of administrative burden, discontinued their role as chairs of commissions, did not require them to preside at overseas conferences and permitted them to reside in the areas where they serve.

1985 General Conference — (1) Elected two or more bishops; and (2) Requested bishops to reside in the areas where they serve.

1989 General Conference — (1) Elected two or more bishops; and (2) Required that the president of the Board of Administration be a person other than a bishop and ordered the organization of an executive leadership team chaired by the headquarters administrator and composed of key denominational executives along with the resident bishop of the area.

(1991 Board of Administration — Adopted a new structure with a headquarters operating committee chaired by the resident bishop plus four denominational executives to implement policies, supervise staff and coordinate denominational programs of the World Ministries Center.)

1995 General Conference — Proposals to increase the number of bishops from three to four were rejected along with a plan to reduce the Board of Administration in size to 15 or 18 members elected from a pool of nominees rather than maintain the current clergy and lay representation of 42 members from all administrative districts.

The General Conference did recommit itself to the principles of equality in clergy and lay representation in church governance and to inclusiveness for women and ethnic members in the representational and leadership roles.

The Dilemma of Executive Leadership

From this review of General Conference and Board of Administration actions dealing with the organization of the church from 1960-1995, the issue of executive leadership runs like a thread through the period. On one hand, there is the administrative overload upon the bishops at the same time that the church needs their pastoral oversight for its ministers and its ministries. On the other hand, there is the reluctance to designate an executive officer for the church from either the ranks of the bishops or the files of individuals with the experience and stature of a chief executive officer.

In 1979 the General Conference authorized the employment of a headquarters administrator, but the position went unfilled until 1985 when the Rev. Earl Schamehorn was appointed as the first full-time administrator for the denomination. During the interim from the time of authorization for the position and Schamehorn's appointment, Bishops W. Dale Cryderman (1981-1984) and Clyde E. Van Valin (1984-1985) did double duty as bishop and "interim headquarters administrator."

As a sidebar on the history of this period, the General Conference of

1979 rejected a proposal for the election of an executive bishop who would reside at the headquarters site and, with the authority of the episcopate position, give administrative oversight to the denomination, supervise its officers and coordinate its ministries.

After serving as headquarters administrator from 1985-1988, Schamehorn resigned the position and was replaced by Dan Wollam, a layperson with credentials in both public administration and Free Methodist higher education. Wollam's term from 1988-1991 included the wrenching experience of relocating headquarters and confronting the most severe financial crisis in the history of the church. He resigned in 1991 and the Board of Administration realized that radical action had to be taken. Chart 2, entitled "Organizational Structure" for the Free Methodist Church of North America, shows the reorganization of 1991, which is currently in effect. [2]

Chart 2

Organizational Structure
Free Methodist Church of North America — 1991

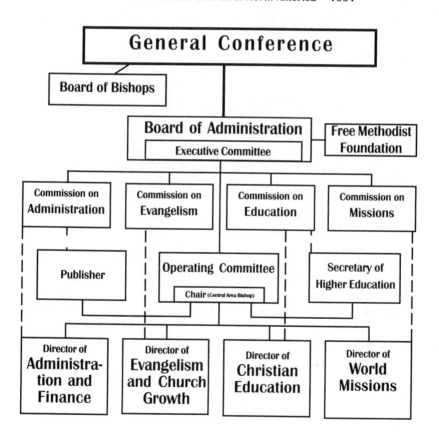

The contrast between Charts 1 and 2 reveals the results of a long and torturous process to resolve the issues that were in evidence in 1960. First, while the General Conference retains the primacy of its position and prerogative for policy-making within the structure, its composition has a direct bearing upon governance in the church. At the 1960 General Conference, out of 167 delegates, four delegates from Japan and Egypt alone represented the international contingent. In 1995, following the action of the 1985 General Conference, which gave full clergy and lay delegate status to overseas conferences, the international representatives numbered 107 or 30 percent of the total delegation. Globalization is a new reality for the church at home and abroad. Certainly, the international representation influenced the character of the General Conference.

Second, the Board of Bishops, with the exception of the central area bishop who chairs the Operating Committee for the World Ministries Center, is taken out of the administrative loop. The *Executive Handbook* defines the board's role: "The Board of Bishops gives general leadership to the denomination. They are charged with spiritual and temporal oversight of the church. The implementation of their vision for the church requires the support of all departments and executives."[3]

Although some ambiguity may still exist, the key phrases "general leadership," "spiritual and temporal oversight" and "vision for the church" describe their role with priority for the planning and pastoral functions.

Third, with the exception of the Free Methodist Foundation, all of the extra-commissional boards and committees have been absorbed into the commission structure. The Free Methodist Foundation, founded in 1987 for the purpose of long-term resource development for the denomination, retains the functions of the former Investment Committee and remains the only department of ministry outside the commissional structure and independent of the executive line of responsibility.

Fourth, and perhaps most important, a clear line of executive responsibility flows from the General Conference, through the Board of Administration and its Executive Committee, and to the Operating Committee chaired by the resident bishop with authority over the executive leadership team of denominational officers who direct their departments and staff.

Fifth, another change in the 1991 organization is the identification of the executive committee of the Board of Administration within the structure. Although not immediately evident from the charts, the power of executive leadership shifted from the Executive Commission in 1960 to the Executive Committee of the Board of Administration in 1991. The Administrative Commission still exists, but its functions are limited. The bishop who chairs the Operating Committee reports directly to the Executive Committee of the Board of Administration rather than to the Commission on Administration.

Sixth, the Judicial Council does not appear in the 1994 Organizational Chart, because its role has been upgraded to legal oversight of the legislative actions of all general conferences.

(Note: A Judiciary Committee of the General Conference still exists to pass on the rulings of the bishops and the legislative body during general conference sessions.)

Consistent with the broadened scope of responsibility for legal overview, a Constitutional Council was formed when the World Fellowship Constitution was adopted at the 1964 General Conference. The first meeting of the Constitutional Council was held in 1966 in Winona Lake, Indiana, to review the legislative proceedings of the general conferences of North America, Japan and Egypt. Meetings are required at least once every five years.

In 1995 the functions of the Constitutional Council were appropriately incorporated into the structure of the Free Methodist World Conference composed of all the bishops of the world church as well as an equal number of lay members. The purpose of the Constitutional Council has been "to maintain fidelity to the provisions of this Constitution ... to decide matters of comity, and to supervise referendums involving more than one conference."[4]

This significant structural change follows the movement toward globalization of the Free Methodist Church and implements the indigenous principle of missions development. Rather than having a North American Judicial Council ruling on the constitutionality of other general conferences, confidence is placed in a fully representative world body.

The Organizational Cycle 1960-1995

To summarize the organizational history of the Free Methodist Church from 1960-1995, we see movement through a full organizational cycle. In 1960 a senior bishop in the person of Leslie R. Marston had the stature and skills for executive leadership that kept a headless organization together. In 1995 the Central Area bishop in the person of Gerald E. Bates served with the portfolio, if not the title, of executive bishop.

No one can second-guess how much farther along the church might be if the time and energy given to administrative starts and stops had been available for the ministry of the church itself. Regrettably, it took the most severe financial crisis to activate a model that both downsized and rightsized the denominational structure. But even more important, the need for executive leadership from the highest office of the church became apparent. Through the throes of this transition, the Free Methodist Church may now be ready for its most effective ministry since the first 30 years of its history.

Internationalizing North America
The Canadian Experience

If history were judged as drama, the story of the Free Methodist Church of Canada would have to be selected for its "journey to autonomy,"[5] which culminated in the period between 1960 and 1995.

A RISING NEED FOR IDENTITY, 1874-1959 — Canada's journey to autonomy began many years before Free Methodism entered its second century. Just 14 years after the church was founded in 1860, Free Methodists were invited to establish churches in Canada. Two years later, the Rev. Charles Sage was appointed as the first Free Methodist pastor in Canada, and within four years the Canadian churches qualified by size for recognition as the Canadian Annual Conference.

In 1895 the continuation of growth led to the division of the Canadian church into the East and West Ontario Conferences. For the next 25 years, the Canadian conferences, which were joined by the Alberta and Saskatchewan Conferences in 1914, continued as full-fledged members of the General Conference of the North American church, even though they were a national minority in representation.

Paralleling these years, the motivation for a distinctive national identity intensified among the Canadian people. Reflecting that drive for distinction, Free Methodist leaders in Canada called together an All-Canada Convention at Sarnia, Ontario, in 1920 for the avowed purpose of developing a strategy and structure for ministry that was uniquely Canadian. As Albert Sims, a clergy delegate, put it, "... the time has come for us to take more advanced ground for the propagation of the distinctive truths we love so well, and for the unifying and more permanent establishment of our work in this rapidly growing country."[6]

Sensitive issues on the table included: (a) the stateside governance of the Canadian church; (b) the monetary assessments for denominational ministries, which were weighted in favor of the U.S. church; (c) the absence of Canadian schools to train ministers; and (d) the need for a publication to tell the Canadian story. In response to these issues, the Sarnia convention adopted resolutions forming the Canadian Executive Board with jurisdiction over education, evangelism and finance in Canada, as well as providing for the founding of Canadian schools for the preparation of ministers and establishing *The Canadian Herald* as a complement to the *Free Methodist* magazine.

Of lesser immediate note, but of greater long-term significance, the Sarnia convention also set in motion the action to incorporate the Free Methodist Church of Canada, an action culminated in 1927 when royal assent was given to the "Dominion Act of Incorporation." Just prior to the centennial year 1960, the church in Canada moved another step forward with the merger of the

Holiness Movement Church into the Free Methodist Church in 1959. The merger brought several hundred members into the Canadian conferences and included 5,000 members of the Egyptian Holiness Church, a church in Belfast, Ireland, and a mission in Hong Kong as an extension of world missions.

AN ENTERPRISING PLAN FOR INDEPENDENCE, 1960-1990 — Once the momentum for national identity gripped the Canadian people in the 1960s with the establishment of a Royal Commission on Bilingualism and Biculturalism (1963-1972) and the redesign of a distinctly Canadian flag (1965), the movement could not be stopped. The climax came in 1982 when the Canadian constitution through the Canada Act became the law of the land.

Free Methodism's journey to autonomy in Canada parallels the path of the nation toward independence. After its centennial year in 1966, the Canadian Executive Board adopted a resolution in 1971 prepared by two prominent laypersons, Selwyn P. Belsher and Alvin Hill, which read: "Moved that we, the East Ontario Conference of the Canadian Free Methodist Church, recommend to the Canadian Executive Board that a committee task force be created to prepare a formal study and discussion regarding the feasibility of organizing a distinct Canadian Free Methodist Church General Conference."[7]

When the report of the committee came out in 1972 with the strong recommendation to proceed toward General Conference status, the study was not without its sting: "The Free Methodist Church in Canada has lived for over 100 years under the hovering wings of the maternal church. Canada will much better develop its own leaders as it accepts its full responsibility for its own destiny. The Canadian Church will be a much stronger partner in the world community of Free Methodist Churches as it becomes fully indigenous."[8]

Resistance to the move could have been expected. Rather than granting the request of the Canadian Executive Board, the General Conference of 1974 approved Canada as a Jurisdictional Conference and elected, for the first time, a Canadian resident bishop in the person of Donald N. Bastian.

From then on, the journey to autonomy picked up speed. In 1982 encouraged by the signing of the Canada Act that gave Canada its own constitution, a resolution, beginning with the statement that Canada has now "come of age," went on to propose a similar maturity for Canadian Free Methodism in the form of a General Conference for Canada. A large majority moved the resolution forward, but not without vigorous debate.

Bishop Bastian focused on the issues in his 1983 Jurisdictional Conference episcopal address: "My question is 'Why should it be brought about?' There can be only one reason: Only if becoming a General Conference will increase our sense of responsibility to preach a full gospel to our own Canadian people and at the same to more fully shoulder responsibility for missionary efforts overseas, is it justified."[9]

Two years later Bishop Bastian himself presented this resolution to the 1984 Canadian Jurisdictional Conference:

BE IT RESOLVED, that this General Conference now approve that the Free Methodist Church in Canada become a General Conference if and when requirements of Paragraph 250.2 a-g are met to the satisfaction of the Executive Committee of the Board of Administration of the Free Methodist Church of North America.

Two resolutions followed to the 1985 General Conference of the Free Methodist Church. One requested total autonomy for the Free Methodist Church in Canada to govern its own financial affairs, and the other asked approval for General Conference status for the Canadian church pending satisfaction of the Executive Committee, Board of Administration and the Free Methodist Church of North America. Both resolutions received the approval of the 1985 North American General Conference.

As would be expected, many issues remained. Most salient were the concerns for administering the General Conference, providing higher education for ministerial prospects, assuring monetary independence, and resolving the question of the Canadian Pacific District, which was a part of the Pacific Northwest Conference centered in Washington state. Still, with an avowed "bias for action," Bishop Bastian pressed on to encourage the formation of a National Task Force on a Canadian General Conference in 1986 with the specific charge to weigh the pros and cons of general conference status, propose a process to bring Canadian Free Methodists together and develop a new ministry vision for the church in Canada.

When the study report came out recommending approval for a time schedule leading to the inaugural sitting of the first Canadian General Conference in August 1990, the process almost tripped on its own feet as the Canadian conferences disagreed among themselves. Finally, however, the internal issues were resolved, and an overwhelming 96.6 percent of the delegates to the three annual conferences of Canada East, Canada Great Lakes and Canada West voted in favor of the resolution.

The desire for Canadian autonomy should not be interpreted as a child divorcing its parent. To assure the continuation of cordial and cooperative relationships, four letters of agreement were written between the proposed Canadian church and its North American counterpart. Three of the letters maintained cooperative working relationships with the Departments of World Missions, Christian Education and Higher Education. The fourth assured the fraternal relationship between the Board of Bishops of the North American General Conference and the bishop(s) of the Canadian church.

All four of these letters of agreement along with the resolution for the establishment of a Canadian General Conference received strong support from the Board of Administration of the North American General Conference at its annual meeting in October 1988. After favorable action, Bishop Clyde Van Valin likened the action to two brothers deciding to work in different fields, but Bishop Donald Bastian countered that it seemed more like a mother giving away a son when he is 108-years-old. [10]

From then on, approval for the Free Methodist Church of Canada followed the formal lines of legislative action. By a standing vote of the 1989 General Conference in Seattle, Washington, the Canadian General Conference was approved.

So on August 6, 1990, Free Methodists in Canada arrived at their destination on the long and labored journey to autonomy when the first General Conference of the Free Methodist Church of Canada was convened at Etobicoke, Ontario. Bishop Donald Bastian voiced the sentiment of all the delegates in his report to the conference when he said, "We are now on the eve of an event we have looked toward for many years — the inauguration of a Canadian General Conference. May the Lord who has brought us safely thus far continue to guide us into the future by His personal presence."[11]

The official organization of the new church then began. In addition to the legal routines required for the organization, special actions were taken to: (1) elect Donald N. Bastian as bishop of the Free Methodist Church in Canada; (2) "Canadianize" the *Book of Discipline* to reflect the history of Free Methodism in Canada; (3) set the interval of the General Conference to convene every three years; (4) study the implications of changing the name of the church from the Free Methodist Church in Canada to the "Free Methodist Church Canada" and/or "*Eglise Methodiste Libre Canada*" when in a French context; (5) make evangelism a priority focus with faith goals at every level of church leadership; (6) emphasize the multicultural setting of Canada in ethnic evangelism; (7) develop ministerial education in a Canadian context for prospective pastors; (8) work toward the inclusion of the Canada Pacific Districts of the Pacific Northwest Conference in the Free Methodist Church in Canada as soon as possible; and (9) seek broad ecumenical relationships with Wesleyan, Methodist and evangelical bodies throughout Canada, North America and globally.

With these actions, the relationship with the Free Methodist Church of North America radically changed. As a full general conference, the bishop of the Free Methodist Church in Canada no longer served as part of the general superintendency of the parent body, and the Canadian Board of Administration governed its own national affairs.

Not all ties, however, were severed. A contractual relationship was established with the denominational body for services of Light and Life Press and the departments of Christian Education and Missions. Also, the bishops of both general conferences retained a fraternal relationship with regular meetings for communication and fellowship. Out of these new relationships came the formation of the North Atlantic Area Fellowship in which Canada, the United States and the United Kingdom joined in strategic alliance among the global partnerships in the Free Methodist World Fellowship.

On a three-year schedule for General Conference sessions, the Free Methodist Church in Canada met in July 1993. History was made again with the retirement of Bishop Donald Bastian, who had served for 19 years as bishop of both the North American and Canadian church. The Rev. Gary Walsh was elected on the first ballot to succeed him. In his acceptance of the office, Bishop Walsh set the tone for his administration by pledging to be a listener to pastors and people throughout the Canadian church.

Further actions were taken to establish the identity of the Canadian General Conference: (1) the Canada Pacific District, long related to the Pacific Northwest Conference, became part of the Canadian church; (2) an outreach strategy session was called to develop a national plan for the outreach of the church with focus upon the ministry of the local church; (3) regional forums were proposed to develop multicultural ministries; (4) a Chair of Wesley Theology was announced at Ontario Theological Seminary; (5) a Canadian Department of World Missions was proposed; (6) the Constitution of the Free Methodist World Conference was approved; and (7) a Canadian Study Committee on Doctrine was formed to deal with theological issues between General Conference sessions. Due to the years of careful planning, the child whom the parent set free at the age of 108 came quickly of age.

AN ENTERPRISING STRATEGY FOR THE FUTURE — All of this history through the journey to autonomy and to the formation of the Free Methodist Church in Canada is prelude to unprecedented actions at the adjourned sitting of the Canadian General Conference at Toronto in December 1994. Along with the election of Bishop Gary Walsh at the 1993 General Conference, the mandate had been given to the Canadian Board of Administration to "begin a thorough study of denominational structures to see how Free Methodist congregations could be better empowered to reach out to their communities."[12]

Knowing the reserved nature of the Canadian character, no one could have guessed the outcome of this study. Utilizing the services of Lyle Schaller, a student of the contemporary evangelical church, the Board of Administration met its mandate and presented a strategic plan entitled "Empowering Kingdom Growth," which qualified as a new paradigm for the ministry of the church. Bishop Walsh stated the mission for the plan when he said, "The Free Methodist Church in Canada exists to empower congregations to fulfill their vision for kingdom growth."

Under the banner "Empowering Kingdom Growth" (or EKG, with the image of a heartbeat), three non-negotiable commitments were identified: (1) the denominational beliefs as outlined in the Articles of Religion; (2) the need to strengthen and multiply congregations; and (3) the need to empower individuals for ministry.

Although similar words of mission and commitments have been spoken and written many times, the model that the delegates to the General Conference adopted by a 90 percent vote is a radical departure from the traditional structure of denominationalism in general and Free Methodism in particular. To start, the four Canadian annual conferences were dismantled, with their functions divided between the local church and a newly named National Ministries Center.

To the local church went the responsibility for developing its own strategic plan for the fulfillment of its ministry in the local community. Furthermore, in place of the conference appointment system for pastors, the local church became the prime participant in selecting its pastors through a "guided transition" system. Resources, then, that had flowed from the local church through a unified budget for support of denominational ministries were returned to the local church for choosing "giving streams" and setting financial goals for the support of five General Conference ministries in Global Missions, Church Planting, Canadian Ministerial Scholarships, Multicultural Ministries and Child Care.

A National Ministries Center was also organized to provide support services so that local congregations could be empowered "to fulfill their vision for kingdom growth." At the center of these services is a National Leadership Team of the bishop and directors of the General Conference departments of Administrative Services, Church Services and Ministerial Advancement. The primary function of this leadership team is to assume responsibility for pastoral development at the local church level, including performance assessment. To implement this plan, regional pastoral team leaders are appointed to work directly in pastoral development with local pastors in their region. One important goal of this new structure is to reduce the overhead costs of administration by estimates ranging from 25 to 55 percent.

Confident that this "lean" approach to denominational administration will win the favor of the people, Canadian leadership is taking the risk of permitting the constituency to set the percentage for a tithe of local church revenues depending upon their perception of the effectiveness of denominational ministries. Bishop Walsh says that he is willing to take the leadership risk that is asked of pastors and people of local churches, "... so the denomination must be willing to enter the same pathway of faith, design our ministry within our support base and do the prayerful work necessary to see the church grow."[13]

As radical as the new structure may seem, the 90 percent vote in its favor indicates that it addressed the felt need for fundamental change in the Canadian church. Specifically, it closed the perceived gap between denominational administration and the local church, downsized the administrative structure, reduced the financial burden, put priority upon pastoral development and placed the power at the point of function in the local church. At the same time, the new structure invited a constitutional test because of the elimination of annual conferences and the guided transition system for the appointment of pastors.

The prospect of legal challenge did not deter the Canadian General Conference from moving forward with the plan. It voted to proceed on a Transitional By-Law until its next Conference in 1996.

THE TEST OF TRANSITION — At the June 1995 meeting of the Constitutional Council of the world-wide Free Methodist Church, the By-Law change and strategy plan for the Canadian General Conference was submitted for approval. After extensive discussion, the Constitutional Council affirmed the transitional proposal, but only as the long term plans for the Canadian church include the formation of annual conferences as growth permits. Thus, the Constitutional Council reserved judgment on the restructuring until the strategy was fully developed and submitted for review.

Additional concerns surfaced at the Canadian General Conference in October 1996. Bishop Emeritus Donald Bastian himself raised the question about a general conference which only hears reports from pre-established administrative committees rather than deliberating issues as a legislative body. Another voice expressed concern that the financing system moved accountability to the local church so that the general conference received no meaningful fiscal reports. And still another voice warned that all of the decisions of the restructured General Conference might be ruled unconstitutional at the next meeting of the Constitutional Council in October 1997.

Despite these concerns, the Canadian General Conference sped forward on its strategic plan for "the strengthening and multiplying congregations and empowering our people."[14]

Today, the Canadian experiment has not shown the results it seeks in membership growth. From a peak of 7,165 members in 1993 and 1994, the Canadian church registered 6,851 in 1995, a loss of 314 or four percent of its total members. The pulse of the EKG heartbeat is yet unsteady as the Canadian church must recover from its losses before it can realize its gains.

All eyes are on the Canadian church as it tests the functional validity of a mission-driven strategy to determine the structure of the organization. Rather than following the usual path of tinkering with the administrative machinery, it has changed the core from which it operates. Few, if any, denominations have dared such a bold venture.

How, one might ask, does this radical change coincide with the passive, institutionalized, socialist and multicultural nature of the Canadian character that started Free Methodists on their journey to autonomy? At first blush, the nature of the change is more consistent with the "revolutionary" character of the United States. But on second thought, perhaps the momentum for independence as a General Conference carried on through to independence for the local church. Also, the multicultural character of the Canadian identity, which prizes diversity, may have taken the indigenous principle to its logical conclusion, namely a self-determining ministry for the local church.

If, however, the new structure is a misreading of the cultural character, the plan may backfire or fail to produce the vitality and growth envisioned by its creators. Whatever the case, the Canadian experiment will go down in Free Methodist history as the boldest venture since the founding of the church. So far in this second century, the Canadians are the revolutionaries.

GLOBALIZING THE CHURCH — While the Canadian experiment must undergo the test of time, the Free Methodist World Fellowship exemplifies the effectiveness of a strategy that dictates the structure. If one crowning event were to be named for the Free Methodist Church from 1960-1995, the formation of the World Fellowship would lead the way.

The Free Methodist Church sent its first missionaries overseas in 1885. Although they were Westerners who might have been accused of imperialism, the history of their ministry belies the accusation. John Wesley Haley, the first Canadian appointed as a missionary, is an example. He went to Africa in 1902 and "pioneered the concept of establishing indigenous churches led by native pastors — a breathtaking venture in an imperialistic age."[15]

Free Methodist missionaries continued to be ahead of their time. Not until 1974, at the World Congress on Evangelization at Lausanne, Switzerland, did evangelical Christians come to grips with the issues of "contextualization." For the first time in a public forum, Christians from the Two-thirds World brought to the table their protest against missionaries whose attitudes made "Christianizing" and "westernizing" synonymous in their work of evangelism and discipleship.

Free Methodist leaders, however, had advanced the indigenous principle as an expression of contextualization long before this time. In a 1953 article in *The Free Methodist*, Bishop Leslie R. Marston wrote, "Increasingly, it seems, the missionary aim must be the evangelization of groups of nationals in strategic centers, these to enlarge by indigenous evangelism and to be stabilized by the development (indigenous so far as possible) of schools, hospitals, and other cultural resultants of Christianization."[16]

Under the impetus of Bishop Marston, general missionary secretary Byron S. Lamson and layleader Hugh A. White, the General Conference of 1960 authorized the study of a plan to create a Free Methodist World Fellowship with the farsighted vision for a Free Methodist Church made up of independent general conferences encircling the globe. Significant decisions followed.

None was more important than the structural change to permit the formation of general conferences in other parts of the world. This led to the recommendation for the organization of a World Fellowship in concert with area fellowships in global regions. Rather than wait for the organization of the World Fellowship, however, the General Conference moved forward to recognize Japan and Egypt as the first Free Methodist general conferences outside of North America.

No time was wasted in the implementation of the actions of the 1960 General Conference. In January 1962 delegates from across the world convened at Greenville College, Illinois, to organize the Free Methodist World Fellowship. A proposed constitution for the World Fellowship stood at the center of the agenda. In that formal document, the purpose of the World Fellowship is stated:

> The Free Methodist World Fellowship is an organization for the coordination of the worldwide activities of the denomination. In harmony with this purpose it shall endeavor to promote closer fellowship and mutual understanding among branches of the Free Methodist Church, serve as an agent for joint planning and cooperative action, carry forward studies helpful to the member conferences and perform such other services as may be required by the members.[17]

Although this statement of purpose is laudable, its implementation is the key to importance of the organization. Article II-C, Organization, describes the powers and duties of the World Fellowship and states that "The World Fellowship shall be responsible to its member conferences for the following:

1. To promote and deepen the spiritual life of the church;
2. To promote the attainment of Free Methodism's aims, goals and objectives;
3. To consider the special needs common to other member conferences and recommend action to meet them;
4. To maintain a continuing study of world trends and opportunities with a view to securing united Free Methodist action concerning the same;
5. To receive reports from member conferences, normally through the executive secretary of the area fellowship, to evaluate the same and

recommend appropriate measures for meeting new challenges;

6. To fix the budget of the World Fellowship and determine the financial apportionment of each member conference on the basis of membership and economic capacity;
7. To receive and act on applications for the establishment of area fellowships; and
8. To assist in defining the leadership needs of member conferences and promote scholarship and other programs of leadership training."

Following the indigenous principle, then, each general conference established would have equal representation in the Fellowship. While the distinction among general conferences, full conferences of mission origin and provisional conferences still needed to be worked out, all of the representatives, by vote and/or voice, were recognized for their contribution.

Closely related to the world organization, area fellowships were proposed for geographical regions where "mutual interests and the need for spiritual counsel and encouragement make it advisable." [18]

While the proposed constitution served as the skeleton for the structure, the discussions of the delegates fleshed out the meaning of the meeting. From the Asia Fellowship Conference, which had already been held in April 1960, came the impassioned challenge:

"Laymen are the evangelists and missionaries of this century. One hundred thousand Free Methodists must be people of the concerned heart. We call the world-wide church to join with us in this second century crusade — the evangelization of every geographical area, every culture, activity, interest." [19]

The African Area Fellowship had its own plea, the kind of plea that would test the intent of Western leadership on the indigenous principle:

"We recommend that the missionary seek for responsibilities he now carries which can be transferred to the national. This should be a matter of first priority for the missionary, thus freeing himself for new fields of service.

"We affirm that the church in each land must become completely at home in its culture and freed from all foreign control." [20]

Another point of potential controversy concerned the finances. A panel from India at the Asia Area Fellowship meeting brought forward the protest: Outside insistence upon self-support as a "must" before self-propagation and/or self-government will only compound confusion and delay revival. Even in the realm of method and good practice, there is a legitimate doubt as to whether the priority of self-support as an absolute necessity for church autonomy or evangelical growth is as correct as assumed. In the first place, it is worthy of notice that most of the voices linking absolute self-support and church autonomy are American voices. [21]

Even with such frank discussion, the spirit of the sessions confirmed the fact that the World Fellowship was an idea whose time had come. Dr. Byron S. Lamson, General Missionary Secretary, set the tone for the meeting with a confession and a vision that could not be denied, "If our policy has been paternalistic with reference to the younger churches on the mission field now we move to a new era — a commonwealth of Free Methodist Churches."[22]

With a stroke of genius, Lamson preempted current management theory that puts a premium upon organizations conserving core values and stimulating creative growth. In memorable words that underscored the purpose of the World Fellowship, he said, "We hope to *conserve the values* of essential Free Methodism and *release the Gospel of Jesus Christ* more effectively in a lost world." [23]

Many visions have been projected and many strategies have been proposed for the Free Methodist Church over the course of its history, but none has results as productive as the World Fellowship. At the time of its founding in 1962, the overseas membership of the church totaled 40,719 persons. At last count in 1995, the numbers had swelled to 314,068!

In 1962 the three general conferences from North America, Japan and Egypt comprised the full membership of the World Fellowship. In 1995 the delegated membership included the 1960 delegation from Japan and Egypt plus the general conferences of Canada and Rwanda, the provisional general conferences of the Philippines, India, Burundi, Mozambique and Zaire. Joining them in 1995 were the provisional conferences of Chile, Korea, Malawi, Northwest Mexico and Paraguay which have the privilege of one full voting member; and the mission conferences of Costa Rica, Ecuador, Puerto Rico and Venezuela with voice but no vote.

Since 1962, minor refinements have been made in the structure of the Free Methodist World Fellowship. In 1964 the constitution for the organization was adopted by the General Conference, and the constitution of the Free Methodist Church was revised to include the provision for new general conferences around the world. To conserve the essential elements of Free Methodism in the constitution of a new general conference, the document must include the Articles of Religion, Membership, General Rules, General Organization, Restrictive Rules and Methods of Amendment. To assure the integrity of the world church, the Constitutional Council functions as the judiciary for ruling on the constitutionality of general conference organization and legislation.

At the General Conference in 1989, a proposal for a Free Methodist World Conference was originated, and in 1995 it was referred to the referendum process. The process itself recognizes that the originating body of the Free Methodist Church of North America is now a partner, not a parent, in the formation of a global church. Assuming this organizational change, the indigenous principle will come of age.

Leadership during this formative time has continued in the hands of

North American bishops: Gerald E. Bates (1989-95) and David M. Foster (1995-forward). Notably, at the 1995 General Conference, the body took leadership in developing a paper outlining eight "Goals for World Evangelism" that will be distributed among Free Methodists world-wide.

1. Continue efforts toward doubling membership by A.D. 2000;
2. Have a missionary program and mission awareness in each conference to reach out crossculturally within the country and outside its bounds;
3. Develop partnership with other conferences in the area for sending missionaries for both short term and long term, and have mutual assistance programs to help the needs;
4. Give priority attention to reaching cities through church planting;
5. Make use of appropriate technology to spread the gospel and to coordinate efforts;
6. Train soul winners, church planters and trainers of soul winners;
7. Challenge each church to plant another church;
8. Concentrate on reaching unreached people groups — especially keeping in mind the 10x40 window and the Muslim world.[24]

A direct cause-and-effect relationship between the organization of the World Fellowship and overseas growth is not claimed. It can be claimed, however, that the World Conference represents the prophetic edge of the Free Methodist Church during the era from 1960-1995. As a rarity among full-fledged denominations, the structure is dictated by strategy. Thus, when the Spirit of God began to move with mighty force through the Two-thirds World and into the Eastern European and Asian blocks north of the equator, Free Methodism had the strategy and the structure to work in concert with the Holy Spirit.

Perspective on Structure 1960-1995 and Forward

The 1995 General Conference produced no major changes in the structure of the Free Methodist Church. Dynamics of a growing church, however, put strains upon the organization and its processes. Most noticeable was the fact that the old mentality of identifying the leadership of the church with the North American or United States bishops no longer held true. While the number of bishops in the United States church has been reduced from four to three in the period from 1960-1995, the number of international leaders in the episcopacy of other general conferences has risen from two to nine.

Even though the World Conference constitution makes structural provision for this change, the full consequences for the mission and the policy of the church are yet to be felt. One thing is certain: The minority representation of the stateside bishops will soon dispel whatever shreds of paternalism or implied imperialism that may remain from the past.

Another dynamic of a growing church put a more severe strain on the 1995 General Conference. Clergy and lay delegates of annual and provisional conferences in the world church made up 30 percent of the General Conference body. Yet their preparation for the issues before the conference proved to be inadequate, and participation in the discussions fell far short of the numbers.

Neither problem was intentional; both problems are fixable. In the case of inadequate preparation, the timeliness of mailing to all delegates faltered on international delays and local processing, especially where understanding of the issues required translation into the language and idiom of the local culture. In some cases, international representatives did not receive the delegate's working manual until they arrived on the General Conference grounds.

Regrettably, then, when the resolutions of the General Conference came to committees or to plenary sessions, the international representatives had to rely on translators to communicate the essence of the issues and interpret the course of the debate. Frustration arose and participation fell as many overseas delegates felt disenfranchised in an honored role from which they expected so much.

As the world church continues to grow in numbers, annual conferences multiply and general conferences are added, further adjustments will have to be made in the organizational structure and governance process to assure the principle of equality that is so fundamental to Free Methodism — past, present and future.

C H A P T E R 7

Governing Our Church

Governance goes hand in hand with structure in understanding the Free Methodist Church as an organization. Structure is the plan for organizing the legislative, executive and judicial functions of the church. It establishes the lines of authority among the governing bodies and defines the roles of denominational officers and representatives. Governance, on the other hand, is the process of decision-making within the structure for visioning, planning, implementing and evaluating the mission of the church.

Both the structural plan and governing process of 1931 remained essentially intact when the Free Methodist Church celebrated its centennial in 1960. From this benchmark in time, changes in the governing process between 1960 and 1995 can be traced, just as changes in the structure during this same period were tracked in the previous chapter.

OPTIONS FOR STUDYING GOVERNANCE — Several options are open for writing this phase of Free Methodist history. One option is to take a *tactical* approach to the policy decisions of the general conference as they are constitutionally reviewed and administratively implemented in the ministries of the church. In a tactical approach, the emphasis is upon the question "How?" and the answers are chronological and functional.

Another option is to take a *strategic* approach to the history of governance in the church from 1960 to the present. With a strategic approach, the emphasis is upon the question, "What?" Beginning with the mission that guides the church, strategic initiatives are identified, follow-up programs are reviewed, and the effectiveness of the outcomes for the ministry of the church are judged.

Our option of choice is to combine the strategic approach with a focus upon the *leadership* of the church. The questions will be both, "What?" and

"Who?" By seeking answers to the question, "What?", we will see the movement of the church at large. By personalizing the role of leadership in the question, "Who?", we will also see the vision of leadership for the ministries of the church at large.

> (In tribute to the bishops, national and international, who have
> served the church between 1960 and 1995, their names lead the
> roll call for "Servant Leaders of Our Generation" in the final words
> of this history [Epilogue].)

Our working principle will be that governance is not an end in itself. Governance, even in a church with a divinely appointed mission, stands accountable to the people whose spiritual destinies are impacted by the visions of the leaders whom they elect to serve them. By selective choice, then, we will center our attention upon the bishops' pastoral addresses that keynoted each of the eight general conferences between 1960 and 1995.

Following this format, three major eras of strategy are identified in the period between 1960 and 1995. These eras are:

    I. Motive to "Double in a Decade" — 1960-1969
    II. Method of Church Growth — 1974-1984
    III. Marketing for a New Day — 1985-1995

I. Motive to "Double in a Decade" 1960-1969

When the second century dawned for the Free Methodist Church, the "Forward Movement" campaign had effectively stalled as a strategy for growth. An attempt was made to restart the movement under the name "New Century Advance."

As Bishop Walter S. Kendall wrote in 1960, "Too often our very perfectionism has brought defeat through our delay, while we despairingly wait to perfect the means we are to employ in the work of the Lord. To reach our goal, we must take to the open road and head for the far-off horizon."[1] A change in attitude, however, needs to be reinforced by the evidence of achievement. In 1960 the Forward Movement needed to be replaced by a new initiative.

The Growth Initiative. Bishop Kendall, addressing the Centennial Conference of 1960, provided the needed initiative in his bold proposal for the church when he said, "With our present organizational framework, enlisting every age group of our membership, and with a larger World Fellowship of Free Methodist Churches united in spirit, and anointed with the Holy Spirit witnessing the redeeming love and power of Jesus Christ, *it is reasonable for us to pray and believe that God will double the membership of the Free Methodist Church in the first decade of our second century.*"[2]

Bishop Kendall's faith for a return to growth that was unprecedented since the founding years of the church came primarily from spiritual confidence not strategic planning. As we noted earlier, he joined with President John F. Kennedy in foreseeing a decade of unprecedented achievements, such as putting a man on the moon and eliminating hunger in America. Sharing the idealistic glow of the era, no intermediate goals were set, no breakthrough strategy was proposed, and no point of accountability was identified. Without being too cruel to that idealistic era and its leaders, "Double in a Decade — Christ is the Answer" must be identified as a slogan not a strategy.

THE PLAN TO DOUBLE IN A DECADE — The recommendations of the pastoral address to the General Conference in 1960 included: (1) Studying denominational finances to relieve the burden on weaker churches and conferences; (2) Computing membership gains including preparatory members; (3) Merging small contiguous conferences for greater efficiency; (4) Coordinating denominational departments for unified advance; (5) Maintaining a sanctified church and promoting union with other holiness churches; and (6) Changing General Conference from quadrennial to quinquennial meetings.

One must surmise that the bishops envisioned the goal of "Double in a Decade" to be achieved by energizing traditional programs of evangelistic outreach with the infusion of spiritual revival, second-century inspiration and management efficiency. No one can fault them. A high tide of evangelism could be sensed in successful crusade ministries, especially engaging the enthusiasm of the youth of the church. Moreover, the Light and Life Hour, the publishing house, Free Methodist colleges, the Sunday school and children's ministries seemed to show unlimited potential. Best of all, the church stood ready to burst into global dimensions through the prospect of the Free Methodist World Fellowship.

Like the rising tide that raises all ships, the bishops had good reason to believe that the local church would rise and grow on the high tide of a new surge in denominational ministries. Accordingly, they personally led the departments of the church in seven "Soul-saving Convocations" in four areas of the North American church.

A year after Bishop Kendall's introduction of the slogan "Double in a Decade," the need for a follow-up strategy became obvious. An attempt was made to unite the motive of the New Century Advance with the means for doubling in a decade. Again, on behalf of the Board of Bishops, Bishop Kendall took the initiative to present four objectives for the program:

1. Each local church shall make a Responsibility List at least ten times the active (or adult) resident membership.

2. Each local church member shall call on at least one person on the Responsibility List each week.
3. "Double in a Decade" is to apply to all measurable progress of institutions and departments at all levels.
4. Every Free Methodist church in its expansion plans shall be alert to opportunities for new Sunday schools intended to become established churches.[3]

Most notable among these four objectives is the call for church expansion through the establishment of Sunday schools as the basis for new churches. Evidently, the call went unheeded, because the number and size of Sunday schools continued to decrease through the era. This objective, along with the other three, appears to be lost in the history of the church.

Organizationally, the Department of Evangelism took on the added name of "Church Extension" as an indication of the tactic for growth. The Rev. Lyle Northrup, director of the department, remained true to his call as an evangelist and counted upon revival meetings in the local church, along with evangelistic crusades, as the major means for denominational growth. At the same time, his evangelistic vision took him to new fields in the British Isles where church extension districts were formed.

MID-COURSE REVIEW, 1964 — Hindsight, of course, is very exact. Looking back upon the bishops' initiative to "Double in a Decade" in 1960, we see the dark shadow of limited resources clouding the vision. Although the Free Methodist Church continued to be among the leaders of all denominations in the United States in per capita giving, the demand of denominational ministries outstripped the supply.

A review of Bishop Leslie R. Marston's pastoral address for the General Conference of 1964, for instance, acknowledges membership growth of only 1,471 persons in North America during the first quadrennium of the second century or 2.5 percent when the goal of doubling in the decade required a 40 percent gain or 22,842 new members in the four-year period. Although no report on the results is given in the pastoral address, the bishops made the following recommendation:

That to implement our goal of doubling in a decade an all-out effort for the salvation of souls and the sanctification of believers be emphasized in the next quadrennium and that each department be urged to gear its activities to this objective.

Complementing this recommendation was the specific proposal "that special training be given in each local [church] in personal evangelism and visitation." This proposal came in response to the new thrust of the Light and Life Men's Fellowship, an auxiliary of the Commission on Evangelism, which was infusing new life into the evangelistic efforts of the church. While not directly identified with the strategy to double in a decade, Light and Life Men's Fellowship gave promise of movement toward that goal.

No other recommendation in the 1964 Pastoral Address came directly to grips with the strategy of the church to Double in a Decade. General recommendations called for a special emphasis upon practical godliness or "holiness of heart and life" and a deepening of prayer life within the denomination. Clues to key issues confronting the denomination, however, came in the remaining recommendations. The need for administrative coordination of denominational departments was evident in the recommendation "that a plan of coordination of the church program be put into operation on the general, conference and local levels." The decline of connectionalism came through in the recommendation "that each local [church] promote church loyalty."

In the mid-1960s, evangelism shifted from crusades among the masses to ringing doorbells in the homes of the local community. Charles Kingsley led a grass-roots movement among men for personal evangelism, and George Delamarter followed with a program of visitation evangelism with the goal of revitalizing the local church. Although often frustrated at the denominational level, Delamarter demonstrated the validity of visitation evangelism when he accepted the appointment to a small struggling church in Wenatchee, Washington. By applying the principles he taught, he set the pace for growth in the Free Methodist Church for years to come.

The cultural revolution in the 1960s also affected the outcome of the bishops' vision to double in a decade. By the time of the General Conference of 1964, established authority within society was being questioned, legitimate leadership was under fire and primary institutions were in shambles. This also affected the church. Denominations, in particular, which had enjoyed unquestioned credibility in the 1950s, found themselves defending a fortress whose foundations were being undercut by privatized religion at the local level. An interesting scenario unfolds in the history of the Free Methodist Church during this time. As the pressure between supply and demand for financial resources took its toll, energy for evangelism gave way to financial problem-solving. Out of these efforts came the establishment of the United World Mission for Christ budget in 1964.

Local churches felt the pressure of expanding needs from denominational departments without the commensurate growth in size and numbers to provide the resources needed to sustain world-wide ministries. Furthermore, as the culture went through the wrenching process of weakened authority and decentralized institutions, the denomination got caught in the middle. In retrospect, the establishment of the United World Mission for Christ budget, with its unified funding, based upon local church and conference assessment, may have represented a good idea trapped in transition.

119

ASSESSING THE RESULTS, 1969 — As a counter to this ongoing cultural revolution, the pastoral address for the 1969 General Conference developed the theme, "The Future Belongs to Those Who Prepare for It." The tone was set to describe a healthy church in a sick culture. Although the address, delivered by Bishop Myron F. Boyd, was not defensive, it described the character of the church by the adjectives — spiritual, biblical, relevant, missional, coordinated, loving, growing, intellectual, discontented, reputable, confrontational, dynamic and confident. With his gift of communication, Bishop Boyd used these adjectives as the rallying cry for significance beyond survival.

Whatever factors may have played into the movement of the Free Methodist Church during the decade of the 1960s, the result was the same. Free Methodism did not double in a decade. The statistics speak for themselves. In 1960 the Free Methodist Church had 57,027 members in North America and 39,057 members overseas. Ten years later, the numbers totaled 69,520 in North America, an increase of 21 percent or 2.1 percent per year.

Overseas, however, the signs of future growth were coming clear as the church increased to 60,433 members, a gain of 54 percent or 5.4 percent per year. As a strategy, "Double in a Decade" fell far short of its statistical goal, even though its spiritual impetus lifted the church on a note of hope during the first decade of its second century.

Dwight Gregory, superintendent of the New York Conference and a student of church growth statistics, reminds us that in some pockets of the church, the church did double in a decade. Without touting his own conference, which he did not lead at the time, statistics for the New York Conference in its urban and ethnic churches show a doubling in the decade. Although it might not have been seen at the time, the view in retrospect shows urban and ethnic growth as a prediction of things to come.

II. Method of Church Growth 1974-1984

Evangelical Christianity, along with the denominations within the broad circle of that community, began to emerge from its minority mentality in the mid-1970s when the Church Growth Movement appeared on the scene. Conceived by Donald MacGavran, a missionary scholar, the church-growth movement integrated the theory of cultural anthropology, the experience of the mission field and the principles of biblical evangelism into a working set of assumptions by which the church could grow at home and abroad. Free Methodist leaders, along with evangelical colleagues, quickly embraced church growth as a methodology for reviving declining congregations, enhancing growing congregations and planting new ones.

STEPS TO CHURCH GROWTH — Steps were taken to implement church growth methods. Early in 1974, all the Free Methodist bishops attended a church growth seminar led by Donald MacGavran. When the General Conference of 1974 convened, Bishop Boyd's pastoral address entitled, "Focus for the Future," endorsed the church-growth movement as the strategy for fulfilling the vision of the centennial conference in 1960.

The address restated the church-growth principles in Free Methodist form: (1) communicating the gospel; (2) converting people groups; (3) preaching cleansing from sin; (4) nurturing Christian growth; and (5) responding with sensitivity to human need. The word "contextualization" became a permanent part of the Free Methodist vocabulary. Contextualization, simply defined, means communicating the gospel with sensitivity to human needs in changing culture but without compromising the salvation message.

The pastoral address of 1974 also set the tone for renewal of the church with a focus upon youth, evangelism, cities and world missions, once again utilizing the methods of church growth. Whereas "Double in a Decade" had a lofty vision and a set goal but lacked a plan for implementation, the church growth movement offered a methodology that could be applied at all levels of denominational ministries. Heavily influenced by sociology and cultural anthropology, the church struck a truce with behavioral science in the 1970s, just as it had befriended psychology and counseling in the 1960s.

The methodology of church growth did not override or displace spiritual renewal as the primary strategy for the Free Methodist Church. The call to prayer, holiness and revival sounded by Bishop Kendall in the pastoral address of 1960 echoes through Bishop Boyd's pastoral address of 1974. Couched in the context of cultural change and national crisis, a sobering tone permeates the address, even while it holds out high hopes for merger with the Wesleyan Church and new growth for local congregations.

MANIFESTO ON EVANGELISM — The church-growth methodology was implemented in the second half of the 1970s in a variety of complementary programs. In 1978, for instance, a "Manifesto on Evangelism" was adopted by the Board of Administration with the pledge: "The Free Methodist Church commits itself to a special mobilization for evangelism. We purpose to marshal our total resources to win lost persons to Christ, to nurture and equip them to become responsible and reproductive church members and servants of Jesus Christ in the world."

Backing up this pledge, the Manifesto cited evangelism as the first priority for the leadership of the church, allocated material resources to reflect this priority, enlisted all denominational institutions and agencies as instruments of evangelism, called upon all denominational ministries at every level

121

to join in the emphasis and challenged all Free Methodists to get "caught up in obedience" to the Great Commission. Consistent with the Manifesto and its relationship to the church-growth movement, the Department of Evangelism and Church Extension was renamed the Department of Evangelism and Church Growth.

BISHOPS' RETREATS — The year 1978 marked a new beginning for the Board of Bishops when they began meeting together annually in a retreat session for spiritual renewal and strategic thinking. Twenty or more years had passed since the bishops had gathered in prayer and planning sessions without the burden of an administrative agenda. But once the retreats began again, the value became immediately evident and resulted in annual retreats from 1978 to the present time. Out of these retreats came leadership initiatives in support of the church-growth strategy.

In 1980, for instance, history was made when a Bishops' School for Renewal for pastors was planned for every region of the church. The bishops, who committed seven weeks of time to the Schools for Renewal, outlined the following goals for pastors:
1. To realize spiritual renewal in our own lives through a fresh emphasis upon the work and ministry of the Holy Spirit;
2. To affirm our ministers, spouses and families as persons and leaders;
3. To clarify the purpose of the Free Methodist Church as it relates to the culture and age in which we live;
4. To clarify the pastoral role as it is set forth in the Scriptures and adapted to the Free Methodist Church needs in the 1980s.

Superintendents' Convocations took on the renewal theme from 1980-1983 in anticipation of 1984, designated as the "Year of Renewal." The agenda set two priorities. One was to challenge the superintendents to lead in the challenge of spiritual renewal from biblical and historical perspectives. The second priority was to forge a relational link between those entrusted with denominational oversight and those responsible for shepherding pastors and supervising programs at the conference level.

TOP GROWTH CHURCHES — Equally supportive of the church-growth movement, in 1976 the bishops began to give recognition to the top 10 or 20 churches that had grown in size to 200 or more members. The decision symbolized a significant shift away from the defensive image of "small but spiritual" churches to a more affirmative position in favor of church growth.

In further support of the church-growth plan, the bishops started the process in the early 1980s that led to a definitive mission statement for the church. Earlier in its history, the church had flourished under the mission statement adopted for the 1862 Discipline, "to maintain the biblical standard of Christianity, and to preach the gospel to the poor."

REVISED MISSION STATEMENT — While the statement was sound, it had been accepted without review for more than 100 years. When the study committee presented its first draft of the mission statement in 1981, it read:
The mission of the Free Methodist Church is to make known to the world God's call to wholeness through forgiveness and holiness in Jesus Christ (Board of Administration, October 1981).
While soundly biblical, Wesleyan and evangelical, critical discussion revealed the lack of a direct link to the local church as a focal point of ministry. Therefore, the statement was revised with the addition of the words, "*and to invite into membership and equip for ministry all who respond in faith.*"
Another revision was made by the Executive Committee of the Board of Administration in 1982 when they reported an amendment to change "*to the world,*" to read "*to people everywhere.*" In this form, the mission statement was adopted by the General Conference of 1985 and continues to serve as the lodestar for church strategy to this day.

ASSESSING OUTCOMES OF THE CHURCH GROWTH METHOD — What about results? Although the church-growth movement did not include specific goals for increases in membership, the test of the concept is still numerical. In 1974 total membership for the denomination in North America totaled 70,782 members when church growth was first enunciated. Ten years later, in 1984, the comparative figures for total membership in North America (including Canada) totaled 84,768, an overall increase of 15.49 percent or 1.54 percent per year.
While recognizing that church growth is a developmental process that takes time, and acknowledging multiple factors that temper the statistics, a general observation can still be made. Neither the motive for "Double in a Decade" nor the method of church growth measurably affected total denominational statistics in North America.
The most important comparison, however, is between the North American and overseas churches during the same two 10-year periods. Between 1960 and 1969, overseas membership increased in numbers from 39,057 to 60,433 for a 54 percent gain or 5.4 percent per year. Then between 1974 and 1984, Free Methodists overseas grew from 72,326 to 126,418 members, a 75 percent gain or 7.5 percent per year.

III. Marketing for the New Day
1985-1994

By now it is no surprise to learn that the strategy for the "New Day" vision under God had its genesis among the bishops during an annual retreat. The pastoral address for the General Conference of 1985 provided the platform for putting the vision into words and setting goals for the church in A.D. 2000. As stated in the pastoral address of 1985, given by Bishop Donald Bastian, ground was also laid for the new strategy in the reiteration of core convictions for changing times:

1. We are evangelicals — without apology;
2. We are Methodist evangelicals;
3. Doctrine and life cannot be separated;
4. Evangelism is the number-one task of the Free Methodist Church;
5. Social concern is a natural outflow of the Christian faith;
6. Evangelism must be undergirded by Christian nurture;
7. In healthy congregations, local churches reproduce themselves;
8. Our mission must be increasingly cross-cultural;
9. Christian unity within our Zion is a biblical mandate;
10. The Lord of the harvest commands us to pray workers into the harvest fields.

GOAL-SETTING FOR THE NEW DAY — Upon this foundation, the bishops declared their vision for the New Day under God:

We believe that the Distinctives of the Free Methodist Church are especially relevant in our times. Our mission today is urgent and clear. God is stirring us to break out of present molds, grow in numbers and impact our world for Christ.

Having prayerfully sought God's guidance, we present the following statements as objectives for the closing years of this century.

— We purpose, under God, that by the year 2000 the Free Methodist Church will be in the vanguard of the evangelical movement and a leading spokesman for the New Testament message of holiness in faith and life as represented by the Wesleyan tradition.

— We purpose, under God, to consolidate with renewed vigor our considerable strengths and resources in order to increase our evangelistic impact and redemptive influence in the world. We believe God would be pleased to make us a dynamic world movement, and His instruments to proclaim and demonstrate the power of grace to heal both individuals and whole nations.

In order to set ourselves on this course for a new day, we present the following goals, inviting all segments of World Free

Methodism to join with us in prayer and work for these and similar endeavors:

WE ENVISION BY THE YEAR 2000:
— 1,000 new church plantings in North America
— 125,000 members in North America
— 300,000 members in the church overseas
— Free Methodist churches in 40 countries
— Six new General Conferences

God promises He will do a new thing among us. "Forget the former things; do not dwell on the past. See, I am doing a new thing" (Isaiah 43:18, 19a). Nineteen eighty-five saw the dawning of this new day. May God lead us as we advance.

New Day Under God General Conference, 1985

The bishops' vision made history. For the first time in 125 years, a full-fledged strategy was consciously proposed and specifically defined for the Free Methodist Church. It was a bold vision, built upon denominational distinctives, guided by a clear mission statement and targeted toward measurable goals that set the church on a course into the future.

IMPLEMENTING THE NEW DAY VISION — Of necessity, the New Day vision required strong support from all sectors of the church. Leading the way was the call for all conference superintendents and pastors to implement the vision at their respective levels by setting New Day goals for their own conference or church. No count was kept on the response. Generally speaking, denominational leaders, who presented the call, point to widespread acceptance of the goal-setting responsibility.

Rather than counting solely upon conference superintendents and pastors to carry the New Day vision, the denominational departments shifted into gear to provide support services for the strategy. With church planting so integral to the New Day vision, it became the major thrust of the Department of Evangelism and Church Growth. Without losing the importance of church-growth methods in existing churches, the thrust of evangelism turned toward church plants, especially in urban and ethnic areas.

The plan took on personality when Dr. Ray Ellis, a specialist in church planting, became director of the Department of Evangelism and Church Growth. His leadership, built upon the work of his predecessor, Dr. Forest Bush, changed church planting from theory to practice, from vision to reality.

The pastoral address for the General Conference of 1989, delivered by Bishop Gerald E. Bates, reinforced the keynote for the New Day vision in

1985. Again, evangelism was first priority backed by doctrinal integrity, church planting, discipleship and sensitivity to ethnic diversity. At the same time, realities of implementing the New Day vision came to light in the 1989 address.

Recognizing the demands upon resources needed to realize the New Day goals, the bishops called for resource development through (1) networking within and without the denomination; (2) recruiting ministers, especially church planters; and (3) urging the stewardship of sacrificial giving.

DEALING WITH FINANCIAL CRISIS — Without a panic call, the bishops' address of 1989 foresaw a financial crisis at the denominational level. The action of the General Conference to relocate denominational headquarters from Winona Lake to Indianapolis, with the purchase of new property but without the sale of the old campus, would be the aggravating factor for a full-blown crisis. But, as we recall from the pastoral address of 1960, the problem had been building for three decades. In the simplest economic terms, expenditures for expanding denominational ministries continued to increase, while revenues from churches and conferences did not keep pace.

Behind the economic problem were sociological and psychological factors. Sociologically, the process of decentralization frayed the cord of connectionalism between the local congregation and the denominational headquarters. Psychologically, the local church became the heart of the Free Methodist Church. True to Christ's Word, the treasure of the people followed the beating of the heart. Denominational ministries were the first to suffer.

Not all the blame can be placed upon the natural movement of all denominations toward hierarchical authority and organizational self-enhancement. A gulf may have been developing in Free Methodism over the years between the leadership and the people, and it took a financial crisis to reveal it. While the tendency is to make finances the "cause" of crisis, the fact is that it is a leading symptom of a more systemic problem with multiple causes.

To address the pending financial crisis without losing the incentive of the New Day vision, fund-raising campaigns were initiated for projects above the United World Mission for Christ budget. To cover the cost of relocating denominational headquarters, a "Home Free" fund, with a goal of $2.5 million, was launched in 1989. Approximately $1.3 million were raised over the next five years (See Chapter 8).

Concurrently, another campaign, entitled "Harvest 1000," was announced for church-planting projects in 1989. The goal of the campaign was $5 million with $2.8 million actually promised and raised. By 1995 the thrust for these campaigns had waned, and, for all intents and purposes, fund-raising ceased, except for occasional gifts or pledges that were still coming in.

PROJECTING A NEW PARADIGM — To restart the New Day vision in 1994, the bishops presented a paper throughout the world-wide church entitled "Century 21 Paradigm." A paradigm, according to Joel Arthur Barker, who popularized the concept for the field of business in the 1990s, is "a set of rules and regulations that does two things: (l) it establishes or defines boundaries; and (2) it tells you how to behave inside the boundaries so as to be successful."[4] From that definition, Barker went on to build a theory of what he called "paradigm shifts" in the culture to which leadership had to respond in order to be successful in the future world.

The bishops adapted Barker's theory for application to the church. Their "Century 21 Paradigm," presented in 1994 by Bishop Richard D. Snyder, defined the boundaries for Free Methodist pastors and leaders between "nonnegotiables" and "desired outcomes" for ministry.

NONNEGOTIABLES FOR MINISTRY:

1. May not live in violation of the Scriptures;
2. May not live in violation of the Articles of Religion and the Membership Covenant;
3. May not live in violation of ordination vows;
4. May not receive members who are out of harmony with our mission and doctrine;
5. May not lead the local church in ways that divert it from the fulfillment of its mission, from growth in Christlikeness, and from the mission of the Free Methodist Church.

DESIRED OUTCOMES FOR MINISTRY:

1. Every church a worshiping community;
2. Every local church a loving, witnessing, enfolding congregation;
3. Every local church producing discipled, growing, holy people;
4. That leaders develop a strategic mindset that plans and implements ways to reach the lost for Christ;
5. That we be a growing world missionary movement;
6. That social awareness will result in ministry to the poor and disenfranchised;
7. That all Free Methodist structures be brought into serving a movement dedicated to evangelizing our world.

Within these boundaries, the Century 21 Paradigm sets no rules and regulations. Leaders of the church, clergy and laity, are urged to demonstrate initiative and creativity as they "strategize and minister in ways that produce the desired outcomes."

By personally presenting this paradigm from the platforms of conferences, area meetings and leadership seminars across the world, the bishops have essentially changed the nature of governance in the church. Rather than relying upon tactical planning at the denominational level for growth in the local church, the new paradigm identifies denominational leadership in its strategic role of monitoring the boundaries of core convictions and desired outcomes, while rewarding initiative and creativity in the leadership of congregations. Questions still remain. How will the nonnegotiables be monitored? How will the desired outcomes be appraised? The test of the Century 21 Paradigm is underway.

CENTERING ON THE LOCAL CHURCH — Coinciding with the public presentation of the Century 21 Paradigm, the bishops made sure that their vision had meaning for local churches. Also, in January 1994 they proposed these targets of strategic planning for the churches:

1. Every church with a clear, written mission statement;
2. Every church with written, measurable goals;
3. Every church with a written plan to accomplish its mission and reach its goals;
4. Every church praying for God to call new ministerial and missionary candidates;
5. Every conference mobilizing for church planting and church growth;
6. Every church participating in the "Adding to the Family" new-member program;
7. Every Free Methodist focusing on neighborhood witnessing and soul-winning;
8. Every pastor and leader going before God and praying for a renewed vision and anointing by the Holy Spirit;
9. Every leader asking God for wisdom in recasting the Free Methodist Church for the Great Commission.

Implementation of the strategy of the New Day in conferences and congregations cannot be guaranteed. No one, however, can fault the bishops for casting the vision of a new paradigm for the denomination, backed up by a feasible plan of action at the local level. In itself, this is a gain over the past.

CREATING INCENTIVES FOR THE NEW DAY — Incentives for advancing the New Day vision as the strategy for the church into the 21st century are also notable, and in some cases almost radical. The incentive for church growth continues in the recognition of the increasing number of large churches. What began as a list of the top 10 churches in 1976 has now been enlarged to the top 50 churches and numbers for the top 10 churches have been increased from 200-plus to 400-plus members.

Near the apex of this growing pyramid are new awards for the largest and fastest-growing churches in each conference. At the peak is the annual honor given to the top church in each U.S. conference with the highest gain in combined membership and morning worship attendance.

Other incentives for meeting the goals of the New Day vision are even more dramatic. Attention will be given to these incentives in appropriate chapters. For now it is sufficient to list them as tactics for the New Day strategy.

1. In recognition of the growth of social, urban and ethnic ministries, Rev. Delia Nüesch-Olver was appointed as the first full-time director of the Division of Social, Urban and Ethnic Ministries under the Department of Evangelism and Church Growth in 1994.

2. To recruit and train pastors and church planters for the New Day strategy, the John Wesley Institute was established on each Free Methodist college campus as the connecting link between the church and pastors-in-training (1987).

   Also, the three-track system of ministerial education and guidance (seminary, college and home study) was given new emphasis, especially in the college and home-study tracks.

3. To preserve the youth for the church, the Department of Christian Education embarked upon a new venture called "MODEL" (Mission, Outreach, Discipleship, Equipping and Leadership), which emphasized leadership development for youth at the grass-roots level of the region, conference and local church.

4. To recognize the resources of women for full participation in the ministry of the church, the traditional organization of the Women's Missionary Society was expanded under the title of Women's Ministries International with a full program of development — spiritual and social, personal and professional, home and church, evangelistic and missionary — for women within and without the church.

5. Consistent with the New Day vision to acknowledge and value diversity in leadership for the church, Women's Ministries International participated in the first International Wesleyan Holiness Women's Clergy Conference in April 1994. Ordained women elders and deacons or candidates in preparation for ordination from the Free Methodist Church were in attendance.

6. With a view toward the New Day of the 21st century, young leaders under the age of 35, from both clergy and laity, participated in a conference at the World Ministries Center in 1993 for a free and open discussion of the future of the church and their role in that future.

These incentives illustrate the fact that New Day was more than a strategy articulated by the bishops and soon forgotten. Follow-up programs engaged the commitment and mobilized the energies of new and diverse leadership at the same time that the existing resources of denominational institutions, departments and auxiliaries were rejuvenated by complementary strategies of their own.

To repeat, the vision of New Day under God is the first fully developed strategy for the growth and vitality of the Free Methodist Church since its earliest years. Vision, mission, distinctives, organization, resources and outcomes all come together in a master plan for the 21st century.

"BY MY SPIRIT" — THE 1995 GENERAL CONFERENCE — When the General Conference convened at Anderson, Indiana, on July 1, 1995, the date marked the 10th anniversary of the New Day under God vision and strategy. With the clarity of its measurable goals, the conference came at the opportune time to assess progress toward the goals, make adjustments if necessary, and reengage the elected leadership of the church in a commitment to its vision, strategy and outcomes.

By choice, however, the pastoral address for the General Conference, presented by Bishop Snyder on behalf of the Board of Bishops, did not specifically mention the New Day vision, assess its outcomes or project its future. Instead, selective facts emphasized the growing places of the church, such as:

— record attendance at denominational conferences and rallies;
— new church plants, especially among ethnic congregations;
— growth upon growth in large churches;
— worship attendance exceeding membership in local churches;
— establishment of the Free Methodist Church in 39 countries;
— increase in per capita giving since 1985, ahead of inflation;
— enrollment of 7,804 students in Free Methodist colleges and universities in the United States.

Within these general statements of growth, however, were statistics both sobering and hopeful. On the sobering side, membership in the Free Methodist Church in the United States had increased only 527 members from a total of 75,392 in 1989 to 75,919 in 1994, a growth rate of less than one percent for the period. Hope was found, however, in the unrealized potential for growth during the same five years. Average annual worship attendance grew by 6,404 from 79,540 in 1989 to 85,944 in 1994, a growth rate of 8 percent.

With even more hope, the bishops also reported that 41,542 persons had received Christ through the ministry of local churches between 1989 and 1994. Taken together, these statistics reveal a mixed account of a church with minimal growth in membership, strong growth in worship attendance and outstanding growth in the number of converts. In sum, the church was effective in attracting non-members and winning persons to Christ, but ineffective in bringing converts to membership.

The pastoral address of 1995 then reaffirmed the foundational principles undergirding the New Day vision in a set of eight core convictions:
1. We must be a holy people.
2. We are to be a praying people.
3. We are to be a people filled with the Holy Spirit.
4. We must be a witnessing people.
5. We are to be a servant people.
6. We must be a church-planting people.
7. We must be a discipled and a discipling people.
8. We must be united as a people.

These core convictions needed to be reaffirmed, but not without attention to the fact that the Free Methodist Church had almost come to a standstill in domestic growth at the same time hundreds of churches were being planted, thousands of people were being converted in local churches, and tens of thousands were being added overseas. On one hand, it might appear as if the church had once again reverted to promoting strategic goals for evangelism without accepting accountability for the outcomes. Free Methodism in 1995 still needed a frank assessment of progress, careful discernment of the reasons for gains or losses, and adjustment of the goals with a balance between faith and facts.

The pastoral address from the Board of Bishops is considered a "State of the Work" report from the perspective of past, present and future with emphasis upon tone-setting for the General Conference. Consequently, the decision not to restate and assess the goals of the New Day vision may have been intentional. The problem, however, is that the General Conference of 1995 provided no other forum for revisiting the strategy and its goals. Earlier pastoral addresses in the period from 1960 to 1989 set the expectation for a benchmark statement on the current status of the church. Bishop Snyder, in response to the question about the New Day vision, explains,

> The pastoral address was born out of New Day Documents and intended to be in full support of the New Day vision. During the past five years, core convictions behind the New Day strategy have been emphasized more than goals. After debating the question of whether or not to make the General Conference the forum for the assessment of the New Day goals, the plan is to give priority to these issues at the 1995 leadership conference for bishops, conference superintendents and denominational executives. The statistics tell us that adjustments will have to be made.

Bishop Snyder's candid response confirms the fact that the Board of Bishops continues to see the New Day vision as the motivating and mobilizing strategy for the growth of the church. They are also aware of the need to assess its actual progress against its announced goals.

From the standpoint of timing for the 1995 General Conference, however, they chose to keep an upbeat tone because of the potentially explosive nature of the membership issue. With that decision, they lost the immediate advantage of General Conference, which would have involved the lay leadership of the church in the assessment of New Day goals.

Perhaps the hope is that changes in the conditions of membership will be the catalyst for restarting church growth with focus upon bringing new believers into membership. If history is the guide, no single strategy, method or procedure will make the difference. But if the change in the conditions of membership has a ripple effect upon the outlook of the church, the outcomes could well follow. Predictions are plentiful, but judgment must be held until the facts come in. Whatever the results, the General Conference of 1995 will not be forgotten.

REVISITING THE NEW DAY GOALS, 1985-1995 — By courageous choice in 1985, the bishops proposed measurable goals for the vision of New Day under God, which required a system for assessing the progress and communicating the results. Furthermore, these measurable goals permitted a comparison of the effectiveness of the New Day vision with the earlier strategies of "Double in a Decade" and the church-growth movement.

In the decade between 1985 when the New Day vision was first articulated and *Yearbook* statistics for 1995, total membership in the United States, Canada and the United Kingdom grew from 81,814 to 82,613. The latter figure, however, is a significant drop-off for the peak of 84,592 total members in 1992 with the most serious loss in the 1995 calendar year when all three sectors of the North American General Conferences experienced decline. The United States annual conferences themselves dropped from 75,919 members in 1994 to 74,735 members in 1995. In contrast, overseas churches (other than the United Kingdom) grew in total membership from 138,994 in 1985 to 314,068 in 1995.

There is merit in revisiting the New Day goals of 1985 in order to have a realistic assessment of gains and losses, within which adjustments both upward and downward can be made. (As a benchmark for assessment, 1995 represents the 10th year on the 15-year New Day calendar which was projected to A.D. 2000. Consequently, 66.6 percent of each goal should be achieved by 1995 for the strategy to stay on track.) The following chart shows the goals and the gains for the New Day vision at the end of 1995:

Goal for A.D. 2000	Goal at A.D. 1995	1995 Actual	% of 1995 Goal Achieved
1000 New Church Plants in North America (a)			
Total Church Plants	666	323	48%
125,000 Members in North America (a)	110,600	82,613	
(Gain of 43,414)	(28,791)	(799)	2.8%
300,000 Members in the Church Overseas (b)	259,200	314,068	
(Gain of 160,500)	(107,337)	(163,144)	157%
Free Methodist Churches in 40 Countries (c)	34	38	
(Net Gain of 16)	(10)	(14)	140%
Six New General Conferences	4	5	125%

(a) Goals for the New Day vision in 1985 and reporting in 1995 include the United States, Canada and the United Kingdom.
(b) In 1990 the New Day goal for overseas membership was increased to 500,000 by A.D. 2000.
(c) In 1990 the New Day goal for Free Methodist Churches in nations other than the United States, Canada or Great Britain was increased to 50 by A.D. 2000.

From this New Day "score card," as the bishops described their report, we see the gains and losses. Leading the way in the gains is overseas growth in membership and new general conferences, which have already exceeded the goals for A.D. 2000. More significant yet, the New Day goals for Free Methodism overseas have been revised upward to envision the church in 50 nations with 500,000 members by the turn of the century!

In the United States, Canada and the United Kingdom, however, the statistics for 1995 fall far short in church membership and church plants. One can argue that the New Day vision is projected forward to A.D 2000, and the momentum is building toward the achievement of the original goals. This may be so, but the 1992 State of the Work Report presented by the Board of

133

Bishops voices the concern that a lag in impetus toward New Day goals in the mid-1990s has replaced the enthusiasm of the late 1980s and early 1990s. Also, Ray Ellis, director of Evangelism and Church Growth, assesses the 1985 goals for 1,000 church plants to be "unrealistic" in light of the history of the church and the requirements for church planting.

Most discouraging, however, is the statistic for membership growth in North America, particularly in the United States, where there is a loss of 1,184 members in 1995 alone. Once again, when the growth statistics for church plants and conversions through the ministries of the local church are added, the net loss is a "soul drain" that no denomination can afford or survive.

One must conclude that the potential for growth exists, but membership development is ineffective as a ministry. To reverse the downward trends and realize its untapped potential, the vision for the church in North America and the United Kingdom will have to be recharged. Otherwise, the New Day strategy for growth will join the earlier strategies as a noble, but unfulfilled, venture.

A CALL TO ACTION, 1995 — On December 8-10, 1995, the bishops of the Free Methodist Church took on the challenge of evaluating the progress of the United States church toward its New Day goals and adjusting them as necessary. All conference superintendents, denominational executives and college presidents were invited to St. Petersburg, Florida, for a New Day Mobilization Conference.

The overall purpose of the conference was announced "to engage the commitment and mobilize the energies of denominational leaders to the mission, manifesto and strategic goals for the future of the church." Seven specific goals were set:

1. To assess the consistency of the mission statement with the ministry of the church;
2. To account for the outcome of the New Day goals 1985-1995;
3. To project the bishops' style as catalysts and models for leadership of the church;
4. To draft a manifesto identifying the New Testament character of the Free Methodist Church and its people;
5. To commit the service and auxiliary ministries of the church to the advancement of mission and support of conference leadership;
6. To set revised strategic goals for the New Day into A.D. 2000 through a "bottom up" rather than a "top down" process;
7. To inspire the leadership of the church to higher levels of devotion and performance.

Three days of intensive and interactive sessions followed. A poll of the superintendents at the end of the meeting revealed unanimous agreement that the stated goals of the gathering had been met, along with the unwritten goal of strengthening the working relationship and camaraderie of the leadership team for the Free Methodist Church in the United States. Labeled as a "summit meeting" for the church as it moves toward the 21st century, the outcomes speak for themselves. First, the mission statement of the church, adopted in 1987, was affirmed as the guide for its ministry into the future.

Second, an accountability report by the bishops on the progress toward the New Day goals of 1985 confirmed the statistics of minimal growth in total membership and losses in the total number of churches. Balancing these sobering statistics, the report also presented evidence of growth potential in the increasing number of new church plants, large churches with membership over 200 and ethnic and urban congregations. Furthermore, they noted that the Free Methodist Church is an exception among Protestant denominations because attendance at worship services exceeds its membership. More than 41,000 persons were converted through the ministry of local churches during the past five years. Realism mixed with optimism prevailed.

Third, the bishops also reported on the general strategies behind the New Day goals. Especially, they wanted to demonstrate changes in their style as catalysts and models for servant leadership in the church. One change noted was their becoming more proactive during the past decades by leading in relocation at Indianapolis, reorganization of the World Ministries Center, restoration of financial stability and cooperation with SCOD in proposing new membership requirements for the 1995 General Conference.

Another change came in the bishops' approach to the regionalization of the North American church. Through the bishops' area cabinets, regional strategies were developed naturally in the context of the culture, rather than artificially from the national level.

Still another change was entitled "permission giving" with particular reference to the Century 21 Paradigm. That model resulted in retaining creative and catalytic leaders who would have been lost to the church if they had not been given freedom within the boundaries of the nonnegotiables for the pastor and outcomes for the local church.

A 10-year scorecard summarized the achievements of the church, including the Young Leaders Conference, 400-Plus Pastors Conference, partnership with the Free Methodist Foundation, development of the pension program, professionalization of screening and selection of conference superintendents, and appointment of the first full-time director of Social, Urban and Ethnic Ministries. While acknowledging the shortfall on achievement of the New Day goals in the past decade, the bishops said they were learning the meaning of a "mission-driven church" and seeing results that gave cause to celebrate.

Fourth, a manifesto addressed to the church under the title, "A Call to Action," was drafted, adopted and signed by the participants. Because the manifesto is intended to be circulated, posted and signed at every level of the church from conferences to local churches, it is a document destined for historical significance.

A Call to Action

Addressed to the Church

The mission of the Free Methodist Church is to make known to all people everywhere God's call to wholeness through forgiveness and holiness in Jesus Christ, and to invite into membership and equip for ministry all who respond in faith.

In order for the Free Methodist Church to achieve its destiny under God, we must rid ourselves of spiritual lethargy. We must ask the God of power to direct us as we end the 20th century. We, as leaders, gathered here in St. Petersburg, Florida, on December 10, 1995, commit ourselves and our people to:

1. *Salvation.* Celebrating the forgiveness of sins, freedom from shame and guilt, cleansing from the power of sin by the Holy Spirit, and the assurance of salvation;
2. *Prayer.* Calling ourselves to the practice of prayer, recognizing our total dependence upon God for the revival, health and growth of His church;
3. *Scripture.* Understanding and obeying the Word of God for growth and wholeness in Him;
4. *Obedience.* Obeying joyfully the lordship of Christ and ruling out any form of casual Christian living;
5. *Worship.* Experiencing the presence of God through worship which is pleasing to Him and meaningful to the people;
6. *Community.* Pursuing a climate of love and trust which makes possible partnership in our common mission;
7. *Reconciliation.* Laying aside all prejudice and bigotry and taking the gospel and love of Jesus to people of all groups and every level of society, leading them to the knowledge of Christ and to full incorporation into His church;
8. *Leadership.* Honoring the God-ordained role of leadership in the church and carefully identifying, developing and supporting gifted and competent women and men who are called to lead;
9. *Mission.* Pledging ourselves to the global mission of the church, ministering worldwide the goodness and grace of Jesus Christ;
10. *Accountability.* Fulfilling our mission to the glory of God with excellence and accountability.

We who have signed below have covenanted together to carry out the above, God helping us, and call on all Free Methodists to join us.

Signatures of bishops, conference superintendents, denominational executives and college representatives were affixed to the document as an example for all Free Methodists to follow.

Fifth, consistent with the goal to develop revised strategic goals for the New Day vision from the "bottom up" rather than coming "top down," the conferees agreed to defer on the projections for membership and churches until the superintendents could further consult with their cabinets and pastors of local churches. This would permit partnership, ownership and accountability for the goals at the level of action where growth must take place. It was agreed that revised goals for A.D. 2000 of the New Day vision would be reported from conference superintendents to their area bishop by March 1, 1996, reviewed for mid-course correction at another summit meeting in 1997 and held for accountability in A.D. 2000.

Needless to say, the New Day Mobilization Conference set a precedent for the Free Methodist Church. For the first time, a summit meeting was called to review and revise the strategy for the church. One conference superintendent expressed the opinion of all participants when he wrote on his evaluation form, "I will take home a new sense that the Free Methodist leadership is united and passionately committed to being a Great Commission church. Accompanying the energy of this sense are specifics that are 'owned' by all of us. I can't wait to see what God will do!"

If his conclusion is right, a mission-driven strategy that mobilizes all Free Methodists in the ministry of a growing church is once again a possibility.

LEADERSHIP FOR THE 21ST CENTURY — Momentum from the 1995 General Conference and the New Day Mobilization Conference summit meeting carried over to the Board of Administration in October 1996. Following his doctor's advice, Bishop David M. Foster submitted his resignation, effective on the date of his 65th birthday in February 1997. Accepting his resignation with regret and expressing profound gratitude for his faithful and effective ministry in leadership since 1984, the Board of Administration proceeded to elect Kevin W. Mannoia, at the age of 41, as one of the youngest bishops to serve the church.

Not only Kevin Mannoia's age, but his advocacy in the 1995 General Conference for changes in the membership requirements, his expertise in aggressive church planting projects, and his leadership in the Southern California Conference of a contemporary expression of Free Methodism in the local churches, represent a new and youthful look for the church. His own words reveal his roots in the history of the church as well as his vision for its future:

The Free Methodist Church is in the midst of healthy transition. Behind us lies the strength of our heritage and the depth of our theology. Before us lies the future of our dreams, under God. As we enter an interdenominational period of church history, we will define ourselves not by our traditional practices, but by common values which will emerge to bond us in mission.

Our diversity will be our strength; our relevancy will be our breadth; our mission will be our drive; relationships will be our trust and holiness will be our character. This identity shift will confirm a New Day in Free Methodism as His kingdom people boldly press forward into the new millennium with creativity and energy that keeps mission ahead of method.

Rise or fall, grow or decline, succeed or fail — one thing is certain. Free Methodism in the 21st century is in for change.

Perspective on Governance
1960-1995 and Forward

Two unspoken questions undergird the strategies advanced by the leadership of the Free Methodist Church during the period from 1960-1995.

Can the Free Methodist Church dramatically grow again?

Can the Free Methodist Church become a dynamic movement once again?

Both these questions are historical because their reference point is in the early years of Free Methodism. In fact, the time line can be narrowed down into the first 30 years of Free Methodist history, when the church grew dramatically and experienced the vitality of a dynamic movement. To what extent, then, did the strategies succeed in giving affirmative answers to these questions? The hard facts of statistics answer the first question. During the period from 1960-1995, none of the strategies produced significant membership growth in the North American church. Overseas, however, Free Methodism recaptured the drama of growth known during its early years.

In response to the second question, there is evidence that strategies for growth revitalized the church in some critical areas of ministry. Beginning with the motive of Double in a Decade, the church left behind its defensive posture and began to look forward. The church-growth strategy introduced a method for the motive so that the restoration of aggressive evangelism as first priority for the church did not ring hollow. Nor did the New Day vision seem incongruous. Without forsaking growth in existing congregations, the New Day goals added a market mentality to the motive and method of the earlier strategies. Centered upon church planting, especially in urban and ethnic areas, the New Day vision represented an affirmative response to the growing edge of a changing culture.

In these sectors, the early signs of dynamic movement are present. Even though increases in total membership are minimal over the period from 1960-1995, and actually on the decline in the 1990s, selected growth among certain regions, churches and ministries is noteworthy. If Free Methodism is to become a movement again, the hope resides in these selected areas where growth and vitality are synonymous.

What can be learned about the governance of the Free Methodist Church from this review? Several observations come forward. One is the fact that none of the strategies, whether centered upon motive, method or market, has had a significant impact upon membership growth in the North American church. Certainly, motive, method and market must come together in a strategy that produces effective results.

Yet a nagging question remains. "Is there still a missing dimension in the conscious strategy of the church today that was unconsciously present in its earlier growth years?" One can only surmise that if that key dimension is present, strategy takes care of itself. But if that dimension is absent, strategy cannot make up the difference. Is that dimension found in spiritual vitality, cultural readiness, seeker sensitivity or the energy of a new movement? That key dimension, whatever it is, defines the search in which the Free Methodist Church is still engaged.

Another observation is the shift in strategy over the period 1960-1995 from denominational departments, through conference superintendents, and to the local church as the action point for realizing the goals of growth. In the 1960s, Double in a Decade counted upon denominational executives and their departments to implement the growth goal.

When the methods of church growth became the strategy in the mid-1970s, with carryover into the early 1980s, attention shifted from denominational executives to conference superintendents as the key to setting goals, training pastors and activating the system. With the market emphasis of the New Day strategy, however, the pendulum of action swung through the full arc from the bishops' vision to the local pastor's program. Theoretically, at least, if the goals of the New Day strategy are to be fulfilled, the power to act is at the point of growth.

Two fundamental fault lines may be seen in all three strategies of the era. Critics will be quick to note that each strategy for growth and renewal has come "top down." The paradox is readily apparent. Bishops are elected with the expectation that they will be visionaries for the future of the church. Yet when they exercise that responsibility, they encounter the natural distrust of established leadership, a legacy of the cultural revolution of the

1960s and 1970s. The dilemma will not go away. In order to engage the commitment and mobilize the energies of the local church pastors and people, the bishops must either "co-create" the vision at the grass roots level or intuitively cast a vision that connects with the imagination of the constituency. Whether or not this observation helps explain the severely limited results of the growth goals for the three strategies is more than a matter of conjecture. Without followers, leadership is a futile exercise.

A second fundamental fault line can be read in strategic planning that sets measurable goals without a designated schedule and system of accountability. Throughout the period from 1960-1995, the failure to meet strategic goals is either spiritualized or rationalized. The full loop of strategy cannot be ignored. As vision demands implementation, implementation requires evaluation. Without accountability, the church jumps from one strategical fad to another. Because the New Day vision is projected forward to A.D. 2000 the church still has the advantage of mid-course correction.

What grade, then, can be given to governance in the period from 1960-1995? Certainly, the bishops did not shirk their responsibility for projecting contemporary visions for the growth and vitality of the church. Overseas and on the growing edge at home their leadership scores high. Their visions, however, often encountered the realities of uncoordinated denominational ministries in the 1960s, diffused executive leadership in the 1970s, financial crisis in the 1980s and congregational inertia in the 1990s. If the effectiveness of strategic leadership is measured by the goals for growth at home as well as abroad, then the search for the missing dimension still goes on.

Max DePree has written in his book *Leadership Is An Art*, "The first responsibility of a leader is to define reality."[5] Reality for the Free Methodist Church at the end of the 20th century is defined by a strategic vision fulfilled overseas and on the growth edges of the church in North America. At the same time, we must recognize the failure to revitalize most of the existing congregations and restore the momentum of a movement. If this is the reality upon which the future rests, the Free Methodist Church must be ready to live with a winnowing process that will test the meaning of governance as both the "management of growth" and the "management of decline."

C H A P T E R   8

Stewarding
Our
Resources

B iblical stewardship is foundational to understanding the Free
Methodist Church. Rising out of creation theology and permeat-
ing the Scriptures, biblical stewardship involves all of the resources
God has entrusted to the church — physical, human and spiritual. Wesleyan
theology not only embraces this conviction at the core of faith but also draws
special focus upon the stewardship of grace, which expresses itself in ministry to the poor.

Bishop Marston, in his book *From Age to Age A Living Witness*, pulled
through this thread of Wesleyan heritage when he listed stewardship as one
of the five founding principles of the church along with doctrine, experience,
worship and piety.[1] In Wesleyan terms, then, stewardship is defined as "faith
working by love."

In more recent years, stewardship in the Free Methodist Church has been
narrowed into financial terms. In 1967 a Department of Stewardship and Finance was established with a director whose specific responsibility was to
raise funds for the denomination. This narrowed definition is not necessarily
inconsistent with either biblical or Wesleyan theology, because wealth is a
central issue of stewardship, both with Jesus in His preaching and Wesley in
his practice. Neither, however, severed the link between stewarding financial
resources and serving human need.

Two errors appear when this linkage is broken. One error is the heresy
of ownership regarding wealth. All of Jesus' warnings about the seductive
power of wealth come into play when Christians, who are blessed with resources, assume they owe God only a portion of their wealth. By implication
and by practice, they are wrong to think that they deserve what they earn,
own what they have, and are accountable to God for only a tithe or a gift.

A second error in the stewardship principle appears when personal resources are given to a denomination in which the organization has become an

end in itself rather than a means of ministry to those who are spiritually and socially poor. Denominations, in particular, are prone to become self-perpetuating bodies requiring ever-increasing resources at the expense of the original purpose for which they were founded. For this reason alone, the percentage of revenues dedicated to administrative expenses or capital overhead becomes a valid stewardship test for denominational vitality.

This chapter will be limited to the issues of the financing, officing and publishing interests of the Free Methodist Church from 1960-1995. At test in each case will be the question, "Does stewardship in the Free Methodist Church still reflect its historical linkage between physical resources and human need as expressed through the mission of the church?" Wesley's General Rules go so far as to make the practice of biblical stewardship a requirement for " ... all who continue in these societies," and continuing evidence of " ... their desire for salvation."[2] If the Free Methodist Church and its members are true to their heritage, history will answer, "Yes" to our guiding question.

Financing Denominational Ministries

As early as 1960 caution flags were flying with concern for denominational finances. At the General Conference of 1960, a freeze was put upon expenditures for all departments in the coming quadrennium. The action came despite the fact that the Free Methodist Church stood at or near the top for all denominations in the United States for per capita giving by its membership. At the same time that the church enjoyed this reputation as a leader in stewardship, rising costs for expanding denominational services were outstripping the limited growth of membership.

THE COMPETITIVE ERA, 1960-1964 — At first, the problem was diagnosed as competition for limited funds among denominational departments, especially home and world missions. Following the trends of the 1960s toward unification of ministries, in 1961 the Board of Administration ordered a study of a unified budget. At the General Conference of 1964, the study committee presented the concept of a World Mission Budget (WMB) and recommended its adoption. At the heart of the concept was the premise, "The World Mission of the local church is to be enlarged by a unified program of stewardship. This plan, enacted by the General Conference, will enable local churches to participate in a stewardship program involving faith and sacrificial giving without competitive appeals for funds."[3]

The World Mission Budget included all denominational departments, offered budgetary guidelines, created a structure and set goals for apportionment from individual conferences.

THE UNIFIED ERA, 1965-1979 — A defining moment in the history of the Free Methodist Church came with the adoption of the concept and the plan for the United World Mission for Christ (UMC) budget at the General Conference of 1964.

(Note: The unified budget went through a succession of name changes from the World Mission Budget in 1964 to the United Ministries for Christ with the division between Home Ministries and World Missions in 1985. To avoid confusion, the current acronym of UMC will be used throughout the text.)

As might be expected, the plan did not become an instant panacea for denominational financing. Spurts and lags in funding characterized the first quadrennium from 1966-1969 while the plan was being put into action. The goals and actual revenues for this period were:

UMC GOALS AND ACTUAL REVENUES, 1966-1969

Fiscal Year	UMC Goal	Actual Revenues
1966	$1,928,500	$1,590,933
1967	$2,158,190	$1,658,841
1968	$1,660,000	$1,655,010
1969	$1,650,000	$1,618,474

As the chart shows, the announced goal for the UMC in 1967 reflected the ambitious hopes for the plan. When giving fell far short, the next year's goal was adjusted downward to the level of giving. Still the UMC fell short.

At the General Conference of 1969, a progress report on the UMC reaffirmed the concept and attributed the lags in apportionment to an adjustment period among constituents. Whether by aggressive promotion or more realistic budget planning, the UMC met its goals in the next period between General Conferences in 1969 and 1974.

UMC GOALS AND ACTUAL REVENUES, 1970-1974

Fiscal Year	UMC Goal	Actual Revenues
1970	$1,677,000	$1,760,000
1971	$2,149,000	$2,319,923*
1972	$1,840,000	$1,912,530
1973	$1,922,000	$2,088,803
1974	$2,056,000	$2,314,305

*16 months due to change of fiscal year
from August 31 to December 31

On this encouraging note, little change in structure or procedure took place in the UMC budget at the General Conference of 1974.

By 1976, however, the threat of deficit operations loomed large. An urgent letter of appeal went out from the Board of Bishops calling the church to increased support for the UMC budget in order to prevent major cutbacks in denominational ministries. Dr. George Ford was also hired as director of Information and Stewardship with the specific task of promoting the budget. Still, during the quinquennium from 1975-1979, UMC revenues began to lag behind goals again.

UMC GOALS AND ACTUAL REVENUES, 1975-1979

Fiscal Year	UMC Goal	Actual Revenues
1975	$2,350,000	$2,358,000
1976	$2,725,000	$2,626,435
1977	$3,000,000	$2,859,300
1978	$3,035,000	$2,921,180
1979	$3,530,000	$3,063,719

At the General Conference in 1979, the cumbersome name of the United World Mission for Christ budget was changed simply to the "United Ministries for Christ" with priority given to evangelism. In recognition of the fact that budget deficits were crippling certain ministries, World Missions in particular, provision was made for Special Growth Projects. Foresight into future problems came with the proposal for an awkward "three-tier" system of financing.

The UMC budget stood alone in the first tier; Special Growth Projects occupied the second tier; and a $1 million campaign for World Missions represented the third. The General Conference tried to give priority to "first-tier" giving in order to meet UMC goals. Sentiment, however, favored the more dramatic appeals of special projects in the second and third tiers.

Also, the General Conference recognized the need for a long-term base of support for denominational ministries by including the deferred gifts in the projects approved for solicitation.

The 1979 General Conference also grappled with the issue of lagging revenues. Riding the high tide of the "Born Again Movement," the glamour stock of televangelism and new networks of interdenominational ministries began diverting millions of dollars from the pockets of members in local churches. To counter that movement, the General Conference of 1979 passed a resolution reaffirming that Free Methodist Church members' "first and wholehearted commitment is to our own denominational ministries. We strongly urge our people to support the programs God has led us as a church to establish."

Revenues lagged behind goals for two more years and cutbacks of 6 percent in 1979 and 10 percent in 1981 were required. Then in 1982 Bishop W. Dale Cryderman, who was also serving as interim general headquarters administrator, could make the jubilant announcement that the UMC goal had been met for the first time in six years. By and large, the encouraging news continued through the sextennium between General Conferences in 1979 and 1985.

UMC GOALS AND ACTUAL REVENUES, 1980-1985

Fiscal Year	UMC Goal	UMC Actual
1980	$3,230,000	$3,063,719
1981	$3,500,000	$3,256,225
1982	$3,400,000	$3,400,000
1983	$3,333,640	$3,438,781
1984	$3,510,000	$3,481,141
1985	$3,712,000	$3,797,008

A hidden factor was at work. Program improvements in denominational ministries were virtually on hold during the period, project funds lagged, and double-digit inflation continued to erode the purchasing power of the dollar. World Missions suffered most, because global ministries were on an unprecedented spurt of growth while tied to the "no-growth" reality at the domestic level. Also, inflation in many countries grew greater than in the United States.

THE BIPOLAR BUDGET, 1985-1995 — At the General Conference of 1985, an impassioned debate resulted in a reversal of the unified budget principle by dividing the funding into "world missions" and "home ministries." In the next quadrennium, the results of a divided budget shows these figures:

UMC GOALS AND ACTUAL REVENUES — 1987-1989

Fiscal Year	UMC World Missions		UMC Home Ministries	
	Goal	Actual	Goal	Actual
1987	$2,101,617	$2,365,925	$1,783,06	$1,700,585
1988	$2,226,579	$2,280,749	$1,901,788	$1,813,320
1989	$2,618,284	$2,793,125	$1,977,450	$1,879,816

Soul-searching by the leadership of the church led to the conclusion that the principle of stewardship and the practice of tithing had broken down in the membership of the local churches. In response to that conclusion, the General Conference of 1989 adopted a paper outlining the tithing issue and the stewardship principle as a working document for regaining the support of the local church.

As added confidence for Free Methodists giving to the denomination, the church became a member of the Evangelical Council for Financial Accountability in 1985. Membership meant that the Free Methodist Church complied with the highest managerial and ethical standards of accounting and accountability in financial matters.

YEAR OF CRISIS, 1990 — Just one year after the 1989 General Conference, mounting deficits compounded by relocation costs and special growth fund appeals required more aggressive action. In 1990 the bishops organized an ad hoc Committee of the Concerned to work toward a short and long-term strategy for funding denominational ministries.

In their *Confidentially Yours* newsletter to ministers, the Board of Bishops published an article with the provocative title "Open Doors and Concrete Shoes." In this article the bishops confronted a cash-flow deficit that included borrowing $750,000 to maintain operation, liquidating a $932,000 debt from the Light and Life Press, carrying an indebtedness of $223,000 from the Winona Lake properties, and funding the principal and interest costs of the new World Ministries Center in Indianapolis based upon a purchase price of $3,100,000.

A bold, turn-around strategy followed. To deal with financial crisis, the bishops proposed to:

1. Develop a network of prayer partners and donors who would give extra to end the year in the black;
2. Form a Stewardship and Finance Task Force to examine the total financial and organizational process and recommend improvements;
3. Launch a church-wide campaign in stewardship and tithing;
4. Make large-scale reductions in general church budgets by eliminating five executive positions, accepting early retirement by Bishop Robert F. Andrews and enacting substantial cutbacks in staff positions;
5. Assume oversight and maintenance management of the new World Ministries Center;
6. Announce the personal pledges of $23,000 from the leadership and staff at the World Ministries Center to help overcome the deficits; and
7. Establish a Home Free committee to raise the funds to pay for the purchase cost of the new World Ministries Center.

Implementation of these actions led to short and long-range strategies for financial turnaround.

Still, in 1990 the deficit for Home Ministries continued to rise, so that more immediate cutbacks were required: (a) A 1 percent increase in the Home Ministries budget combined with inflation meant a 5 percent cut in purchasing power; (b) seminary scholarships were lowered from 60 to 40 percent of tuition costs; (c) Free Methodist Futures grants for college students and the funding for the Historical Center were eliminated; (d) loan service on the Indianapolis properties totaling $250,000 was to be raised from sources outside the budget; (e) off-site staff office help was discontinued; and (f) no annual pay raises were given to denominational and departmental executives.

THE TURNAROUND ERA, 1991-1995 — After the financial brinkmanship of 1990, the effects of budget management quickly took effect. In 1991 income from all sources exceeded expenses by $8,000 to set the pace for balanced operations in the future.

Spurred by early evidence of financial turnaround, a Task Force on Services was established in 1991 to survey local churches and conferences with the aim of determining the relevance of denominational services to the constituency and with a view to adjusting budget priorities. Fifty-six clergy and lay leaders were asked to rate the importance of the services of denominational departments to the local church. The primary concern of grassroots leadership did not center in the value of departmental services, but in questions of confidence about the organizational structure, executive effectiveness and financial accountability.

When the Task Force on Services presented its recommendations to the Board of Administration, they centered upon radical adjustments in the organization and finances in order to restore confidence in the leadership of the church. Almost all recommendations were adopted by the Board of Administration and became the basis for restructuring and downsizing which led to financial turnaround.

Soon the full impact of financial discipline and organizational streamlining could be felt. In 1992 income exceeded expenses by $1,158,000 and in 1993 by $791,000. The meaning of these figures goes beyond balanced budgets and sound fiscal management. No longer did the church have to borrow funds to maintain cash flow, but the budgets provided for the elimination of past deficits, carried the load on capital debt and permitted the reestablishment of the reserve fund. At the close of the fiscal year 1994, financing had been stabilized for the fourth consecutive year with income exceeding expenses by $105,293 as evidence of operating efficiency.

The turnaround story of the Free Methodist Church in financing its denominational ministries needs to be told. The 1991 appointment of the resident bishop, Gerald E. Bates, as overseer, and the 1992 appointment of Gary Kilgore as chief operating officer, with the title of director of Administration and Finance, set the tone for the turnaround.

Credit, however, does not belong to one individual or group. Rather, from the policy of the General Conference and the Board of Administration, through the executive leadership of the bishops and denominational officers and to the crisp decisions of the Operating Committee of the World Ministries Center, the turnaround was achieved.

The fact remains that financial solvency came from the internal reduction of expenditures, rather than external increases in revenues through the United Ministries for Christ funding. Also, UMC budget goals are established on the basis of conference pledges that are compiled directly from local church pledges. From 1990 through 1995, the UMC goals and actual revenues were:

UMC GOALS AND ACTUAL REVENUES, 1990-1995

Fiscal Year	World Missions		Home Ministries	
	Goal	Actual	Goal	Actual
1990	$2,469,899	$2,743,976	$1,950,988	$1,875,850
1991	$2,672,531	$2,855,713	$2,050,865	$1,937,196
1992	$2,739,634	$2,839,473	$2,048,792	$1,999,248
1993	$2,838,692	$2,798,311	$2,101,639	$2,026,115
1994	$2,945,417	$2,845,712	$2,130,707	$2,038,513
1995	$2,962,236	$2,968,296	$2,196,482	$2,149,402

World Missions exceeds its funding goals four of six years, while revenues for Home Ministries continue to lag behind. This does not mean that World Missions is overfunded, because missionaries and missionary programs still suffer from severely limited resources.

Home Ministries face a different challenge. Funding for denominational services is always a dilemma unless there is direct evidence of benefit to the funding source. The Task Force on Services took commendable steps toward identifying the World Ministries Center as a "resource center" at the service of the church. Still, the radical cutbacks in the early 1990s did not bring an outcry of dissatisfaction due to reduced services from the World Ministries Center. With the natural momentum of decentralization in the culture and the loosening bond of connectionalism in the local congregation, indifference rather than dissatisfaction may be part of the answer. Most likely, funding for World Missions and Home Ministries will remain on tight budgets and limited improvements for years to come.

SPECIAL PROJECTS AND FUND CAMPAIGNS, 1979-1995 — Beginning in 1979, Special Growth Projects were authorized by the General Conference in a second and third tier of giving beyond the UMC budget. Later, these Special Growth Projects were extended to major fund-raising campaigns, sometimes with multimillion dollar goals and church-wide promotion.

A partial list of these Special Growth Projects and/or campaigns, with goals compared to total funds received, illustrates how the concept of a unified budget was modified beginning in 1979:

Special Project	Year	Goal	Total Funds Received or Pledged
World Evangelism	1981	$1,000,000	$ 379,483
Home Free Fund	1989	$2,500,000	$1,317,000
Harvest 1000	1991	$5,000,000	$2,832,000
Operation Hope	1994	$1,000,000	$ 268,890

Without being unduly critical, it is easier to initiate special projects and fund-raising campaigns than it is to assure adequate preparation, follow-through and evaluation of results. No one is at fault, and the Free Methodist Church is not alone. Let the lesson of history be learned.

Managing Denominational Investments

During its first century, the Free Methodist Church operated upon the traditional "faith" principle of financing. Annual needs were met by gifts with regular appeals from denominational departments. A unified budget represented a move to a sustaining base of support through the apportionment system with the hope that special projects would not be necessary. Like United Way, the church adopted the appeal, "Give Once For All," as the means for more efficient and effective giving. Also, like United Way, the assumption was that Free Methodists would regularly give more each year to meet ministry needs at home and abroad.

New economic realities advanced funding for Free Methodism another step with the introduction of deferred-giving programs in 1972. As background for deferred-giving, Americans were accumulating wealth in their estates that would continue beyond their lifetime. Without planning for the distribution of these assets, estate and inheritance taxes imposed by the government would leave little for heirs or charities. Favorable legislation on the use of wills, bequests and annuities, however, made it possible for a person to save and defer taxes while determining the use of the funds even after death.

Free Methodists, who had stewarded their resources to the church through tithes and offerings and were now accumulating wealth in their estates, became natural prospects for a deferred-giving program. As a continuing expression of a life of stewardship, their wealth and estates could be given to advance the ministries of the church in perpetuity.

Deferred giving requires a new paradigm for biblical stewardship. Historically, a "faith" position for the funding of ministries implied a day-to-day and hand-to-mouth existence. Deferred giving is intended to provide a sustaining base for the future that alleviates the anxiety of uncertain funding. Some fear that ministries are spoiled when dependence upon daily faith is lost. Others, however, foresee mature stewardship exercised by those who project their faith into the future in order to provide sustaining, long-term gifts for the ministry of their choice.

Through the establishment of a standing Investment Committee at the time of the reorganization in 1931, the Free Methodist Church had already adopted a long-term view on the stewardship of assets. As a follow-up to this philosophy and with the initiative of Hugh A. White, Howard Fear presented a proposal to the Board of Administration in 1972 for a deferred-giving program. The plan met with the favor of the board, and plans began to develop for a planned-giving program.

In 1974 another step was taken with the authorization for the employment of a planned-giving specialist. These actions led to the establishment of a Division of Planned Giving in 1974 by consolidating all deferred-giving contacts from among individual departments and inaugurating deferred-giving seminars throughout the church.

Early success of the program led to the appointment in 1975 of Dr. Stanley B. Thompson as the first full-time director for the Division. Four years later the Division of Planned Giving as well as the Ministers' Pension Fund were more specifically added to the responsibilities of the Investment Committee, which continued to function under the oversight of the Board of Administration but independently of the Commission structure.

Assets of the Division of Planned Giving continued to grow when regional representatives across the United States were employed to write wills, bequests, annuities and other life-income plans. Capturing this opportunity, the Board of Administration in 1987 approved the establishment of The Free Methodist Foundation (FMF) to promote programs in planned giving and manage all investments of the church. The investment portfolio of the Foundation grew again by action of the Board of Administration in 1994, when the Church Extension Loan Fund (now the Free Methodist Loan Fund) was added to its responsibilities.

The organizational plan for the Foundation included the election of a board of directors by the Board of Administration, a president elected by the board, regional vice-presidents throughout the nation, a headquarters staff and a Foundation office at the site chosen by the Board of Directors. Implementation of this plan led to the election of Stanley Thompson as the first president of the Foundation with headquarters located in Spring Arbor, Michigan.

The directors of the Foundation adopted the following mission statement:

> The Free Methodist Foundation supports the mission of the Free Methodist Church by providing planned giving assistance, investment services, trust services, loan assistance to Free Methodist churches, and fund-raising counsel.

Since its founding in 1987, the Foundation has grown to a major ministry for the church, with assets of $109,534,618 according to the 1995 annual report. These total assets are divided into the following managed funds:

FUNDS MANAGED BY THE FREE METHODIST FOUNDATION, 1995

Free Methodist Church Pension Funds	$57,883,837
Life income Plans	$31,362,698
Free Methodist Loan Fund	$16,088,869
Endowments	$4,199,214
Total	$109,534,618

The economic relationship of the Foundation with the Free Methodist Church can best be seen in the percentage of these funds designated specifically for its ministries:

FOUNDATION FUNDS DESIGNATED FOR FM MINISTRIES, 1992-95

	Amount	Percentage
World Ministries Center	$14,162,873	30.9%
Local Churches	$13,699,320	25.1%
Colleges/Universities/Seminaries	$9,410,522	14.7%
FM Conferences	$4,515,513	9.5%
Other FM Ministries	$4,726,433	8.8%
Non-FM Ministries	$6,275,791	7.5%
FM Social Service Agencies	$1,845,909	3.5%
Total	$54,636,361	

A foundation for planned giving starts slowly and then builds momentum as donors and assets increase. Growth of donors and assets since 1991 attest to the success of the Foundation. From 1992-1995, total assets increased from $79,092,467 to $109,534,618. In 1995 alone $17,122,605 was added to the funds for the which the Foundation is responsible. During this period, the investments had average annual weighted gains of 10.4 percent. These gains, in combination with wills, bequests and annuities that matured upon the death of the donor, not only helped increase the assets of the Foundation but permitted the following distribution of funds from matured estate and outright gifts for the designated ministries:

FUNDS RECEIVED BY DESIGNATED MINISTRIES
FROM MATURED ESTATE AND OUTRIGHT GIFTS, 1992-1995

	Amount	Percentage
World Ministries Center	$3,217,931	43.3%
Local Churches	$1,718,626	23.1%
Colleges/Universities/Seminaries	$1,047,904	14.1%
Other FM Ministries	$ 983,453	13.2%
FM Conferences	$ 256,469	3.5%
FM Social Service Agencies	$ 114,849	1.5%
Non-FM Ministries	$ 95,398	1.3%
Total	$7,434,630	

Over the same period of time from 1992-1995, outright gifts channeled through the Foundation to designated Free Methodist ministries totaled $3,521,582. Large single gifts to the World Ministries Center, a Free Methodist college and specified local churches accounted for the large majority of this total amount. When the matured estates and outright gifts are combined for the period 1992-1995, the grand total was $7,434,630 with 43 percent of the amount designated for support of the World Ministries Center.

Retired ministers received $6,916,448 from 1992-1995 from the Pension

Fund, and local churches borrowed $7,803,670 for capital projects through the Free Methodist Loan Fund. These disbursements determined the effectiveness of the Foundation and the achievement of its essential purpose. The disbursements have had limited impact upon the funding base for the designated Free Methodist ministries, with the exception of the World Missions department and the World Ministries Center. Administrative expenses for World Missions were totally funded by deferred gifts and endowments, while the World Ministries Center received a growing percentage of its operational costs from the FMF during this period. As the Foundation grows in assets and time brings deferred gifts to maturity the impact will undoubtedly increase.

Organizationally, the relationship between the Free Methodist Church and the Free Methodist Foundation is delicate. Because of the independence of the Foundation, only a line of trust can assure a common commitment to the mission and priorities of the church in the cultivation of donors, investment of assets, management of funds or evaluation of performance.

President Stanley Thompson voiced the delicacy of this relationship in his report to the FMF Board of Directors in 1995 when he said, "The Free Methodist Foundation will continue to build and maintain its strength to serve other parts of our church effectively only as long as we are able to maintain a loyal, healthy, but independent relationship apart from the bureaucracy of our denomination ... Our directors must continue to function as proactive churchmen (women) who establish the parameters for the day-to-day direction of the FMF. As president, I want to be a good steward of the autonomy which has been granted to us."

Nevertheless, the Board of Administration in 1996 called the Foundation to closer accountability to the church. The "autonomy" of which Stanley Thompson speaks does not exempt the Free Methodist Foundation from detailed reports regarding its policies, operations and performance. Accordingly, the Board of Administration reaffirmed the Free Methodist Church of North America as the parent body of the Foundation and called for review of such policies as the distribution of unrestricted funds, the sphere of operation for the FMF and fees for its services.

The Board also called for detailed reports to the Executive Committee on items ranging from current budgets to annual, five and 10 year returns on portfolios. These expectations are consistent with the standards of credibility that have been developed for charitable foundations in the crucial areas of fund-raising costs, administrative costs, and reserves held over and above operational costs. For the future, the relationship between the Free Methodist Church of North America and the Free Methodist Foundation can best be described as "autonomy with accountability."

The Free Methodist Foundation is both old and young. Spawned out of the Division of Planned Giving that was established in 1974, the Foundation has functioned as an entity since 1987 and gained momentum ever since. At the same time, the Foundation is rapidly coming of age with a history of planned gifts going back 22 years and an institutional identity focused on fund-raising going back almost 10 years. The test of its significance in providing a sustaining financial base, endowments or project dollars for the multiple ministries of the church is not far in the future. Its promise, then, is even greater. Even though Americans are the most generous givers in the world with the largest share of $150 billion in gifts going to religion each year, the percent of income, even for Free Methodists, is far below the tithe.

Furthermore, within the next few years, the largest transfer of wealth in history — estimated as high as $8 trillion — will move to the next generation. If Free Methodists of the current and future generations are faithful stewards of their resources, the Free Methodist Foundation holds the promise of being one of the most effective instruments for financially resourcing the ministries of the church.

Relocating Denominational Headquarters

Physical facilities represent the resource of space that must be stewarded as wisely as money. Free Methodism's history in the stewardship of space is a study coincidental with strategic moves of the church itself. In 1935 the publishing house led the way in a move from a high-priced urban plant in Chicago to the more compatible and less costly Christian conference setting of Winona Lake, Indiana. The move made sense. Publishing is not space-bound. Literature can be printed and transported from any site at competitive costs in the national and international mailing system.

The advantages of Winona Lake with its small-town setting, modest living cost, and conservative Christian culture symbolized Free Methodism in the relatively stable environment of the 1930s. It should be no surprise to learn that a General Conference mandate in 1955 ordered that all denominational offices be relocated with the publishing house on the Winona Lake campus.

From the beginning, Winona Lake was intended to become the permanent headquarters of the Free Methodist Church. Reinforcement of this intention came with the construction of the Light and Life Press building, along with the remodeling of the headquarters offices in 1961, acquisition of the Westminster Hotel in 1970 and the purchase of an adjacent warehouse in 1971. An addition to the Word Music building was completed in 1976 and further improvements were made in subsequent years. All told, the assets of the investment in Winona Lake campus peaked at a total $2.25 million by the end of 1985.

153

Yet the inevitable winds of social change were blowing. Not only were the antiquated Winona Lake properties requiring costly maintenance investments on top of increasing operating costs, but the location no longer symbolized the exploding dimensions of the world church. Signs began to point toward the need for a centralized metropolitan setting with savings in time and money for serving the expanding needs of an emerging world church.

The issue of relocation surfaced as early as 1972, when the Christian Service Fellowship was engaged to consult on the church and its future. The Christian Service Fellowship report recommended that no more money be invested in the deteriorating facilities. However, the church had already entered into a combined gift and bargain sale agreement with Mr. and Mrs. James Thomas (a sister to the late Homer Rodeheaver) for the acquisition of the Westminster Hotel and a parcel of property for the construction of a new building as the distribution center for the Rodeheaver Music Company. The building was then leased to Word Music, Inc., on a long-term contract. While assuring adequate returns for the facility itself, the earnings did not assist in the losing venture on the main campus.

In 1974 the first call came from the General Conference to study the feasibility of relocating the world headquarters of the church. The study stalled through the 1979 General Conference, but in 1985 the General Conference authorized the Board of Administration to "carry forward a thorough study of location and facilities for the Free Methodist headquarters, and the Light and Life Press in the immediate future with a report to the 1989 General Conference."

To implement this action, the Executive Committee of the Board of Administration appointed a working committee chaired by David McKenna, with Norman Edwards, Leslie Krober, John Minshall, Kathy Ogles and Wesley Skinner, Jr., as members. In its initial meeting, the committee defined its charge under three tasks: (1) to appraise the Winona Lake property for renovation or sale; (2) to evaluate the Winona Lake location as the continuing site for world headquarters; and (3) to compare optional sites for buying, leasing or building a new world center for the church.

The committee assumed that the decision on location should be driven primarily by the mission of the church, with economic feasibility as a supporting premise. The committee also concluded that its recommendation to the Board of Administration, in anticipation of the 1989 General Conference, should be stated as a "stay-or-go" choice relating either to renovation of the existing facilities or relocation to a new site based upon preestablished criteria for the decision.

After more than 18 months of concentrated study, the committee recommended against renovation of the Winona Lake campus and for relocation of a newly named World Ministries Center at an available site in Indianapolis. The committee identified Indianapolis, among 11 cities in the United States, as the one which best met the preestablished criteria:

1. To advance the mission of the church into the 21st century, especially in support of the "New Day" vision of 2000 Free Methodist churches by A.D. 2000.
2. To symbolize the movement of the church toward evangelism, urbanization and internationalism.
3. To serve efficiently and economically the current and developing world ministries of the church, especially at the local level.
4. To steward the resources of the church in capital, operational and relocation costs.
5. To cooperate with other denominations to create a "Wesleyan presence," improve services and save money.
6. To provide a quality working environment for executives and staff, and if relocated, to assist them in relocation.
7. To facilitate local, national and international travel to and from the site, saving both time and money.
8. To offer a quality living environment — socially, culturally, educationally and spiritually — for the executives and staff.
9. To assure reasonable costs for housing, goods and services, taxes and wages, construction and leasing.
10. To include adequate conference facilities, e.g., housing, dining and large-group meetings.

As would be expected, a recommendation of this magnitude produced emotionally charged responses on both sides of the question. Long-time members identified Winona Lake as "home" for the church; economic realists feared the hidden costs of a move while acknowledging the "sink hole" of debt on the old campus. Most of all, the Winona Lake staff felt traumatized by the thought of being uprooted from their homes or losing their jobs.

When the 1989 General Conference convened in Seattle in July, emotions had peaked. Opponents of the move appeared at the conference wearing buttons that read, "DON'T MOVE," and sides were drawn at dining tables and coffee breaks. Parliamentary maneuvering began the moment the proposal reached the floor of General Conference. Opponents moved for a two-thirds majority vote and proponents angled for a simple majority. The advocates of a plurality won the point and the vote was taken. A total of 64.7 percent of the delegates voted for relocation, a decision that would have been lost by three or four votes on the requirement for a two-thirds majority.

Of course, the decision of General Conference did not dispel all the problems of relocation. Even with financial assistance, denominational executives and staff members had to decide whether or not to relocate their homes and families. Negotiations had to be conducted for the $3.1 million purchase of a building, which originally housed the National Hardware Association located on the west side of the city on Interstate 465 within four miles of the international airport. The Winona Lake property had to be put up for sale in an area with a depressed real estate market.

In response to these issues, not enough credit can be given to the staff members who made the sacrifice to relocate because of their sense of call to ministry and their love for the church. Healing took place faster than expected so that in 1995, five years after the move, the consensus of the staff can be spoken through the words of a senior member who has served the church for more than 30 years. When asked to speak honestly about the morale of the staff in the new setting, the staff member answered, "We are more together as one body now than ever before. By and large, those who made the move feel that relocation was the right thing."

To purchase the hardware building without creating a capital debt that would further imperil existing deficits in the denominational budget, a "Home Free" fund was established at the 1989 General Conference with a goal of $2.5 million to make the purchase with minimum debt. Although the total raised by the Home Free campaign fell short of the goal, the gifts of $1,317,000 assisted the church in meeting the obligations of a $2,066,000 5-year bank mortgage based upon 20 years amortization at 10.4 percent interest, which was later refinanced at rates of 8.9 percent then 8.05 percent. Additional loans were negotiated with Deaconness Hospital and Bank One in order to purchase the building. These latter loans have been paid in full.

To service this capital debt out of the UMC Home Ministries budget, however, exposed the severity of an economic crisis. Critics may place the blame for operating deficits on relocation, but in reality the denomination was already overextended and underbudgeted. Notwithstanding, the added burden of a long-term debt on the Indianapolis facility, while still maintaining the unsold Winona Lake campus, might still be considered the proverbial straw that broke the camel's back.

The Winona Lake campus is only now being sold. Maintenance and utility costs have been substantial. Early attempts to sell the property met with frustration after frustration. The specialized nature of the facility, the depressed real estate market, the inability of investors to finance the purchase, and the reluctance to sell below the appraised value all militated against the sale. In the Committee on Relocation's report in 1989, the property was appraised at approximately $1.2 million.

With the sale of the Winona Lake property and other gifts which have come in, the remaining principal on the Indianapolis property stands at under $1.2 million. Of note is the fact that the property which cost $3.2 million in 1990 now has an estimated worth of $4.2 million. The Partners in Ministry program under the Free Methodist Foundation continues its efforts to pay off the remainder and endow the operational costs of the World Ministries Center.

In 1995 the financial status of the World Ministries Center reflected the discipline of stewardship that led the church through crisis to recovery. Both the principal and interest on the loan for the purchase of the facility are serviced within a balanced denominational budget. Looking back, the decision to relocate now bodes well.

Promoting Denominational Publishing

Free Methodism inherited the legacy from John Wesley of the effective use of the printed word as a medium of communication and an instrument of connectionalism. Through the leadership of B.T. Roberts, a prolific author and publisher, the Free Methodist Church became identified with the widely circulated paper, *The Earnest Christian*. B.T. Roberts and other leaders, such as T.B. Arnold, considered a denominational paper so essential to the connectional relationship and evangelistic outreach of the church that they took personal responsibility for the ownership and financing of *The Earnest Christian*.

In 1886 the church purchased the publishing business of T.B. Arnold at a price of $8,000, named him the first publisher, and elected B.T. Roberts as editor of *The Free Methodist*, which had been published independently since 1868.

Publishing continued to be a growing and influential ministry of the church through its first century. The publishing house, through its circulation of printed materials for local Free Methodist churches, symbolized the connectional strength of the church. As publisher B.H. Gaddis noted in 1936, the publishing house served as "... a monument to the loyalty and support of publishing interests on the part of the membership of our church, expressive of the loyalty unsurpassed by any other church." [4]

The strength of Free Methodist publishing at the opening of the second century in 1960 can best be attested by its contributions, out of its own operations, to other ministries of the church and particularly by its investment in facilities for the general church at Winona Lake. In 1960 a deed was executed by the publishing house board in favor of the general church whereby the church became the owner of the old publishing house property, plus nearly eight acres of land.

Subsequently, the publishing house built its own attached addition to the general church headquarters. For this exchange the general church agreed to make payments of $5,000 a year over a 10-year period. The payment was to be applied to the six-percent interest charge on the loan that the Investment Committee made to the Publishing House for the construction of the new press building. Later on, the loan was locally refinanced to the advantage of the church until paid in full in January 1967.

Throughout the decade of the 1960s, successful operations of the Free Methodist Publishing House permitted its board to demonstrate its value as a ministry of the church by continuing to contribute from their surpluses to the activities of the general church. But in 1969 the opportunities for extension of the publishing house ministry prompted publisher Lloyd Knox to recommend that any profits of the operation should be reinvested in publishing itself. This policy prevailed through the 1970s and into the 1980s with the effect of making Free Methodist publishing a major force shaping the direction of the church, especially in the development of curriculum materials.

During that time the publishing house, operating under the name of Light and Life Press, rode the high tide of the evangelical movement, which led the nation in the growth of its books, periodicals, curricula and other printed materials. In 1978 the evangelical press was reputed to have published one-third of all books printed in the United States.

The publishing interests of Light and Life Press reached their apex in 1985 with the $325,000 purchase of a new state-of-the-art Heidelberg Press with its four-color printing and nonstop loading to produce 10,000 impressions per hour. This purchase vaulted Free Methodist publishing into public prominence in 1986, when the trade journal *Inplant Reproductions and Electronic Publishing* honored the Light and Life Press as number two in the nation for in-plant printing utilizing the newest technology.

The national award, however, came at the expense of rising costs and mounting deficits in the printing operations. Especially with the demise of the Aldersgate Curriculum, the high-tech printing press geared for volume turned overnight from an award-winning asset to a deficit-mounting liability. By 1989, just three years after the award, accumulated operating deficits forced the sale of the Heidelberg Press for $330,000, discontinuation of all printing operations, liquidation of the remaining equipment, and contract services for the printing of *Light and Life* magazine.

According to the Board of Bishops' letter *Confidentially Yours* of November 1990, the liquidation of the press and three straight years of operational deficits totaling nearly $500,000 left a debt of $932,000 that the general church had to assume. The size of this debt, along with other operating deficits and capital obligations, echoes again the meaning of the dramatic turnaround in finances that began in 1990, eliminated cash flow deficits by 1993, and met all of the obligations of principal and interest on both operating and capital debt, including Light and Life Press.

With the liquidation of printing operations and the sale of the press building to the general church, Light and Life Press opened a new chapter in its history. In 1990 as part of the management plan to turn around finances, the recently appointed publisher, John Van Valin, presented the first budget for Light and Life Press. The budget included balanced operations based on the new initiatives, particularly the Light and Life Bookshop in Indianapolis, which was rapidly rising to prominence as one of the top 10 Christian bookstores in America. Other management initiatives included competitive off-site printing, cooperative publishing with other Wesleyan denominations and, of course, tight budgetary control on expenditures to avoid future deficits. As a result Light and Light Press returned to a balanced budget position in 1991 with a surplus to assist the general church by repaying its debts to the church which had been accumulating since 1985.

To assure the continuation of balanced budgets and long-term viability, the Board of Administration, which also serves as the Board of Directors for Light and Light Press, instructed the publisher to prepare one- and three-year plans for the program. In September 1994 the plan was presented with such specific targets as: (1) More efficient employment of fewer persons; (2) Reduction and/or repayment to the general church of old accounts payable; (3) 15-percent gain in subscriptions for *Light and Life* magazine; (4) Printing 30 book titles a year that are initiated in concert with Free Methodist ministry needs and requests; (5) Marketing for increased sales ranging from 10 to 30 percent within three years; and (6) Increased cooperative marketing with members of the Holiness Publishers Alliance (Church of the Nazarene, Wesleyan Church and Church of God — Anderson).

The purpose of this plan was to implement the following Mission Statement of Light and Life Press:

Light and Life Press, the official publishing house of the Free Methodist Church, is a not-for-profit corporation that exists to serve in partnership with its parent body, the Free Methodist Church. Its primary purpose is to publish and distribute materials which enable the church to fulfill its stated mission. Light and Life Press also offers its services and materials to all who seek to make Christ known. In a world where information is wealth, communication is instant and competition is fierce, Light and Life Press will continue to face the challenge of disciplined and creative stewardship in both mission and market.

Ministering Through Print

The centerpiece for Free Methodist publishing throughout the history of the church has been a magazine that has served as a communications bond for the membership. Even before the founding of the church in 1860, B.T. Roberts wrote with a powerful and eloquent pen in the publication *The Earnest Christian*. After the church was founded and began to spread westward, the periodical was continued under the private auspices of B.T. Roberts and others, because the infant organization lacked the funds to publish its own denominational magazine.

On January 6, 1868, the first issue of *The Free Methodist* was published as a private venture headed by Levi Wood. Strange as it may seem, the ownership and publication of *The Free Methodist* stood at the center of one of the church's most controversial eras. Crisis after crisis rolled through the church as the debate over the establishment of a publishing house, which would take over the financial responsibility for publication of a denominational paper, dominated the agenda of general conferences through the 1870s and into the 1880s.

Meanwhile, B.T. Roberts continued as the editor and publisher of his own paper, *The Earnest Christian*. Finally, the General Conference of 1886 established the Free Methodist Publishing House and ironically, elected B.T. Roberts as editor of *The Free Methodist* in direct competition with *The Earnest Christian*.

Once the Free Methodist Publishing House was established and *The Free Methodist* put under denominational ownership, the magazine gained the status as the official organ of the church. By the centennial year of 1960, Bishop Marston noted that *The Free Methodist*, a weekly magazine, had a circulation of 30,000 and the reputation as the flagship of Free Methodist publications.[5]

Under the editorship of James F. Gregory, the editorial policy of 1960 sets the benchmark for tracing the movement of the magazine through the era from 1960-1995:

> It is the purpose of *The Free Methodist* to inform its readers doctrinally, to shed light on Christian experience, to enliven the truth of the Scriptures, to unify the church in a program of evangelism through every department, to act as an organ of promotion, and to cover the news of the church. Special attention is given to the centrality of the Bible as God's book. The importance of Christianity in family life is a major concern. Considerable attention is given to religious news that the denomination must be aware of its responsibility to the church universal.[6]

Gregory carried this agenda through the years of his editorship, from 1960 until his death in 1964. Awards for Christian journalism and denominational magazines were received in 1962 from the Associated Church Press and the Evangelical Press Association. But the awards did not alleviate the pressure of finances or editorial workload. In 1962 the Board of Administration made the decision to change *The Free Methodist* from a weekly to a biweekly publication.

When James Gregory died, publisher Lloyd H. Knox assumed the role of Acting Managing Editor until the 1964 General Conference, when Byron S. Lamson was elected as editor. In the same General Conference, the shift toward a family magazine was proposed for *The Free Methodist*, with the call for an in-depth study of its purpose. The discussion continued without resolution through the tenure of Lamson until the name of the magazine was changed to *Light and Life* by the Board of Administration in 1970.

The board offered this rationale:

We exist, not [for] ourselves, but for the world. We are committed without reservation to the Free Methodist Church as a means of fulfilling God's purposes for mankind. We must therefore do all we can to get the attention of persons who need God in their lives. Both the name and the cover, we hope, will invite further reading. We want to exalt Christ. He must come before denominational sponsorship. It is our earnest prayer that *Light and Life* will be an evangelistic tool for every subscriber. Let us share the good news of God's redemptive acts.

Light and Life is a meaningful name. To Free Methodists it is as well known as our denominational designation. From the uninitiated it should evoke interest. It is distinctly biblical and theological. Jesus said, "I am the light of the world; he that followeth me shall not walk in darkness, but shall have the light of life." The Apostle John wrote of Christ, "In Him was life; and the life was the light of men."

Light and Life — symbolic New Testament words that speak of the revelation of Christ and suggest the Christian's role in society. They emphasize the delicate and required balance between warm, personal Christian experience and social outcome, between our relationship to God and to one another, between the heavenly and the earthly, between the vertical and horizontal.

The words *Light and Life* speak of the light that breaks upon our dark planet giving greater hope than the rising of the sun. In fact, they characterize our reasons for existence.[7]

Within this statement of purpose is a change in direction for the magazine. From the comprehensive news magazine with a strong doctrinal emphasis under the editorship of James Gregory and Byron Lamson, the shift was not toward the family-type magazine as proposed in 1964, but toward an evangelistic tool of outreach for the Free Methodist Church with non-believers as the primary market.

Another major change in leadership for *Light and Life* magazine took place in 1970. For the first time, the periodical did not have a single editor at the helm. Rather, four off-site editors were appointed — Robert M. Fine, Donald

E. Demaray, U. Milo Kaufmann and H. Frank Van Valin. This editorial team functioned under an Editorial Board and shared rotating responsibility for issues of the magazine, with coordination by a managing editor. Jay Benson served as the managing editor from 1969-1971 when G. Roger Schoenhals assumed the role and served until 1981.

During this time, special efforts were made to promote the magazine. Named the Love-Care concept, subscriptions were drastically reduced in 1975 so that the magazine could be placed in the homes of all constituents of the church. Under this plan, *Light and Life* subscriptions in 1977 totaled over 58,000. Strong support came from the Board of Bishops for pastors to submit mailing lists of local constituents for follow-up promotion of the magazine. Two years later, as financial pressures increased, the magazine came under scrutiny and a revised plan of action was advanced.

Once again the mission of the magazine shifted back toward the needs of the church, not to the neglect of an evangelistic motive, but with priority given to communicating with the membership. The editor of the magazine was also restored to status as a denominational executive, even though he continued to report to the publisher, who held parallel status as a denominational executive. Under the new plan, a goal of 65,000 subscriptions was proposed along with the goal of making the magazine self-sustaining by 1981.

For the next five years, *Light and Life* continued to be published by committee. An Editorial Advisory Committee set the policy, editorial consultants reviewed the content, an executive editor provided overview supervision and a managing editor did the work. Although the organization was cumbersome, the magazine continued to advance in quality and recognition under its managing editors. After G. Roger Schoenhals resigned as editor in 1981 to take a pastoral appointment in the Northwest, Lyn D. Cryderman assumed the role and continued until 1986, when he moved to *Christianity Today Institute* as managing editor.

In 1986 leadership for *Light and Life* returned to the pattern of the 1960s when Robert B. Haslam was employed by the Board of Administration as the new editor. With his employment, the position of managing editor was discontinued and Bishop Bastian's title as executive editor was changed to chairman of the Editorial Advisory Committee. Haslam immediately advanced a new philosophy for publication of the magazine. The primary objective was to build up the church, reach out to new persons and families and assist in winning and discipling of non-believers.

Haslam said, "*Light and Life* strives to illuminate and enhance human life from the perspective of the Free Methodist Church's mission (forgiveness, holiness, ministry, faith) with interesting and engaging articles that conform to high journalistic standards."[8] In support of the New Day emphasis in this philosophy, the Board of Administration set aside $3,700 in the budget for 1986 for 500 *Light and Life* subscriptions to be distributed among church-planting projects.

Has *Light and Life* accomplished its purpose? Awards of national recognition as the top denominational magazine came to *Light and Life* in 1992 and 1994 from the Evangelical Press Association, and in 1995 circulation stood at 24,043. Furthermore, as a rarity among denominational magazines, *Light and Life* has either operated in the black or come within a few dollars of the goal of being a self-sustaining periodical.

Results of a reader survey done in 1992 further confirm the quality of the publication. More than 400 readers in the sample agreed that the magazine is interesting, appealing, biblically based and spiritually helpful. The quality of the cover, the bishops' column and the editorial page stood out in their minds. Major benefit to the readers were up-to-date news of the church and articles that aid spiritual growth. When they received the magazine, they read first the letters to the editor.

There is no doubt that the readership is loyal. Even with a random survey, the average years of reading *Light and Life* was 28.2. As might be expected, 85 percent of the respondents were members of the Free Methodist Church, and more than 96 percent professed to be born again. With a large dose of human interest stories and articles on holiness counterbalanced by minimal promotion of the Free Methodist Church, the magazine clearly serves the purpose of a devotional publication ministering to the spiritual and relational needs of members of the church.

The vision of its use as an evangelistic tool has not been realized and probably cannot be. A monthly publication of limited size must be aimed at one constituency or another. To combine a devotional emphasis with an evangelistic one in the same publication reduces the effectiveness of both ministries.

In 1995 Robert Haslam retired as editor of *Light and Life*. His successor, Douglas Newton, came to the post from the position as president of Oakdale Christian High School in Kentucky. Although his agenda for the future is still being formed, Newton will find meaning in the valedictory words of his predecessor, Robert Haslam, "As we approach a new century, what will our leaders ask of us? Where will they challenge us to go? What will they call upon us to accomplish? The answers to those questions will impact the story of the church that is ever unfolding in the pages of *Light and Life*."[9]

Despite the changing priorities and leadership models for *The Free Methodist* and *Light and Life* from 1960-1995, there is continuity with history in the emphasis upon a periodical that bonds Free Methodists as members of the church and seekers of spiritual growth. Even as the church enters the Age of Information in the new millennium, and electronic media dominate the information highway, there will be the need for a denominational magazine. "In fact," Newton says, "the fast-paced, visual nature of modern communication media, which tends to elicit unreflective responses, makes the need for print media more pronounced. Since Christian discipleship requires careful thinking, one of the primary goals of the magazine must be to invite people to slow down and choose a lifestyle of quiet, biblical reflection."

Light and Life Press started a new publication, *Youth's Temperance Evangel*, a take home paper for young people in 1897. In 1912 it was combined with several other youth papers and retitled *Light and Life Evangel*. Sixty years later — March 1972 — the title became simply, *Evangel*.

Though the name of the paper and editors have changed, the mission to share the Good News of Christ has remained the same. In 1997 *Evangel* celebrated 100 years of providing solid, inspirational reading resources for adults.

A wide range of other publications have come and gone in the period between 1960 and 1995. Other periodicals that were prominent in 1960 — *Youth in Action, Sunday School Journal*, and *Transmitter* — are no longer in publication. Also, the loss of *Arnold's Commentary on the International Sunday School Lesson, Uniform Series*, combined with the reduction in Free Methodist Sunday school literature due to competing publications, has had a direct bearing on the strategy of Light and Life Press. Many departmental periodicals were started and stopped in the 35-year period between 1960 and 1995. Rather than listing them individually, a sample of publications from Light and Life Press in 1995 shows the wide-ranging scope of the print media as ministry:

Laughter, Joy and Healing — Donald E. Demaray
Does Doctrine Matter? — Donald N. Bastian
Church Planting — Kevin Mannoia
The God of our Salvation — Paul Livermore
Dark Providence, Bright Promise — Ken Leech
Book of Discipline
On a Hill Far Away: Journal of a Missionary Doctor in Rwanda
   — C. Albert Snyder, M.D.

Ministry through print has undergone several changes in the period from 1960-1995. General church publications now include *Light and Life* magazine, *Update, Today* and *World Mission People* magazine (which is published through the World Missions department). Books are being published as a major product line of the publishing house. The 1960 emphasis upon Sunday school literature has been expanded into comprehensive curricular tools in support of many facets of the New Day vision.

Publisher John Van Valin sees continuity in the axiom, "we become what we teach," as the theme that has defined the publishing ministries since their inception. As for the future, he sees Light and Life Press as a serving arm for the church and its departments, assuring the theological integrity of its publications and cooperating with sister denominations through such networks as the Holiness Publishers Alliance, to expand its offerings and explore new avenues of communication through electronic media. Accordingly, in 1996 the name of Light and Life Press was changed to Light and Life Communications. A new mission statement was formed:

Light and Life Communications serves the Free Methodist church and the world by providing resources that proclaim Christ's love, declare God's sanctifying grace and strengthen the integrity of our church community.

Perspective on Stewardship
1960-1995 and Forward

In retrospect, has the Free Methodist Church advanced the biblical and Wesleyan principle in its stewardship of finances, space and services during the past 35 years? The answer is, "Yes" if the church continues to exercise the discipline of hard lessons learned in order to apply limited resources more effectively to the achievement of its mission.

Without doubt, *Free Methodists can still be identified as a "tithing church."* A comparison can be made between per capita giving for Free Methodist members between 1960 and 1995. Marston noted that Free Methodists stood in the top ranks of per capita giving in 1958, but no rank or dollar amounts were cited. In 1962, according to *The Yearbook of American and Canadian Churches*, Free Methodists ranked high among North American denominations with average annual per capita giving of $177.66 for each of its 59,222 members.

By comparison in 1995 a total membership of 74,735 in the United States conferences gave $78,982,200 through their churches or $1,057 per capita. As commendable as the increase may be over the 33-year period, inflation has eroded the purchasing power of the dollar and severely limited available resources. If the limited growth of membership and the increased competition for funds from other evangelical ministries are added to the inflationary factor, one understands why the denomination has not been able to fund major expansions in denominational ministries.

An encouraging note for the future is the 1995 year-end report on income for the UMC budget. World Missions reached 100 percent of its goal for the year and Home Ministries reached the level of 97.86 percent. In comparison with the financial crisis of 1990, one can say that the Free Methodist Church is living within its means on a lean, realistic and "no-growth" budget.

While the inability to expand and improve denominational ministries may tend to be discouraging for Free Methodists, the downward trend in per capita giving has affected all denominations, especially in the mainline sector. Evangelical churches, while not exempt from the downward trend, sustain a higher level of giving from their members than other denominations because of their orthodox theology, evangelistic outreach and emphasis on tithing. The Free Methodist Church meets each of these criteria, and the prospects for future funding depend upon the commitment of the next generation to these foundation principles.

During the 1960s and early 1970s, the denomination came perilously close to feeding upon the expectation of ever-increasing resources out of a shrinking pool. A financial crisis hovering on the brink of bankruptcy awakened the church to its responsibility for the management of decline at home as well as overseas growth. Heeding the alarm in the 1990s, Free Methodism proved that the discipline of stewardship in turnaround management could hone denominational operations to greater efficiency in ministry and effectiveness in mission.

Still ahead for the Free Methodist Church is the test of stewardship between current giving and deferred giving. People who give regular tithes and offerings are the best candidates for future deferred gifts. The Free Methodist Foundation is designed to cultivate this potential for the future of the church. Assessment of its effectiveness will include achieved goals for writing deferred-giving instruments, a reduced percentage of administrative expenses against increasing assets, a favorable return on managed funds, significant disbursements to denominational ministries and retired ministers as well as an increasing volume of capital loans to local churches at favorable rates. Momentum along each of these lines gives high promise that the Foundation will be a major contributor to the viability of the church in the near future.

Relocation from Winona Lake to Indianapolis has turned from a trauma to an asset for the future of the church. As the dream of a global church comes true and Indianapolis speeds toward identity as a world class city, Free Methodism will be well situated for entry into the 21st century.

Light and Life Communications must walk the razor's edge between new communications technology and financial solvency. It will also have to anticipate a quantum leap into electronic and visual media for its ministry. Competition from other ministries in the evangelical network will continue to tempt local churches and conferences to buy more popular and cheaper materials rather than to put first priority upon Wesleyan theology and denominational loyalty in their choices. Because communications are inseparable from connectionalism in the Free Methodist Church's history, Light and Life Communications must be envisioned as essential to the future creative edge.

When all is said and done, adequate resources in the Free Methodist Church depend upon its clarity in teaching the biblical doctrine of stewardship and its commitment in practice to the Wesleyan distinctive of "faith working through love." If oncoming generations wholeheartedly embrace these convictions, the Free Methodist Church is ready to leave its concrete shoes behind and run with new confidence through its ever-opening doors.

C H A P T E R 9

Centering Our Ministry

Decentralization is a dominant trend in the history of the Free Methodist Church between 1960 and 1995. Power has shifted from episcopal authority to congregational leadership, and the center of action has moved from denominational events planned by headquarters to grass-roots ministries in the local church.

The culture went through the social revolution of the late 1960s and early 1970s with the breakdown of authority. The result was loss of confidence in leadership and the rise of individual freedom. On this same path, the trend toward decentralization in the church picked up speed.

In 1995 the Free Methodist Church had a radically different profile than it had in 1960. Bishops had been reduced in number, moved into the areas where they served, replaced in the chairmanship of the Board of Administration, and guided by a rewritten job description to emphasize their pastoral role. At the same time, laity have come into their own as leaders at all levels of church governance. Congregations have a direct voice in the evaluation of pastoral performance, the continuation of pastoral appointments and the assessment of church effectiveness. Pastors are perceived as equippers for ministry more than the doers of ministry, and enjoy a wide range of freedom in determining the mission, nature and style of the church.

The results of these trends toward decentralization come to focus in the changing profile of the local church. Fundamentally, Free Methodist churches are more diverse in doctrine, worship and lifestyle than ever before. The diversity is compounded by regional, generational and ethnic differences. Old criteria for justifying denominations are lost in this changing scene. Doctrinal identity may be more evangelical than Wesleyan; worship motif may be more contemporary than traditional; personal lifestyle may be more free than disciplined; and loyalty to the church may be more relational than connectional.

Free Methodism is not exempt from the phenomenon called "cocooning" of the local church — self-contained in nature and loosely connected to the historic church. But networking goes on across doctrinal and denominational lines to find benchmarks for new methods of ministry and new relationships for the congregation. With cocooning, of course, comes the danger of a "Mercator Map" view of the world, which pictures the local setting as the enlarged center of the globe with all other continents reduced in size, so that world missions and social compassion become selective, secondary and safe in the mission of the church. Conformity may be out, but is there still unity in diversity among Free Methodist churches in 1995?

Defining Moments in Decentralization 1960-1995

History takes us back again to the turning point in 1975 when Free Methodist leaders sponsored their first Church Growth Seminar. This represented a shift in focus from denominational ministries to local-church development. Through their spokesperson, Myron F. Boyd, the bishops made church growth at the local level their first priority. They confirmed their action in 1976 with the dual emphasis upon revitalizing smaller churches and celebrating larger churches. A Task Force on Smaller Churches was created by the General Council of Church in Mission to study the problems of these churches and recommend the methods for more effective evangelism leading to growth. At the same time, the first convocation was held for pastors of churches with more than 200 members to celebrate their size and discern the reasons behind their growth.

The failure of the merger with the Wesleyan Church turned the energies of leadership back to "growth from within" rather than by "multiplication from without." Also, the election of three new bishops, Donald Bastian (1974), Elmer E. Parsons (1974) and Clyde E. Van Valin (1976) represented a changing of the guard. They brought with them reinforcement for the agenda of evangelism and pastoral ministry. All of these forces converged in the second half of the 1970s to create momentum for the church-growth movement in local churches as the driving force for the next two decades.

The 1979 General Conference took action to recognize the establishment of "fellowships" that were on the way to becoming full-fledged Free Methodist societies. The following year, the bishops sought to close the gap between denominational leaders and local church pastors by conducting Bishops' Schools of Renewal.

Goals for the schools were: (1) *to clarify the pastoral role* as set forth in the Scriptures and adapted to the need of Free Methodism in the 1980s; (2) *to identify the leadership role of the pastor* in worship, pastoral services and administration, and to show how these are integrated in effective pastoral leadership; (3) *to develop in pastors a holy optimism* toward their task, grounded in a living faith in God; (4) *to raise evangelism to first priority* as the natural activity of a healthy church; and (5) *to pinpoint methods for leading a church* in worship, ministry and membership growth.

By 1989 the General Conference was ready to formalize the procedure for planting fellowships and growing Free Methodist churches through a section in the *Discipline* entitled "Formation of New Churches." As part of that action, fellowships were permitted to receive members into the church.

As early as 1980, the issue of Free Methodist membership requirements had been raised, especially in church plants where prospective members and new converts did not understand the history behind the standards of a separated lifestyle, which once characterized a Free Methodist. Pastors of these church plants struggled with the standards for membership that required a high level of spiritual maturity when new converts needed first a sense of belonging to the body of Christ. Preparatory membership, the traditional mode for discipling new converts toward Christian maturity, did not adequately address this need.

For the next six years, the issue boiled beneath the surface as the Study Commission on Doctrine (SCOD) studied the issue and prepared a recommendation. In its deliberations the General Conference of 1995 gave first consideration to SCOD's recommendation for a revision in the criteria for membership. The unity of the church was at stake. But when the final action was taken in favor of the change, the local church won the case.

In recognition of diversity in Free Methodism, individual churches could exercise a local option, either to continue the traditional practice of preparatory membership with discipling toward Christian maturity or adopt the new procedures, which brings the new convert directly into membership with discipling to follow. This action of the 1995 General Conference indicates that the locus of power has turned full cycle. The local church has replaced denominational headquarters as the center of action for the Free Methodist Church.

Profile of the Local Church 1960-1995

Free Methodist churches are committed to grow. The Great Commission of Jesus Christ, the example of the New Testament church and the mission statement of the Free Methodist Church are explicit mandates for growth. Every strategy for evangelism the church adopted between 1960 and 1995 had as its goal the evidence of growth in numbers of converts, members and churches.

Comparative statistics for 1960 and 1995 are one indicator of whether or not the church has met its mandates and achieved its goals. At best, statistics make up the skeleton that can come alive only with the flesh and blood of people and the life the Holy Spirit. While growth is not an end in itself, it is the natural consequence when the church is meeting its mandates and achieving its goals. A profile of change and growth in the local church in the United States, Canada and the United Kingdom can be drawn from comparative statistics between 1960 and 1995.

LOCAL CHURCH TOTAL MEMBERSHIP, 1960 AND 1995 — Membership in the Free Methodist Church in North America totaled 57,027 in 1960 and 81,586 in 1995 (including the Canada General Conference but not the United Kingdom, for comparative purposes). This is total growth of 43 percent over a period of 35 years or an average of 1.2 percent per year. The greatest growth came in the 1960s when membership increased by 21 percent or 2.1 percent per year.

The 1970s and 1980s slumped back to 9 percent in total growth or less than one percent per year. On a comparative basis, the first half of the decade of the 1990s slowed even more, moving into a loss position in 1993.

These grim facts are once again accented against the growth of the Free Methodist Church overseas. In 1960, membership overseas totaled 39,057 compared to 57,027 in North America. By 1974 the overseas church had caught up and passed the North American church with 72,326 members compared to the 70,782 in the United States and Canada. Statistics for 1995 now show a total of 395,681 members worldwide with 314,095 overseas.

TOTAL NUMBER OF CHURCHES, 1960 AND 1995 — Growth can be also measured by the number and size of churches. In 1960 the Free Methodist Church in the United States numbered 1,201 local churches. Ten years later the total had declined to 1,102 and then to 1,029 in 1980. But six Free Methodist fellowships and two new church plants that were not yet eligible for status as societies raised the total number to 1,037.

By 1990 the number of societies had fallen further to 1,003; but 37 fellowships and 56 church plants increased the total to 1,096 ministry units. The next five years, from 1990-1995, saw the number of societies decline to 939, and fellowships decreased to 33 and church plants to 45. In 1995, local societies, fellowships and church plants totaled 1,017.

Three facts come forward from these figures. First, the number of church closures and mergers exceeded the number of new societies, fellowships and church plants between 1960 and 1995. A count in 1993 indicated that while 250 new churches had been started between 1960 and 1993, 400 had been closed. Second, without the development of fellowships and church plants, the total number of units would have decreased to 840 in 1995, a drop of 38 percent from 1960. Third, the membership of the church plants totaled more than 7,000 persons. Without these numbers, the church since 1985 would have been in membership decline rather than having experienced minuscule growth. But, fourth, the rate of new church plantings has recently decreased so that it has once again slipped behind church closings.

Another revealing statistic relates to the size of the membership in local Free Methodist churches. In 1960 the local church averaged 47 members per congregation, while in 1995 the average had increased to 77. Behind this increase in average membership is a story of uneven growth that highlights a new phenomenon in Free Methodism. In 1995 Free Methodist churches were widely diverse in size. One half of the local churches served fewer than 50 members and the other half served over 100 members. One group is skewed toward hundreds of churches that serve fewer than 25 members, and the second group is skewed toward the few churches of 400 or more members.

Dwight Gregory, superintendent of the New York Conference and unofficial demographer of church statistics, helps us understand these figures with a technique he calls a composite "Growth Index" that he has applied to both conferences and local churches.

According to the growth index in 1993, 29 percent of Free Methodist churches were growing, 25 percent had plateaued, 37 percent were in decline and 9 percent were newly planted churches. Gregory's statistics pinpoint the dual purpose of the New Day vision to revitalize churches that were either on a plateau or in decline, and to plant new churches if Free Methodist membership in North America were again to grow in total numbers.

The profile of the size of local churches in Free Methodism also exposes a point of tension between the past and the future. Historically, the Free Methodist Church is a product of a rural culture, where small churches serve a homogeneous population. Such churches still exist, many in a sizable group of plateaued or declining churches with fewer than 50 members. Their growth is limited by their location and their population, but their service may still be essential even if inefficient. In fact, some of the large and growing churches are in the rural and small town setting.

At the other extreme are growing and new churches that are basically a response to an urbanized culture, where the population is growing and the diversity of age, sex, race, ethnic origin and religious background is increasing. Current facts indicate that the future growth of the Free Methodist Church will be primarily determined by the effectiveness of its ministry in this new culture.

In 1976 the Board of Bishops decided to celebrate growth in Free Methodist churches. A convocation for local churches with 200 or more members was called with pastoral and lay representatives from each of the churches invited to attend. Perhaps to the surprise of many, 50 Free Methodist churches were identified in this category. A discernible shift was already becoming evident at that time. In 1960 Free Methodist churches in college centers held six of the top 10 positions based upon a composite of membership and Sunday school attendance.

Although all of the college churches have remained in the top 20 through 1995, the new entries are sending a message to the whole church. In 1992 for the first time, Wenatchee, Washington was second in size only to the college church at Spring Arbor, Michigan. This is the first time that a church not located in a college center was among the top three largest churches.

Also noteworthy is the fact that a Canadian and a United Kingdom church were listed in the top 20 that year. Saskatoon, Saskatchewan, had 372 members in 1992 and Fulwood, England, reported 292. Even more encouraging is the fact that three of the top 20 churches in 1992 were formed since 1970. They are located at Fulwood, England; Timberlake, Washington (293 members), and Temecula, California (The Lamb's Fellowship with 354 members).

A large church forum was held in 1993 for pastors who ministered to the 19 churches with more than 400 members. Dwight Gregory notes that the most dramatic conference gains have come in the Northeast and South, even though the United States population is shifting to the West and South. He also notes that the planting and growth of ethnic churches account for much of the growth, namely in Florida in the South and in New York and Centenary conferences in the Northeast.

Growth in Free Methodist churches is shifting away from college centers to suburban and ethnic church plants in the Northeast, West, Northwest and South, although the bulk of Free Methodist membership is in Midwest and North Central states. But if trends predict the future, the center for Free Methodism may well be shifting from the rural to the suburban location, from college churches to new church plants, from Anglo-European dominance to newer ethnic peoples and from the center of the nation to its coastlines.

ETHNIC AND URBAN CHURCH DEVELOPMENT, 1960-1995 — Ethnic churches have a story of their own in the history of Free Methodism from 1960-1995. In 1960 there were 38 predominantly ethnic churches with 2,080 total members. Twenty-two of the churches were Hispanic, eight were Japanese and four were African-American. German, Italian and Native American people made up the other ethnic congregations.

By 1992 the number of language groups had increased to 15, including Haitian, Native American (Canada), Chinese and Asian Indian congregations. Membership in these churches totaled 7,232, with the largest numbers in Hispanic, Japanese and Haitian congregations. Free Methodist churches in 1995 also include Cambodian, Korean, Portuguese, Samoan, Arabic and Filipino congregations. Gregory notes that the Free Meth. ferences with the highest growth index are either distinctly ethnic con. ences or conferences with a strong ethnic component. Conversely, the conferences with the most seriously negative growth have no distinctly ethnic congregations.

A shadow in the growth pattern of ethnic churches between 1960 and 1995 is the limited number of African-American churches. In 1960 a Department of Interracial Evangelism had a prominent place in the Quinquennial Report of the general secretary of Evangelism. Under the leadership of the Rev. and Mrs. E.E. Shelhamer, Dr. and Mrs. Gilbert James, and the Rev. Glen Williamson, interracial work was occurring in Shreveport, Louisiana; Crewe, Virginia; Washington, D.C.; Pontiac, Michigan; Detroit, Michigan; Windsor, Ontario; South Bend, Indiana; Portland, Oregon; and Los Angeles, California. By 1995, however, the number of churches was limited to Shreveport Central with 132 total members, Portland Immanuel with 103 total members and Los Angeles Second with 75 total members.

These figures may help account for the concern expressed in the 1995 manifesto, "A Call To Action," which confesses prejudice and bigotry that must be laid aside in order for the church to take the gospel and love of Jesus Christ "to people of all groups and every level of society."[1] While serving other ethnic groups fairly well, is it possible that the Free Methodist Church missed an opportunity to be at the forefront of reconciliation with the African-American community? It may be a case of abandoning the field when liberal Christians took up the cause of civil rights. Whatever the reason, the leadership of the church in 1995 is now seeking reconciliation with African-American peoples and invites them to be full partners in the future of the Free Methodist Church. Statistics for integration in the local church as well as new church plants will test the mandate.

Another key trend in the Free Methodist Church between 1960 and 1995 was the shift in cultural direction from a small, rural church to a growing, suburban church. We must not forget that 100 years ago the Free Methodist Church was predominantly English in language and rural in location. In 1995 Free Methodism initiated an "urban presence" in metropolitan areas and extended its ministry to a dozen or more language groups. Astute observers, however, will note that in 1990 only 5 percent of Free Methodist churches in North America were located in urban areas with a population of one million or more.

No challenge is greater for the future. How will the Free Methodist Church handle the diversity between small, rural and homogeneous churches of its tradition along with the growing, urban and diverse churches of its future?

LOCAL CHURCH EFFECTIVENESS, 1960-1995 — Other statistics in the profile of local Free Methodist churches come closer to revealing quality as well as quantity in the effectiveness of their ministry. One such statistic was attendance in Sunday morning worship services. Contrary to many denominations, attendance at Sunday morning worship services in Free Methodist churches exceeds the membership of the denomination itself.

A 10 year study of morning worship attendance by Robert Logan, for the period from 1983-1993, showed a spurt in worship attendance that began in 1990 and rose to an average of 84,719 in 1993 compared to 76,419 members for the same year.

From this potential pool for church growth, a second statistic was even more meaningful. In 1971 the *Yearbook* began reporting adult and youth conversions in the United States, Canada and the United Kingdom. Statistics in 1971 showed 10,938 conversions for a membership of 68,540, or a ratio of one convert for every 6.3 Free Methodists. Comparatively, in 1995, conversions of 9,831 were reported for the United States, Canada and the United Kingdom for 82,613 members or a ratio of one convert for every 8.4 Free Methodists. Within the declining number of converts from 1971-1995, the major loss was in youth conversions while the adult numbers have remained stable.

With membership barely holding steady, attendance at Sunday morning worship on the rise, a declining number of conversions, particularly among youth, and a higher ratio of Free Methodists required to gain one convert, the potential for evangelistic growth is cause to celebrate. At the same time, a reduction in evangelistic effectiveness is cause for concern.

Bishop Emeritus Elmer E. Parsons brings special insight to these statistics. Using the number of conversions reported in 1971, he traced the net gains or losses in total membership during the 20-year period from 1971-1990 in order to determine the percentage of converts assimilated into church membership. His report for the 20 years showed 191,939 conversions and 29,175 additions to membership or 15.2 percent of the converts assimilated into the church.

Bishop Parsons concluded that the slow but consistent growth in membership was welcome, but the poor performance in assimilating new converts into the church "... is a call to greatly intensify our acceptance, training, encouragement and incorporation into the body of the church those who enter salvation by repentance and faith in Christ."

The changing nature of ministry in the local church can also be read from Robert Logan's study. While Sunday morning worship attendance rose slowly over the period from 1983-1990 and began to soar from 1990-1993, Sunday school attendance fell from 63,803 in 1983 to 54,107 in 1993, a drop of 16 percent. Midweek services showed a more gradual decline, from 38,004 in 1983 to 35,484 in 1993, a loss of 11 percent. Sunday evening services, however, plummeted from 37,974 in 1983 to a low of 27,348 in 1993, a 37 percent loss. *Yearbook* figures do not show whether other specialized ministries, such as cell groups, have compensated for these losses, but future statistics will need to reflect changes from the more traditional model.

Diversity Among Local Churches

The new diversity of Free Methodist Churches is not confined to statistics of size and location. Even the nature of ministry is spread along a line of differences. As radical as it may seem, there may be more diversity in the nature of ministry *among* Free Methodist churches than *between* Free Methodist and other evangelical churches. In 1960 this was not the case. Although there was some diversity among the local churches, major differences were limited. A visitor at a Free Methodist worship service almost anywhere in the nation would find common elements of program and style that characterized churches of the denomination.

In 1995, however, the same visitor might well be confused by the variety of programs and styles to be found in local churches. One might be a semi-liturgical service with a carefully programmed order of worship closely akin to the formality often associated with United Methodist or Presbyterian churches. The other might be a free-flowing contemporary service with Spirit songs, rock musicians, charismatic praise and a "seeker sensitive" sermon. In between, a visitor can find a variation on these themes. Free Methodist churches with shouting saints, revival meetings, traditional programs and separated lifestyles still exist. But most local churches are adjusting to the new realities of changing needs in a changing culture.

To illustrate these changes in the profile of the Free Methodist Church, five churches were chosen from different regions of the nation to represent the diversity of ministries at the local level. Although not intended to be all-inclusive of diversity in the local church, vignettes of their ministry will embrace many similar churches.

I. NEW GROWTH CHURCH — A midwestern Free Methodist church dates back to the first decade in the history of Free Methodism. Initial services were held in 1856, and the society was officially recognized in 1872. For almost 100 years, the membership remained fairly stable. In 1960 the *Yearbook* showed 57 members. By 1985 its membership had grown to 199, with attendance at Sunday morning worship averaging 377. Ten years later the attendance averaged 487, while membership had declined to 158.

The passing of the generations was evident in these figures. While retaining elements of traditional worship and declaring its commitment to the doctrine and polity of the Free Methodist Church, its senior pastor emphasized contemporary communication through music and message as an entry point for full-service ministries offered to young families. The result was a ministry to 215 non-member households in 1994 compared to 87 non-member homes in 1985.

A sampling of the congregation showed a strong cohort of young, white and professional adults of upper-middle-class status. They rated the core convictions and denominational distinctives of the Free Methodist Church as moderately important. Therefore, the challenge for the church was twofold. One challenge was to realize the potential of new growth for membership in the Free Methodist Church; the other was to engage the commitment of the new generation to the contemporary and relevant meaning of those convictions and distinctions as part of their growth to Christian maturity.

II. ETHNIC CHURCH — A western Free Methodist church ministers primarily to persons of Japanese origin. Founded in 1919 by women leaders, the history of the church was written in chapters of faithfulness for a congregation buffeted by social change and personal tragedy. Begun as a mission to Japanese immigrants, the church struggled for stability during the 1920s and 1930s only to be decimated by the war-time policy of evacuating its members to internment camps along the West Coast. After the war a new generation of Japanese immigrants brought the church to its peak with 625 worshipers in attendance at an Easter sunrise service in 1965. But the momentum was lost when an arsonist burned down the sanctuary just as the remodeling was completed to accommodate growth.

Relocation and rebuilding also rekindled the spirit of the church and brought the challenge of ministry to a third generation of Japanese families, most of whom represented marriage across ethnic lines. Consequently, the ministry of the church included two separate language divisions, Japanese and English, to serve different generations. Membership in the English division totaled 232 in 1994, a gain of 40 in a 10-year period. Average attendance in Sunday morning worship was 206 and almost equally divided between member and non-member homes.

The Japanese division of the church reflected the changing culture with 122 members in 1994 compared to 139 in 1985. Sunday morning worship attendance ran an average of 71 with the number of member homes doubling non-member households in the congregation.

Worship services tended to be traditional but with a touch of the contemporary in music. Families, many of whom were related to long-time members, gave stability to the church and provided a natural base for small groups and specialized ministries. In keeping with the strengths of tradition and the continuity of long-time members, the congregation held all the core convictions and denominational distinctives of high importance, in fact, of highest importance among all of the congregations in the sample.

For the future, the church has the challenge of growth with another new generation of Asian-Americans whose spiritual quest may be more like their contemporaries than their ancestors.

III. SUBURBAN CHURCH PLANT — A suburban fellowship did not exist until seven years ago. The pastor transferred to the Free Methodist Church because of the open door of opportunity he saw for its ministry in the Northwest. Meetings were held in a junior high school located in an up- and-coming bedroom community for baby boomers. These services are called "Main Events" in a full week of spiritual, social and recreational activities.

Contemporary in the style of music, worship and communication, the church identified with Free Methodism in its welcome package by short paragraphs outlining its history, purpose, guiding principles and present ministries. First-timers were introduced to a simple statement of Christian faith, with details left for further instruction. Contemporary worship services, including a regular feature of dramatic ministries, were designed to provide the first-time attendee with "a safe place to get practical help for everyday issues." This seeker sensitive approach to young, professional and relatively affluent families was consistent with the patterns of growth for other fast-growing churches in the same suburban area.

The growth of this Suburban Church Plant, identified by name as a community fellowship, increased from 110 in 1990 to 196 in 1995. Non-member households to which the church ministers grew from 52 to 814 during those same years and conversions increased from 80 to 162.

Such explosive growth in community outreach was not at the price of fundamentals for Free Methodism. A very limited sampling of the congregation showed relatively high importance given to the core convictions and denominational distinctives of the church. The exception was with the symbols of connectionalism and associations with other Wesleyan groups. Clearly, the challenge of the future was to convert its attendees and disciple its converts into Christian maturity, church membership and effective witness through sacrificial service.

IV. TRANSITIONAL URBAN CHURCH — In 1960 the First Free Methodist church in a north, central city was the 9th largest church in the denomination with 278 members. Even more significantly, the church stood third in size among non-college churches at that time. Recently relocated near the edge of a relatively stable blue collar community of the automobile industry, the church also cooperated with a small, but effective mission serving African-Americans in the adjacent inner city. At the peak of its growth in the 1960s, Sunday school attendance numbered over 600 persons.

The 1970s saw the beginning of social change that literally turned the city upside down and inside out. Following the pattern of many mid-size cities, citizens of the central city, who became part of the "white flight" to the suburbs, took their homes, stores, schools and churches with them. In addition, an adjacent urban giant expanded north and west to embrace the smaller city as a part of its metropolitan area. As community clusters grew up around shopping malls, the city lost an identity of its own.

The decline of First Church followed the decline of the city itself. By 1985 membership had dropped to 135. The interracial mission struggled for survival under the persevering leadership of a long-term pastor but eventually merged into First Church. Although lacking denominational visibility, the moral influence of the mission far outweighed its size. When race riots threatened to burn out the central city, the Free Methodist pastor took his credibility to the streets and calmed the restless crowds of African-American youths who were on the verge of violence.

More recently, Free Methodists have refocused their ministry in a new identity as a "community church." A small multiracial and multigenerational congregation was gathered to restart the church. Retired persons, who had been members of First Church during its growth years, made up a majority of the members. Another 35 percent came from persons of African, Asian, and Hispanic-American origins.

The year 1995 proved to be a time of setbacks when the mission pastor died and the senior pastor moved on. Total membership of 98 and average morning worship attendance of 73 in 1994 dropped another 20 or more persons so that only a small core remained upon which to rebuild. Yet the character and composition of the church represented the diversity of the central city where the moral, social and spiritual needs were so desperate.

The challenge of survival for this Transitional Urban Church extends beyond city and conference to the denomination. Will Free Methodism have an "urban presence" in the future? Students of the inner city believe the presence of a strong church, fully representative of its racial, ethnic, economic and generational composition, may again be the hope that will defuse the powder keg. The Transitional Urban Church is one point of test for that future.

V. TRADITIONAL TOWN CHURCH — Another midwestern Free Methodist church stands at the center of history in Free Methodism's march across America. Located in a midwestern town of approximately 10,000 people, it can be identified as a "Town Church" and typifies the strength of Free Methodism within the heartland of the nation.

Within a year after the denomination was founded, Free Methodist pioneers organized societies in midwestern states and used them as a jumping-off place for evangelistic thrusts to the north, west and south. Even the name of the place where Town Church is located had special meaning in that early history. Migrants, moving to the West, frequently gave the same names to the towns they founded as the names of the towns from which they came. Town Church is the namesake of a sister town in the eastern United States, which, in turn, was named for one in England.

Town Church was organized out of a series of successful camp meetings in 1913. By 1960 the membership of the church totaled 140. Twenty-five years later, in 1985, membership totaled 217 members. Statistics in 1995 showed a total of 244 members, or an increase of 27 over the period. In 1995 after a long period of decline in church members, worship attendance and Sunday school, the church was experiencing a turnaround with small but hopeful gains.

Members of the church characterized the ministry as a stable, middle-class, middle-aged and Caucasian congregation that depended upon traditional programs, including short-term revivals, for the impact of its witness. The population of their town had remained fairly stable with fluctuations between 8,000 and 10,000. In 1995 the town was just beginning to recover from economic and population losses in earlier decades. The pattern of decline in the community helped explain the fact that the church served 156 member families and 101 non-member households. The senior pastor saw potential for growth in the new families coming to the community and was leading the congregation in planning programs and facilities to serve increased numbers.

A sampling of the congregation further confirmed its identity as a Town Church defined for its stability rather than its growth or decline. With the exception of a low rating of importance given to a separated lifestyle as evidence of personal holiness, members of the congregation gave high ratings of importance to all of the core convictions and denominational distinctives benchmarked in 1960. The congregation of Town Church was made up of a solid core of spiritually mature people who were loyal Free Methodists. Their worship services were built around singing of hymns and preaching of the Word. The church facility showed simplicity with quality, and the publications of the church spoke to members and visitors with warmth and class.

No one can doubt that Town Church has a continuing role in the future of the denomination. The ministry matches the culture. But the challenge rests in the reality of changing generations. Will the needs of the next generation in this typical midwestern town remain the same, or will their needs and expectations match those of their contemporaries in urban and suburban settings?

THE SURVEY IN PERSPECTIVE — A sampling of these congregations

.caled additional divergence. Traditional, ethnic and inner-city church congregations tended to rate almost all of the historic core convictions and denominational distinctives higher than the new-growth church or the suburban church plant. Highly significant differences were found in the importance of the doctrine of entire sanctification, symbols of denominational connectionalism and cooperation with other Wesleyan associations. The importance attached to crusades and revivals as the primary means of evangelism was also divergent. Contemporary congregations rate these forms of evangelism as low in importance, while traditional congregations still hold them as moderately important.

Other core convictions and denominational distinctives did not vary significantly among the five types of churches. The importance of sacraments in worship, compassion for the poor, the value of Christian higher education, the role of the clergy and laity in leadership, funding denominational ministries, personal tithing and the global mission of the church were all rated as moderate to high in importance. Particular attention, however, was given to the importance of well-trained clergy as pastors for the local church.

To summarize the new diversity, it appears as if the generation upon which the ministry focuses determines the character of the church. If the focus is upon baby boomers and their needs, the church grows and its character changes. If the focus is upon an older generation, the church holds its own or enters into decline. In one sense the statistics suggest that there is no middle ground. Stable churches that do a mix and match of worship styles and ministry programs experience limited growth, if any at all.

Our sampling of the churches indicates that the generational focus supersedes the regional location. The culture of different regions may have a bearing upon the breadth of style for the ministry of the local church, but the generational needs appear to be similar across regions.

Central to the understanding of this new diversity is the role of the pastor in the local church. When a visionary pastor is appointed to a "ready" or new church, the potential for growth multiplies greatly. In each case, it appears as if pastoral leadership may supersede generational focus and regional culture. The subject is worthy of exploration.

Pastoral Leadership in Local Churches 1960-1995

Our sampling of the congregations of the five types of churches showed the continuing importance of pastoral leadership. Despite the shift toward lay leadership in the local congregation and the change of expectations for the equipping role of the pastor, members of the congregations still gave a high rating of importance to well-trained pastors.

EMPOWERING THE PASTOR, 1960-1995 — The section in the *Book of Discipline* on the role of the ordained minister has undergone several revisions since 1960. At that time the qualifications for the person called to preach still tended to reflect the language and expectations of historical Wesleyanism and Methodism. Major revisions reflective of changes in the church and the culture were made in 1969 and 1974.

In 1983 a summary statement was adopted by the Board of Administration as a guide for the pastoral mission:

> The mission of Free Methodist pastors is to propagate the gospel; preaching and teaching the Word of God with clarity and power, giving pastoral care with faithfulness and vision, overseeing the administration of the local church in accordance with the *Book of Discipline*; and in all their labors, to carry out the mission of the church.

This statement is sound but general. The vision of the New Day, with its emphasis upon church growth and church planting, required a more specific look at the role of the pastor. Consequently, in 1994 the Board of Bishops proposed a new paradigm for the pastor of the local church under the title, "Century 21." Utilizing the outline of strategic-planning theory, the bishops created a model that defined nonnegotiables for the individual pastor and desired outcomes for the local church.

The importance of these statements cannot be overemphasized. A full range of initiative and creativity is encouraged as "leaders are free to strategize and minister in ways which produce the desired outcomes." Such freedom is not without its risks, because it speeds the process of decentralization from the general church to the local church and invites additional diversity in the nature of the local church and its ministry. This is a radical turnaround in the history of a church that has come close to division over Pentecost Bands in the 1890s and membership requirements in the 1990s.

No judgment is made on the change, except to repeat that the new paradigm is a catalyst for the trends toward decentralization and diversity. Even more important, the pastor of the local church has been empowered to lead with the initiative and creativity, which, according to our survey, the congregations expect.

The 1995 General Conference made extensive revisions in the *Book of Discipline* under the section entitled "The Ordained Ministry." This thorough revision of the job description recognized the changing role of the pastor, the diversity among local churches and the centrality of pastoral leadership at the local level.

The intent of revision was as crucial to defining the God-ordained role of the Free Methodist pastor as giving specific details of the job. In the trends speeding away from clerical authority and toward lay leadership, the ordained ministry can lose the distinctions of its divine calling, sacramental authority, prophetic proclamation and biblical accountability. The New Testament and Wesleyan standards for ordination still set apart a person who is true to the Word and blameless in character. Perhaps with this truth in mind, the General Conference of 1995 also limited the use of the term "pastor" to those who are ordained while encouraging the application of the term "minister" to all Christians who are called to serve.

EVALUATING THE PASTOR, 1960-1995 — The development of the process for evaluating the performance of pastors in the local church is another unmistakable symbol of the trend away from episcopal authority and toward congregational leadership. The Methodist tradition gives the authority for pastoral appointments directly and almost exclusively in the hands of the presiding bishop. John Wesley himself gave precedence to this power when he insisted on personally ordaining all of the clergy coming to the Methodist church. He also was affronted at Francis Asbury's decision to take the title "bishop" of the North American church without Wesley's approval.

In 1960 the presiding bishop of annual conferences in the Free Methodist Church still held control over pastoral appointments. Pastors and spouses anxiously awaited the reading of the appointments at the closing session of the annual conference and steeled themselves for the surprises of new appointments without any prior knowledge. A crack in the system, however, developed in 1955 when the General Conference permitted the local congregation to cast a confidential vote on the return of a pastor. This permission included a stipulation that this vote was "advisory to the stationing committee and not determinative."[2]

Once the door for congregational participation in the evaluation of pastors was opened, their role grew progressively larger throughout the period from 1960-1995. A running history of General Conference, Board of Administration and Board of Bishops decisions showed the shift toward the congregation:

1960 General Conference — The stationing committee is to be informed of the results of the vote.

1964 General Conference — The pastor is to be informed of the results of the vote.

1969 General Conference — The vote on the return of the pastor may now be taken in a Sunday morning worship service designated as an annual society meeting.

1977 Board of Bishops — Non-members are denied the right to vote on the return of the pastor, but permits the conference superintendent to use an opinion survey, which must be separated from the members' vote.

1979 General Conference — Guidelines are set for vote by ballot on the return of the pastor every second year and with comments by full, preparatory and associate members.

1985 General Conference — Evaluation forms designed by the Board of Bishops will be prepared annually (after second year of pastoral tenure) by all full members on the quality of pastoral leadership and church effectiveness. The superintendent will confer with the pastor on results and also provide results on church effectiveness to the delegates.

1989 General Conference — Paragraph A/403 added to the *Discipline* an "Evaluation of Pastor Leadership and Church Effectiveness" and "The Pastoral Return Survey" with details of the full process and formalized procedure.

1995 General Conference — All references to the "Pastoral Return Survey" were deleted from the *Discipline* in order to shift the evaluation of ministry effectiveness away from a negative tone and toward mutual improvement of the local church among all participating parties.

Between 1960 and 1995 the purpose of pastoral evaluation moved from a "yes" and "no" confidential and non-debatable vote of the membership to an assessment of pastoral leadership and church effectiveness according to the goals set by the pastor and the congregation on a three-year schedule. Communication of the results of this evaluation is openly given to the local church as well as to the bishop, superintendent and conference bodies responsible for the development and appointment of the pastor.

Positive gains are seen in the process, which confirms the professional status and developmental potential of pastoral leadership. At the same time, the new process serves as a significant symbol of shifting the center of action from the general church and its leadership to the local church.

In further support of pastoral leadership, the church has taken progressive steps toward benefits for pastors that are conducive to personal development and professional security. In 1964 the General Conference authorized a pension plan (effective January 1, 1969) for pastors of all local churches.

At the 1995 General Conference, another major step was taken toward recognition of effective pastoral leadership when a sabbatical plan based upon a three year cycle of service was referred to the Board of Administration. It was approved for implementation by that body in October of the same year. Each of the actions indicated a sensitivity to the responsibility for stewarding the valuable resource of pastoral leadership.

Perspective on the Local Church and Pastoral Leadership 1960-1995 and Forward

The future of the Free Methodist Church depends upon the effectiveness of the local church and the leadership of its pastor. For the local church, diversity will continue to test its viability.

At the extremes, traditional churches, with small congregations in rural or town settings, will be stretched to minister to the changing needs of a new generation. Contemporary churches with fast-growing congregations in an urban setting will be pressed to disciple their converts and transplants in the essence of the core convictions and denominational distinctives that give meaning to the name "Free Methodist."

In between, the majority of local churches will be pushed and pulled by the extremes in a search for identity. The Free Methodist Church itself will be challenged to clarify a biblical and Wesleyan theology of the church and find its niche as a denomination in a "post-denominational" period. This is no small challenge, but the rewards are worth the risk.

As the local church is central to the denomination, the pastor is central to the local church. While a premium is being set upon church growth as an indicator of pastoral performance and church effectiveness, the qualitative measure cannot be neglected. Pastors have the responsibility to communicate with contemporary relevance the essence of the core convictions and denominational distinctives that give the Free Methodist Church both its identity and its integrity. As the center of action for the Free Methodist ministry moves more and more toward the local church, the denominational distinctive of a vision that balances the local church with the global mission must be a priority.

If the shape of the Free Methodist Church in the past was a pyramid with episcopal leadership at the apex, the shape of the future may well be an ellipse drawn around the twin poles of the local church and the local pastor. While the changing shape may appear to be radical, the work of the Holy Spirit is not confined either to pyramids or ellipses. In the past as in the future, the empowerment of the Spirit is the promise for leadership at the center of action.

CHAPTER 10

Extending Our Witness

Evangelism is the heartbeat of the Free Methodist Church. Its history is written between the bookends of mission statements that are aggressively evangelistic in character. In 1860 B.T. Roberts called for the organization of the church under the evangelistic mandate, "To maintain the Bible standard of Christianity, and *to preach the gospel to the poor*"[1] [emphasis added].

One hundred thirty-five years later the official mission statement of 1995 resounds with the same ring of evangelism even though the wording is more general: "The mission of the Free Methodist Church is *to make known to people everywhere God's call* to wholeness through forgiveness and holiness in Jesus Christ, and to invite into membership and to equip for ministry all who respond in faith" [emphasis added].

History of a Heartbeat
1860-1995

Effectiveness in evangelism has not always kept pace with the verbal commitment of these mission statements. In the first 33 years of its history, a finger on the pulse of the fledgling church would have felt a fast and pounding beat echoing the drive of aggressive evangelism. When B.T. Roberts died in 1893, the Free Methodist Church had grown to 812 churches in 33 annual conferences with 23,326 members. During the seven years preceding his death, church membership increased 51 percent. If the same evangelistic zeal had continued from the 1890s to the 1990s, the Free Methodist Church of North America in 1995 would total over 1 million members![2]

By 1894 the pulse beat for evangelism could barely be detected. A State of the Work report warned that the church was growing too fast, and pioneer

185

ere starting too many churches. The role of general conference evan-
gcmot was established to do the work of evangelism, so pastors could devote
themselves to "earnest, faithful pastoral work, and to feeding the flock of
God" rather than "running hither and thither as evangelists."[3]

Momentum from its evangelistic past carried the Free Methodist Church
for the next six years. By 1900 the number of churches had grown from 812 to
944 and total membership to 28,588. But then the heartbeat almost stopped.
Not even the reestablishment of a General Board of Aggressive Evangelism
in 1919 could make the difference.

In 1931 an appropriation from local churches for evangelistic outreach
disappeared with the reorganization of the church. Consequently, statistics
for 1960 show that Free Methodist churches in North America numbered 1,201,
a growth rate of only 24 percent in 60 years. As Free Methodism closed its
first century, the unavoidable question had to be asked, "Can the Free Methodist Church recover the heartbeat of aggressive evangelism and start growing again?"

The Beat Goes On
1960-1995

While the strategy for evangelism traditionally came through the vision
of church leadership, tactical decisions for the implementation of that strategy came through the Commission on Evangelism and the denominational
department charged with the responsibility for outreach programs. An overview of the department of evangelism for the period from 1960-1995 revealed
another perspective on the search of the church for the secret of growth.

EVANGELISM AND CHURCH EXTENSION, 1960-1969 — As the Free
Methodist Church turned into its second century in 1960, the Rev. Lyle
Northrup, a noted evangelist in his own right, headed the Department of
Evangelism and Church Extension. Out of the compelling motive of his own
calling, Northrup gave priority to the role of the evangelist and the results of
local church revivals in his administration. In 1962, he sponsored a Conference on Evangelists for the 42 ministers officially designated as either general
or annual conference evangelists by the church. Later, he cooperated with the
Board of Bishops to inaugurate soul-winning convocations throughout the
church with an emphasis upon local church revivals.

"Church Extension" represented the other side of Northrup's portfolio.
By definition, "church extension" meant the evangelization of areas where
Free Methodism was not represented in order to assist in the organization
and supervision of churches until they became part of existing or new annual
conferences. It also meant a support base of funding from the department for

the building of new churches through donors who were partners in funding grants and loans under the designation of the Church Extension Loan Fund (CELF) or the Total Enlistment League (TEL).

Northrup's reports to the General Conferences of 1960 and 1964 contained statistics that defined total evangelism modeled after his own personal style. He traveled back and forth across the country holding revival meetings in local churches and preaching an average of 180 times a year. He served as the exemplar for general and annual conference evangelists when they were still looked upon as specialists in the field. Scanning North America and the Western world, he got the Commission on Evangelism to declare New England, Nevada and Mississippi-Alabama as districts for church extension. Although the results were limited, Northrup's vision could not be faulted. In 1963 he requested Forward Movement funds through the Board of Bishops to assist evangelistic efforts in New York City. The request was rejected on grounds that the Forward Movement did not give help to a department for ongoing programs.

In his 1960 report to the General Conference, Northrup stressed the strength of interracial ministries. Four years later Northrup's report to the General Conference carried the tone of de-emphasis upon interracial evangelism. The Shreveport church was in leadership transition; the Shelhamer Memorial Mission was struggling to exist and the scholarship fund for "needy colored students" was falling behind the demand and the opportunity.

Northrup's vision reached beyond North America when he proposed that the United Kingdom be declared a church extension district under his department. Beginning with the Belfast Crusade in 1960, the team of evangelists included such youthful Free Methodist leaders as Mervin Russell, Donald Bastian and Robert Crandall as well as Lyle Northrup and Lowry McKeown, more senior leaders.

The Rev. and Mrs. Carl Anderson were appointed as pastor/superintendent couple for Northern Ireland. Their work soon showed the promise of an established work when Victor Trinder, a British national serving in another denomination, joined the Free Methodist Church in 1965 and became superintendent of the United Kingdom district in 1968.

Although he died at the early age of 54 in 1988, Trinder left an indelible mark on Free Methodist history in the United Kingdom. Under his leadership, 16 churches were organized by 1980, two United Kingdom annual conferences (Great Britain and Northern Ireland) were organized in 1986, and a British broadcast of the "Light and Life Hour" was instituted with Trinder as speaker.

Tragedy continued to dog the footsteps of Free Methodism in the British Isles following Trinder's untimely death due to a heart attack. Each time that the church gained momentum, its leadership was struck down by illness or accidental death. Superintendent Ronald Taylor retired after one three-year term, and Barrie Walton had to resign for health reasons in 1994. His protégé and successor, Kenneth Leech, assumed the superintendency in September 1994. Within two months, however, Leech and his lay assistant, Alan Ramm, died together in the crash of an American Eagle flight as they headed home from Board of Administration meetings in Indianapolis.

In 1995, under the superintendency of J. Allan Ellershaw, 22 churches and 1,114 members continued as an annual conference with the aspiration of becoming a provisional general conference before the turn of the century. The maturity of their partnership with the church was attested by their membership along with the general conferences of the United States and Canada in the North Atlantic Fellowship of the Free Methodist World Fellowship.

In the short history of 35 years, Free Methodism in the United Kingdom models the meaning of "church extension" as understood in 1960. Beginning with an evangelistic crusade, following with missionary and then indigenous leadership and advancing to annual conference status, the Free Methodist Church in the United Kingdom represents the concept of church extension at its best.

MASS EVANGELISM TO PERSONAL WITNESSING, 1967-1974 — With the retirement of Lyle Northrup (1967), Dale A. Woods was elected as general director of Evangelistic Outreach, a title that was shaped by the changing emphasis in the department. In the mid-1960s, crusade evangelism and local church revivals gave way to a new thrust toward personal witnessing.

Charles Kingsley felt frustrated by the limited results of mass evangelism and marshaled the men of the church who shared his passion for personal witnessing. He led the way into the streets, ringing doorbells with a testimony for anyone who would listen. Although some might have considered this maverick approach a threat to the officially sanctioned strategy for evangelism, the General Conference of 1964 recognized the Light and Life Men's Fellowship as an auxiliary arm of the Department of Evangelism and Church Extension, operating through the Commission on Evangelism but with its own constitution and by-laws.

Looking back upon the personal witnessing movement, one might see it as the mid-1960's Free Methodist forerunner to the "Promise Keepers" network of the 1990s. At least the issues are similar. Both movements reflect the realization that Christian men need to step forward with a visible declaration of faith, penetrate the rotting core of a secular society and witness with boldness to the saving grace of Jesus Christ. The intent to mobilize Christian men for social witness was the same. Kingsley must be remembered as a man ahead of his time who goaded the conscience of the church and rallied men around the cause of personal evangelism.

George Delamarter put method behind Kingsley's motive. Under the name *Salvation By Appointment*, Delamarter fashioned a step-by-step process that began with a community canvass for personal witnessing and progressed to a program for discipling converts in the local church. After proving the process by the test of experience, Delamarter joined with John Maxwell, a Wesleyan Church pastor, to write *Reaching Out In Love* as a field manual for a program of personal evangelism in the local church.

When Dale Woods reported to the General Conference in 1969 as the new director of Evangelistic Outreach, he brought with him an agenda of personal evangelism that had superseded the earlier emphasis upon city-wide crusades and local church revivals. Lay witnesses, especially, began to move into prominence as replacements for the professional evangelists of an earlier era. Woods carried the title of director of Evangelistic Outreach to represent the change.

In his report Woods rejected the tactics of what he called "unconventional evangelism" in favor of the need "to go and do what we already know."[4] He saw his responsibility to provide the tools for annual conferences and local churches to do the work of evangelism. Thirty-five outreach programs were identified. Although almost all of these programs disappeared over time, they represented the shift in the primary emphasis of the director's role from a "doer of evangelism" through revivals to a "manager of outreach" through denominational resources.

Two other changes appeared in the 1969 Quinquennial Report for the Department of Evangelistic Outreach. One is the addition of responsibility for the "Light and Life Hour" following the election of its speaker, Myron F. Boyd, as bishop in 1964 and the subsequent election of Robert F. Andrews as the new director-speaker in 1965. Earlier the "Light and Life Hour" had carried its own departmental identity, even though Boyd had recommended closer integration between its ministry and the departments of missions and evangelism. After reorganization in 1967, the broadcast became specifically identified as an instrument of evangelistic outreach.

The second major change in the 1969 report involved the status of Light and Life Men International as auxiliary under the Commission on Evangelism. In confirmation of their ministry the General Conference of 1969 recognized Christian Witness Crusades as a major thrust of evangelism in the church,"... thus making the winning of men to Christ our major concern."[5] By this act of recognition and coordination, Christian Witness Crusades became one of the department's most active and aggressive tools for evangelism. With emphasis upon training pastors and laymen for personal evangelism through community canvass, door-to-door visitation and home Bible study, the structural move also signaled the shift away from mass rallies and local church revivals.

Woods' tenure as director of Evangelistic Outreach was short-lived. In 1970 he resigned the position because of the lack of financial and staff resources to accomplish the task he felt that he was given to do. Although the whole church was feeling the pressure of financial shortages, evangelism seemed to be in a holding pattern at the denominational level. To replace Woods, the burden shifted to Robert F. Andrews, speaker for the "Light and Life Hour," who also struggled with tension between opportunities to expand the radio ministry worldwide and the handicaps of severely limited resources. Consequently, in his report to the 1974 General Conference, Andrews spoke of his passion for evangelism but within the frustration of trying to coordinate the outreach programs that he had inherited.

EVANGELISTIC OUTREACH TO CHURCH GROWTH, 1974-1984 —
To move from Christian Witness Crusades to church growth was more than a small step. Christian Witness Crusades were conceived within the boundaries of individual witnessing and the rules of door-to-door evangelism, with the goal of establishing home Bible studies. Church growth, on the other hand, tended toward corporate boundaries of the local church and rules of readiness for the unchurched, with the goal of growth through homogeneous groups.

Even more important was the cultural background from which the two movements come. Christian Witness Crusades grew out of protest against the relative ineffectiveness of city-wide crusades and local church revivals, which represented a lingering form of frontier evangelism. Church Growth, however, came out of the discipline of cultural anthropology as successfully applied on the mission field. Rather than giving a random witness in a diverse culture, evangelism centered upon reaching homogeneous groups of unchurched people who were most ready to receive the gospel. Although critics of the Church Growth Movement might claim that the Great Commission neither made distinctions among people or nations to whom the gospel was preached nor limited the message to those who were ready to receive it, the fact was that church-growth principles had proved to be a more effective tool as the culture changed.

Free Methodism and its leaders enthusiastically endorsed church growth as the energizing force to restart evangelism within the church. To promote its principles, a Conference on Mission and Strategy was held for superintendents and pastors, a Small Church Task Force was established to help small churches grow and a Top Fifty Convocation was instituted for the largest churches in the denomination.

The Board of Administration took action in 1978 to rename the department once again. Thus, the Department of Evangelistic Outreach became the Department of Evangelism and Church Growth. Shortly thereafter,

Forest Bush, a leading advocate of church growth, was named director of the department. Bush immediately reorganized the department into four divisions: Church Planting, Evangelism, Discipleship and Home Ministries.

Under the aegis of what he called "Mission America," Bush saw North America as a mission field where the church-growth principles could be applied as effectively as they had been overseas. Symbolic of this new thrust, at the General Conference of 1979 the Manifesto on Evangelism (see Chapter 7) was introduced and referred to the Board of Administration with power to act on evangelism as the first priority of the church. The Board decided to write into the *Book of Discipline* a new section on "Formation of New Churches."

Consistent with these actions making evangelism the first priority of the church, Bush advanced an agenda of aggressive evangelism for the department. He continued with such programs as the Christian Witness Crusades under the Division of Evangelism and the *Decision-to-Disciple* materials of the Light and Life Men International under the Division of Discipleship. Under the Division of Church Planting, grants from the Total Enlistment League were given to Hispanic ministries. The metropolitan centers of Miami, Denver and Atlanta were targeted as strategic for church plants. Metro Research was set up to identify urban areas for church plants or relocated churches. In support of these projects, Bush pleaded for a doubling of the existing $2 million Church Extension Loan Fund for the building of churches.

At the General Conference of 1985, the report of Bush again took the theme of "Mission America" with a focus upon new church planting as the "... single most effective evangelistic methodology known under heaven."[6] Bush reported that an average of 23 new churches per year had been planted between 1982 and 1985 compared with 10 new churches per year between 1979 and 1981. These numbers also compared with an average of 3.8 new churches per year between 1966 and 1979.

Staying on course with the 1979 call to plant churches among people in urban centers, Bush also reported three new extension districts. One was in the Southeast with special attention to Hispanic and Haitian populations in Miami. The second covered the Gulf Coast with its burgeoning populations. The third involved the Atlantic Southeast where sensational growth in churches, membership and giving were now following years of decline. Members of the church were urged to become Partners Assisting Church Extension (PACE) by volunteering to participate in a church-planting project. Another appeal was made for gifts to the Church Extension Loan Fund, and Volunteers in Action (VIA) was created to enlist persons with specialized skills for ministry in urban and ethnic church plants.

As the Free Methodist Church came to General Conference in 1985, the theme of "Mission America," the focus upon urban and ethnic centers, the

191

principles of church growth, the method of church planting and the tools of church-growth institutes, volunteer programs and informational resources held the promise of a new day.

CHURCH GROWTH TO CHURCH PLANTING, 1985-1995 — The year 1985 marked a catalytic moment for evangelism in the Free Methodist Church. The Board of Bishops brought a New Day Document to the Board of Administration with the general objectives and specific goals for the church in the final 15 years of the 20th century.

While the New Day vision came "top down" from the Board of Bishops, it served its purpose to catch the rising tide of interest in church growth and church planting. In 1986 two pace-setting planning sessions were held in what might be considered the Free Methodist "wastelands" of the Northeastern and Southeastern United States. Confronting the hard fact that Free Methodism was woefully weak in these areas, the planning sessions called for aggressive action to revitalize existing churches and plant new churches.

Nine years later the New York Conference showed spectacular results from the follow-up of the 1986 planning session. Whether counting new conversions, membership growth, average church size or the number of churches planted and sustained, New York represented a region where the New Day was in evidence.

Perhaps even more important was the fulfillment of the vision for "Mission America" in its urban and ethnic context. Penetrating into the heart of the inner city of the New York area, the growing edge of Free Methodism was represented by Hispanic, Portuguese, Haitian, Japanese and Indo-Pakistani churches. Historically, these people were represented by the poor who could not afford to rent pews. Today they are urban people who struggle to survive against the blight of the city, or they are ethnic minorities seeking to find their rightful place in a free society.

Many threads in the history of evangelism came together in 1988 with the appointment of Ray Ellis as the director of Evangelism and Church Growth. Coming from the position as superintendent of the Florida Conference and director of Church Planting for the southeastern region, Ellis brought with him the unique combination of a published student and proved practitioner of church planting. His first report to the General Conference in 1989 shows the priority that he gave to the Church Revitalization, Church Planting, and Urban, Ethnic and Social Ministries through the development of church-growth resources for local churches.

Picking up where Forest Bush left off at the time of his retirement, Ellis reported that a total of 153 churches had been planted between 1985 and 1988 as part of the New Day vision, and wrote, "Our goal of adding 1,000 churches by the year 2000 is possible."[7] To reach that goal, Ellis took leadership of church-growth conferences across the nation, offered training sessions for consultants in church growth, published a manual, *Strategizing for New Churches,* and named the Rev. Paul Olver as the first part-time director of Social, Urban and Ethnic Ministries (SUE).

When Ellis once again reported to the 1995 General Conference, the program he foresaw in 1989 was well on its way. A mission statement for the department left no doubt about its direction:

The Department of Evangelism serves as a catalyst and resource center to assist conferences and local churches in fulfilling the Great Commission through church planting and church revitalization.

Reporting for the decade between 1985 and 1995, Ellis noted that there were 323 church planting start-ups with 253 organized and 171 still active. This is a success rate of 71 percent for the organized churches, well above the average for other denominations and measurably better than earlier efforts.

Church revitalization also held priority in the direction of the department. One-half of Free Methodist churches averaged 50 or fewer in morning worship. The report of 1995 recognized that the options for revitalization were limited. Some of these churches will die a natural death; some will be restarting with the strategy of a church plant; others will merge with other Free Methodist churches. In the same period between 1985 and 1995, when 323 church plants were initiated, 241 Free Methodist churches either closed their doors or merged with another Free Methodist church. Of particular interest was the proposal that small and stagnant churches be restarted with the same strategy used for planting a church.

The principles of church growth and the strategy of church planting now permeated the programs of evangelism throughout the denomination. A National Growth Network, staffed by regional growth consultants, had been established with specialists in the field appointed to positions at Greenville and Spring Arbor colleges. A resource center developed by the department provided such services as Church Planters Assessment Centers, New Church Incubators, the Parent Church Network, Cluster Strategy Consultations, the director of Social, Urban and Ethnic Ministries, Partners Assisting Church Extension, Volunteers in Action and Craftsmen for Christ — all focused upon church planting. What began in 1974, when leaders first attended a conference on church growth, had become the priority for evangelism in the future.

While the emphasis in church growth and church planting tended to be corporate in context, the importance of personal witnessing was not lost. Integrated into the methods of both church growth and church planting was the concept of Lifestyle Evangelism, which was based upon the premise that, "Evangelism operates best when each individual believer sees the opportunities for sharing Christ in his everyday affairs, and develops a lifestyle that responds in Christian love to the needs of those around him."[8] The familiar steps of witnessing, winning and training, which characterized the Christian Witness Crusades, were present in the process of Lifestyle Evangelism. A major difference, however, was evident in the statement, "Evangelism thus becomes not something that you *do* but something that you *live*." Christian Witness Crusades, as the name implies, were conducted as specialized ministries of lay volunteers who canvassed the community and witnessed to strangers at random. Lifestyle Evangelism, however, began with the assumption that the most effective Christian witness was something you live.

In place of the random witness, Lifestyle Evangelism utilized the decision-making model of church-growth methodology, which focused witnessing on the readiness of unchurched people to respond to the gospel. Also, in place of the community canvass, the "FRAN Network" (Friends, Relatives, Associates and Neighbors) became the sphere of influence for which the witnessing Christian was responsible. Church-growth and church-planting methods were quick to use telemarketing as an upgrade on the community canvass. Again, if there was a difference, it was between the random approach of the community canvass in Christian Witness Crusades and the targeted approach of telemarketing to "readiness" groups in the church-growth strategy.

REDEFINING LIGHT AND LIFE MEN INTERNATIONAL — The history of evangelism in the Free Methodist Church cannot be written without citing the latest chapter in the story of Light and Life Men International (LLMI). The organization that championed Christian Witness Crusades has continued as a viable and expanding ministry under the Department of Evangelism and Church Growth. After the retirement of its founder, Charles Kingsley, in 1975, LLMI went through a succession of directors who had to struggle with funding, the marginal identity of the organization in the eyes of the church and the shifting emphasis toward church growth. The crisis came in 1984 when the Board of Administration decided to discontinue the auxiliary ministry due to lack of funds.

Loyalists of the movement, led by Lucien Behar and U. Milo Kaufmann, would not let LLMI die. At the 1985 General Conference, members of the organization voted to resurrect LLMI and accept the responsibility to erase an operating debt of more than $60,000. In 1986 then, Lucien Behar, a general conference evangelist and protégé of Charles Kingsley, became executive director and leading advocate of men's ministries in the church.

January 1989 is remembered as a banner day for Light and Life Men International when President U. Milo Kaufmann could report that the debt of $60,000 had been retired and that the Board of Directors had approved a plan to marshal the resources of men in helping reach the New Day goals of founding 1,000 new churches by the year 2000. LLMI volunteered to be a training unit for lay witness teams of men in church-planting projects and to coordinate a new ministry called Craftsmen for Christ, through which volunteers would assist in the construction of new churches. Since its beginning in 1989 Craftsmen for Christ projects have ranged from church plants in the United States to lay witness teams in the United Kingdom.

Equally effective was the development in 1993 of a cooperative ministry of compassion with the Women's Ministries International called Project Barnabas. Through this agency, containers of supplies in response to urgent needs are sent to such distant fields as Rwanda, Haiti and Hungary. LLMI moved from the margins of Free Methodism into full partnership with the vision of church planting for the New Day at home and the compassion of world missions abroad. To encompass this large purpose, the name of the organization was changed in 1994 to Men's Ministries International (MMI).

ASSESSING THE ERA OF CHURCH GROWTH AND PLANTING — It is too early to make a full assessment of the effectiveness of church-growth methods as a turn-around tool for revitalization and growth in the Free Methodist Church. More than a decade has passed since the principles of church growth and the priority of church planting undergirded the goals of the New Day vision. As Ray Ellis reported to the 1995 General Conference, 253 church plants have been organized into societies since 1985 and 171 are still active.

This is a success rate of 71 percent, above the average for church plants in most denominations, but below the goal of 90 percent that has been achieved when the recruitment of church planters is highly selective. Even then the number of church plants in the decade between 1985 and 1995 has not kept pace with the New Day goal of 1,000 new churches by 2000.

Reflecting upon the original goal, Ellis now says the lessons of experience show it to be unrealistic and proposes a revision that is still optimistic, but tempered by facts that determine the outcome of church planting — the motive of the people, the training of ministers, the investment of money and, of course, the passage of time. New goals based upon these facts call for planting an average of 30 churches per year between 1995 and A.D. 2000 with a 90 percent success rate.

If these goals are achieved, a total of 385 new Free Methodist churches will have been planted in the 15-year period since the inception of the New Day vision. Ellis also looks forward to A.D. 2010 when church planting as an evangelistic strategy is fully implemented throughout the church. The proposed goal for the next 15 years from 1995 to A.D. 2010 is to plant 550 new Free Methodist churches with active and growing congregations.

Church revitalization is the companion goal to church planting through the remainder of the decade and into the 21st century. In 1994 the Free Methodist Church in the United States and the United Kingdom was represented by 1,031 organized societies and fellowships. Of that number, 835, or 81 percent of these ministry units, counted 99 or fewer members, and a majority of that number had 50 or fewer members. These small churches served only 40 percent of the total membership of Free Methodist Church. This means that 228 churches, representing only 19 percent of the total number of societies and fellowships, minister to 60 percent of the membership in North America. Thus, the goal of church revitalization for A.D. 2010 is to see the statistics reversed with 80 percent of the churches growing to membership above 100 and only 20 percent still at 99 or fewer members.

To achieve this goal, the church-growth and church-planting strategy is invoked once again. By involving every pastor in a Cluster Strategy group, led by other pastors of growing churches and training local leadership in church growth and church-planting methods, the plan is to recognize that 25-50 people make a strong nucleus for a church-planting project. Therefore, with a new vision and trained leadership, many small and struggling churches can be restarted as church plants.

For stable churches above 100 members, the same principles would be applied for growth and eventually to birth other churches. This would be done by spinning off a nucleus of their membership for the project, or by adopting church-planting projects in or across conferences and cultures.

The potential for the Free Methodist Church has been revealed in both church-growth and church-planting statistics. Average attendance in Sunday morning worship services in 1995 exceeded the membership of the church by an average of more than 13,000 worshipers. But far more important, the number of conversions through church ministries averaged about 9,000 a year between 1990 and 1995. The discrepancy between the growth of membership by tens and the potential of conversions by thousands lends justification to the emphasis of the Department of Evangelism and Church Growth upon personal discipleship and corporate reproduction to close the loop of soul-winning.

Standing out as a good word among these denominational statistics is the percentage of growth in new-church plants, especially those serving urban and ethnic congregations. At last count, ethnic congregations represented 13 percent of all Free Methodist churches and fellowships serving 8,079 members. Taken together, these facts point to the promise that the Free Methodist Church can grow by reaping the harvest of its potential.

A Ministry to Remember
"The Light and Life Hour"

A veiled note of sadness accompanied the reports of the denominational executives who had been responsible for evangelism during the period from 1960-1995. Through these reports, the rise and peak, decline and demise of the "Light and Life Hour" radio broadcast could be read.

By action of the General Conference of 1943, the "Light and Life Hour" radio broadcast was launched a year later out of Ferndale, Michigan, on over 49 radio stations, under the directorship of LeRoy M. Lowell. In August 1945, Myron F. Boyd succeeded Lowell as the new director and speaker. At the Centennial General Conference of 1960, Boyd outlined the achievements of the "Light and Life Hour" as a world-wide broadcast reaching 10 million listeners in six languages. The program had won awards at the annual convention of the National Religious Broadcasters as the best in religion radio, and its speaker, representing the Free Methodist Church, had been vaulted into national and international prominence in evangelical circles.

Boyd foresaw a larger future in which the broadcast would reach into such an evangelical wasteland as France and behind the closed doors of Russia, China and the Middle East. Also, on the distant horizon, he foresaw the telecasting of the "Light and Life Hour" over the rapidly expanding national networks.

Four years later at the 1964 General Conference the "Light and Life Hour" celebrated its 20th anniversary. With a note of caution and tone of nostalgia, he summarized the 20-year history of the broadcast in the words, "During the past 20 years, radio has made it possible for the Free Methodist Church to minister to more people than the apostle Paul and John Wesley did in a lifetime. This is the 'Miracle of Radio.' The 'Light and Life Hour' is a great advertising medium, a strong evangelistic arm of the church, a great missionary project and a means of spiritual nurture for Christian people in all denominations."[9]

As for the future, Boyd expressed his continuing confidence in the ministry of the "Light and Life Hour" as an "evangelistic-missionary endeavor," but within a "more united program of planning, promotional literature and activity between the departments of Evangelism, Missions and Radio."[10] Throughout the report, his prophetic intuition was readily apparent.

Robert F. Andrews became Boyd's successor as director of the "Light and Life Hour" in 1965. Equally impassioned for world evangelism, Andrews carried on the legacy of Boyd, which included the recommendation to merge the free-standing Department of Radio into the newly named Department of Evangelistic Outreach headed by Dale A. Woods. The purpose of the merger was to provide better coordination of outreach ministries, but the result tended to take the edge of distinction away from the "Light and Life Hour."

By 1969 when Woods reported to the General Conference on the silver anniversary of the "Light and Life Hour," the report had been reduced to three paragraphs. Both the number of stations and the number of broadcasts had been reduced from the peak time in the mid-1960s. Neither the quality of the broadcast nor the competence of the speaker was the question because in

1969 the "Light and Life Hour" again received the Honor Citation by the National Religious Broadcasters. Finances appeared at the heart of the problem. Rising costs of network time coupled with decreasing support from the members of the church and the inability to solicit funds under the United Mission for Christ budget all became nails in the coffin of the broadcast.

When Woods resigned as general director of Evangelistic Outreach in 1971, the role of Andrews was enlarged to encompass all of the programs of the department, while still serving as director-speaker of the "Light and Life Hour." His report to the 1974 General Conference illustrated the heavy weight of administrative responsibility that he carried for multiple programs, all of which were suffering for resources and searching for direction.

In 1982 an attempt was made to revive the media ministry of the Free Methodist Church. A Department of Communications was established under the direction of Rev. Donald Riggs. "Light and Life Hour" was placed under his direction also. Created for the purpose of promoting the denomination at the local-church level, raising funds for media ministries and exploring the potential of television broadcasting, the department faced insurmountable odds.

Neither the promotion of existing ministries nor the attraction of new programs could stop the slide of diminishing resources for denominational ministries. Consequently, at the Board of Administration meeting of October 1982, the "Light and Life Hour" was discontinued. Residual programs at the international level were transferred to the Department of Missions. A touch of irony had to be felt at the General Conference of 1989 when tapes of the British broadcast of the "Light and Life Hour" were offered to the North American church as a ministry from abroad.

More than the "Light and Life Hour" died October 1982. An era of evangelism passed from the scene. Through the "Light and Life Hour," the concept of evangelism, which served national and international masses at random from a denominational level, gave way to the church-growth concept of evangelism, which served unchurched people at the local level who were most ready for the gospel. But more than a concept of evangelism might have been lost. No longer could Free Methodist churches carry the words on the street sign, "The Church of the Light and Life Hour." And who knows how much the radio broadcast served as a "unifying agent" for the church?

Perspective on Evangelism 1960-1995 and Forward

The Free Methodist Church has not lost its heartbeat for evangelism. If anything its pulse picked up speed during the period from 1960-1995. The reason is not in the motive, strategy or even the method of evangelism. In each era of the church between 1960 and 1995, the call to evangelism was sounded, a strategy advanced and a method proposed. But the difference was found in the concentration upon evangelism as the all-consuming purpose of the church. In 1960 "Total Evangelism" meant the specific program of the Department of Evangelism and Church Extension. In 1995, however, the New Day vision engaged every department in the evangelistic enterprise.

Free Methodist colleges served as the best example. Although clearly distinguished for their academic mission in Christian higher education, they also participated in the New Day vision through the appointment of regional church-growth consultants to faculty positions within the institution.

Even with this new emphasis, the continuities in evangelism, which ran through the era from 1960-1995, were important to remember. In the articulation of church extension in 1960, for instance, the priority of church planting was evident. In the 1960 General Conference call to "Double in a Decade," the principles of church growth were implied. And in the Interracial Department of 1960, the image of urban and ethnic ministries was foreseen.

What evidence do we have that evangelism in the new mode will make a difference? We must return to the potential seen in the statistics of growing churches, attendance exceeding membership in worship services, the number of conversions in Free Methodist churches, the increasing percentage of urban and ethnic churches and the growth rate of church plants. To date, the potential has not been translated into membership growth in the North American church as it has overseas. The difference is not in the method because the principles of church growth and the methods of church planting are the same at home and abroad. Furthermore, the Free Methodist Church, through the action of the World Fellowship in 1995, wholeheartedly adopted the most sophisticated evangelistic strategies.

The issue comes to rest in the question of motive. Can comfortable and affluent Americans become self-sacrificing with a sense of urgency? The tendency is to preserve both comfort and affluence by accommodating the gospel to the "seeker sensitive" needs of a gospel-ready congregation. Cheap grace must give way to costly grace at the risk of losing those who are not willing to pay the price of being mature disciples of Jesus Christ. Free Methodism defines that relationship as "entire sanctification" in which the motive is pure love and the method is self-sacrifice.

Sooner or later, as the theology of self-sacrifice is explained, the Spirit of God will ask all believers the same question that Jesus asked His first disciples in a moment of truth, "Will you also go away?" This is the question that must be constantly monitored and unabashedly asked in each generation of evangelistic outreach, whether by revivals in city-wide crusades or church-planting projects in local churches. Without the urgency of motive for evangelism, no method will be effective. But if the urgency of motive is present, no method is faulty.

Early Free Methodists practiced church planting as their method of evangelism from 1860-1890 and witnessed by lifestyle evangelism in the practice of holy living. Perhaps a full cycle has turned once again. If self-sacrificing Free Methodists with a sense of urgency can find the new frontier of unchurched people for Mission America in the 1990s, the march will begin again.

CHAPTER 11

Embracing Our World

The glory of Free Methodist history can be summarized in one sentence, "From 1860 to the 1890s, Free Methodism marched across America; from 1960 to the 1990s, Free Methodism marched across the world."

When Bishop Marston wrote his centennial history in 1960, he predicted that membership of the overseas church would overtake North American membership within 10 years. He missed on his prediction by only four years. In 1974 overseas membership passed the domestic church, and in 1995 it represented three of every four Free Methodists in the world.

Reaping the Harvest of World Evangelization

Statistics are only the skeleton of a growing church. Still, neither the skeleton nor the statistics can be ignored. In the Acts of the Apostles, no apology was made for the statistical report that the number of men who believed "grew to about five thousand" (Acts 4:4). So, before proceeding to give flesh and blood to the story of Free Methodist world missions between 1960 and 1995, we need comparative statistics to see how large the body has grown.

1960 GENERAL CONFERENCE — At the time of the 1960 General Conference, world missions accounted for 37,000 members, or 38 percent of the Free Methodist Church. No general conferences existed outside of North America. Mission conferences were limited to the Dominican Republic, Japan, South Africa and the South Africa Provisional Mission Conference. The Pacific Coast Japanese and the Pacific Coast Latin American conferences were also designated as mission conferences.

A Free Methodist missions presence, however, was reported in a total of

16 nations, including Brazil, Congo Nile, Continental China, Egypt, Formosa, Hong Kong, India, Paraguay, Philippine Islands, Portuguese East Africa, Southern Rhodesia and Transvaal in addition to the nations of the four missions conferences. Congo Nile, the largest of the fields, had 8,465 members, followed by Portuguese East Africa with 5,423 members and Japan with 3,939 members. Through the 1959 merger with the Holiness Movement Church of Canada, 5,000 new Free Methodists had just been added in Egypt. By action of the 1960 General Conference, both Japan and Egypt were given general conference status, but not before the 1960 statistics were published.

1974 GENERAL CONFERENCE — Between 1960 and 1974, Free Methodist world missions continued to grow. The pivotal year was 1974 when overseas membership passed domestic membership. As noted earlier, between 1960 and 1974 overseas membership increased by 33,269, at a growth rate of 85 percent, while domestic membership increased by only 13,782, at a growth rate of 24 percent. Although there were still only the two general conferences of Japan and Egypt and four provisional conferences, 33 general conference delegates came from 13 annual conferences and comprised 14 percent of the legislative assembly. Their presence forever changed the character of the general conference.

Not only did the international delegates represent a formidable voting block on pivotal issues, but they also brought with them vision and vitality of a growing world church. As Charles Kirkpatrick, general secretary of World Missions, introduced his report at the 1974 General Conference, he quoted Dr. Donald MacGavran, world authority in church growth, who said we are in the "sunrise of missions."[1]

1995 GENERAL CONFERENCE — By 1995 the full momentum of growth in the overseas church could be counted in statistics. Free Methodist churches overseas registered 314,068 members, or 79 percent of total world membership of 396,681. General conferences numbered 10, annual conferences 10, provisional annual conferences four, and mission districts seven.

Between the 1989 and 1995 General Conferences alone, Free Methodist churches had been officially organized in 14 new countries — Cameroon (1989), Nigeria (1989), Costa Rica (1990), Korea (1990), Argentina (1994), Bolivia (1994), Colombia (1994), El Salvador (1994), France (1994), Kenya (1994), Myanmar (Burma) (1994), Nicaragua (1994), Peru (1994) and Tanzania (1994). Never shortsighted, the vision for world missions now foresaw a Free Methodist presence in Cambodia, Ethiopia, Uruguay and even Cuba sometime in 1996.

Behind each of these statistics is the fact that Free Methodist world missions had raced ahead of the New Day goals set in 1984 for A.D. 2000. As noted earlier the New Day goal for the overseas church in A.D. 2000 was

300,000 members in 40 countries and six new general conferences. The growth continues. By the end of 1995 the Free Methodist Church overseas totaled 314,068 members, or 104 percent of its goal for the turn of the century.

Also, the church was organized in 38 countries against the New Day A.D. 2000 goal of 40, and five of the six projected general conferences had already been organized. The New Day goals for world missions were revised upward by the Commission on Missions to 500,000 members in 50 countries with six new general conferences by A.D. 2000

Almost every sign points forward to the fact that Free Methodist world missions will meet or exceed its revised New Day goals. A note of caution, however, is read in the 1994 *Yearbook* of the church. For 1994, statistics showed a mix of gains and losses that tended to slow growth in the overseas church. Strong gains in such countries as Zaire and Malawi were modified by relatively large losses in Korea, Nigeria and Mozambique, so that a total gain of 3,207 members represented only a 1.1 percent increase for the year.

These volatile statistics show the fragile nature of rapid growth in world missions. Government crackdowns, tribal warfare, competitive religions, intrachurch conflict, refugee migrations and cultural shifts can have a direct effect upon the growth pattern of overseas churches. Sometimes these forces are catalysts for evangelism; at other times they become deterrents to the Christian movement. Yet the principle still holds. A suffering church is a growing church, and the Free Methodist Church overseas is no exception.

Strategy for World Missions

In the 1974 report of the General Missionary Board, the strategy for Free Methodist world missions unfolded with a currency that helps account for the spectacular growth of the movement. Leading the way was *a vision for world evangelization*. Years ahead of the home church, that vision foresaw the overseas missions targeting urban areas, planting satellite churches, searching for unchurched peoples at home, crossing national boundaries and anticipating the time when its own missionaries would be sent abroad. The vision also saw fertile fields where Free Methodism had no foothold. In 1974 Indonesia, for instance, represented an open door.

Close behind this vision for world evangelization came *an emphasis upon theological education and leadership training* at the grass roots level of national churches. Theological Education by Extension (TEE) served as the primary instrument for this thrust, with the goal of developing a powerful evangelistic force of both pastors and people. Complementing TEE, advanced theological education and leadership training were provided through denominational and cooperative seminaries and Bible colleges. For students identified as future leaders of the church, postgraduate training was offered in the United

States or Europe with a long-term view toward nationalizing the administrative leadership of the overseas institutions.

Free Methodist missions strategy also found *an open door of opportunity in primary and secondary schools*. With the desperate need for educating children in developing nations, Free Methodist missionaries founded Christian schools that served public needs with the blessing of local governments.

Although this relationship teetered on a razor's edge because of the threat of governmental takeover, the quality of these schools made them an indispensable part of national development. The same could be said for secondary schools. Free Methodist missionaries responded to a desperate need for secondary education in such countries as Rhodesia, Rwanda and Zaire by building schools and providing national leadership through its educational system.

Partnering with education as a social ministry to the people of these nations, the Free Methodist Church also built and staffed hospitals and mobile clinics in undeveloped areas as visible symbols of its compassion for human suffering, without regard to spiritual condition, social status or religious affiliation. Thirty percent of all missionaries in 1974 were engaged in educational, medical, construction or professional staffing for these ministries.

Again, in recognition of the fact that the majority of the population in developing countries was made up of youth under the age of 21, the strategy of Free Methodist missions put *a priority on reaching the next generation* through youth groups, youth hostels and youth camps.

The General Missionary Board carefully planned *a literature and multimedia ministry* as a means to reach the masses, ranging from Bible translation to radio broadcasting, bookstores, cooperative publishing and literature distribution.

Through the *Volunteers in Service Abroad* (VISA), begun in the early 1960s, clergy and laity in local churches were recruited and deployed for short-term missionary assignments abroad. Thousands of youth and adults participated in these work-related ventures in which churches, schools and hospitals were built; evangelistic crusades were conducted; literature was distributed; classes were taught; medical services were performed. Most importantly, cross-cultural relationships were formed to create permanent bonds in the body of Christ.

Adjustments have been made as cultures have changed, churches have grown and resources have been limited. But the vision for world evangelization into urban areas, among unreached peoples, and across national boundaries still fires the passion, and the support system of trained leadership among clergy and laity, backed up by evidence of social compassion, still turns the vision into reality. This strategy is based on principles that are neither culture-bound nor time-bound. For this reason, the same drumbeat that led Free Methodism's march across America in the last four decades of the 19th century can still be heard leading Free Methodism across the world in the last four decades of the 20th century.

LEADERSHIP FOR WORLD MISSIONS, 1960-1995 — The indigenous principle is only theory until it is put to test in the leadership of the church. As noted earlier, Byron Lamson, general missionary secretary, articulated the principle early in the 1950s. The 1960 proposal for a Free Methodist World Fellowship depended upon the principle for its success, and the strategy articulated in 1974 depended upon implementation of the principle across the world. The growth and maturity of Free Methodist missions between 1960 and 1995 was enhanced by denominational leaders, whose gifts matched the needs of the developing world church.

Embracing Lamson's vision, his successor Charles D. Kirkpatrick (1964-1985), brought skills of goal-setting for missions strategy. Since then, career missionaries whose experience added another dimension to the leadership role have served under the title Director of World Missions. Elmore L. Clyde (1985-1989) realized the importance of giving authority to area administrative assistants in order to meet their goals. M. Doane Bonney (1990-1996) has built upon the contributions of his predecessors by upgrading the title of area administrative assistants to area directors, appointing national leaders as executive secretaries of the Area Fellowships, and bringing area directors together as a team for the world-wide ministry.

Area directors who report directly to the director of World Missions have been career missionaries who are thoroughly dedicated to the indigenous principle of leadership. A full roster of the names of these leaders is in the Epilogue "Servant Leaders of Our Generation," but a quick glance reveals three potential bishops of the church — E.C. John, Asia; Elmer E. Parsons, Asia; and Gerald E. Bates, Central Africa. Also on the roster are the well-known names of missionary statesmen who served in the role, such as Victor Macy, Africa; K. Laverne Snider, Asia; Robert Cranston, Asia; and Harold H. Ryckman, Latin America.

To name only the administrators of World Missions is to miss the missionary servants who day by day, year by year, decade by decade give themselves in ministry to the people. These faithful servants are represented by the names of missionaries who served on the field for 25 or more years in the era between 1960 and 1995. The Epilogue of this history honors these missionaries among the servant leaders of our generation. (See Epilogue.)

Ultimately, the effectiveness of general directors, area directors or field missionaries is determined by the quality of national leaders who are identified, recruited, trained and empowered to serve their people. Again, a full roster of national leadership is included in the Epilogue. We can read, however, the growth and stature of the world church in the names of current bishops elected by their general conferences, all of which have been established since 1960: Daniel Ward, India; Luis Uanela Nhaphale, Mozambique; Robert Nxumalo, South Africa; Sukenari Iwamoto, Japan; Mounir H. Gindy, Egypt; Noah Nzeyimana, Burundi; Aaron Ruhumuriza, Rwanda; Jim Tuan, Philippines; Bya'ene Akulu Ilangyi, Zaire; and Gary Walsh, Canada.

A salient fact emerges from this list. The episcopal leadership for the Free Methodist Church has shifted from four North American bishops in 1960 to 10 international bishops and three United States bishops in 1995. The majority has become a minority in partnership with a team of world leaders.

LEADERSHIP FOR THE 21ST CENTURY — At the Board of Administration meeting in October 1996, the retirement of M. Doane Bonney was announced after serving six years as Director of World Missions and a total of 40 years in Free Methodist missions and ministry. In his place, Larry E. Houck, Director of Personnel for the Department of World Missions since 1994, was elected.

Houck, while not a career missionary, foresees the strategy for world Free Methodism as being built upon the past but responsive to the future in this vision: "Free Methodist missions in the 21st century will be a global network of churches from North America and overseas. Cross cultural teams from different national, ethnic and racial origins will be matched for urban missions. The role of the missionary will change to that of partnering with nationals for church planting and opening new fields. Most important of all, Free Methodists worldwide will see persons of other cultures and colors as brothers and sisters in Christ for whom they bear mutual responsibility."

To work out this strategy is the task for tomorrow.

Model for a New Testament Church

By its own definition, world missions involves a scope of cultures and a variety of ministries that defy written description. Even if volumes were written, some distant outpost would be bypassed, some unsung saint would be neglected and some miraculous event would be missed. As the company in the upper room learned at Pentecost, language itself falls short when the Holy Spirit comes as a rushing wind and a flaming tongue.

How then can we tell the story of Free Methodism's march across the world in our generation? After hearing, reading and weeping through epic stories of our overseas churches, one thought kept coming to mind: *In the mirror of Free Methodist world missions, we see the image of the New Testament church.* It is the image of a church maturing in the crucible of the culture, being purified by the fire of the Holy Spirit and becoming refined on the full cycle of a growing church. A sampling of mission churches details the story.

A VISIONING CHURCH — In 1990 there were no Free Methodist churches in Central America. But Free Methodist history was about to be repeated. A United Methodist pastor named Jorge Gomez from Colombia had stopped in Costa Rica for seminary training on his way to a missionary appointment in Spain. Temporarily, Gomez and his family were assigned to a church in Alajuela, Costa Rica. Immediately, the church began to grow as a demonstration of evangelistic fervor punctuated by a message of heart purity. United Methodist leaders, however, opposed the ministry and message of Gomez, because he refused to preach and teach Liberation Theology. When it became clear that Gomez would not change his ways, the leaders of the church removed him from his pulpit, expelled his family from the parsonage and piled their belongings on the curb!

What would Gomez do? He was a Methodist in belief, experience, fellowship and loyalty. The answer came quickly. Lay members of his congregation told him, "They threw us out *with* you!" Hence, a new church was born — a parish with roots in Methodism, the message of holiness, a heart for missions and a natural for Free Methodism. In 1990 Costa Rica became a mission district under the leadership of Jorge Gomez, who is called by Clancy Thompson, Latin American area director from 1990-1997, "The B.T. Roberts of Central America."

Since becoming a mission district in 1990, Costa Rica has grown to 402 members with five churches and preaching points. Behind the growth is the vision of Jorge Gomez, which centers in San Jose, the capital of Costa Rica, and extends in ever-larger circles to encompass Costa Rica, reaching out to El Salvador and Nicaragua, finding a point of penetration in Communist Cuba, and coming full circle with the planting of a Free Methodist church in Colombia, Gomez' native land. As point man for his vision, Gomez rides the Central American circuit finding people, training leaders and planting churches. In February 1995 for instance, the first Free Methodist church in Nicaragua was organized with 35 members.

A PLANTING CHURCH — The turning point for the Free Methodist church in Rwanda occurred in 1974. Aaron Ruhumuriza, a Free Methodist pastor, represented Central Africa and Rwanda as a delegate to the International Congress on World Evangelization at Lausanne, Switzerland. Profoundly influenced by the potential for world evangelism seen in the conference, he returned home with a new and fresh vision for his own immediate world, the nation of Rwanda.

Since its founding in 1942, the Free Methodist Church in Rwanda had been confined with limited growth to a few provinces in the western part of the country. Inspired with boldness to back his vision, Aaron told his colleagues, "God wants all of His lost children to be found everywhere. We need to reach all of the areas of Rwanda." His vision met opposition. Almost in the words that stifled aggressive evangelism in the North American church in the 1890s, the leaders replied, "Let us strengthen first the work already started and find out all the unreached in this area. Then we will plan to move toward new areas in the future."

Aaron's Spirit-guided response defined the future for the Rwandan church and established a working principle that may well have been the secret of church growth for which Free Methodists world-wide were searching. He said, "... If the missionaries who brought us the good news had waited until all of their countrymen had been converted, today there would still not be a single Christian in our country." Hearing these words, pastors fell to their knees, educated laity heeded the call to ministry, and together they left the comfort and security of their homes to relocate in distant provinces for the sake of the gospel.

By the end of 1990, eight of the 10 provinces in Rwanda had Free Methodist churches in their capital cities, and rural works had begun in the other two provinces. Membership had grown to 46,464 members by 1994 and, in a dramatic reversal of most long-term plans, Area Director Virgil Kirkpatrick reports that 15-year strategic goals set for Rwanda in 1986 had been revised to a five-year and then a four-year schedule. Under the impetus of a planting church, Free Methodism has a presence throughout the whole nation of Rwanda.

A DISCIPLING CHURCH — Discipling is an educational process that begins with the quality of preparation for pastoral leaders. When the first Free Methodist church began in Malawi in 1973, the poor and uneducated people of the rural nation had no core of potential leadership for the infant church. Missionaries Henry Church and Phil Capp grappled with the problem and, in 1983, came up with the idea of beginning a new type of Bible school with an unconventional curriculum, designed uniquely for the needs of the developing church in Malawi.

Rather than taking future pastors away from their families, churches and villages for two or three years of schooling, students of the Bible school attend one month at a time in three or four month intervals. These modules of schooling are tucked in between the seasons of planting and harvest, so crucial to an agricultural economy. Rather than waiting until graduation to begin ministry, each student must plant three churches as a graduation requirement. Rather than pricing some students out of an education because of tuition and living costs, a future pastor can attend and graduate for little more than the cost of a round-trip bus ticket to the capital city once every few months. Rather than learning theory in school with a view toward practice later on, the students are required to apply the principles of their learning during each of the intervals between classes when they are at home serving as pastors and planters. Although it takes an average of five years to graduate from the Bible school in Malawi, 33 pastors graduated in the first decade between 1983 and 1993. Thirty-two future pastors are currently enrolled.

The Free Methodist Church in Malawi is the fastest growing denomination with a growth rate above 15 percent for each of the past 20 years. At last report there were 14,178 members of the provisional conference, 38 ordained clergy, 63 organized churches, more than 200 preaching points and two missionaries to other nations. Convinced that the structure of the Bible school has been a major contributor to the growth of the church, Henry Church is now restructuring the Bible school in Zimbabwe along similar lines.

THE SUFFERING CHURCH — A holocaust of suffering is another side of the story for the growing Free Methodist churches of Burundi and Rwanda. Exact statistics are lost in the maelstrom of persecution, exile and martyrdom that has swept through these nations since 1993. Earlier, tribal conflicts between Tutsi and Hutus had pushed thousands of refugees from Burundi across the border into Rwanda. The picture took a violent turn in 1993 when the ruling minority of Tutsi began a systematic process of "tribal cleansing" with the goal of killing all of the educated Hutus.

A soul-wrenching tally emerged from the slaughter for the Burundi Free Methodist Church. At least 450 Free Methodists were murdered, 114 died of dysentery, 43 churches were destroyed and 804 homes of members were burned. Neighboring Free Methodists in Rwanda became part of equally appalling statistics: 21,374 members in refugee camps, five ordained pastors killed, 503 starved to death in one district, and 931 murdered in another district.

By 1995 more than 31,000 members from Rwanda had fled as refugees from their home country, primarily into Zaire and Tanzania. Bishop Aaron Ruhumuriza is in exile in Kenya along with his fellow leader, Bishop Noah Nzeyimana of Burundi. Almost certain death awaits them if they return home. Yet in exile they have continued to give leadership to their people, especially those who are interred in refugee camps. Free Methodist pastors have been appointed to serve in each camp, and lay ministers appointed to complement their ministries.

Worship services and prayer meetings are held regularly in the camps; conversions are common, and baptisms are frequent. Young people are accepting God's call to evangelism in the camps, and pastoral-training programs are being set up inside the fences. Free Methodists, in particular, are known as people of compassion because their church has given food, clothing, medical supplies and help for children to non-members as well as members through Operation Hope, the Bishops' Famine and Relief Fund and International Child Care Ministries.

Humanly, the situation is almost hopeless for Free Methodists who are people without a country. To go home is to risk death; to stay is only to survive because they are unwanted by the nations that are their temporary hosts. Spiritually, however, the "refugee church" of Free Methodism is growing in the midst of suffering — another sign of its New Testament character. Late 1996 saw the beginning of refugees returning to Rwanda, signaling hope for unity in the nation and renewed vision for the church.

THE SERVING CHURCH — Zaire is among the poorest of nations. In 1990 the country teetered on the brink of total economic and political collapse when tribal warfare broke out in the neighboring nations of Burundi and Rwanda. Refugees by the hundreds of thousands poured across the border, only to encounter new hostility. Zaire could not feed them, heal them, house them, educate them or offer plots of land for more than 2 million exiles. As a tactic of desperation, Zairian troops finally resorted to force as they pushed the fleeing people back across the border.

The Zaire Free Methodist Church and its people were equally victims of their nation's impoverishment. Yet putting aside national and tribal suspicions, as well as their own self-interest, they determined that their Free Methodist brothers and sisters would not have to go behind the barriers of refugee camps. Their churches, schools and homes filled up with visitors. With true biblical hospitality they shared their food, even though they and their children had gone hungry for years. The public witness was powerful; the spiritual bonding miraculous. Free Methodists with differences came together in the unity for which Christ longed when He prayed to His Father, "that they may be one as we are one" (John 17:11).

When refugee camps became the only alternative for handling the continuing flood of Free Methodist refugees, Bishop Bya'ene Akulu Ilangyi of Zaire joined with Bishop Aaron Ruhumuriza of Rwanda to appoint pastoral leaders for the camps. No wonder delegates from Burundi and Rwanda were visibly moved at a Free Methodist conference in 1995 as they gave thanks for "the serving church" of Zaire.

THE SENDING CHURCH — A church planted by missionaries comes to a measure of maturity when it mothers other churches and funds its own missionaries to other mission fields. The Free Methodist Church in the Philippines represents "the sending church," which is fast becoming an identifying quality of overseas churches as they mature.

Pol Guazon, a pastor in the Philippine church, began praying in 1990 about becoming a missionary to another nation. Hong Kong never came to her mind. But in the providence of God other forces were at work. Polly Ho, a Free Methodist pastor in Hong Kong, had been appointed as missions coordinator for the conference. Her vision was to start a Filipino church in Hong Kong among Filipina women, who temporarily served as domestics away from home in order to support families left behind in the Philippines. At an Asian Area Conference in 1991, Pastora Pol (as she is called) heard that Free Methodists in Hong Kong were praying for the Lord to send them a person from the Philippines to minister among more than 80,000 Filipinas who were living among them. When Pastora Pol heard the word, she answered, "This is it!"

By February 1992 Pastora Pol had moved to Hong Kong, but without formal training as a missionary and without personal contacts among the domestic workers. In fact when the Filipinas gathered in the parks on Sunday afternoon, they divided themselves by regional groups and spoke in their regional dialects.

Alone, lacking training, facing language barriers and confronting unexpected hostility when the women learned that she was a missionary, Pastora Pol might have given up. In that moment, God took over. Just as Jesus made an innocent request for a drink of water from the Samaritan woman at the well, Pastora Pol innocently asked a Filipina for help getting home through the streets of the unfamiliar city. The woman responded by introducing her to someone who could help her, a domestic named Imelda, who came from Pastora Pol's home town!

Barriers began to fall, and within seven months Pastora Pol held her first church service in a Free Methodist primary school with 12 new Christians. Three years later, in 1995, more than 100 Filipinos attended service each week, and a second missionary, Pastora Edna Bacus, had come from the Philippines to assist in the expanding ministry.

The story of a "sending church" does not stop here. The 100 Filipinos who attend services each week do not include the many domestics who had to return home at the end of their two-year contract in Hong Kong. Back in the Philippines, they planted a church at Tarlac, a new area for Free Methodists located 180 miles northeast of Manila. The cycle of world missions does not stop with the mature response of a "sending church."

POSTSCRIPT — Now, as the church comes to the end of the 20th century, the silent leaven of its passion for world missions continues to surprise us. Out of Red China comes the word as many as 1 million Chinese consider themselves "Free Methodists." They know little about the denomination and have never been counted among its members. Yet, they claim the heritage because the pastor, layperson or missionary who introduced them to Christ had also been influenced by the Free Methodist Church in its pastoral, education or missionary ministry. The hidden church of Red China is a reminder that the Great Commission makes "disciples" the only statistic that counts.

The stories could go on and on — from Haiti to Brazil, from Egypt to Japan, from Mozambique to Taiwan. Wherever Free Methodist missions has touched down at any place in the world, the story of struggle against insurmountable odds has become the story of abounding grace.

Not that the Free Methodist church overseas is perfect. But when the angel of the church begins to write their story, they will hear the promise, "To him who overcomes and does my will to the end, I will give authority over the nations" (Revelation 2:26).

Perspective on World Missions 1960-1995 and Forward

Free Methodism's march across the world in our generation has been fueled by indigenous principles and inflamed by the Holy Spirit. Aggressive evangelism, coupled with the refining fire of leadership and compassionate service, has put Free Methodist world missions into a position of leadership for the church at the end of the 20th century.

As Free Methodist churches overseas continue to lead in the growth of membership and the maturity of character, even the terms "Home Ministries" and "World Missions" will be obsolete. For Free Methodists of the future, the church will mean the "world" and every local church will be a mission station called "home."

Lest We Forget

Over what do Free Methodists weep?

With tears we remember ...

... our brothers and sisters
who have fled as refugees
by the thousands,

... our pastors, lay leaders,
spouses and children
who have died as martyrs
by the hundreds,

... our bishops and church leaders
who have been driven into exile
by the score.

Their blood and our tears
write the heart of our history
at the end of the 20th century.

Nurturing Our Generations

Christian Education in the Local Church
1960-1995

E ducation and evangelism are partners in Free Methodist history. Consistent with its Wesleyan heritage, the Free Methodist Church has developed educational ministries that represent an affirmative answer to Charles Wesley's unforgettable prayer, "Let us unite these two, so long divided, learning and vital piety."

In 1960 the educational ministries of the Free Methodist Church ranged from Sunday school to seminary, served all generations, represented the majority of denominational departments, attracted top leadership to executive positions, captured a good share of the denominational budget, and thus represented the weight of an unwritten priority in the balance between education and evangelism. Perhaps the shift only brought the two ministries into balance. Evangelism in 1960 still held central focus in the vision of the leaders of the church, but education had certainly come into its own. One hard fact remained. The Free Methodist Church was not growing in membership, either from evangelism or education.

Benchmarks for Christian Education
1960

Three benchmarks for Christian education in the church were most prominent in 1960. From these starting points, the changes in Christian education from 1960-1995 can be tracked and interpreted.

THEOLOGY — *Theologically, the relationship between education and evangelism was uncertain in 1960.* Marston, in his history, gives evangelism precedence over education in the divine plan of salvation. He reasons that the goal of evangelism is to transform human nature and renew the human mind by the transforming touch of God. Christian education is defined as the post-regenerative process through which the individual learns by experience to know God's "good, acceptable and perfect" will. Few would disagree that evangelism is central and crucial to the work of salvation, but many might disagree that the context and vitality of education are limited to human experience.

Perhaps for this reason the relationship between education and evangelism in the history of the Free Methodist Church is sometimes out of balance. Even though Marston sought to define a "both-and" rather than an "either-or" relationship between education and evangelism, the balance does not always hold up in practice. Without a clear theology that articulates its relationship to evangelism and its role in the plan of salvation, Christian education will have to earn its viability in each generation.

EDUCATION — *Educationally, the philosophy of Christian education in 1960 was formal and classical.* Bishop Marston accepted the purposes of Christian education proposed by Frank Gaebelein within the premise that evangelism is central. In 1960 those purposes were defined as:
— the transmission of the Judeo-Christian heritage;
— the application of the specific teachings of the Bible to life and conduct;
— training in the approach to God through Christian worship;
— directing the student to the transforming experience of faith in Jesus Christ;
— leading the student to increasing stature in Christian character.[1]

While these purposes cannot be faulted, they lack the power and specificity of evangelism to engage the commitment and mobilize the energies of pastors and people in the ministry of Christian education. They also fall short in defining the relationship of Christian education to the history, theology and mission of the church. With limited attention to the context of the local church or the changing culture, they pointed forward to a more formal and institutionalized program of Christian education for the Free Methodist Church.

ORGANIZATION — *Organizationally, Christian education in the Free Methodist Church in 1960 was highly specialized and departmentalized.* The sheer number of departments reporting to the 1960 General Conference attests to the specialization and departmentalization of Christian education at the denominational level. General secretaries or departmental directors reported for the Sunday school, Christian Youth Crusaders (CYC), Free Methodist

Youth (FMY), Higher Education, Service Training, Ministerial Training, John Wesley Seminary Foundation and the Servicemen's Department. Although all of these departments made up the portfolio of the Commission on Christian Education, they were essentially independent of each other.

Sometimes the departments were competitive. The CYC, for instance, overlapped with the Junior Missionary Society (JMS). Occasionally the departments were cooperative. When the FMY began to develop leadership training courses for youth, a cooperative program with Service Training was developed. By and large, though, Christian education lacked integration in funding, programming and goals.

Within these major benchmarks, the department of Christian Education in 1960 also had specific characteristics that served as anchor points for change in the future:

— Sunday school enrollments were in decline after peaking in the decades of the 1930s and 1940s;

— Intermediate youth, through the CYC, was rising to its peak in the number of programs in local churches, the number of members and the enrollment in summer camps;

— Free Methodist Youth was best known by crusades at home and abroad where young people were introduced to the methods of mass evangelism;

— Ministerial training had moved away from the home-study curriculum in favor of collegiate or correspondence study and a preference for graduate theological training through the John Wesley Seminary Foundation;

— Higher education among Free Methodist colleges was on the verge of new growth as national priorities in the post-World War II period shifted toward opportunity, access and quality in American higher education;

— Service training offered accredited courses for lay leaders in the local church; and

— Servicemen's ministries continued for Free Methodists still serving in the armed forces.

The unfolding ministry of education in the Free Methodist Church from 1960-1995 is a story of change. It is written by the lofty vision of leaders within the church, prevailing theories of education in the academy, and changing needs of the society outside the church.

In his report to the General Conference of 1960, the General Secretary of the Sunday school wrote, "The church is always one generation from extinction." The corollary could also be written, "The church that grows must save its own." These two simple sentences establish the mission and the motivation for Christian education in the local church.

The Era of Departmental Promotion 1960-1967

By 1960 the Free Methodist Church had more than compensated for the neglect of Christian education in the local church that caused the alarm at the General Conference of 1907. Seven different directors or secretaries of departments under the Commission on Christian Education reported to the 1960 General Conference.

An overview of these reports suggests an approach to Christian education that is heavily departmentalized and highly specialized. Promotion of departmental interests naturally follows. Strong leaders with a vision for their departments carried their case directly to the General Conference in order to win support for their programs and proposals. Although a common commitment to the church took the competitive edge off efforts of the individual directors, evidence of cooperative programming was limited and administrative coordination was almost nonexistent. At the same time, the sheer number of programs reported to the General Conference of 1960 gave witness to the fact that the church took seriously the challenge of Christian education.

The departmental reports of 1960 are too extensive to review in detail, but the essence of their content provides benchmarks against which changes can be seen in the approach to Christian education in the local church over the period from 1960-1995.

DEPARTMENT OF SUNDAY SCHOOL, 1960-1967 — In the last 20 years of its first century, the Free Methodist Church experienced phenomenal growth in Sunday school enrollments. But then the growth slowed down, particularly in the quinquennium between 1955 and 1960.

General Secretary of the Sunday School, Royal S. Nelson, reported that the Sunday school in 1960 totaled 147,400 enrollees in comparison with 58,975 members of the church. He also compared the growth lines over the first century to show that church membership had increased from 6,684 in 1870 to 58,975 in 1960 while Sunday school enrollments had increased from 6,231 to 147,400 or almost three times the growth rate of the church over the same period. Even more pointedly Nelson carried his case for the evangelistic role of the Sunday school by noting that 90,000 of the 147,400 enrollees came from outside the membership of the church. Unabashedly, then, Nelson identified the "promotional" role of his department:

Our function is to foster in our denominational program of Christian education greater efficiency, improved skills, concepts and techniques, in order that we may achieve greater effectiveness in Sunday school and church growth.[2]

To accomplish this promotional purpose, General Secretary Nelson pro-

216

jected a plan for the Sunday school improving its planning, process and teaching techniques, and developing an enlargement campaign with an evangelistic emphasis.

Four years later, Nelson's report to the 1964 General Conference unveils the disappointment that had been under the surface of the 1960 report. With obvious grief he said, "... At the close of the last quadrennium it was apparent that this passion for the Sunday school was decreasing." Responding to his own challenge, Nelson called for a philosophy of the Sunday school as an evangelistic arm of the church to convert an estimated 80,000 unsaved students attending Free Methodist Sunday schools, and as a growth arm of the church to bring at least 7,000 of these students into membership in the church.

Nelson's final report to the 1964 General Conference proved to be prophetic. Sunday school enrollments continued to decline, Christian education in the local church became more generalized, and within three years, the Department of Sunday Schools was absorbed into an integrated program along with Departments of Intermediate Youth, Youth and Adult Ministries.

DEPARTMENT OF INTERMEDIATE YOUTH, 1960-1967 — Closely related to the Sunday school, but still independent, was the report of Floyd Todd, general director of Intermediate Youth. Todd reported that the department, which had been established by General Conference in 1939, had come of age with organized chapters in more than 50 percent of the local churches and coordinated by grades with the Sunday school.

Within the CYC program, Heralds were children from 6 to 8 whose ages matched the Primary Department of the Sunday school, Cadets from the age of 9 to 11 were matched with the Junior Department, and Crusaders aged 12 to 14 were matched with the Junior High Department. At the age of 15, then, the FMY took over responsibility for youth and continued with young adults to the age of 35.

Four years later, Todd's report to the General Conference of 1964 outlined the progress of each of these programs. Statistical growth showed a 60 percent gain in CYC registrants, Bible quizzing had been introduced, 80 summer camps were being held annually across the country, Free Methodist colleges had introduced camping courses in their curriculum, and the CYC had become the model for ministry to intermediate youth for other holiness denominations. A permanent office and staff in the general headquarters building symbolized the benchmark of CYC as a full-fledged denominational department.

DEPARTMENT OF FREE METHODIST YOUTH, 1960-1967 — Youth from the age of 15 and young adults to the age of 35 represented the constituency of the FMY in 1960. General superintendent of the FMY, C. Mervin Russell, reported that the department centered its attention upon promoting youth ministries through publications such as the magazine *Youth In Action;* organizing chapters in more than 800 local churches; educating leaders for the teaching, quizzing and youth camp programs of these chapters; and introducing youth to the ministry of world evangelism by becoming members of evangelistic crusades at home and abroad.

Of these activities, the crusade ministry, especially on the world scene, exudes the excitement of the leadership in 1960. Crusades, held by Supt. Russell and other youth leaders, were reported for the Dominican Republic in 1959 and planned for Belfast, Ireland, in 1960.

Russell also reported on his responsibility as director of the Servicemen's Department of the church, a carryover ministry from World War II. More than 33,000 men and women in the armed forces had been served through written correspondence, formal publications and personal contacts. Russell reported a continuing ministry for the department through Free Methodist chaplains in the field and literature sent from the home office.

Shortly before the 1964 General Conference, Robert Crandall assumed the directorship of the FMY, inheriting the "Decade of Diligent Witness" from his predecessor. He reported on progress toward its threefold target of enlistment, training and outreach for youth in the name of Christ.

No statistics of enlistment are given, but the popularity of youth rallies, camps and the annual Winona Youth Advance are noted. Perhaps as a reflection of Crandall's expertise in the field of curriculum, training comes through as the emphasis in his report. Through officer-training schools, leadership curriculum, publications for FMY officers and pastors at the local level, a stronger support base for youth ministries was beginning to develop. Crusades still represented the edge of outreach for the FMY, but with reduced emphasis on leadership and with more coordination among departments, especially with world missions.

Realistically, however, Crandall reported that the department was either overextended or underfunded and voiced his plea for financial resources to meet the high expectations for youth ministries. By 1967 the drive to promote the department on the glamour of crusades had begun to wane. A new direction was in the offing.

The Era of Curriculum Development
1967-1988

When Robert A. Crandall assumed the directorship of the Department of Christian Education, he brought with him advanced academic preparation in the fields of curriculum and instruction. Early on, he combined his ministerial and academic credentials to remind the church that the great commission began with the words, "Go ye therefore, and *teach* all nations ..." (Matthew 28:19, KJV, [emphasis added]). He also put Christian education at the center of a growing church with the reminder that 95 percent of all conversions and church members come through the educational ministries of the local church. Accordingly, the threefold purpose of his department was to assist the local church in converting, nurturing and equipping all generations from infants to senior adults through the agencies of Christian education.

Crandall's vision set the primary agenda for the Department of Christian Education through the 1970s and into the late 1980s. The core of the program was based upon a *theological* understanding of the nature of persons, a *psychological* understanding of the needs of persons, and an *educational* understanding of new teaching and learning techniques to meet those needs.

In his report to the 1974 General Conference, Crandall outlined a five-year plan in six areas of development for Christian education with integral connectors to the budding church-growth movement.

Those six areas were: (1) *Basic Programming Resources* so that every local church would have "A Total Program for the Total Person"; (2) *Communication* of the ministry of Christian education primarily through promotional materials; (3) *Training* through leadership training texts and Leadership Education and Development (LEAD) seminars; (4) *Field Service* information, instruction and inspiration led by executive members of the department in conferences and local churches; (5) *Organization* for a comprehensive Christian Education program in the local church that ranged from children through youth to adult ministries; and (6) *Evaluation and Research* with each local church setting five-year goals for Christian education with periodic evaluation of the results.

By the 1979 General Conference, Crandall could report substantial progress in each of the six areas outlined for the work so that the department was "recognized as a leader in development of curriculum and program ministries for local churches both within and beyond the denomination." The direction of the department was further reinforced by the report that the executive team in Christian education now included persons who held three Ph.Ds and seven master's degrees with more than 300 years of educational service among them.

Most representative of this leadership was the Aldersgate curriculum. Initiated by publisher Lloyd Knox in the early 1960s, edited by Dr. Donald Joy in the 1970s and completed by Dr. Catherine Stonehouse in the 1980s, the Aldersgate curriculum provided thorough Christian education on a biblical foundation for all ages.

The emphasis upon curriculum resources for teaching and learning in the local church continued through the General Conference of 1985. Catherine Stonehouse, the first woman to hold the directorship of a denominational department, added further educational stature to the role with her earned doctorate and expertise in the development of curricular tools and teaching techniques. Again, the 1985 report emphasizes the progress made toward the six working goals for the department, but with added weight given to information and communication resources. A denomination-wide conference called "C.E. '84" served as the capstone of this emphasis and perhaps represented the culmination of the teaching era.

Stonehouse also reported significant shifts in the field programs of the department. Free Spirit, for instance, was a popular singing group of youth initiated by the Rev. LeRoy Kettinger when he served as director of Youth in the late 1970s and early 1980s. Free Spirit traveled throughout the church from 1981-1984, but as leadership for youth in the department changed, priorities also changed.

An assessment of the youth ministries in the local church showed the need for greater involvement of youth in the mission of the church. Project HELP (Helping, Evangelizing and Loving People) was organized in 1983 as a response to that need. Bible quizzing among juniors also enjoyed a resurgence of interest, and adult ministries stretched out to include Marriage Encounter and Engaged Encounter programs as these specific needs were identified. The Sunday school, however, continued to decline.

The Leadership Development Era 1988-1995

When Dr. Daniel L. Riemenschneider was named director of the Department of Christian Education in 1988, he brought with him a perspective for the ministry directly from the field.

"Building the Church through Christian Education" became the watchword that tied the mission of the department to the vision of the New Day. As the introduction to his report to the 1989 General Conference, Riemenschneider wrote, "Christian education is the best place to start when revitalizing an established church or planting a new church." The new director utilized the principles of organization and management that had come into prominence during the 1980s. Words such as "vision," "strategy," "networking" and especially "leadership" reveal the change in approach to Christian education. Riemenschneider also notes a complete turnover in the departmental staff.

To implement the mission of "Building the Church through Christian Education," Riemenschneider brought forward plans for adjusting to changing times in the ministry of the local church. CYC, the program for intermediate youth, serves as an example. With more mothers working outside the home, most children having little knowledge of the Bible, and more "hi touch" required in a "hi tech" age, the CYC program was revised to become the Christian Life Club (CLC) with a six-year plan stressing Bible study sources for use in the local church.

Youth ministries underwent revision as well. While retaining the established programs of Project HELP, regional, national and international youth conventions and Bible quizzing, a major change was enacted with a return to regional representatives in the field who were on staff in local churches, and a National Council for Youth Ministries was developed and made up of youth ministers.

Symbolic of the transition from the era of curriculum development to the era of leadership development were two decisions made by the Board of Administration in 1988. One closed the printing operation of Light and Life Press; the other created a cooperative with other holiness denominations to develop and select resource materials for Christian education that would reflect changing needs of learners and the changing nature of the church.

When Riemenschneider reported to the General Conference in 1995, the mission he had proposed for the department in 1989 could now be described in the management terms of "core values." He said:

1. "Together, we are servant leaders" as he described the executive team of the department working with regional and conference leaders;

2. "Together, we are a MODEL ministry" as he defined the new acronym for the strategy proposed for every church:
   "God calls the church to a mission (M). Achieving this mission requires a balance of outreach (O), discipleship (D) and equipping (E) programs. These programs are implemented through leadership (L) teams."

3. "Together, we are networking" as he cited working relationships with conferences and local churches, other Free Methodist departments and outside organizations.

4. "Together, we are changing lives" as he passionately foresaw the strategy of MODEL ministry in action throughout the church.

Looking back upon the five-year period from 1990-1995, the report confirmed two major changes in philosophy. First noted was the shift away from curriculum development to leadership development. Second noted was the decentralization of the department as age-level executives remained off-site and working in local churches in their respective regions. Phone, E-mail and fax kept the members of the National Christian Education Leadership network in close contact with each other.

Looking forward to A.D. 2000, Riemenschneider saw progress toward fulfillment of the mission of the department, primarily through implementation of the MODEL strategy in every conference and local church. He sounded the warning given by George Gallup whose 1991 survey showed, "Overall, the Sunday school and religious-education system in this country is not working." In response to this warning, he quoted the Search Institute report of 1990, which said that the "revitalization" of Christian education "must move to center stage."[3]

Although statistics are absent from the reports of the Department of Christian Education in 1989 and 1995, Gallup's reference to the Sunday school prompts interest in its growth or decline in the Free Methodist Church. In 1974 Robert Crandall reported that 95 percent of conversions and church memberships came through Christian education ministries. In 1985 Catherine Stonehouse had expressed her concern for the 29 percent decline in Sunday school enrollments between 1960 and 1985.

What, then, are the statistics 10 years later? Figures from the 1996 *Yearbook* of the Free Methodist Church show that the decline has continued. Sunday school attendance in 1985 totaled 62,490 students out of an enrollment of 102,304. In 1995 attendance figures had dropped to 50,649 out of an enrollment of 88,962, representing another drop of 15 percent in enrollment and 19 percent in attendance for the 10-year period. Against the benchmark year of 1960 the comparative Sunday school statistics for the United States in 1995 show a total drop of 34 percent in enrollment and 43 percent in attendance.

If it is true, as Royal Nelson said in 1960, "The church is only one generation away from extinction," is the church winning its own through the Christian education programs of 1995? The answer may not come in specific statistics of growth for each of the Christian education departments in the church, but it must come in the facts showing that converts are being received into the church, discipled toward Christian maturity and equipped for multiplying the ministry. Contrary to the past, when accountability was limited, the strategy for Christian education today is not complete until the loop is closed and the bottom line is drawn.

Perspective on Christian Education 1960-1995 and Forward

If Christian education in 1995 is viewed against the benchmarks of 1960, dynamic movement is seen in the theological understanding, educational theory and structural relationships of the Department of Christian Education.

THEOLOGY — *Theologically, Christian education has moved toward a working alliance with evangelism to fulfill the Great Commission.* This is not to say that education and evangelism were adversaries in 1960. Their relationship, however, seemed uncertain. Even though Bishop Marston defined their relationship in "both-and" rather than "either-or" terms, evangelism clearly had first priority and education found its meaning in an evangelistic context. Consequently, in 1960 the multiple departments under the Commission on Christian Education functioned as agencies with little connection to the strategy of "Double in a Decade." But we cannot forget that practical theology is the strength of the Wesleyan tradition.

Perhaps the change began in 1974 when Robert Crandall struck the keynote of the Great Commission to emphasize the biblical mandate for the work of Christian education, "Go ye therefore, and *teach all nations, ...*" (Matthew 28:19, KJV, [emphasis added]). His call echoed the church-growth movement with its emphasis upon discipling and equipping believers.

Then in 1985 when the New Day vision was projected with its view of growth through the revitalization of existing churches and the planting of new churches, Christian education found the niche in the mission of the church that evangelism alone could not fill. For the first time the purpose of Christian education became integrated with the strategy of the church. Even though this relationship is still under test, education and evangelism appear to be new partners as Free Methodism heads toward A.D. 2000.

EDUCATION — *Educationally, the concept of Christian education has moved toward the contemporary theory and language of leadership theory and strategic planning.* As a benchmark of 1960, Christian education was defined in the language of classical pedagogy as an individual learns by experience and grows in grace to know God's "good, acceptable and perfect" will.

Later in the decade the concept of Christian education took on the nuances of theology, which described the nature of the individual; psychology, which described the needs of the individual; and education, whose curriculum addressed those needs. Christian education took a more radical turn in the late 1980s when the theory of systems, the language of management and emphasis upon leadership development became prominent. Recast in biblical, evangelistic and church-growth terms, the new and enlarged concept of Christian education depends upon the quality of strategic thinking and planning communicated through national and regional networks to the local church by the leaders who are skilled in the implementation of MODEL ministries.

ORGANIZATION — *Organizationally, the primary emphasis of Christian education in the local church has moved to a full-service, multigenerational and seven-day-a-week program.* Specialized ministries especially designed for children and youth represented the benchmark for Christian education in 1960. Before the end of the decade, these ministries were reorganized as Children's, Youth and Adult Ministries under the Department of Christian Education. Priority for the department also shifted from "doing" conferences, camps and crusades at the denominational level to "managing" the development of Christian educational programs and leadership in the local church.

Further change was evident in 1995. In response to the changing culture and the influence of the megachurch, Christian education is rapidly moving toward the model of a full-service program on a seven-day-a-week schedule. Children's ministries are designed to accommodate the schedule of working mothers, Sunday school may be taught on Wednesday evening and Adult Ministries may specialize in serving singles.

Today the relationship between education and evangelism has taken on new meaning. Theologically, there is recognition that the Great Commission is more than an evangelistic mandate. "Go into all the world and make disciples" gives equal weight to both evangelistic and educational ministries. Especially in the Two-thirds World where persons are coming to Christ by the thousands, the need for the educational ministry of discipling as the follow-up to evangelism is central and crucial. Now the same truth is coming home to the North American church. With statistics in the 1990s showing thousands of conversions in Free Methodist churches while membership growth is measured in the tens and hundreds during the same period, the crisis in Christian education is self-evident.

Whether at home or abroad, there is also the recognition that the growth of the church cannot depend upon the "outreach" of evangelism to unchurched peoples without the "inreach" of education to bring the oncoming generations into membership in the church. A survey by George Gallup leaves no doubt that growing churches pay attention to the nurture of children and youth.

The future of Christian education in Free Methodism is not guaranteed. If the church is "only one generation from extinction," every generation is a crisis. If the church must win its own in order to grow, every generation is a challenge. To achieve the evangelistic goals of the New Day vision for the 21st century, the Free Methodist Church must ask an educational question, "Will its 'inreach' equal its 'outreach'?"

C H A P T E R 13

Educating
Our
Leaders

rom its beginning in 1860, the Free Methodist Church has prized the value of higher education. As a university graduate himself, Roberts modeled the unity of a tough mind and a tender spirit. With equal passion, he could preach at a camp meeting, teach a Sunday school class, plant a church or found a college.

Because of Roberts' enlightened leadership, the Free Methodist Church stands tall among holiness denominations for its commitment to Christian liberal arts colleges, rather than following the typical path of revivalistic churches into the founding of Bible colleges or ministerial training institutes. When Roberts founded Chili Seminary (later Roberts Wesleyan College) in 1866 for the specific purpose of providing general education for all students who desired higher learning in a Christian context, he added another dimension to the meaning of "Free" Methodist. Just as he envisioned "free churches" for the ministry to the soul, Roberts also foresaw "free colleges" for the ministry to the mind.

As an exception to other holiness denominations, the Free Methodist Church has never exercised control over its colleges by a centralized board of higher education and the restrictions that follow. The relationship between the church and its colleges has been more missional than legal and more fraternal than paternal. Free Methodist institutions of higher education cannot be classified as "church-controlled" or even "sectarian" in strictly legal terms. Their boards of trustees are independent; their policies are not subject to review; their budgets are not significantly underwritten by the denomination; and their assets are not assigned to the general church in the event that their educational corporations were dissolved. At best they must be classified as "church-affiliated" with Free Methodist representation on the boards of the trustees, in the person of the president and in the religion faculty.

From time to time this relationship is tested. During the 1960s it was tested in the merger negotiations with the Wesleyan Church. While a compromise was worked out in the merger agreement, neither party was fully satisfied. In the 1980s the issue surfaced again in the perennial struggle over church-state relationships. After the State of Washington charged Seattle Pacific University with religious discrimination in hiring, the university sued the state for the right to select its employees as an "arm of the church."

Needless to say, the Free Methodist Church and its colleges walk a fine line in maintaining their relationship. Yet in testimony to the leadership of both the church and colleges throughout Free Methodist history, none of the colleges have followed the downward path of defection from the faith that so many other church-affiliated schools have taken. To the contrary, in 1995 the bond of mission and moral affiliation between the church and its colleges is stronger than ever.

Free Methodist Higher Education 1960-1995

Between 1960 and 1995 the dramatic story of growth in Free Methodist higher education is second only to the more dramatic story of growth in the overseas church. Few Free Methodists understand the impact of the colleges on the growth of the church, and fewer understand the value of the spiritual, human, financial and physical resources invested in its schools.

Comparative enrollments for Free Methodist higher education between 1960 and 1995 show the growth of the sector. According to the 1960 *Yearbook*, Free Methodist colleges enrolled 3,050 students, of which 1,454 or 48 percent were Free Methodists. In 1995 a total of 13,268 students enrolled at AFMEI schools (Association of Free Methodist Educational Institutions), of whom 909 or 7 percent are Free Methodists. If the enrollment of Azusa Pacific University, a cooperating institution, is deducted from the figures in 1995, the total enrollment drops to 8,667 with 888 Free Methodist students or 10 percent of the enrollment. As another means of comparison, the 888 Free Methodists enrolled in the colleges represented 1 percent of the 81,586 members of the church (including Canada for an equal comparison) in 1995. This compared with the 1,422 Free Methodist students in the colleges in 1960, who represented 2.4 percent of the 58,975 members of the church at that time.

As another facet in the history of Free Methodist higher education between 1960 and 1995, a comparison of the financial status of the institutions over this period of time borders on the unbelievable. The total operating budgets for Free Methodist schools in 1960 (including the Moose Jaw Bible College, Lorne Park College, Los Angeles Pacific College and Wessington Springs College, which either closed, merged or became foundations during this period) was $3.04 million. In 1995 the AFMEI schools show operating budgets totaling more than $165 million! Adding to these growth figures, the value of the physical plants on these campuses went from $2.1 million in 1960 to $146 million in 1995. Student financial aid in these institutions has also multiplied during this 35-year period from the 1960 total of $200,000 in comparison with $21.7 million in 1995.

Slower growth is evident in endowments for the AFMEI schools. In 1960 total endowments were listed at $1.2 million, and in 1995 at $34.5 million. Operating and capital debts have been managed during this period, even though each school has gone through financial crisis at one time or another. In 1960 the five schools showed a total operating deficit of approximately $750,000, with two schools debt-free. In 1995 these same schools showed approximately $20 million in current operating deficits. Two schools were debt-free in their operations. Capital debt in 1960 among the five totaled $2.5 million with one school debt-free. By 1995 all schools carried some capital debt, a total of $29 million among the five.

From these figures, the magnitude of the ministry and the wealth of resources invested in Free Methodist higher education verified its importance to the church. Enrollment growth in the sector exceeded the growth in American higher education. But, the number as well as the percentage of Free Methodist students has decreased. Other changes included the marked increase in graduate students and adult degree completion or enrichment programs. Enrollments continued to grow despite the rising costs of tuition. All the schools were dependent upon increasing student financial aid to sustain their enrollments. This dependence was both a strength and a weakness.

Financial growth also multiplied during the era. With total operating budgets exceeding $100 million, Free Methodist higher education must be recognized as equal to a major corporation in the American economy and the greatest financial asset of the church. Its current role, however, was ill-defined, except for the expectation that the schools would rally to the New Day vision in support of ministerial education. The most evident weakness in the financial picture for Free Methodist higher education was the failure to increase endowments over the period from 1960-1995. Without such sustaining income, the schools would continue to be enrollment-driven, tuition-supported and aid-dependent. A change in any one of these factors could upset the narrow margins of financial operations upon which the schools depended.

Profiles of the Colleges and Universities 1960-1995

Each of the AFMEI member schools has a story to be told for one of the most eventful periods of change in American higher education. These stories deserve a book of history in itself. For our purposes, however, the stories must be limited to a profile of change in the schools, with emphasis upon the turning points.

(Presidents who have served Free Methodist institutions of higher education between 1960 and 1995 are honored by name among the Servant Leaders of Our Generation [Epilogue].)

ALDERSGATE COLLEGE (Moose Jaw Bible College) — Founded in 1940 to serve students in the western conferences of Canada, the name of the school was changed to Aldersgate College in November 1963. Enrollment in 1960 totaled 30 students and five faculty members. Ninety percent of the students were Free Methodists. Throughout the era from 1960-1995, the college struggled with small enrollments and marginal finances.

Nine presidents tried different strategies to stabilize the school until finally in 1995 the school made the transition from a campus ministry to a scholarship ministry under the Aldersgate College Foundation. This was similar to the scholarship ministry developed out of the assets of Lorne Park College for Eastern Canada. The purpose of the foundation was to provide undergraduate and graduate scholarships for Canadian Free Methodist students, not just for Free Methodist colleges and universities in the United States but also approved Bible colleges and a Christian university in Canada.

When the Aldersgate College campus is sold and debts are cleared, it is estimated that the net assets will provide an endowment of $300,000 for the scholarship fund.

CENTRAL COLLEGE — Central College was founded as Orleans Seminary in 1884. By 1960 the two-year college registered 102 students plus 60 in the high school. Of the total head count, 115, or 71 percent, were Free Methodists.

After years of an uphill struggle to develop a cost-effective enrollment for both college transfer and terminal curriculums, Central College came to its defining moment between 1960 and 1995, when the school achieved the goal of regional accreditation with the North Central Association. Its student enrollment in 1995-1996 totaled 303 students, of whom 105, or 35 percent, were Free Methodists. These numbers included students taking the first four-year degree offered by the college in the field of pastoral ministry.

GREENVILLE COLLEGE — Founded in 1892, Greenville College followed in the path of Free Methodist pioneers who established, in order, their homes, their church and a college at the intersection of a railroad and a river for the education of their youth. In 1960 Greenville enrolled 625 students, of whom 48 percent were Free Methodists. Notable at that time was the fact that one out of five Free Methodist ministers in the United States and Canada was a graduate of Greenville.

During the 35-year period between 1960 and 1995, Greenville remained relatively stable in its tradition as a Christian liberal arts college, noted for the contributions of its faculty to the church and the influence of its graduates in scholarly and service careers. In 1995-1996 the enrollment totaled 827 students, of whom 26 percent were Free Methodists. Fifty percent of the full-time faculty of 86 are members of the Free Methodist Church.

LOS ANGELES PACIFIC COLLEGE (Azusa Pacific University) — As the last of the Free Methodist colleges in the United States to be founded by evangelists and church planters, Los Angeles Pacific Seminary began in 1903 with a view to serving Free Methodists in the burgeoning basin of Southern California. Between 1903 and 1960, the name of the two-year school was changed from "seminary" to "college" as part of the efforts to build enrollment and finances.

By 1960 students in two-year programs numbered 241, with 42 percent Free Methodists. In that same year, the college added a Bachelor of Theology degree as part of its service ministry to the church in the Southwest because of the distance to the seminary program at Asbury Theological Seminary in Kentucky.

Before the end of the decade of the 1960s, Los Angeles Pacific College confronted the reality of closure, primarily because of finances. A merger agreement was negotiated with Azusa College, which gave Free Methodists the advantage of education in a sister school of Wesleyan roots and supported by several holiness denominations. The merger was completed in 1965, and Azusa changed its name to "university" in 1981 as it added a graduate school of theology among its advanced offerings.

Because of its unique relationship to the Free Methodist Church as one of its supporting denominations, Azusa was classified as a "cooperating institution" in its membership with the Association of Free Methodist Educational Institutions. In 1995 Azusa enrolled a total of 4,229 students, of whom 21, or a fraction of one percent, were Free Methodists.

LORNE PARK COLLEGE — Coordinated with the development of Canadian Free Methodism in the 1920s, Lorne Park Seminary was founded in 1924 with a particular interest in the education of students in Ontario. The curriculum centered upon ministerial education, along with a secondary program for students at the high school level. By 1960 the school enrolled 76 students, of whom 41 percent were Free Methodists. In that same year, Lorne Park added a Bachelor of Theology degree in an upgraded program for ministerial education.

Finances, the common cause of college closures, caught up with Lorne Park College in the mid-1960s. As an alternative to the loss of educational quality in the campus curriculum, officials decided to close the college and use the assets to fund scholarships for Canadian students at Free Methodist and other church-approved schools.

In 1994, 120 Canadian students received grants through the Lorne Park College Foundation, including a dozen ministerial candidates who received Wesley Scholarships at Ontario Theological Seminary, the newly established affiliate of the John Wesley Seminary Foundation. At Ontario Theological Seminary, a Chair of Wesley Studies has been founded at the initiative of Free Methodist leadership.

ROBERTS WESLEYAN COLLEGE — Carrying the name of the founder of Free Methodism and distinguished as the oldest of the Free Methodist educational institutions, Roberts Wesleyan College was founded as Chili Seminary in 1866 by B.T. Roberts. The stated purpose was to provide "general education" in the spirit of Free Methodism for all students.

By 1960 Roberts moved toward its own centennial with 356 students. At the time of its centennial in 1976, Roberts represented both the strength and the struggle of Free Methodist higher education. Its strength was in its unswerving dedication to the Free Methodist Church without legal bonds. Its struggle was represented by organizational changes from a seminary to a two-year college in 1921 and then to a senior college in 1953.

On the path of this change, Roberts Wesleyan College had 1,267 students in 1995 with 201 Free Methodists, or 16 percent of its total enrollment. These enrollment figures included students in degree-completion programs for adult learners on and off campus as well as graduate students in newly developed master's degrees in selected fields.

SEATTLE PACIFIC COLLEGE (Seattle Pacific University) — When Free Methodism reached the Northwest in 1885 and before the Washington Conference was formed in 1896, Seattle Seminary was created in 1891 by a gift of land from the Peterson family expressly for developing a school for the training of missionaries. Not unlike other Free Methodist schools, Seattle Seminary gave way to Seattle Pacific College in 1915 and carried that name as a fully accredited four-year college, which also offered master's degrees in such fields as education, religion and nursing.

In 1960 a total of 1,196 students were enrolled in the college, with Free Methodists representing 24 percent of the student body. True to its founding mission, 36 percent of all of the missionaries of the church were graduates of Seattle Pacific College.

In 1960 Seattle Pacific flourished along with other colleges as veterans returned home and the federal government invested in higher education. Later in the 1960s, however, the tide turned and the college went through a down cycle in enrollment and finances. Recovery came in the early 1970s and continued through the decade with increased enrollments, new programs and financial stability.

In 1977 Seattle Pacific took the step of becoming the first university in Free Methodist higher education, with nine schools of liberal and professional studies as well as several graduate programs of recognition. This growth has continued. A total head count of 3,437 students registered for the fall semester 1995-1996, including 134 Free Methodists, approximately 4 percent of the total enrollment.

SPRING ARBOR COLLEGE — Shortly after the founding of Chili Seminary in New York State, the Rev. and Mrs. E.P. Hart extended B.T. Roberts' vision for evangelism and education to Michigan, where Free Methodists organized a conference in 1866 and founded Spring Arbor Seminary seven years later.

In 1960 Spring Arbor Junior College enrolled a total of 264 students, with 225 in the junior college and 39 in the high school. Of the junior college enrollees, 80 percent were Free Methodist. Future plans called for the closure of the high school and the development of a four-year Christian liberal arts college.

Three years later Spring Arbor offered its first junior and senior courses, with the distinction of being the first Free Methodist institution fully accredited by the North Central Association in advance of its first graduating class in 1965.

Growth of the college continued through the next 30 years so that 1995-1996 enrollments totaled 2,247, including 164 graduate students and over 1,400 off-campus registrants. Free Methodists numbered 251, or 11 percent of the total student body. The total enrollment was bolstered by the alternative education program offered in satellite centers in metropolitan areas of Michigan. In the early 1990s, Spring Arbor introduced graduate study into its curriculum, including teacher education and business management.

WESSINGTON SPRINGS COLLEGE — As Free Methodism marched westward in the 1880s, rugged pioneers of the Dakota territory wanted a school of their own. Their persistence produced Wessington Springs Seminary in 1887. The number of prospective students, funding potential and the Dakota weather all militated against the success of the school. From the time of its founding to 1960, the school survived the leanest of times. In 1960 the enrollment stood at 102, with 68 of the students coming from Free Methodist homes.

The struggle for survival continued through the 1960s when the hard facts required a merger with Central College. Yet out of its rugged 81-year

231

history, Wessington Springs College is remembered for its parenting of Free Methodist ministers, missionaries and scholars far beyond its numbers or its resources.

GRADUATE STUDENTS' THEOLOGICAL SEMINAR, 1964-1995 — A report on the history of higher education in the Free Methodist Church between 1960 and 1995 would not be complete without recognition of an innovation rising out of desperate need in the early 1960s. An air of suspicion, left over from the liberal-conservative conflict over the authority of Scripture, tended to follow Free Methodist students pursuing graduate study in theology and biblical studies in prominent universities.

Frank Thompson, a doctoral student in Old Testament at Princeton University in 1964, felt the stigma of that suspicion and appealed to Dr. George Turner, Professor of English Bible at Asbury Theological Seminary, for proof that the prevailing motto "The Church that Cares" applied to university scholars as well as military personnel. Turner responded with that care, and together with Byron Lamson, general missionary secretary, organized the first graduate students seminar at Nyack, New York, in 1964.

Free Methodist graduate students in theology and biblical studies were invited at the expense of the mission board. They were joined by churchmen and professors, including Lamson, Turner and Lloyd Knox, denominational publisher. Frank Thompson, a founding member and lifetime professor of Old Testament at Greenville College, recalled the accepting atmosphere. He likened it to the "first morning of Creation" as students and executives "simply poured out our hearts one to another."

In 1995 the Graduate Students' Theological Seminar convened for the 32nd consecutive year. Over 125 graduate students and approximately 40 denominational representatives, including bishops and seminar alumni in professorial positions, have attended the seminar. Follow-up has been informal, but a reading of the roster confirms the need and the vision that brought the seminar into being. Leaders of the church, professors in Free Methodist colleges and affiliated seminaries, authors of scholarly publications and other representatives in the evangelical academy are witness to the fact that the seminar stopped the "brain drain" of outstanding young scholars. The Free Methodist Church demonstrated its confidence in God's truth and gave new meaning to the motto, "The Church that Cares."

Department of Higher Education and the Ministry 1960-1995

A formal linchpin in the relationship between the Free Methodist Church and its colleges is the Department of Higher Education, which functions under the Commission on Christian Education. Because of the independence of the colleges, the general secretary of the department must rely upon persuasion rather than power to fulfill the leadership role mandated by the 1989 *Discipline* through two divisions: (1) The Division of Educational Institutions, "Responsible for promoting and helping to maintain adequate opportunity for college and graduate training of the young people of the Free Methodist Church" (Par. B/470, 8b-1); and (2) The Division of Ministerial Education and Guidance, "Responsible for setting up or approving and supervising the various programs in the church for the education and training of ministers" (Par. B/470, 8b-2).

Within the department and these divisions, the church-college relationship between 1960 and 1995 had fluctuated widely as different directors brought their own interpretation to the role and its responsibilities. Some discernible shifts are evident in the reports of the general secretaries to each of the general conferences during this period.

THE JURISDICTIONAL STRUGGLE, 1960-1964 — When Bishop Charles V. Fairbairn, chair of the Commission on Christian Education, reported as the acting secretary of Educational Institutions, he saw his role as a holding action in a jurisdictional struggle. Each of the colleges had carved out conference boundaries within which they recruited students and raised funds. When Free Methodist college presidents met in annual sessions, the agenda invariably included the question of jurisdictional boundaries. Each year the issue was aggravated as alumni became more mobile and the boundaries became fluid. So the best the acting secretary could do was to mediate the conflict and rely on the goodwill of the presidents.

In the 1960 report to the general conference, Bishop Fairbairn especially noted the one point of leverage that the *Discipline* gave him over the colleges. He approved fund-raising campaigns and construction of new buildings on Free Methodist college campuses. But even then the critical question took cover under the goodwill of the presidents, "What if the Department of Educational Institutions refused to grant permission for fund-raising or construction?" Because the department had no legal control over the colleges and provided no funding for their operations or capital projects, the question would have been rendered moot.

THE ASSOCIATIONAL EFFORTS ERA, 1964-1979 — In 1964 Dr. C. Hoyt Watson, president-emeritus of Seattle Pacific College, reported as the educational secretary. As an insider among presidents and founder of the Forward Movement, he brought a special educator-churchman's view to the department. Under his leadership the Association of Free Methodist Educational Institutions (AFMEI) was formed to promote cooperation among Free Methodist colleges.

In recognition of this new unity, the Board of Administration granted the AFMEI two seats on the Commission on Christian Education with full voice and vote on behalf of Free Methodist higher education. Out of the AFMEI came area workshops on college cooperation, along with lobbying efforts to promote the cause of Christian higher education at annual conferences and throughout the church.

Watson's report in 1964 was not without a woeful note. In 1937 the church established and funded by church-wide subscription a $100,000 endowment for the benefit of the colleges and with a view toward building a fund that would significantly assist Free Methodist students to attend the schools. While reporting that the initial $100,000 fund was still intact, Watson poignantly said, "The sad part, however, is the fact that this fund has not been increased by even $1.00 in 45 years."

As a companion report in 1964, Watson also reported as executive secretary of the Central Board of Ministerial Training. In keeping with the trend toward higher education in the church at that time, he reported that the transition in ministerial education from the home-study curriculum to college and seminary preparation was nearly complete. Home study, the track to ordination in the church from 1860-1931, had now been replaced by formal and advanced education with correspondence courses as the option. Surprising statistics reveal that of the 182 deacons ordained as elders during the quadrennium from 1960-1964, 96 had attended college, 80 percent had graduated from college, and 29 had graduated from seminary.

A.D. Zahniser assumed the position as general secretary of the Department of Higher Education and the Ministry in 1966 and reported to the General Conference in 1969. At that time the threat of public higher education mounted as Free Methodist students faced the choice of a convenient location at a lower cost in public institutions in lieu of Free Methodist colleges.

Students of American higher education predicted the demise of hundreds of private and church-related colleges due to rising costs and falling enrollments. Therefore, while maintaining strong relationships with Free Methodist colleges through the AFMEI, Zahniser also launched a program of Aldersgate Fellowships on public college and university campuses. Chapters were established with a cadre of Free Methodist students at the universities of Illinois, Michigan, Kansas, Ohio State and Central Michigan. With a view toward creating a network of fellowships across the country, the thrust was strong but short-lived. At the 1974 General Conference, Dr. Lawrence Schoenhals, the new general secretary of the department, did not include the Aldersgate Fellowships in his report but focused upon the colleges, especially their survival.

A prophetic note was struck in the report to the 1979 General Conference when the new name appeared, "Department of Higher Education and the Ministry." The portfolio for ministerial education had already been moved to the department between 1974 and 1979. With that move came the Central Board of Ministerial Training, the Department of Service Training, and the Servicemen's Department with its reemphasis upon chaplains, both military and institutional, e.g., hospitals.

Free Methodist college presidents convinced the general church that it must demonstrate concern for preserving its college-age youth for the church. The Free Methodist Futures Fund was established as a line item in the denominational budget (with some income from the long-established, but nongrowing Educational Endowment Fund) providing a $100 grant to Free Methodist students attending Free Methodist colleges.

THE ERA OF MINISTERIAL DEMAND, 1985-1995 — Dr. Bruce Kline, former president of Central College, made his first report as general secretary of Higher Education to the 1985 General Conference. He described the status of Free Methodist colleges as "awakening giants," and then focused upon the specifics of ministerial education in relationship to the New Day vision. Neither composite statistics on enrollment and finances for the higher education sector nor individual reports for the colleges were included in the report. Rather, the AFMEI and its member schools were generally recognized for health and growth under the "awakening giant" theme.

Kline's report reflected the new responsibility given to the Department of Higher Education and the Ministry by the General Conference of 1979 for developing and credentialing pastors. In addition to the credentialing function for entry into the ordained ministry, continuing education credits were required for all pastors.

In a reversal of the direction toward graduate theological education set in 1960, a renewed emphasis was given to ministerial education for second-career persons who did not have the opportunity for college or seminary education. In 1982 the department inherited from the Department of Service Training a 16-day program called the "January Term" with courses taught by Free Methodist professors for either ordination or continuing education credit.

Perhaps to keep pace with the hopes for the New Day vision in the church, the quantity as well the quality of ministerial candidates had come to the fore. Not that the John Wesley Seminary Foundation was forgotten. The report to the 1979 General Conference showed that 62 Foundation students were enrolled at Asbury Theological Seminary and 37 more at Western Evangelical Seminary in Portland, Oregon. A total of $129,157 in United Mission for Christ funds supported these students through John Wesley Seminary Foundation grants. These scholarships were far below the level of 70 percent of tuition costs mandated by the Board of Administration.

Beginning in 1979 it was obvious that the general secretary of the Department of Higher Education and the Ministry must carry water on both shoulders. On one shoulder weighed the persuasive role of keeping strong the linkage between the church and its colleges. On the other shoulder balanced the powerful role of developing and credentialing a new and larger contingent of pastors. As the church anticipated growth, the weight inevitably shifted toward the shoulder of ministerial education.

So when General Secretary Kline reported to the General Conference of 1985, he echoed the dual themes that the church inherited from the contemporary educational and religious culture. Kline prefaced his report with this statement of priority for the department: "Overseeing the training, certifying and continuing education of leaders." His role in Free Methodist higher education was then recognized as equally awesome in, "... Providing liaison for the colleges and universities of the denomination through the AFMEI. These institutions educate pastors and lay leaders, and a high percentage of other persons in local churches."

Kline turned to ministerial education. Over 900 ministerial candidates were under the guidance of the department in 1985, and during the six-year period between 1979 and 1985 a total of 1,298 persons had been certified as candidates or ordained as deacons or elders under the guidance of the department. Kline's report noted the growth of enrollments in correspondence study, J-term programs, and continuing education, along with a rising number of John Wesley Seminary Foundation (JWSF) students, especially at Asbury Theological Seminary.

A good and bad news report on seminary students followed. A 10-year study of JWSF graduates announced the good news that 83 percent were serving the Free Methodist Church, but during this same period JWSF grants had fallen from 73.7 percent of seminary tuition in 1979 to 42.2 percent in 1985. The reality of low pay for pastors and missionaries in the church had consequences that prompted the general secretary to sound the alarm.

The Servicemen's Department, a leftover from World War II, took a new turn in 1983 with the organization of the Free Methodist Chaplains Association. Annual meetings of military chaplains, awards for chaplaincy service and the inclusion of institutional chaplains were joined with the role of the general secretary who officially endorsed chaplains of the church.

By the 1985 General Conference, the direction established in 1979 was now set. Secretary Kline's report was exclusively directed to the role of the department in support of the denomination and its New Day vision. The AFMEI report, for instance, cited the new curricular developments in ministerial education for each school. Most notable among these developments were a Bachelor of Religious Education at Aldersgate College, a Bachelor of Science in Ministry at Central College, a Bachelor of Arts in Pastoral Ministry at Greenville and Bachelor of Arts in Contemporary Ministries at Spring Arbor College.

Roberts Wesleyan College was reported as assessing its curriculum in ministry, Seattle Pacific University was exploring the possibility of establishing a seminary, and Azusa Pacific University was noted for the approval of its Graduate School of Theology as a John Wesley Seminary Foundation affiliate. Through these reports, Free Methodist colleges and universities expressed their commitment to serve the church in its mission of evangelism and church growth.

Together with the AFMEI, the Department of Higher Education and the Ministry also launched the John Wesley Institute in 1984. A combination of college courses on AFMEI campuses, short courses in the J-term and correspondence studies was designed to serve the needs of second- and third-career candidates for ministry.

Behind this twofold thrust of collegiate-level ministerial education and the John Wesley Institute was The Pastoral Supply 2000 study, conducted by Wayne McCown. The results of the study showed that there must be a marked increase in the number entering Free Methodist pastoral ministries during the final 15 years of the century or the church would be "painfully short of qualified ministers before the year 2000."[1] The conclusion had its base in the premise that the church would grow to achieve the New Day goals of 1,000 new churches and 125,000 members in North America by A.D. 2000.

The new direction is also evident in developments reported to the General Conference in 1989. Even with the Graduate School of Theology at Azusa Pacific University joining with Asbury and Western theological seminaries as affiliates of the John Wesley Seminary Foundation, enrollments of Free Methodist students in these schools fell from a high of 102 in 1984-1985 to 68 in 1988-1989. These statistics confirmed a reversal in the direction of ministerial education. In 1960 a seminary education was designated as the preferred track to ordination; in 1989 the church now counted upon the collegiate curriculum and the John Wesley Institute as major tracks for supplying its pastors for the future.

Prior to the 1995 General Conference, the leadership of the Department of Higher Education and the Ministry changed. General Secretary Bruce Kline left the post he had held since 1981 to continue his educational ministry in the development of the John Wesley Bible Institute in Hungary. Dr. Timothy Beuthin succeeded him and reported as general secretary to the 1995 General Conference. As might be expected, the report represents the continuity of transition as Beuthin noted changes during the period between general conferences rather than proposing a full-fledged agenda for his own administration. Those changes were significant.

Leading the way in significant change between 1989 and 1995 was the turnover of Free Methodist college presidents. Only President William Crothers of Roberts Wesleyan College continued in the role during this period. All other institutions had a changing of the guard, and some more than one. Also, Aldersgate College followed the path of Lorne Park College in the 1960s and closed its doors, with the residual resources redirected to scholarships for Canadian students through the Aldersgate College Foundation.

Still another important change between 1989 and 1995 was the appointment of Sylvia Fox as director of Ministerial Credentialing Services within the department, with special responsibility for the ordination process, J-Term and the correspondence school of the Free Methodist Church. Her appointment indicated the increasing importance and growth of these two tracks in ministerial preparation for the church.

On the other side of the ledger, Beuthin announced the discontinuation of the Free Methodist Futures scholarship program, which had granted approximately 900 scholarships to Free Methodist students attending AFMEI schools between 1982 and 1992. Originally begun as a line item in the UMC budget, the Free Methodist Futures program became the first victim of budget cuts during the 1980s. To keep the program alive, AFMEI schools agreed to share equally the funding with the church. Even this 50-50 share disappeared as the church faced further financial crises so that the colleges carried the full cost for a short period of time.

At the same time, the number of seminaries affiliated with the John Wesley Seminary Foundation had been expanded to include Wesley Biblical Seminary (Jackson, Mississippi) and Ontario Theological Seminary (North York, Ontario, Canada).

The general secretary reported that the percentage of tuition paid by JWSF grants had again slipped from 59 percent to 38 percent, far below the Board of Administration's mandate of 70 percent. The specter of debt facing Free Methodist seminary graduates entering ministry rose again.

Picking up the leadership theme that permeates all of the reports of the denominational executives in 1995, Beuthin pledged himself to the task of serving as spokesperson and liaison between the church and its educational institutions in the future. Primary to that role was assisting the institutions as they address the needs of the church, with attention to the development of lay and clergy leaders for the denomination, its educational institutions and the local church.

Future relationships between the church and its colleges will also change. At the annual meeting of the Board of Administration in October 1996, a proposal was presented to the Commission on Christian Education to reduce the required percentage of Free Methodist trustees and faculty as stipulated by the *Discipline*. Although the proposal is undergoing further study, it reflects a new reality in Free Methodist higher education.

As Free Methodist colleges and universities have grown in size and diversity, the church has not grown to keep pace with the need for trustee leadership in resource development and faculty leadership in academic fields. Some would argue that this proposed shift is the path of defection for the colleges from their church relationship.

The history of Christian colleges in American higher education tends to confirm their opinion. Others, however, would point to the fact that the genius of Free Methodist higher education has never been determined by legalistic restrictions enforced by church funding. Rather, the bond of affiliation between the church and its colleges has held firm for more than 135 years on moral and spiritual grounds.

Beuthin takes this position as he reflects upon the proposal and response by the Board of Administration, "A relatively new Commission on Education has established an initiating posture toward its educational institutions. It is committed to serving them as a resource in historical and theological foundations, funding, recruitment, planning and information dissemination. This represents a fundamental shift from a paternal relationship to a covenantal partnership responsive to the challenges and opportunities of the future."

Some might disagree. Free Methodist colleges have always been identified as "church-related" rather than "church-controlled." In a sense, then, a "covenantal partnership" rather than a "paternalistic relationship" has prevailed from the beginning. If so, it means that the future of church-college relationships depends upon the strength and quality of the continuing covenant if and when the percentages of Free Methodist trustees and faculty are reduced.

The issue comes into focus with the question, "What is the critical mass of Free Methodist trustee and faculty leadership needed to maintain the strength and quality of a covenantal partnership between the church and its colleges?"

An exact percentage may not be the answer, but the issue is pivotal to the future of church-college relationships. With the prediction that there will be winnowing among Christian colleges in the 21st century, this is one of the most urgent and far-reaching issues with which the Free Methodist Church must grapple.

Perspective on Ministerial Education 1960-1995 and Forward

Comparative statistics for 1960 and 1995, showing the number of ministerial candidates in the three tracks toward ordination, are not available due to the lack of a centralized system of reporting in 1960. Statistics for 1995, however, show the following breakdown of ministerial candidates in the three tracks:

MINISTERIAL CANDIDATES:

Track I — Seminary	(M. Div. completed)	61	12%
Track II — College	(B.A. completed)	407	53%
Track III — Correspondence	(B.A. not completed)	294	35%
	Total	762	100%

It can be assumed that a record number of persons pursued ordination in 1995. This assumption comes from a 1989 study, conducted by Bruce Kline on the pastoral supply and demand with a view toward the needs in A.D. 2000. Kline reported that the current system of supplying ministers through education and transfer would balance the losses due to retirement and drop-out. However, if the New Day goal for 1,000 new churches by A.D. 2000 were to be realized, 70 additional pastors would be needed each year, bringing the total, including replacements, to 130. Because the growth in the number of new churches has not kept pace with the 1985 goals, it can be assumed that the pastoral supply probably balances current demand.

Another revealing statistic in Kline's study shows that 76 percent of 2,312 ordained Free Methodist pastors, serving in all capacities, have completed four or more years of college, and 39 percent have completed the Master of Divinity degree. Also, 73 percent of all pastors under appointment in 1989 had attended a Free Methodist college or university.

As it stands in 1995, the supply of ministerial candidates will exceed the demand for pastors in A.D. 2000. If so, the selection of the best qualified candidates may require new criteria for educating and guiding prospective pastors. A release valve on the oversupply may be a quickened race toward New Day goals, church planting projects, development of multiple staff positions in growing churches or specialized alternative ministries for "tentmakers" who hold both secular and church employment.

The Free Methodist Church is in the enviable position of attracting pastors by transfer from other denominations. Lacking a natural identification with the history and theology of the Free Methodist Church, their orientation courses and continuing education present their own challenges. Both the quantity and quality of Free Methodist clergy will continue to be issues with which the church and Ministerial Education and Guidance boards will have to grapple in the future.

Perspective on Higher Education
1960-1995 and Forward

When the sector of Christian education represented by the Association of Free Methodist Educational Institutions, the Canadian foundations and the John Wesley Seminary Foundation is seen in total, the magnitude of the ministry boggles the mind. The multiples of growth in enrollments, curriculum and physical plant make it one of the most valuable assets of the church; the recognition of its academic standing makes it one of the most significant witnesses of the church; and the potential for Christian leadership among both clergy and laity makes it a powerful force in the society. Free Methodist higher education is companion with world missions in its extended impact within and beyond the church. Also, in companionship with world missions, Free Methodist higher education between 1960 and 1995 has the amazing story of a "growth ministry" during a time when the church fluctuated on the rising and falling tides of membership.

Several issues summarize the history of higher education in the Free Methodist Church from 1960-1995. They also pose the challenge for the church and its educational programs for the future. First, the mission of Free Methodist colleges and universities must reflect the distinctive character of a Wesleyan theology of education and the spirit of Free Methodist history. A winnowing process is predicted for American higher education in the future as educational costs rise with the grim prospect of pricing middle- and lower-class students out of the college market.

The Free Methodist colleges and universities that survive with significance in the future will reflect a character, quality and spirit that positions them, not only in the academic marketplace, but also within the evangelical community and the Free Methodist constituency. The choice of public colleges based upon lower cost and convenient locations can be countered only by the campus climate, academic quality and spiritual convictions of the Free Methodist college.

Second, the continuing leadership of presidents, trustees and faculty must be assured to maintain the relational bond with the Free Methodist Church. Free Methodist colleges are unique in American higher education. Without the stringency of legal ties to the church or without a centralized board of control from the church, the historical pattern of denominational colleges is to defect from the faith and lose their identity as church-related schools. Free Methodist colleges are just the opposite.

Between 1960 and 1995 the voluntary bond of church relatedness has been strengthened because of the common commitment of church and college leaders personally to Jesus Christ and collectively to the mission of the Free Methodist Church. With the harsh reality that Free Methodist colleges are no longer attracting Free Methodist students to retain the number or percentage of their presence on campus, the spiritual, theological and educational bonds are at risk. If the past is a predictor, the personalized commitment of college leadership to the church and church leaders to the college is also the holding power for the future.

Third, the mission of Free Methodist colleges must be integrated with the mission and vision of the Free Methodist Church. In recent years the colleges made a commitment to the vision of the New Day primarily through the preparation of ministers at the collegiate level for the purpose of church planting. This represents a limited start on an integrated mission. The partnership of the church and its colleges needs to be expanded to include the development of lay leaders and members for the church, educational and evangelistic service to non-Free Methodist constituencies whom the colleges serve, and the moral and spiritual impact of the colleges on their communities and the culture.

Fourth, Free Methodist colleges must maintain the integrity of their mission in Christian higher education against the pressures of being driven by the marketplace. If Christian higher education has a fault line traceable through the period from 1960-1995, it is the shift in balance from mission to marketplace. The motive for the expansion of curricular offerings into professional studies, graduate degrees, adult learning programs and satellite centers must constantly be tested against the mission of the institution. If they detract from that mission or dilute the quality of education in order to increase revenues, they carry within themselves the fatal flaw by which a college loses the keen edge of its Christian character. Free Methodist colleges must continue to be mission-driven without losing their sensitivity to the marketplace.

Fifth, Free Methodist colleges must develop endowments as a sustaining base of support for the future. All Free Methodist colleges are enrollment-driven, tuition-supported and aid-dependent. These factors are out of the control of the colleges. From 1960-1995, enrollments have fluctuated with changing demographics and revolutionary cultural patterns. Tuition has continued to rise ahead of inflation or family income throughout the era, with the constant danger of pricing students out of the Christian college market.

Consequently, over this same course of time, Free Methodist colleges have become more and more dependent upon student financial aid from governmental and institutionally funded sources. Funds from federal and state governments are always subject to political whimsy, and institutionally funded student aid usually comes directly out of total tuition revenues. At best, the financial future of Free Methodist colleges is on a razor's edge. A major drop in enrollments, tuition or financial aid would jeopardize the quality, if not the existence of the schools.

The church needs to support its Free Methodist schools and students financially. The Educational Endowment Fund of $100,000 that was established in 1937 has never received additional funding, and the colleges remain woefully underfunded in endowments. The Free Methodist Foundation provides the vehicle for the development of endowments. If, however, the schools are to survive the fluctuations of the future, an all-out effort is needed from the church, the Foundation and the colleges themselves. The Free Methodist Futures fund for support of the Free Methodist students in the colleges needs to be revived as an indicator that the church cares about the students, as an investment in the future, both for them and the church.

Sixth, Free Methodist colleges must maintain their independence as church-related institutions. From 1960-1995 storm warnings were posted in church-state relationships affecting Free Methodist colleges. Seattle Pacific University went to court over its right to discriminate on the basis of religion in its employment policies. Roberts Wesleyan College confronted the definition of sectarian higher education in its application for Bundy aid for students from the state of New York. Spring Arbor College faced bitter opposition to state support for convicts enrolled in its educational program at Jackson prison. All indications point to increased tension for church-state relationships.

Free Methodist colleges will be at the point of the controversy because of their employment policies and their student aid programs. As the integrity of Free Methodist colleges depends upon their consistency with their mission, the independence of Free Methodist colleges depends upon the clarity of their rights and privileges with the state.

In 1989 Bruce Kline called Free Methodist higher education an "awakening giant." By 1995 it appeared that the giant was fully awake.

One of the major challenges for the Free Methodist Church in its New Day vision for A.D. 2000 is to capitalize on the full potential of this awakened giant. Rather than taking them for granted and expressing concern only in crisis, Free Methodist higher education must be an integral part of strategic planning for the future of the church.

C H A P T E R   14

Showing
Our
Compassion

ree Methodists are heirs to a social conscience as keen as their spiritual thirst, and a social compassion as ardent as their evangelistic fervor. Their legacy comes directly from the founding purpose of the church.

When the first mission statement of the Free Methodist Church was written in 1860, an inseparable link was forged in the twofold purpose "to maintain the Bible standard of Christianity, and to preach the Gospel to the poor." In a follow-up paragraph, this mission statement was grounded in the ministry of Jesus Christ. The *Discipline* read, "In this respect the church must follow in the footsteps of Jesus. She must see to it that the gospel is preached to the poor."

FREE METHODISM'S MISSION TO THE POOR — From this first mission statement came the character and identity of the Free Methodist Church. The *Discipline* continued, "Thus, the duty of preaching the gospel to the poor is enjoined by the plainest precepts and examples."

Even more specifically the first *Discipline* (1860) made reaching the poor the priority for evangelism in the church. In the same paragraph that links the mission of the Free Methodist Church with the ministry of Jesus, the church declares its intention to make "special efforts" to reach the poor.

B.T. Roberts embodied the mission of the church in his own leadership and ministry. In an article published in *The Earnest Christian*, January 1865, he wrote, "My special mission is to preach the gospel to the poor. ... The work is progressing and I expect to live to see free churches all over the land — especially in the cities where the poor are congregated. This is a blessed work!"

Roberts forged yet another link in his compassion for the poor. His stand against human slavery, which became the position of the church, is well-known. In retrospect, to link evangelism among the poor as the priority for the church with legislation for social justice among the races may seem to be a natural connection, but in the 1860s it put Roberts' leadership at risk. Individual redemption not social reformation was expected to be the role of the evangelist.

At even greater risk, in his 1886 book, *First Lessons of Money*, he revealed an economic philosophy that would open him to the charge of being a liberal today. Drawing upon biblical principles of economic justice, particularly as found in the Old Testament, Roberts opposed the political influence of money upon governmental leadership, proposed laws that prohibited vast accumulations of wealth in the hands of a few and even argued for the equal division of property among the populace.

Roberts' stand for social justice may have come at a time when the popular tide had already turned toward abolition. Equally controversial might have been Roberts' interest in the welfare of the farmer. He helped his son organize the Farmers' Alliance of New York as a labor union protecting their interests against the moneyed interests of railroads and banks.

B.T. ROBERTS' LEADERSHIP TEST — Roberts' leadership suffered when he made his plea before the 1890 General Conference for gender justice, namely the ordination of women in the Free Methodist Church. Far ahead of his time, Roberts saw the natural extension of the mission of the church to include those who were disenfranchised from ministerial ordination and leadership roles because of gender. When his plea for the ordination of women was repudiated by the 1890 General Conference, Roberts lost his leadership role. For generations to come, the keen edge of social conscience in the Free Methodist Church seemed to be blunted, and the hot fire of its social compassion seemed to be banked.

Benchmarks of Our Compassion
1960

When Bishop Marston wrote his centennial history of the church in 1960, he put strong emphasis upon the heritage of social compassion in the ministries of John Wesley and B.T. Roberts. Neither one of them wrote a theology that linked the doctrine of holiness with the mission of evangelism to the poor. Most likely, they felt no need to explain what to them was self-evident from the example of Jesus Christ.

Each of them, however, embodied this connection in their denominational leadership and personal ministry. Marston recognized this heritage in his summation of the founding principles of Free Methodism. Stewardship expressed as "full consecration of service to God and man" was one of those principles understood by "a sensitive social conscience" and expressed by the phrase "no slaveholding."

AGENCIES OF COMPASSION — In 1960 Bishop Marston did not describe the character of the church as pervasively influenced by its mission to preach the gospel to the poor or pointedly focused in its strategy of evangelism to reach the poor. Rather, he redefined social holiness primarily as "philanthropy," which was demonstrated either regionally in benevolent institutions or locally in congregations serving their community.

Because the purpose of his history was historical in perspective and denominational in scope, no specific examples were given of local churches continuing the ministry of outreach to the poor. But in the chapter entitled "The Outreach Through World Missions," Free Methodist mission stations in North America were included, with brief descriptions of ethnic ministries among Japanese, Hispanic and Native American peoples as well as among the poor of Appalachia. Social compassion was present in the Free Methodist Church of 1960, but not with the same pervasive influence or evangelistic priority of its guiding mission.

RESOLUTIONS OF CONSCIENCE — As the Free Methodist Church came to the close of its first century in 1960, its social conscience was expressed in a number of resolutions that had been passed by general conferences and confirmed from time to time. Industrial labor relations, a major concern of B.T. Roberts, continued to hold the attention of the church into the 20th century. At one time the church censured labor unions because of their secrecy, violence and communist influence.

In 1915 Free Methodists were forbidden to be members of labor unions, but through a succession of revisions and deletions a more balanced approach was taken in 1955 when the proposal of the Committee on Social, Moral and Economic Action was adopted. It made required union membership a violation of individual freedom and called both labor and management to moral, legal and financial accountability.

Other resolutions, which formed the moral and social stance of the church in 1960, included protests against militarism, with provision for Free Methodists to serve as conscientious objectors; endorsement of the temperance movement, while avoiding official alignment with the Prohibition Party; and the confirmation in 1955 of the historic stand against racial discrimination taken by resolution in 1886. This latter resolution came at the time of the Supreme Court ruling of 1955 declaring unconstitutional any form of racial segregation.

As a footnote on the social conscience of the Free Methodist Church, the 1951 General Conference passed a resolution in favor of the separation of church and state with specific disapproval of a presidential representative to the Vatican and public aid for parochial schools. The nomination of John F. Kennedy for the presidency in 1960 would test this resolve.

THE PENDULUM SWINGS — If the benchmarks of social conscience and compassion for the poor in 1960 are compared with the early mission of the Free Methodist Church, a swing of the pendulum is seen. First, the character of the church is no longer shaped by the drive to "preach the gospel to the poor." Second, the strategy to reach the poor is no longer the top priority for evangelism. Third, the leading vision for the church is no longer to see Free Methodists in every city of the nation where the poor are congregated. Fourth, the call for justice in the structures of the society continues in the stance of the church against racial discrimination, but with a shift away from economic issues and toward matters of political conservatism and personal morality.

Bishop Marston explained this shift in the character, priority and vision by the amount of leadership energy required to form and fund the Free Methodist Church as a denomination during its early years. Evidently, those same energies were applied to the continuing organization and reorganization of the denomination in the first 60 years of the 20th century.

When the Free Methodist Church celebrated its centennial year in 1960, the benchmarks were clear. The church still had the voice of social conscience and the hand of social compassion. But now these convictions were expressed primarily through resolutions passed by the general conference, benevolent institutions organized at the regional or conference level, North American missions among ethnic peoples, and local church ministries in response to the needs of its community. Energies of leadership at the denominational level were focused upon forming and funding denominational development, evangelism for church growth and overseas missions.

Against this background our question is: "What are the issues of social conscience and the ministries of social compassion that have helped shape the character, priorities and vision of the church between 1960 and 1995?"

Speaking Our Conscience

The prophetic voice of B.T. Roberts still echoes through the halls of Free Methodist history. The keenness of his social conscience matched the white heat of his evangelistic fervor. He confronted the issues of social justice and national morality. Looking backward we would prefer to remember his stand on issues of personal morality, such as abstinence from alcohol, tobacco, dancing, gambling and the like. There is less risk in speaking about these vices.

How faithful has the Free Methodist Church been to the social conscience of its founder from 1960-1995? A review of the resolutions passed by the general conferences of the church during this time will lead us toward an answer.

ISSUES OF SOCIAL JUSTICE, 1960-1995 — Since liberal Christianity took over the agenda for social justice at the turn of the century, conservative Christians have been relatively quiet in these matters for fear of being smeared as liberals. If the timing for a resolution comes after the risk is past, the prophetic voice is lost.

The record of the Free Methodist Church as prophetic risk-taker in matters of social justice is spotty at best. In 1964 the General Conference passed a resolution confessing its failure to speak out against the wartime injustice that put Japanese-Americans, including Free Methodist members, in internment camps along the West Coast. Although the apology came late, it spoke to the wounds of Japanese-American Free Methodists and laid the groundwork for rebuilding the Pacific Coast Japanese Conference as a model of ethnic ministries.

In 1964 a "Human Rights" resolution was passed by the General Conference and incorporated into the *Discipline*. In response to both human oppression in Communist and other dictatorial governments overseas and racial discrimination at home, the church went on record as a champion of human rights.

In 1969 another resolution passed by the General Conference specified racial discrimination as a violation of its stand on human rights. The year of 1969 signaled an era of peaceful protest in the African-Americans' March on Washington, counteractive violence in the assassination of Martin Luther King, Jr. and a myriad of policies and regulations aimed at ending racial discrimination by affirmative action.

Two questions remain. One is to ask whether or not the church could have passed a resolution against racial discrimination in 1964 during the heat of protest when Rosa Parks was ordered to the back of the bus, Martin Luther King, Jr. led the march on the bridge at Selma, and James Meredith was denied admission to the University of Mississippi.

The other question is to ask whether or not the resolutions made a difference in the direction of the church. The ongoing history of racial and integrated ministries shows some gain. In 1995 the church was still struggling with the issue and asking, "What should we do?"

One other resolution speaking to an issue of social justice has roots that go deep into the earliest years of the church. As B.T. Roberts spoke to the issue of labor relations in 1872, the General Conference of 1995 acted upon it, but with a difference.

Roberts advocated a labor union to protect farmers, and the General Conference of 1995 acted to protect the laborer from the union. As the pressures of "closed shops" mounted in secular employment and labor unions took on some of the characteristics of secret societies, the church came to the side of its members by supporting those employees who refused to join unions as a matter of religious conscience. As a specific protector of individual rights, the resolution may have been an effective tool for many Free Methodist employees.

Notably missing among the resolutions dealing with social issues between 1960 and 1995 are instances when the church took a position on economic justice for the poor. On such matters as tax and welfare reform to benefit the poor today or deficit reduction to benefit the next generation, the church has been silent.

ISSUES OF PERSONAL MORALITY, 1960-1995 — Because the Free Methodist Church has historically had well-defined behavior standards for its members, resolutions on personal morality have seldom come before the general conference.

Between 1960 and 1995 five resolutions fit this category. Two of the papers reaffirmed the position of the church on abstinence from alcoholic beverages. The first, presented to the 1964 General Conference, reaffirmed the position, while the second, presented in 1979, enlarged the position to include drugs and other forms of substance abuse.

Resolutions urging Free Methodists to exercise their rights as citizens were passed by the General Conferences of 1964 and 1969. In 1964 pastors were asked to challenge their members to be "active and aggressive" at the ballot box. In 1969 Free Methodists were urged to become more involved as citizens in community, political, social and service activities.

At the General Conference of 1995 a relatively new dimension of personal morality was addressed in a resolution dealing with entertainment. Recognizing the influence of new technology through E-mail, Internet and World Wide Web, the paper proposed adding "electronically distributed media" to the section of the *Discipline* dealing with entertainment. After referral to the Board of Administration, the paper was accepted so that the section now reads: "Many forms of entertainment (television, videos, movies, recorded music, printed material, electronically distributed media, etc.), though not inherently evil may have content that arouses fleshly impulses, rather than nurturing life in the Spirit."[1]

Except for the last resolution, which represented a response to developments along the "Information Highway," the genesis of these positions on personal morality is unknown. They are refinements of earlier positions of the church. They keep the church in pace with change but do not radically alter the expectations for personal morality of Free Methodists.

ISSUES OF NATIONAL MORALITY, 1960-1995 — As a moral voice in society, the Free Methodist Church addressed a large number of moral issues at the General Conference level between 1960 and 1995. A listing of these issues and the year of their adoption show wide range and timely relevance:

Family — 1969
Sex Education — 1969
Biblical Creation — 1974
Prayer in Public Schools — 1974
Abortion, Sexuality, Homosexuality — 1979
Pornography — 1985
Gambling — 1985
Abortion — 1995
Political Correctness — 1995
Abortion/Euthanasia — 1995
New Age Movement — 1995
AIDS — 1995

The issues of national morality which the Free Methodist Church has spoken about since 1960 tend to coincide with the debate over these matters in the public forum. Homosexuality, for instance, became a national issue in the late 1970s, when public polls showed changes in sexual morality and the Moral Majority began to speak out against the practice.

Most issues are a match for the conservative political agenda of the time whether secular or religious. Pornography, gambling and abortion have comprised the core of the conservative agenda throughout the 1980s and into the 1990s. Activity on issues of national morality picked up at the 1995 General Conference when the church spoke to such new moral concerns as euthanasia, political correctness, the New Age Movement and AIDS.

THE POWER OF RESOLUTION — What is the impact of these resolutions upon the church and society? For the most part, they state a position for the church on personal and social matters. In Chapter III of the *Discipline* on "The Christian Life," the section (Par. A/330) entitled "As Regards Myself and Others," many of the key resolutions passed by the church since 1960 are included as official statements, including human rights, abortion, war and peace, education of children and youth, entertainment, misuse of drugs, gambling, pornography and employer-employee relations. With the authority of the *Discipline*, clergy and laity have support for social action.

For example, since 1985 the Free Methodist Church has been identified with the National Coalition Against Pornography, with one or more of its leaders actively participating in its lobbying efforts. Generally, however, the resolutions are neither given to the press nor sent directly to organizations with influence in these matters. More often than not, they also grow out of individual concerns that are brought before the general conference and passed or referred without vigorous debate.

Resolutions give the Free Methodist Church a strong conservative voice in moral matters at the personal and social level. By their lag in timing and conservatism of content, the prophetic note of Free Methodism's early history is generally missing.

Struggling With Racial and Ethnic Diversity

Although the Free Methodist Church took a strong stand against human slavery as a part of its founding principles, the church did not follow through with equally aggressive action to bring the newly emancipated people into the fellowship of the church. At best, the history of the church between 1960 and 1995 was a story of starts and stops, gains and reversals, action and inaction in relationships with racial and ethnic minorities, especially members of the African-American community.

INTERRACIAL EVANGELISM — In 1960 the Department of Interracial Evangelism stood alone as the agency with the specific purpose of evangelism and ministry among African-Americans. With a view to the future, proposals were made for fund-raising projects to advance the work of the department among annual conferences and establish the Julia Shelhamer Reserve Fund to assure the survival of interracial churches caught in financial crisis or racial tension.

By 1964 the tide had turned. The Department of Interracial Evangelism had been absorbed into the Department of Evangelism and Church Extension without a separate director who carried a passion for the program. Inevitably, the thrust was lost and the only mention made of the ministry in the general director's report to the 1969 General Conference was to identify a church extension district named "Louisiana Interracial."

MINORITY MINISTRIES — In that same year, the General Conference took action to eliminate the term "interracial" from the denominational vocabulary and replace it with the words, "all peoples" in order to embrace the full range of racial and ethnic groups. Consistent with this change, assertive action was taken ordering the commissions on Education, Evangelism and Missions to collaborate in sponsoring a Council on Social Action for the specific purpose of "establishing a general church program of ministering to minority groups."[2]

At the 1974 General Conference, the Council on Social Action presented its first report. In that report, the original charge was enlarged to encompass "keeping abreast of the current crucial social issues" and "developing programs ministering to all human needs." No specific recommendations followed, and the original charge of "ministering to minority groups" had been generalized.

252

While the church was gearing up for social action in 1974, another report struck a note of sadness. When the general secretary of Evangelistic Outreach reported to his commission that same year, he included a brief paragraph commending the growth of the Shreveport Central Free Methodist Church and School. With enthusiasm he spoke of a "real breakthrough" when the pastor of the church and principal of the school visited the Louisiana Conference grounds and were "well received." He concluded the paragraph by saying, "We're hoping and working for the day soon when these wonderful people are fully accepted by the other churches and people of the Louisiana Conference."

TRIBUTE TO A JUDGE — The sadness is deepened by the fact that the most prominent African-American leader in the history of the Free Methodist Church came from Louisiana and the Shreveport church and school. Late in the 1940s, Gilbert James, pastor of the Shreveport interracial mission, stopped along a dirt street to invite a small African-American boy to leave his game of marbles and come to Sunday school.

Paul Lynch answered that call, came to Christ and brought his family with him. Nurtured in the ministry of that church and its school, Paul received a scholarship to attend Spring Arbor High School and Junior College. After graduation with an Associate in Arts degree, he transferred to Roberts Wesleyan College, where again he distinguished himself in scholarship, athletics and Christian witness.

The drive to excel led Paul Lynch to law school at Southern University. After graduation with a doctorate in jurisprudence *magna cum laude*, he married Doris, fathered a daughter, entered the military, rose to the rank of major as chief of military justice for the 24th Division of the U.S Army in Europe and then returned home to become the first African-American appointed as a Federal District Judge in Louisiana.

His denomination honored him as Layman of the Year in 1981 in recognition of his prominent witness as a Christian in public circles as well as his faithful stewardship to Free Methodism as a member of the local church, a member of the general church Committee on Ethnic Representation and trustee of Spring Arbor College. An untimely and tragic death took Judge Paul Lynch on October 4, 1982, at the age of 43, just after his morning jog and just before he was to address a legal convention in New Orleans. His funeral brought together the leadership of the church, the legal community at state and federal levels, and citizens, black and white, who had been influenced by his witness.

Other successes of Free Methodist interracial missions confirm the multiplied impact of the ministries of such pioneers as E.E. and Julia Shelhamer, followed by Gilbert and Esther James. Gene Alston, who was converted through the ministry of the Julia Shelhamer mission in Washington, D.C., earned a doctorate in education and became a prominent educator in both Christian and public schools. Major Brock, Jr., another alumnus of Shreveport Central School, rose to the position as chief administrative officer for the city of Shreveport. Together, they stand with Paul Lynch as tributes to the work known as "interracial evangelism."

AN UNEASY CONSCIENCE — The struggle of conscience for the Free Methodist Church in race and ethnic relations is not over. On one side of the ledger is the growth rate of ethnic churches. According to 1994 data, 150 ethnic churches with 8,338 members comprise 13.8 percent of all Free Methodist churches and 11.1 percent of the membership in the United States and Great Britain. Their growth rate, especially in urban settings, is pace-setting for the church.

The other side of the ledger cannot be ignored. Among these ethnic groups, only seven African-American churches with 423 members are listed. The lack of growth in this sector may be the effect of shifting focus from the African-American community through interracial evangelism in the 1960s to ethnic evangelism for "all peoples" in the 1990s. In any case the social conscience of Free Methodists rests uneasy.

As part of the Manifesto adopted at the New Day Mobilization Conference in December 1995, there occurred a telltale sentence of confession calling for reconciliation with the African-American community in particular. Together, the leaders committed themselves and their people to: "Reconciliation. Laying aside all prejudice and bigotry and taking the gospel and love of Jesus to people of all groups and every level of society, leading them to the knowledge of Christ and to full incorporation into His church."

At the 1979 General Conference the church grappled again with its social conscience for ministry among racial and ethnic minorities. A Committee on Ethnic Representation was ordered and implemented with the charge to work within the fundamental principles of the church and: (1) Correct our representational imbalance and strive for wide representation by establishing appropriate funding and selectional procedures; (2) Develop more appropriate leadership concepts which not only harmonize with, but will lead us toward attaining the stated principles of our church in these areas of great importance and sensitivity; (3) Prioritize the providing of denominational resources presently not available to our ethnic groups; (4) Institute a denomination-wide educational program through our publication channels and our educational and curriculum materials, by our own life and example, to create better understanding of the ethnic groups within the Free Methodist Church.

Bishop Parsons chaired the committee with representative members from the African-American, Japanese, Latin American, Arabic and Hispanic churches.

At the Board of Administration meetings in October 1981, the committee recommendations were as forceful as their original charge. For Free Methodist ministerial education through the colleges and seminaries, recommendations were made to recruit ethnic students, provide scholarship aid, adapt the curriculum to their cultural needs, and allow emergency certification for urgent church demands. The committee called for action on communication, education, church planting and leadership for ethnic persons in response to the evidence that one in five Free Methodist churches in North America was an ethnic congregation. From this committee also came the resolution of apology to Japanese Americans who had been forcibly relocated during World War II. The Board of Administration adopted the resolutions, but the record of follow-up was lost.

Recognizing Women as Clergy and Leaders

When Roberts carried his case for the ordination of women, at the risk of his leadership, to the General Conference of 1890, he had thoroughly researched his position from a biblical and historical perspective. Yet, he failed, not just by a vote of opposition against his recommendation, but also by a counter proposal stating the case negatively and positioning the church in strong opposition to women in ministry. An amendment was proposed to have the motion state opposition to the ordination of women even when "called of God ... and duly qualified." The amendment lost, but the main motion of opposition won by vote of 35 to 29.[3]

A LEADER'S LEGACY — Roberts died before the 1894 General Conference but not before his case was published under the title *Ordaining Women — Biblical and Historical Insights.* His conclusion in the book was the landmark toward which the Free Methodist Church steered on a zigzag course throughout the next century, "We come, then, to this final conclusion: the gospel of Jesus Christ, in the provisions which it makes, and in the agencies which it employs, for the salvation of mankind, knows no distinction of race, condition, or sex, therefore no person evidently called of God to the gospel ministry, and duly qualified for it, should be refused ordination on account of race, condition, or sex."[4]

From 1890-1911 the church seemed to go backward in its attitude toward the role of women in ministry. Then at the 1911 General Conference a proposal to permit annual conferences to ordain women as deacons failed in committee, but not with the necessary two-thirds vote that would have kept it from the conference floor. There the resolution passed, but with the clear understanding that the ordination of women as deacons "... shall not be considered a step toward ordination as elder."[5]

For the next 63 years women suffered the same injustice of *de facto* discrimination against ordination as elders and ministerial leaders as African-Americans did in the South after the Emancipation Proclamation. It is not surprising, no women held elders orders as the Free Methodist Church celebrated its centennial year in 1960.

BELATED LEGISLATION — Not until 1974 did the General Conference pass the resolution giving women equal status with men in the ministry of the church. This action cleared the way for women to be ordained as elders and serve in leadership capacities previously reserved for men.

History was made by this action, and within a few days after general conference, M. Jean Perry of the Pittsburgh Conference was ordained as the first woman elder in the Free Methodist Church. Ina Ellis, stepmother of Bishop Paul Ellis, followed almost immediately as a member of the Wabash Conference. Within a year, Mona McKeown became the third with her ordination in the Pacific Northwest Conference.

Throughout the remainder of the 1970s and most of the next decade, the women's movement in the Free Methodist Church continued along the parallel tracks of individuals coming to ordination as elders in annual conferences, along with the vigorous program of the Women's Missionary Society (WMS).

CATCHING UP WITH THE CULTURE — In the 1980s, American culture went through another social revolution that included the rising role of women as equals with men in their created personhood and full partners with men in social and professional life. Suddenly, the narrower focus of ordination as the definition for women in ministry exploded into the larger issue of the role of women in leadership for the church. The issue came forward at the 1989 General Conference with the proposal to change the name of Women's Ministries Fellowship, International (WMFI) to Women's Ministries International (WMI).

Under the directorship of Carollyn Ellis, in 1995 WMI was represented in the highest councils of the church. Ellis, for instance, held a place on the Executive Leadership Team of the World Ministries Center. She reported directly to the 1995 General Conference, even though WMI was still organized as an auxiliary ministry of the Department of World Missions. Representatives of WMI also hold membership on the Commission on Missions, along with a partnering voice on the Commission on Evangelism.

LEADING WITH PURPOSE — No department of the church has been more active in the 1990s developing programs to fulfill its avowed purposes.

256

In her report to the General Conference of 1995, Ellis listed more than two dozen projects that were either completed or in process. Projects aimed at meeting the first WMI purpose to "encourage women in areas of personal growth, stewardship, outreach and discipleship" included Bible studies, support groups, aerobics, community ministries, parish nursing and leadership materials for WMI chapters in annual conferences and local churches.

The second purpose to "broaden missions awareness through instruction of children, youth and adults" centered on various projects. These included missions education for children and publication of *Soul Afire*, the story of Free Methodist missions in Central Africa written by Bishop Gerald E. Bates.

The "stimulation of financial support for Free Methodist missions" continued to be a priority as the third purpose of WMI. Between 1989 and 1995 several millions of dollars had been contributed to World Missions. Funds were provided for the construction of the Women's Training Center in Cameroon, to establish a women's literacy program in India and to pay half the cost of an ambulance for Umri Hospital in India.

These projects also connected with the fourth purpose of WMI, to "interact with international women." During the six-year period, they fulfilled this purpose by sponsoring and funding area fellowship events for Free Methodist women in Asia, Latin America, South Africa and England.

As WMI gained visibility for its extended ministries, new opportunities came for women's leadership. The fight against pornography took Olive Hodson, vice-president of WMI, to a position on a national task force.

In response to requests, WMI published sex education materials written by Joyce Northrup Dodge. Again, WMI developed a program in Parish Nursing, led by Helene Kahlstorf, as a ministry through health care for the local church. To communicate the progress of all of these programs and create an interactive network among its members, WMI published a quarterly newsletter called *On Line*.

WOMEN IN MINISTRY AND LEADERSHIP — In 1994 WMI funded the Free Methodist segment of the Wesleyan Holiness Women's Clergy Conference in New Mexico. Free Methodist women clergy and students attended the meeting in response to the theme "Come to the Water." Out of the conference came the WMI publication *Common Call*, which joined 25 active pastors, 52 associate pastors, 23 retired pastors, missionaries or associates, 19 ministerial students and 75 clergy women in special ministries.

All of this evidence of the rising influence of women in leadership and ministry narrows down to their representation among general conference delegates, in executive officer positions, and on boards, commissions and committees at the denominational, annual conference and local church levels. In the 1960 General Conference five women were delegates, and no women were in executive leadership or on the Board of Administration. In 1995 women elected as delegates to General Conference numbered 41, or 13 percent of the total membership. Carollyn Ellis held a position equivalent to a denominational executive, seven out of 13 departmental executives were women, but only Betty Ivers served as a member of the Board of Administration.

The comparison shows that gains have been made for women in leadership, but not at a level commensurate with their numbers, influence and leadership potential. Opportunities for women in ministry and leadership continue to be a challenge on the growing edge of the Free Methodist Church.

Ministering Through Social Service Agencies

What Bishop Marston called "benevolent institutions" in 1960 are now "social service agencies." He used "philanthropy" rather than "stewardship" to describe Free Methodism's motivation for fulfilling its earlier commitment to social compassion through these institutions. With apology, the bishop also noted that these benevolent ministries were accredited by the general church, but founded by the initiative of the local church, annual conference or regional leadership. Even more apologetically he expressed regret that the denomination gave only token financial support to these social ministries.

According to the 1960 *Yearbook*, 3,000 persons were served through five benevolent institutions accredited by the church: Deaconess General Hospital and Home of Redeeming Love, The Gerry Homes, The Jolley Homes, Life Line Children's Home and The Woodstock Homes. In that same year their combined operating budgets came to approximately $750,000 and their combined net assets totaled $1.5 million.

A HIDDEN RESOURCE — The growth in size and significance of benevolent institutions between 1960 and 1995 is another of the hidden stories of Free Methodist history. Under the new title of the "Association of Social Service Agencies," five institutions have grown to 11 agencies. The Jolley Homes of Conyers, Georgia, are no longer included. So the seven new additions to the accredited agencies included Anvil Time, The Birth Connection, Clawson Manor, The Retirement Village at Copper Lake, Lighthouse Community Outreach Center, Olive Branch Mission and Warm Beach Senior Community.

These agencies continue to service the wide range of human needs from unwed mothers and inner-city people, including children, to retired senior citizens. In comparison with a ministry to 3,000 persons through five agencies in 1960, these 11 agencies now serve more than 121,984 persons annually. Combined operating budgets total $102.4 million and net assets approximate $102 million.

Denominational support, however, has not increased. The Easter offering, collected regionally, continues to be the primary source of church-wide stewardship for institutional compassion. In addition to the status of recognition by the church through its Commission on Administration, these institutions have also found cooperative strength through joint membership in the Association of Social Service Agencies.

David Fairchild, president of the Association, agrees with his predecessor John Ellis who stated, "The purpose of the Association is to bring together for fellowship, encouragement and cooperative planning leaders of the various social service agencies supported by the Free Methodist Church." The Association should also "establish a framework to assure that the mission and financial control of each agency meets the standards of the denomination."

Abbreviated descriptions of the agencies give us a small glimpse into their history and current ministry:

Anvil Time (Rochester, New York) is a national nonprofit organization dedicated to the restoration of inner-city, front-line youth through innovative, culturally relevant programs and services and dynamic leadership.

The Birth Connection (Sacramento, California) provides unconditional support, education and an alternative to abortion for women in unplanned pregnancy situations. The Birth Connection also offers community education and support groups.

Clawson Manor, New Life, Inc. (Clawson, Michigan) provides high-rise-apartment care for well, elderly senior citizens and the handicapped of all ages capable of living independently. Fully occupied are 179 efficiency and 85 one-bedroom apartments.

Deaconess Hospital (Oklahoma City, Oklahoma) offers medical, surgical, maternity and senior psychiatric care, and a wide range of state-of-the-art radiological procedures in its 250-bed hospital and 20-bed out-patient clinic. The Deaconess Home (formerly The Home of Redeeming Love) provides counseling, medical care and adoption services for women in crisis-pregnancy situations.

Heritage Village, formerly The Gerry Homes, (Gerry, New York) is a Christian retirement community with four levels of care for 300 senior citizens.

Life Line Homes, Inc. (Kansas City, Kansas) functions as a permanent endowment fund that provides grants for worthy projects in youth ministries upon written application from local churches, annual conferences, camps and other agencies.

Lighthouse Community Outreach Center (St. Louis, Missouri) provides recreation, educational support and substance abuse and violenceprevention programs for children, youth and adults in south central St. Louis.

Olive Branch Mission (Chicago, Illinois) consists of three ministries: Hospitality serving 500 meals per day and providing shelter to homeless people along with basic educational classes; Discipleship involving 18 men and women at a time who live and work at the Mission in a residential rehabilitation program for cocaine, heroin and alcohol addiction with the goal of independent Christian living; and *Christian Center for Urban Studies* through which 13 Christian colleges and seminaries send 400 students a year to Olive Branch for practical and accredited urban experience.

The Retirement Village Copper Lake (Edmond, Oklahoma) is an independent-living community of 119 apartments and nine townhomes for retired persons.

Warm Beach Senior Community (Stanwood, Washington) offers seniors a variety of housing opportunities including 48 mobile home units, 97 individual apartments, 32 residential-care units and a health care center with 81 beds and 24 boarding home units. The community began in 1967 as a ministry to retired ministers, missionaries, professors and lay leaders who had dedicated their lives to Christian service.

Woodstock Christian Care (Woodstock, Illinois) ministers through three divisions: *Sunset Manor* offers long-term care for 138 persons; *Carefree Village* provides 117 apartment units for independent living; and *Woodstock Day Care Center* offers day care for 123 children.

During the past 35 years, Free Methodists have continued to show their social compassion through their social service agencies. The number of agencies has more than doubled, and the operating budgets and net assets have multiplied many times. Local, conference or regional initiative still creates and sustains these social service agencies. While identified with the Free Methodist Church, funding support is, in some cases, significant but never large.

Most of the agencies are economically self-sustaining with some grants, gifts and contracts. While their ministries benefit Free Methodists in the region where they serve, the agencies demonstrate the axiom of Christian social compassion of being organized to minister to the needy beyond the denominational family.

Personalizing Our Compassion

Within the scope of social compassion demonstrated by the Free Methodist Church are projects that are more personal than institutional and more *ad hoc* than organizational. Only samples of these ministries can be cited.

BISHOPS' FAMINE AND RELIEF FUND — As a response to human suffering in Africa, the bishops established the Bishops' Famine and Relief Fund in 1975. According to the guidelines for the fund, the primary objective is to give a Christian response through financial assistance in cases of natural disaster or critical human need with priority in the areas where the church is in ministry.

Since the time of its founding, the Bishops' Famine and Relief Fund has received and distributed over $1,425,116 to people of impoverished areas and responded to such disasters as famine in Africa, hurricanes in Bangladesh, tornadoes in Canada, flood relief in the U.S. and cases of individual distress.

INTERNATIONAL CHILD CARE MINISTRIES — Still another expression of church social compassion is the program for International Child Care Ministries (ICCM). At minimal cost, a child is sponsored for food, clothing, educational opportunity and needed medical care in 23 countries of the world where Free Methodists minister.

The Rev. Alton Gould initiated the ministry in 1966 as part of the "rooftop" schools in Hong Kong. By 1990, the program had been expanded to an international base of sponsors with more than 4,950 children in the program. Five years later, under the leadership of Ann Van Valin who was appointed as director in 1990, the ministry has expanded to sponsor 11,100 children in 1995 with many thousands more either sponsored or helped in its 30 year history.

As a salient symbol of Free Methodist compassion for children overseas, a total of $15,630,233 has been given to International Child Care Ministries in the same period of time. With an administrative cost of only 15 percent, 85 cents on every dollar given to ICCM goes directly to support for the basic needs and the education of the children.

VOLUNTEERS IN ACTION — VIA, as it is known, began in 1972 under the direction of the Department of Evangelism. It is the domestic counterpart for North America and Great Britain for Volunteers in Service Abroad (VISA), a program of the World Missions Department. VIA gives opportunity for individuals and teams to donate their skills and time in service to other churches that need help, ranging from building construction to evangelistic outreach in urban, ethnic and racial communities.

Since its founding, VIA has engaged 28 individual volunteers and 140 workers in teams for projects such as building the Central Free Methodist Church in Shreveport, Louisiana. Rev. Donna Saylor is one example. She has served as a VIA volunteer in the inner city of New York since 1975.

THE LOCAL CHURCH A CENTER FOR COMPASSION — VIA illustrates the fact that social holiness is still a vital and voluntary impulse in companionship with personal holiness among Free Methodists. If that same impulse were traced through the community outreach of the local church, the list of creative and compassionate ministries would be endless.

Each new issue of *Update* newsletter and *Light and Life* magazine carries human interest stories of Free Methodists finding a mission field for ministry within their own community. Prison ministries, homeless shelters, police chaplaincies, parish nursing, pre-abortion counseling, anti-pornographic crusades, day care centers, hospice homes, and care for AIDS patients, unwed mothers, orphaned children, broken families and lonely or helpless senior citizens represent just a beginning of the continuously untold story of social compassion in local Free Methodist churches.

Both social conscience and social compassion in the Free Methodist Church are alive and well. If all the stories could be collected and communicated, the Free Methodist Church would stand out as a church that speaks its conscience and cares about its community.

Organizing a Caring Denomination

Free Methodists have always found a way to organize their social conscience and express their social compassion. At times, the organization is a task force in response to an urgent issue; at other times, it is a standing committee charged with responsibility for social action; and at still other times, it is a department or division integral to denominational organization reporting through a board or commission of the church.

COMMITTEE ON SOCIAL, MORAL AND ECONOMIC ACTION, 1960 — In 1960 a Committee on Social, Moral and Economic Action provided the leadership for resolutions coming to the general conference. The newspaper headlines of the times can be read in the resolutions brought to the 1960 General Conference and adopted as the church's official position.

Through the same committee, the General Conference of 1964 took another stand for human rights and social justice in the resolution confessing the failure to speak against the internment of Japanese Americans during World War II or minister to their needs. Along with the apology, the paper commended the Pacific Coast Japanese Provisional Conference for their progress toward full conference status.

Other social issues to which the 1964 General Conference spoke included a reiteration of the historical stand of the church in favor of total abstinence from alcohol for the individual and prohibition against the manufacture, distribution and sale of alcoholic beverages in the society. Free Methodist ministers were also urged to call their congregations to exercise their right to vote at the ballot box.

COUNCIL ON SOCIAL ACTION, 1969 — By 1969 the name of the committee had been shortened to the Council on Social Action. Again, their recommendations reflected the social revolution of the late 1960s, especially in the breakdown of the family and the continuing gap between the church and racial minorities. The resolution on the family put the church at the center of responsibility for building the family, ministering to broken families, working with disadvantaged children and monitoring sex education in the public schools.

The church entered an era in which position statements on the new complexities of marriage, divorce, remarriage and homosexuality would become a prominent part of its social stance. Racial discrimination resurfaced as an unresolved issue for the church. Whereas the 1960 resolution spoke generally against racial discrimination, the 1969 version put forth a proactive program for local churches.

At the 1974 General Conference the Council on Social Action moved directly in the mainstream of organization for the church. Gaining its authority and membership from the Board of Administration, the council took on the responsibility for keeping the church alerted to current social issues, formulating recommended positions for the church on those issues and developing seminars or conferences to assist members of the church to respond to them.

Evidently the lack of funding kept the Council on Social Action from becoming a functioning unit in the interim between general conferences. Consequently, at the 1979 General Conference a new proposal was made to establish a denominational Council on Social Action with essentially the same responsibilities as proposed in 1974 but under the Commission on Christian Education. A Committee on Ethnic Representation was formed with the responsibility to study the issues related to ethnic imbalance in the leadership of the church, ethnic disadvantage in denominational resources and ethnic bias across the membership of the church.

CONTINENTAL URBAN EXCHANGE, 1974 — In 1974 the Light and Life Men's Fellowship and the Department of Evangelism cosponsored the first Continental Urban Exchange (CUE) conference under the banner, "Consider the City." The conferees foresaw the future of Free Methodism in urban evangelism. From the stimulus of this inaugural conference, a new direction was set for the church, particularly among members of the younger generation of pastoral and lay leaders, whose heartbeat echoed B.T. Roberts' call for the church to preach the gospel to the poor in cities across America.

From the small beginnings of the first CUE conference in 1974, the *ad hoc* groups identified as the Committee on Social, Urban and Ethnic Ministries (SUE) and the Free Methodist Urban Fellowship (FMUF) were born in the early 1980s. Basically, these groups represented a younger generation of clergy and lay leaders who were staunch loyalists of the church, but concerned about the loss of its early compassion to preach the gospel to the poor in the major cities of the continent.

DIVISION OF SOCIAL, URBAN AND ETHNIC MINISTRIES, 1985 — The two groups came together at the General Conference in 1985 when the mandate was given to create a division of the church entitled Social, Urban and Ethnic Ministries, with a full-time director under the Department of Evangelism. The action was only partially implemented in 1987.

In 1994 the Continental Urban Exchange celebrated its 20th anniversary, and a long-time vision of the church became reality in the same year when Rev. Delia Nüesch-Olver, an ordained clergy person, was appointed as the first full-time director of Social, Urban and Ethnic Ministries for the Free Methodist Church.

AGENDA FOR COMPASSION, 1995 — With this definitive action came the agenda for the social, urban and ethnic ministries of the Free Methodist Church for the 1990s and beyond. Because that agenda is now official policy for the church, the essence of its 12 points is repeated here for historical purposes:

1. The future of the Free Methodist Church has an increasingly urban, culturally diverse future;
2. The Free Methodist Church cherishes the growing cultural, ethnic and racial diversity in our church;
3. As Free Methodists we are recovering the profound biblical convictions on social consciousness that are part of our history;
4. The challenge before Free Methodists is to face the reality of ingrained cultural prejudice, paternalism and sexism;
5. Recognizing the global dimensions of our ministry, overseas missions and North American ethnic ministries will network in planning initiatives within linguistic groups and in productive exchanges of leadership;
6. Ethnic/urban/minority leadership development is a priority of the church;
7. Regional metropolitan networks are being developed;
8. The thrust of social, urban and ethnic ministries is church planting;
9. Successful models of social, urban and ethnic ministries are being analyzed and the insights shared;
10. New Free Methodist social-service agencies will be launched to meet people's felt needs as an integral part of evangelism;

11. Every local church is challenged to get involved in some significant intentional social ministry to its community.
12. Social, urban and ethnic ministries carry the gospel to too many strongholds of evil and thereby require vigorous prayer, great faith in God and the overcoming power of the Holy Spirit.

At the Board of Administration meeting in October 1996, action steps were proposed and adopted to implement this ambitious agenda in every annual conference and department of the denomination. Particular attention was given to cross-cultural awareness and sensitivity as well as leadership development and organizational restructuring with a view to social, urban and ethnic ministries at every level of the denomination. Thus, this agenda in its action plan is now the benchmark for social action in the Free Methodist Church as it moves into the 21st century.

The agenda encompasses every denominational expression of social conscience and compassion that has been developing over the past 35 years. The statement penetrates to the roots of the church. Rather than being a denomination identified with small, rural, white and middle-class churches, the agenda forecasts a future of planting and growing racially mixed and culturally diverse congregations in urban areas.

Perspective on Social Compassion 1960-1995 and Forward

Once again the vision of B.T. Roberts is seen. If the agenda is enacted, there will be "free churches all over the land — especially in the cities where the poor are congregated." Roberts expected to live to see the day when this vision would become reality. The vision is still before us. Through the penetrating points of conscience and compassion as expressions of our social holiness, Free Methodism can once again discover "the blessed work" of ministry to the poor.

CHAPTER 15

Multiplying
Our
Witness

After its first 30 years of evangelistic extroversion, the Free Methodist Church turned inward in 1890 in order to form and fund a denominational organization. Bishop Marston, in his history, saw this introversion continuing to grow in the first half of the 20th century, until it characterized the personality of the church itself. With the inception of the "Forward Movement" in 1947, however, an attempt was made to change the outlook of the church.

By 1960 Bishop Marston saw the church exercising its rediscovered self-esteem through affiliations with "the larger fellowship" of the body of Christ. Rejecting sectarian bigotry, Marston characterized Free Methodists as "loyal denominationalists" with the confidence to extend the hand of fellowship to other Christian groups.

Marston reminded his readers that the preamble to the constitution of the Free Methodist Church stated that one of the purposes for the framing of the document was "to prepare the way for the evangelization of the world and a *more effective cooperation with other branches of the church of Christ* in the advancement of Christ's kingdom among men"[1] [emphasis added].

With this motive for cooperative affiliations reaffirmed in 1960, how has the Free Methodist Church continued to fulfill one of its founding purposes in the period between 1960 and 1995? Three discernible eras mark the relationship between the Free Methodist Church and other denominations or associations from 1960-1995.

ASSOCIATIONAL MEMBERSHIPS — As the Free Methodist Church crossed the threshold of its centennial year in 1960, the spirit of interdenominational cooperation and denominational merger engaged the energies of Free Methodist leadership. With the church as a charter member of the Christian Holiness Association, the National Association of Evangelicals and the World

Methodist Council, bishops and officers of the church held prominent positions in each of these organizations.

If concentric circles were drawn for each of these three organizations, based upon the commitment of the church and its leadership to their cause in 1960, the Christian Holiness Association would occupy the inner circle, the National Association of Evangelicals would be in the second circle and the World Methodist Council in the outer circle.

The Christian Holiness Association (CHA) held annual conventions to promote the cause of Christian holiness against a tide that had turned against the belief, experience and practice of entire sanctification as a second work of grace subsequent to regeneration. Presidents from our ranks were Bishop Myron Boyd 1968-72, and Bishop Robert Andrews 1986-88.

In recent years Bishop Clyde Van Valin, Dan Riemenschneider, Ray Ellis and John Van Valin have represented the Free Methodists as commission chairmen, members of the executive committee and board of administration, giving evidence of the denomination's continuing commitment to the message and influence of CHA.

Bishop Myron Boyd gave strong leadership to the effort to form a Federation of Holiness Churches. One of the proposals was for a joint complex for denominational offices and publishing efforts, short of actual merger. Many hours of study and dialogue were not successful, however, in forming a more cohesive bonding of the various holiness interests. The CHA continued to be the forum for such cooperative efforts.

The National Association of Evangelicals was born in 1943 as a reaction to the extremes of liberalism and fundamentalism in theology. Bishop Leslie R. Marston was one of the early leaders and served as president from 1944-45. He states the purpose of the organization was for "united evangelical action." It has been "effective in representing evangelicals where Bible-believing Christians need to be heard."[2]

The Free Methodist Church has had representation on the board of administration and several commissions over the years. Bishop Boyd served as president 1972-73, and Bishop David Foster has served on the board and executive committee 1989-97.

Other conferences of national and international participation in which Free Methodists have contributed are noted: U.S. Congress on Evangelism, Minneapolis, 1969; World Conference on Prophecy, Jerusalem, 1970; Strategy for Evangelism Conference, Morecambe, England, 1972; Conference on Evangelism, Lausanne, Switzerland, 1974; National Workshop on Race and Reconciliation, Louisiana, 1975; Continental Congress on the Family, 1975; Consultation on World Evangelization, Thailand, 1980; Task Force on the Family, Chicago, 1987; National Coalition Against Pornography, 1989.

The World Methodist Council was a different kind of association. Made up of denominations with a common Wesleyan heritage, the council ranged widely from liberal to conservative theology. Certain denominations, such as Free Methodism, took on the cause of preserving and advancing the historic position of Methodism in orthodox theology and evangelistic outreach. Some cooperative programs were developed in each of these associations but never with a view toward organic unity.

If the same concentric circles were drawn in 1995, the order would remain the same, but not with the same intensity of interest that characterized the earlier years. The Christian Holiness Association would still be at the center with a strong commitment of the church to its continuation, even though the group has struggled to justify its existence. The National Association of Evangelicals would still be in the second circle but with decreased visibility in top leadership from the church.

As for the third circle in which the World Methodist Council (WMC) is located, the church withdrew from status as a full member in 1980 and has since limited its participation to a fraternal relationship. The decision to withdraw from full membership centered in several live issues.

First, the WMC promoted the ecumenical movement. In this regard the role of the council was frequently misunderstood among laity, especially in overseas churches where there may have been confusion between the names and acronyms of the "World Methodist Council" (WMC) and the "World Council of Churches" (WCC).

Also, when the World Methodist Council opened dialogue with the Roman Catholic Church in the 1970s, Free Methodist churches in countries such as Ireland and Central America, where Catholicism is militant and sometimes oppressive against religious freedom, interpreted the conversations as compromise.

Perhaps most important, in many parts of the world substantial segments of Free Methodism came out of larger Methodism as protest movements over issues of liberalism and its outworkings in lifestyle issues. In eastern Europe, Free Methodism's attitude has been influenced by the experience of its sister church, the Hungarian Evangelical Fellowship (HEF), which views conciliar Methodism as one of the collaborators with the Communist regime and being actively among HEF's persecutors.

Still, with a solid core of leadership in the World Methodist Council being bold advocates of Wesleyan holiness and world evangelism, in 1984 the WMC chose to name the author of this history as one of five vice-presidents of the North American section and a voting member of the World Executive Committee. This opened the opportunity to include a portrait of B.T. Roberts among the founders of Wesleyan and Methodist denominations in the WMC museum at Lake Junaluska, North Carolina; to present the keynote address for the 1986 world conference in Nairobi, Africa; and to host the first international teleconferencing for world Methodism at Asbury Theological Seminary in 1994 to demonstrate the theme "The World is Our Parish."

In 1996 Bishop Richard D. Snyder was appointed by the Board of Bishops to continue representation of the church as a fraternal member, serving as a vice president of the North American section of the World Methodist Council.

Outside the third circle is the National Council of Churches and the World Council of Churches. In 1955 the Free Methodist Church had to decide how it would respond to an invitation for membership in these bodies. Because of their liberal policies on both theological and social issues and their rising interest in organic unity of participating denominations, the church summarily rejected the invitation.

DENOMINATIONAL MERGER — As early as the 1943 General Conference, the Free Methodist Church formally expressed an interest in exploring the possibility of merger with other holiness denominations. In that year serious negotiations began for merger with the Wesleyan Methodist Church (later named the Wesleyan Church) and received continuing support from the General Conferences of 1951 and 1955. But in their own General Conference in 1955, the Wesleyan Methodist Church terminated negotiations and put a temporary end to a courtship that had originally begun in the early 1900s. Despite the turndown, Free Methodist and Wesleyan leaders still nursed the hope for merger in 1960.

Specific interest in merger with the Wesleyan Methodist Church and general interest in union with other holiness denominations became a priority item on the general church agenda in 1968. In that year the Wesleyan Methodist Church merged with the Pilgrim Holiness Church and voted to reopen merger talks with the Free Methodists.

For the next five years the energy of the church and its leadership centered upon the articles of agreement, a massive document in which the polity, procedures and practice of the two churches were reworked in order to form a new church.

Sometime between the General Conferences of 1969 and 1974, the dynamics of interest in merger began to change. Prior to the 1974 General Conference, the Board of Administration of the Free Methodist Church expressed concern that the Wesleyan General Conference of 1972 required that certain key issues in the merger agreement must be stated in accord with their viewpoint. Those who remember that moment in history believe that an inerrant view of Scripture was a case in point.

Even though the Committee on Merger Exploration presented a finished document for vote to the General Conference of 1974, the Board of Administration recommended delay on the final vote until action was taken by the Wesleyan General Conference in 1976. Debate on the recommendation from the conference floor led to a vote of more than two-thirds of the delegates favoring merger in principle, but refusing to take final action until the 1976 Wesleyan General Conference formally expressed its intentions.

Whether the Wesleyan Church response in 1976 interpreted the Free Methodist action implicitly as a negative vote, represented continuing concern over issues of doctrine and governance, or reflected the fact the movement lost its momentum with the passage of time is a matter of conjecture. Perhaps all three factors played a part in the negative response of the 1976 Wesleyan General Conference

For all intents and purposes, merger talks died between the Free Methodists and Wesleyans. It was not a natural death. The death was traumatic.

When the issues were finally drawn, the two churches parted ways because of three fundamental differences. One, on the inspiration of Scripture, the Wesleyans tended toward inerrancy, while Free Methodists preferred a plenary viewpoint. Two, in Christian higher education, Wesleyan schools were church-controlled, while Free Methodist colleges were independent but church-related. Three, regarding the superintendency, the Wesleyans preferred the title and role of the "general superintendent," while the Free Methodists still esteemed their leaders as "bishops."

While these three factors were critical, they were not decisive. The leadership of both churches had taken the initiative to move ahead, but someplace in the process their followers turned a corner and left them out in front all alone.

The churches went their separate ways. Wesleyan interest in merger with other holiness denominations has stayed alive, but Free Methodists turned away from growth by merger in order to devote their energy to church growth at home and abroad.

The General Conference of 1989 revived interest in cooperative relationships with other holiness churches and groups but not with merger in mind. Rather, the mode of cooperation that the church fostered in the 1990s has been the development of specialized resources for denominational ministries with the goals of enrichment and efficiency. In 1995 ecumenism in spirit was still alive, organizational merger was dead and cooperative resourcing was being born.

TRANSDENOMINATIONAL NETWORKS — Throughout church history God has raised up *ad hoc* movements to meet changing spiritual and social needs that the institutional church has either neglected or forgotten. In the 1960s, the parachurch movement, particularly among high school and college youth outside the church, became a formidable force in evangelical

ιity. Headed by charismatic personalities and fired by the enthusi-
_____, outh, movements such as Youth for Christ, Campus Crusade, Young
Life and Navigators ran parallel to the youth ministries of denominations
and often threatened them.

Historical reflection sees similarities between these parachurch movements and the Pentecost Bands that challenged the flexibility of the Free Methodist Church in the 1890s. Also, like the Pentecost Bands, the church was not
quite sure how to handle the parachurch phenomenon. Not by coincidence
the most vigorous years of Free Methodist Youth as an organization overlapped with the heyday of the parachurch youth movement.

Many Free Methodist youth might have been members of both church
and parachurch organizations, but most observers of that era in the 1960s
saw these ministries running on parallel tracks past each other. To their credit
and in contrast with their predecessors in the parachurch movement, today's
transdenominational networks have stayed connected to the church and therefore have become instruments in spiritual renewal in local congregations. They
have shown promise of being vehicles for moral and spiritual awakening on
a national and even global scale. Still, they present a challenge to denominations and local churches that must be willing to share the time and money of
their members with these networks in return for renewal in the church and
awakening in the world. If there is a crunch to come, it is yet ahead.

Perspective on Cooperation 1960-1995 and Forward

One of the most dominant trends shaping the future of the church can
be detected in the attitude toward cooperation. Between 1960 and 1995, Free
Methodists, especially at the congregational level, turned their attention more
and more upon the local church and away from denominational loyalty, ecumenical cooperation and global mission. This observation reinforced the process of decentralization that was evident in church governance during the
same period.

Although no formal survey was conducted of congregational attitudes
in the mid-1970s, the inference seems clear that the Free Methodist-Wesleyan
merger failed because it lacked support at the grass-roots level in both denominations.

Be that as it may, there are lessons to be learned. One lesson is to acknowledge that the current climate of the Free Methodist Church tends to be
post-denominational. The prior assumption that congregations will follow
the initiative of top-down leadership no longer holds. Likewise, church leaders cannot assume that the traditional symbols and events that developed
denominational loyalty will still be effective today.

The basis for denominational distinction has changed. Some contend that denominationalism has outlived its usefulness. Others believe that denominationalism is going through another stage of metamorphosis on the way to a new form.

Robert Wuthnow, author of *The Restructuring of American Religion*, sees denominational loyalties giving way to a new division between religious conservatives and religious liberals. If so, how will the Free Methodist Church relate to the new configuration? For the future a "federation" of local churches serviced by the World Ministries Center may be more accurate than a restructured "denomination." In such a case Free Methodism would also have to redefine "connectionalism" around relationships other than organizational structure.

Another lesson from the findings of this survey comes with a touch of irony. Contrary to expectations, the advent of electronic media, which brings news and pictures instantaneously into our homes, may have enlarged our global perspective but not sharpened our sensitivity to human need. By withdrawing into the local scene, the individual chooses a manageable situation where he or she can make a difference.

Almost all of the cultural forces shaping the church today are moving inwardly and centering on the local church as a self-contained unit with a limited worldview. Missionaries may still be honored, missionary education may still be taught, and missionary offerings may still be taken, but they are peripheral to the purpose of the church.

The Free Methodist Church may be caught in this dilemma as it pursues a mission with two center poles. One pole is the outward look toward a world church; the other pole is the inward look toward the local church. Ideally, the outward look and the inward look are complementary.

Byron Lamson, general missionary secretary in 1960, saw that as ideal when he foresaw the growth of the world church. He declared, "If we give ourselves without reserve to save the lost world, God will take care of our church."

Even more emphatically, Bishop Marston wrote in the same year, "One of World Free Methodism's crucial needs in the decade immediately ahead is more rapid strengthening and expansion of the home base to insure financial support and missionary personnel commensurate with the world-encircling opportunities God has opened before the church. ..."[3]

Both visionary leaders would be disappointed by the evidence that the importance of Free Methodism's global mission has not kept pace with the rise of importance of the local church, especially in the minds and hearts of the congregation. While giving for world missions still exceeds giving for home ministries in the United Ministries for Christ budget, the budget is far below the opportunities and minimal when compared with increases in personal income, inflation and local church revenues. Special projects for world missions and North American church planting fared even worse. Whether from a limited perspective of world ministries or limited sensitivity to world need, special fund drives struggle to meet their goals and often fall short.

Free Methodism cannot avoid this dilemma now or in the future. For denominational leaders and pastors of local congregations, the challenge is to balance the vision of a world church with the vitality of the local congregation. Also, for the denomination, ways and means must be found to retain the values of a connectional church while respecting the individuality of the local congregation. The church must also decide its policy and priority for participation in cooperative associations, consortia and networks.

C H A P T E R 16

Profiling
Our
People

The movement of the Free Methodist Church from 1960-1995 is now recorded history. How has the character of the church been shaped by these changes?

In Chapter 3, "A Calling to Fulfill," the founding principles of the church were advanced as biblical convictions and denominational distinctives that characterized the church as it celebrated its centennial and anticipated its second century. These convictions and distinctives can now serve as benchmarks against which changes in the character of the church between 1960 and 1995 can be read.

As part of research for writing this history, a church-wide survey was conducted among more than 750 clergy and lay denominational leaders as well as local pastors and members of local congregations.

Ninety-three denominational leaders responded to the survey, including bishops, conference superintendents, denominational executives and both clergy and lay members of the Board of Administration. The group was then divided among those designated as past leaders who served the church in the 1960s and 1970s, present leaders who are currently in positions of leadership and future leaders under the age of 35 who have been identified for their potential in denominational leadership roles.

One hundred local pastors completed and returned the survey form. They represented a range of educational preparation from correspondence courses to graduate theological study and in appointments from small to mid-size and large churches. Sixty-eight members of five congregations also answered the survey. They represented churches in five regions of the nation identified by type — a traditional church, a new growth church, a church plant, an inner-city church and an ethnic church (see chapter 9).

Respondents to the survey were asked to rate the biblical convictions and denominational distinctives for their level of importance in the life of the church today. Their answers ranged along the line of five choices: very important, important, somewhat important, less important and no longer important. From their responses, changes in the character of the church could be read and comparisons made between the various groups of respondents. Statistical comparisons were run to validate the findings of the survey.

For the purpose of this history the report on the findings will be limited to comparisons between two groups of respondents: (1) past and future leaders of the church; and (2) present pastors and congregations of local churches.

For these two groups the findings of the survey showed: (1) The present level of importance given to the biblical convictions and denominational distinctives in the church today by past leaders, future leaders, local church pastors and members of local church congregations; (2) Significant differences between past and future leaders, pastors and congregations on these historic benchmarks; and (3) The effectiveness of the church as it balances pairs of biblical convictions and denominational distinctives along the line of a common dimension, such as the importance of education in balance with evangelism and the importance of the global mission in balance with the local church.

These findings test the working assumption that:

"The effectiveness of the Free Methodist Church as an organization is directly related to its ability to balance competing values in its biblical convictions and denominational distinctives at a high level of importance with minimal differences between past and future leaders and between local church pastors and congregations."

Through the Eyes of Past and Future Leaders

PERSPECTIVE ON BIBLICAL CONVICTIONS — A comparison of the level of importance that past and future leaders attach to the biblical convictions showed generational changes in the perspective of the church between 1960 and 1995. The following chart displays the comparative level of importance that the past and future leaders gave to the 1960 benchmarks of biblical convictions.

Dimension	Biblical Convictions — 1960	Level of Importance — 1995	
		Past Leaders	Future Leaders
Faith	Entire Sanctification	Very Important	Very Important
	Crisis Experience	Very Important	Important
Worship	Order (Sacraments)	Important	Somewhat Important
	Freedom (Visitation of Holy Spirit)	Important	Important
Growth	Education (Higher Education)	Very Important	Important
	Evangelism (Revivals and Crusades)	Important	Less Important
Witness	Personal Holiness (Separation from the World)	Somewhat Important	Less Important
	Social Holiness (Compassion for the Poor)	Somewhat Important	Important

From this chart, the following observations could be made. First, past leaders placed higher importance on the biblical convictions of 1960 than do future leaders in 1995. The key exception was the doctrine of entire sanctification on the faith dimension, which both past and future leaders rank as very important.

Second, past leaders gave significantly higher ratings of importance than future leaders on the crisis experience and on revivals and crusades as the primary mode of evangelism. In turn, future leaders gave significantly higher ratings than past leaders to social holiness as expressed through compassion for the poor.

Third, past and future leaders were in relatively balanced agreement on their rating of importance for the dimensions of faith, worship, growth and witness in the character of the church.

Only in the case of evangelism did the past and future leaders differ by more than one level of importance. Past leaders rated evangelism by revivals and crusades as important while future leaders dropped their rating of evangelism by traditional methods to the level of low importance.

To summarize these observations, the doctrine of entire sanctification continued to be the most important identifying characteristic of the Free Methodist Church in the minds of past and future leaders. In contrast, revivals and crusades as the primary mode of evangelism were no longer important from the perspective of future leaders under the age of 35. Other biblical convictions were less important to them, but not to the extent of reducing the effectiveness of the church by imbalance along the dimensions of faith, worship, growth and witness. Future leaders gave greater importance than past leaders to social holiness with emphasis upon compassion for the poor.

When this return to historic Free Methodism is combined with the high level of importance that they give to the doctrine of entire sanctification, there is reason to conclude that the church of the future can be stronger in its convictions and clearer in its identity than in the past.

PERSPECTIVE ON DENOMINATIONAL DISTINCTIVES — While biblical convictions tend to be grounded in the theological position of the church, denominational distinctives reflect the organization, governance and functions of the Free Methodist Church as an institution. The following chart shows the perceptions of past and future leaders related to the present importance of the 1960 benchmarks of denominational distinctives.

Dimension: Denominational Distinctive — 1960		Level of Importance — 1995	
		Past Leaders	Future Leaders
Governance	Episcopal Leadership (Clergy)	Important	Important
	Congregational Leadership (Laity)	Very Important	Important
Stewardship	Unified Budget (Denominational Ministries)	Important	Important
	Personal Tithing (Local Ministries)	Very Important	Important
Focus	Local Church (Well-trained Clergy)	Very Important	Very Important
	Global Mission (Indigenous Leadership)	Very Important	Somewhat Important
Direction	Connectionalism (Denominational Symbols)	Somewhat Important	Somewhat Important
	Ecumenism (Wesleyan/Holiness/ Evangelical Cooperation)	Less Important	Less Important

A reading of the chart revealed some fundamental changes in the importance of denominationalism to past and future leaders. First, past leaders rated all of the denominational distinctives as high in importance, with episcopal governance, the local church, global mission and a unified budget as very important. Future leaders also rated the local church and the global mission as very important, but rated down in importance the other denominational distinctives, especially a unified budget, connectionalism through denominational symbols and ecumenical cooperation.

Second, past and future leaders gave significantly different ratings of importance to key denominational distinctives. Past leaders rated as highly important episcopal governance under clergy leadership and stewardship for denominational ministries through a unified budget. Future leaders reversed the level of importance given by past leaders to governance by rating congregationalism with lay leadership along with personal tithing for the ministry of the local church as very important. Future leaders differed significantly from past leaders in their perception that connectionalism through denominational symbols was only somewhat important and that ecumenical cooperation with other Wesleyan, holiness, and evangelical denominations or associations was of low importance.

Third, despite their divergence from past leaders on many denominational distinctives, future leaders retained a balance on the dimensions of governance, stewardship, focus and direction for the church at a level of importance that retained denominationalism in a more decentralized, democratic and relational context. Reengineering denominational governance, reordering denominational functions and reworking denominational symbols to maintain the strength of connectionalism in the church were needs of the present and tasks of the future.

Through the Eyes of Local Church Pastors and Congregations

Another perspective on the character of the Free Methodist Church in 1995 can be gained by comparing the ratings of importance on the historical benchmarks of biblical convictions between pastors of local churches and members of local church congregations. The following chart shows the comparative ratings of importance on biblical convictions for pastors and congregations.

Dimension: Biblical Convictions — 1960		Level of Importance — 1995	
		Pastors	Congregations
Faith	Doctrine (Entire Sanctification) Experience (Crisis)	Important Very Important	Somewhat Important Somewhat Important
Worship	Order (Sacraments) Freedom (Visitation of the Holy Spirit)	Important Very Important	Important Less Important
Growth	Education (Higher Education) Evangelism (Revivals)	Important Less Important	Important Less Important
Witness	Personal Holiness (Separation from the World) Social Holiness (Compassion for the Poor)	Somewhat Important Somewhat Important	Less Important Somewhat Important

Surprising insights into the changing character of the local church were revealed in this chart. First, pastors of local churches gave lower ratings of importance to the biblical convictions that characterized the church in 1960 than did past and future leaders. A gap was also shown between pastors and people, meaning that congregations were even farther removed from the leadership of the church on the importance of biblical convictions.

Second, pastors diverged most significantly from the congregation in their higher rating of importance for freedom of worship involving the visitation of the Holy Spirit and the crisis experience. Also, while the pastors rated personal holiness with emphasis upon separation from the world as somewhat important, the congregations gave it a rating of low importance. For the doctrine of entire sanctification as well, while pastors rated it important, the congregations rated it somewhat important. Both groups agreed on the low importance of revivals and crusades as the mode of evangelism for the growth of the church.

Third, the biblical convictions that served as benchmarks for the church in 1960 were balanced at a relatively low level of importance for pastors and congregations of local churches. Generally speaking, it appeared that the pastor leads the way in setting the standard of importance for the congregation. Whatever level of importance the pastors gave to the biblical convictions of the church, the congregation tended to rate those convictions one step lower.

PERSPECTIVE ON DENOMINATIONAL DISTINCTIVES — Pastors of local churches and members of local congregations also rated the continuing importance of denominational distinctives that characterized Free Methodism in 1960. The following chart shows their responses.

Dimension: Denominational Distinctive – 1960		Level of Importance – 1995	
		Past Leaders	Future Leaders
Governance	Episcopal Leadership (Clergy)	Important	Important
	Congregational Leadership (Laity)	Very Important	Important
Stewardship	Unified Budget (Denominational Ministries)	Important	Important
	Personal Tithing (Local Ministries)	Very Important	Important
Focus	Local Church (Well-trained Clergy)	Very Important	Very Important
	Global Mission (Indigenous Leadership)	Very Important	Somewhat Important
Direction	Connectionalism (Denominational Symbols)	Somewhat Important	Somewhat Important
	Ecumenism (Wesleyan/Holiness/ Evangelical Cooperation)	Less Important	Less Important

Once again, we saw that pastors and congregations of local churches served as barometers for changing attitudes toward denominationalism. First, the most obvious shift from past leadership was the very important rating given the local church by both pastors and congregations. Pastors also rated as very important congregationalism with lay leadership, personal tithing and the global mission of the church. Congregational members separated from the pastors by giving balanced importance to clergy and lay leadership in governance. Most dramatically, however, congregations rated down the importance of the global mission of the church to only somewhat important. Both pastors and people agreed that ecumenical cooperation with Wesleyan, holiness, and evangelical denominations or associations was of low importance in the life of the church today.

Second, pastors and congregations of local churches differed most significantly on matters related to the global mission of the church, the leadership role of laity in church governance, personal tithing for support of local ministries and connectionalism as represented by denominational symbols. The pastors gave each of the denominational distinctives ratings of higher importance than members of the congregations, suggesting that they were guardians of a denominational perspective for the ministry of Free Methodism.

Third, despite their differences, pastors and congregations were relatively well balanced on the dimensions of governance, stewardship, focus and direction in their relationship with the denominations. The functions and symbols of denominationalism might be less important to them but they were not lost.

Profile of the Free Methodist Church 1995

Measured by the benchmarks of biblical convictions and denominational distinctives that characterized the church in 1960, a profile of the Free Methodist Church in 1995 showed both continuity and change.

FIRST, the identity of the Free Methodist Church as a Wesleyan/holiness denomination was still intact, but at a reduced level of clarity due to less importance placed upon its Wesleyan theological positions and its traditional denominational functions. This change was particularly evident among future leaders, clergy and laity, under the age of 35 and among laity in local church congregations.

SECOND, the center of Free Methodism had shifted away from a centralized headquarters and toward the local church, away from episcopal governance superintended by the clergy and toward congregational governance led by the laity. These changes reflected trends toward decentralization and democratization in the culture at large.

THIRD, while pastors and congregations differed on the importance of many biblical convictions and denominational distinctives, they were as one in the expectation that a well-trained clergy was very important.

FOURTH, major changes in the identifying characteristics of the Free Methodist Church since 1960 have been in evangelism focused upon revivals and crusades and in ecumenism with an emphasis upon merger and/or cooperation with other Wesleyan/holiness/evangelical denominations or associations. The change in evangelism was primarily a matter of method with the new emphasis upon church-growth principles and church-planting programs. The change in ecumenical interest reflects not only the general shift in religious direction, but also the focus of the vision of leadership in different generations.

FIFTH, the major imbalance in the vision of the Free Methodist Church in 1995 was in the importance of the local church at the expense of the global mission, especially among members of local church congregations.

SIXTH, the Wesleyan doctrine of entire sanctification had lost some importance, but the spiritual experience of crisis in conversion and sanctification had lost more. Semantics might help explain the loss of the importance for the doctrine of entire sanctification because polls showed that the thirst for holiness had not diminished in this generation. The influence of developmental psychology and evangelical theology might account for the lower level of importance attached to the crisis experienced by Free Methodists today. Each case warrants further study.

SEVENTH, members of congregations, despite the narrowing of their focus upon the local church, still held as important order in worship, higher education, episcopal leadership and an unified budget.

EIGHTH, changes in the shape and character of the Free Methodist Church between 1960 and 1995 tended to be generational and congregational. With each new generation, less importance was being attached to the 1960 benchmarks of biblical convictions and denominational distinctives. Also, laity in local church congregations placed less importance upon these benchmarking characteristics than the local church pastor and still less than denominational leaders. With each new generation of Free Methodists and with each new or growing congregation the gap was widened.

NINTH, personal holiness with emphasis upon separation from the world and social holiness with emphasis upon compassion for the poor have both suffered the loss of importance in the profile of the church for 1995. The identification of personal holiness with external regulations on lifestyle might account for a reaction against its importance and the rise of the denomination toward middle-class status might partially explain the lessened importance of identifying Free Methodism with compassion for the poor.

TENTH, the clergy of the church, at both the level of denominational and local church leadership, were the primary guardians of denominational distinctives.

ELEVENTH, future leaders of the Free Methodist Church put highest importance upon the doctrine of sanctification, social holiness as expressed through compassion for the poor, personal tithing, the local church and the global mission.

In sum, the profile of the Free Methodist Church in 1995 showed a strong church in its faith, a weakened church in its denominational connections, a searching church in its identity, a shifting church in its pattern of governance, a changed church in its methods of evangelism, a wealthy church in its human and institutional resources, a struggling church in its stewardship, a different church in its leadership, a transitional church in its congregations, a quiet church in its social holiness and a confident church because of its future leaders. With this profile silhouetted against the background of its recent history, the Free Methodist Church must now turn and look forward to the challenges of the 21st century.

Part IV

INTO THE
21ST CENTURY

The Years Ahead

A ll history leans into the future. Just as the past can be seen in the
present, a glimpse of the future can be seen in both the past and
the present.

Details of the future cannot be written with accuracy. Only a tentative
agenda for tomorrow can be projected from the trends of today. Even then,
future predictions are shaky in a world where chaotic change is constant.

Part IV is not a pre-history of the Free Methodist Church as it moves
into a new millennium. It is an invitation to open conversation about the church
of the future, and in a small way, to prepare the church for that future. By
realistically noting the challenges to the church along the trend lines of today
and even more realistically assessing the readiness of the church to meet those
challenges, a tentative agenda for the 21st century can be written.

C H A P T E R   17

Challenges
to the
Church

I s the past of the Free Methodist Church prologue to its future? A
simple answer will not do. A church, like the human personality, is
shaped both by its heredity and its environment. The Free Methodist Church has the heredity of history as represented by the belief, experience
and practice of biblical holiness. Not unlike the genetic code in the human
personality, Free Methodism is stamped with this image from the past, which
is also prologue to its future. If the church forfeits or denies this imprint of its
history, its essential character will no longer be Free Methodist.

Free Methodism is also a product of its environment. It began not only
as a reaction to the spiritual malaise of the Methodist Episcopal Church in
1860 but also in response to the moral issue of human freedom that divided
the nation. Environment continued to be a major influence on the church in
its first century.

Free Methodism from 1860-1960 followed the path from sect to church
and church to denomination as it searched for its niche in American society.
Likewise, between 1960 and 1995 the history of the Free Methodist Church
parallels the history of the evangelical movement through its stages of mass
evangelism, personal evangelism, church growth and church planting as
well as in its conservative stance on social, sexual, political and economic
issues.

Standing on the threshold of the 21st century, the Free Methodist Church
is an institution shaped by its past and a movement following trends into the
future. In this reality the church finds its strength. Along with all social organizations caught in the tumultuous times of accelerating social change, Free
Methodism in the future must be built upon the stability of its historical mission and the risk of change in its contemporary ministry.

Two questions must be asked: "What must the Free Methodist Church
preserve of its history to be true to its mission?" Also, "What must the Free

Methodist Church change in its future to be true to its age?" Inevitably, in response to these questions, there will be old endings and new beginnings for the church in the 21st century.

Benchmarks for the Church

The Free Methodist Church has had two historical benchmarks against which to measure change in its history. First, the founding principles of 1860 served as benchmarks for Bishop Marston's centennial history in 1960. Second, our review of those principles from a contemporary perspective provided benchmarks for the history from 1960-1995. But what about the future? What benchmarks can be set from which we can project the Free Methodist Church into the 21st century?

Certainly, from the history we have written, we can assess the current status of the church as it comes into the final years of the 20th century. Also, we can trace verifiable trend lines into the future. But can we predict the outcomes of those trend lines in order to begin writing an agenda for the Free Methodist Church of the future? At high risk we must try.

A wise futurist once said, "If you must predict, predict often." Forecasts of the future depend upon the predictability of trends and the stability of conditions for their accuracy. Neither of these factors is holding as we approach the 21st century. The speed of change is accelerating so rapidly that predictability has been replaced by uncertainty, and stability has given way to chaos.

Observers of social change say that there has been more change in the first 95 years of the 20th century than in all of the centuries since the birth of Christ. They contend that more change is taking place in the 1990s than in all of the nine preceding decades of the 20th century. Reflecting upon the changes in Free Methodism between 1960 and 1995, which have been chronicled in this history, could not the same be said for our church?

Yet most of these changes followed trends that could have been detected 10 years ago. Neither the spectacular growth of the overseas church, for instance, nor the continuing decline of membership in small, rural and static churches came as a surprise. Even the financial crisis of 1990 represented the culmination of a trend detected as one of the rising issues of the church in 1960.

So with some confidence in the discernible trends of 1995, a 21st century setting can be portrayed on the large screen showing a changing age with global and national trends that directly affect the mission and ministry of the Free Methodist Church. Conservatively, the trends can be traced along a rising straight line into the future, meaning that current movements will be magnified by A.D. 2001. Admittedly, this approach assumes some predictability for these trends and some stability in the speed of change along these trend lines.

If the past is prologue, however, we can expect surprises along these trend lines as technological or social change accelerates at revolutionary speed. The impact of the computer upon society in the last 10 years is one of these surprising speedups. Then again we must make room for intervening events, beneficial or tragic, that cannot be predicted. A nuclear war or a worldwide spiritual awakening could nullify all straight line predictions into the future.

No futurist of the 1960s, for instance, predicted the born-again movement of the mid-1970s. While Christians are called to discern the signs of the times in order to be more effective in ministry, we must hold lightly our predictions and be ready to welcome new trends initiated by God's intervening grace.

Futuring is a full-time occupation with many Christian writers. Book after book has been published on the church in the 21st century. Projections, paradigms and predictions abound in these writings. Many are relevant to the future of the Free Methodist Church; others are not. Our choice is to select from this myriad of forecasts three major trends that most directly affect the Free Methodist Church as it speeds toward the new millennium. These trends are related to changes in (1) communications technology, (2) demographic patterns, and (3) denominational development.

The Message of the Media

By now it is a well-accepted fact that our Western civilization is caught in the trauma of transition between the Age of Industry and the Age of Information. On a global scale the transition is even more traumatic because nations of the Two-thirds World are being dragged from the pre-industrial Age of Agriculture into the Age of Information with only an abbreviated stopover in the Age of Industry. For them as well as for us, Kipling spoke about our worldwide dilemma when he said we are "caught between two worlds; one dead, the other helpless to be born."

In the Age of Information, values take on new meaning. Wealth is no longer money but information. Power is no longer control of capital but control of information. The medium of communication itself affects the message. And with the bombardment of information upon the masses, leadership is the ability to make meaning out of the mush. Although the terms tend to be technical in definition, "data" are the raw bits of facts, numbers and ideas that are transmitted to the general public over the media, such as a statistic on the murder rate.

"Information" is data that has been classified into groups, such as crime statistics including murder rates. And "knowledge" is a perspective on information that includes value judgments and human insights, such as an interpretation of the meaning of crime statistics.

To advance these definitions one step further, "truth" would be a perspective on the meaning of information disciplined by a particular worldview. For us, "truth" is the interpretation of information from the Christian worldview as revealed in the Word of God and centered in the incarnation of Jesus Christ. John Naisbitt analyzed the frustration of our age so succinctly when he said that we are, "drowning in information, but starving for knowledge."[1] We would add, "... dying for the Truth!"

In the Age of Information options multiply. As information becomes available to the masses, people are empowered for decision making. Hierarchies break down because their leaders no longer have control of privileged information or the timing for its release to the public. Instead, communication media become instruments for individualism and consumerism as the masses are bombarded with information, given multiple options for personal choice, and urged to exercise self-interest in decision making.

Idealists assume that the discerning masses will sort out truth from error and right from wrong in order to make wise decisions that will advance the democratic process. Jacques Ellul, however, raises a warning flag on what he calls the "technological bluff."[2]

In the Age of Information, civilization can swing between the extremes of anarchical self-interest and authoritarian manipulation as well as come to balance in a democracy of informed and discerning citizens. Already, observers of the contemporary scene are seeing the manipulation of moral values and lifestyle standards by the "sports-entertainment complex" that dominates media programming and advertising. According to Robert Bellah in *Habits of the Heart*,[3] the pendulum is swinging toward the extreme of individualistic and utilitarian self-interest.

Another warning flag must be raised on the hope that global communications will create an alert and sensitive citizenry linked together in a world community. Initially this hope may seem true as viewers see both good and bad news of global consequences seconds after it happens. But then because the viewers feel powerless to act, recipients of world news tend to withdraw into the cocoons of their own homes, churches and communities, where they feel as if they can control their lives and have some influence on local outcomes.

As ironic as it seems, just when we can see to the four corners of the earth through communications technology, the prominent church historian, Martin Marty, rues the evidence that religious people are becoming more private, parochial, provincial and prejudiced in their world outlook. A "global village" populated by world citizens is still an idealistic dream.

A CHALLENGE TO THE CHURCH MESSAGE — Christianity is a world religion whose mission should be served by the Age of Information. Global systems put world evangelization within reach. Global news can sensitize Christians to the needs of hurting people in distant places. Global networks can turn the whole world into a classroom for teaching the Word of God and discipling the nations. Global interdependence offers the promise of a unity within the diverse body of Christ never before known. In a very real sense the Age of Information gives the Great Commission greater feasibility than any generation has ever known.

Hard truth also shows the downside of the Age of Information for the mission of the church. Rather than accepting the racial, ethnic and cultural diversity of the body of Christ around the world, Christians can divide over these differences. In place of sacrificial giving for the needs of suffering people, Christians can send tokens to assuage their conscience. But at the heart of the communications revolution is the question of truth. Instead of developing spiritual discernment for the values of the media, Christians can become victims of its individualistic outlook and pawns of its consumer mentality. In a worst-case scenario, the interpretation and application of the Word of God would become a private and subjective matter fashioned to justify the whims of self-interest.

One might say that the Age of Information has taken us back to the Garden of Eden, where the potential for good or evil has eternal consequences. Or perhaps we have already lost our innocence and are running through flaming swords toward a hostile world.

In either case we are in a crisis of truth. How do we sort out truth from error? How do we determine right from wrong? How do we retain the integrity of Christian faith? How does the Word of God discipline our minds as well as our lifestyle? What is the role of the church as the agent of the Holy Spirit in a truth-starved age? As with our Edenic ancestors, the answers to these questions have eternal consequences.

The Demographics of Diversity

In 1995 the globe was occupied by approximately 7 billion people. By A.D. 2001 those numbers may increase to a world population of 10 or more billion. The sheer weight of these numbers presents a challenge to Christianity with its commitment to world evangelization. But hidden within the population statistics are demographic facts that are even more challenging to the church.

Evangelization of the world's growing masses must be conceived in the context of ever-increasing diversity among people and groups. If, for instance, we assume that the world population in 1995 could be compressed into a

village of just 100 people, it would look like this:
There would be 57 Asians, 21 Europeans, 14 North and South
Americans and 8 Africans; 70 of the 100 would be non-white, 30
would be white;
70 would be non-Christians, 30 would be Christians;
50 percent of the wealth of the village would be in the hands of six
people; all six would be citizens of the United States;
70 would be illiterate;
50 would suffer from malnutrition;
80 would live in sub-standard housing; and only one would have
a college education.

As the world grows in numbers the demographics of diversity will become more pronounced. As reported by American Demographics, "You will know that you are in the 21st century when everyone belongs to a minority group!"[4]

It is not enough to see that these demographics are changing the world. With even greater force they are turning the Western world, especially North America, upside down. Although the population of the United States is projected to increase only 7 percent between 1995 and A.D. 2000, African Americans and immigrants, primarily from Asia, will combine to account for the majority of the increase. In fact, due to declining birth rates, Caucasians are expected to reach zero population growth by 2000 and represent the bulk of the aging population over the age of 65.

Along with the demographic shifts in race, age and ethnicity will come an ever-widening range of religious pluralism. African Americans, Hispanic and Asian churches are predicted to grow rapidly along with Muslims, Hindus, Buddhists and Baha'i. Also, what Robert Ellwood calls "alternative altars" will be erected in the name of cults, the occult, science, ecology, self-help and feminism.[5]

Demographic change will be further complicated as the new diversity among minority groups in the United States leads to new segmentation among people.[6] Racial differences will lead the way in the coloring of America. Close behind will come the segments of age as the nation grows gray. Gender differences will create other segments as women enter leadership fields, including the clergy, and demonstrate gifts traditionally attributed to men. Generational segments will widen the gaps between baby boosters (those born before 1945), baby boomers (those born between 1946 and 1964), baby busters (those born between 1961 and 1981) and baby boom echoes (those born after 1981).

Diverse family patterns will further complicate the segments. With only 27 percent of families fitting the nuclear model of two parents and children living together in the home, there are other growing segments such as the two-career family, single-parent family, blended family (after divorce and re-marriage), adoptive and foster family, extended family, cohabiting family and, if legal changes allow, the same-sex family. On and on the list of diversity could grow as segments are added for differences in geographical region, rural or urban location, socio-economic class, educational level and the ever-widening division between the "new-poor" children of single parents and the "new-rich" children of aging parents who are in line to inherit their wealth.

A CHALLENGE TO THE MINISTRY OF THE CHURCH — If the 21st century church is to be a growing and effective force in North America, it must come to grips with the demographics of diversity and the segmentation of people groups. More specifically the church of the next century must be a multiracial, multicultural, multigenerational, multifamily, multiclass and multilocational community of faith, not unlike Isaiah's vision of the Temple of the Lord as a "house of prayer for all nations" (Isaiah 56:7).

For most evangelical churches this requires a revolution. As predominantly white, urban and traditional churches ministering primarily to rising social classes and geared to the needs of middle-aged and older people, the demographics of the 21st century pose a threat as well as a challenge. Vision and attitude, mission and ministry must change if the church is to be effective in evangelism, discipleship and witness in the years to come.

As in the 20th century the melting pot became a salad bowl, in the 21st century the salad bowl will become one of the stations in an international buffet featuring food for every taste. Yet we know that not even megachurches and metachurches can be everything to all people. Spirit-guided leadership of the future will rediscover, communicate and act out the culture-free essence of the gospel in which diverse peoples and segmented groups once again become "one in Christ."

The Decline of Denominations

It is an understatement to say that the forces of global and national change are militating against the future of denominations in North America. As individualism and consumerism increase in the Age of Information, the commonality of old differences upon which denominations depend will decrease. Theology, ethnic origin, race, socio-economic class and governance patterns will no longer be adequate to justify denominational differences and breed "brand" loyalty.

Even the strong connectionalism of doctrine and experience giving identity to Wesleyan and holiness churches will suffer. To assume that denominations can continue to find their vitality and effectiveness in 20th century assumptions is to fulfill the cynical prediction that denominations will be the "cultural dinosaurs" or "irrelevant self-appointed regulatory agencies of the 21st century."

Lyle E. Schaller, in his book *Strategies for Change*, lists major functions from which denominations get their authority.[7] These functions center in the development and authorization of doctrine, worship, ordination, world missions, publications, church-state relations, benevolent institutions, ecumenical relationships and pastoral placement.

In each case Schaller sees the erosion of denominational authority. Doctrine is diluted; worship is free-style; ordination is devalued; world missions becomes individualized; publications are cooperative; new church plants are quasi-independent; brand loyalty has given way to denominational switching; seminaries are irrelevant; coalitions confront government; benevolent institutions must go it alone; and congregations want to choose their own pastors. As denominational differences are reduced and denominational authority is weakened, it is the clergy who become guardians of its values. Regrettably, this guardianship can widen the gap between pastors and people.

A new iconoclasm that denies the icons of traditional symbols adds to the dilemma of denominations. Whether rejecting the denominational name for local churches, letting teen-agers serve Communion, substituting song sheets for authorized hymnals, preferring parachurch rallies to denominational events, buying interdenominational publications for educational ministries, preaching without attention to the church year or winking at lifestyle expectations for membership, the new iconoclasm is with us.

All of this culminates in the sobering footnote that economics will determine the future of denominations. Without the financial resources provided through personal tithes given to the local church and appropriated for church-wide services, denominations cannot sustain the functions from which they get their authority.

A CHALLENGE TO THE MODEL OF THE CHURCH — While mainline denominations are the first victims of this malaise, evangelicals are showing the early symptoms of the same disease. Following the developmental pattern of their mainline predecessors, evangelical denominations that lose the "adhesive and dynamic principles" that brought them into being will turn to the functions of "regulating, granting, consulting, franchising, marketing and training"[8] in a desperate grasp to maintain their credibility. But as the scholars note, these functions "do not energize, do not adhere, do not unite the denominations in the way that the grand cause of a Christian America once did."[9]

Consequently, local congregations chart their own courses, appeal to consumer motives and follow the success syndrome of megachurches and metachurches with their "mall-like congregations offering both superstore and boutique religion."[10] For many members there is more loyalty to trans-denominational networks, often created around a single issue, than to the denomination itself.

As dire as these words may sound, religious scholars do not foresee the demise of denominations in the 21st century. To the contrary, they see them regaining their vitality as they represent a new set of distinctive religious communities. Schaller envisions growing denominations in the 21st century as those that emphasize five top priorities: "resourcing of congregations, mobilizing of resources for world-wide mission, planting of new churches, encouraging the emergence of more large congregations and enlisting a new generation of highly competent and deeply committed pastors."[11] With these priorities, the denominations must "display a high level of trust toward congregational leaders."

To this affirming vision, Robert Wuthnow adds what he calls Christianity's greatest resource, an orientation to the future with its central message of hope. In this, he sees the adhesive and dynamic principle for which denominations are groping in the era called "Post-denominational Confessionalism," as characterized by the privatized faith of a growing number of believers who are not belongers. Sooner or later they will return. When they do, the denominations that symbolize hope in a community of historical memory, spiritual support and sacrificial service are due for resurgence in the 21st century.

21st Century Challenges for the Free Methodist Church

Out of these trends come three major challenges for the Free Methodist Church in the 21st century. First, as communications technology becomes a companion with culture in advancing the secular values of self-indulgence, individualism, self-interest and a consumer mentality, the message of the church will be challenged. At stake will be the doctrine of holiness and its theological implications. Personal holiness as expressed in heart cleansing and holy living are contradicted by self-indulgence. Social holiness as expressed in self-sacrifice and servanthood runs directly counter to the motivation of self-interest. Individualism as well undermines the nature of the biblical community and the theology of the church. A consumer mentality is the archenemy of the principles of stewardship in which Christ becomes the Lord of life as well as the Savior of the soul. No challenge is greater for Free Methodism in the 21st century.

Traditionally, Wesleyans are considered to be weak on systematic theology and strong on practical theology. In preparation for the 21st century, the key is biblical holiness clearly and concisely stated for the core doctrines of personal and social holiness, the nature of the church and the whole life character of stewardship. These doctrines must be communicated in relevant and meaningful terms to assist laity in developing discernment for making Spirit-guided theological and ethical decisions out of the morass of information offered through the media. Most of all, the Free Methodist Church in the 21st century must sound the keynote of the Wesleyan message, which blends "believing, being and doing" into faith, experience and practice in the totality of the Christian life.

The demographics of diversity present the second challenge to the Free Methodist Church in the 21st century. With the sheer weight of growing numbers and the increasing diversity among people, contemporary as well as traditional concepts of evangelization are challenged. Although the term "aggressive evangelism," which characterized the Free Methodist Church in its early years, has fallen in disrepute because of its implied militancy, Christians under the mandate of the Great Commission cannot adopt a "live-and-let-live" attitude of tolerance in a pluralistic society.

At the risk of misunderstanding and hostility, the Free Methodist Church must be engaged in the mission of "intentional evangelism" based upon the scandal of particularity regarding Christ and salvation without belligerence or condescension. Furthermore, demographic diversity will challenge a "market-orientation" that leads the church to establish its "market niche" based upon the readiness of people to respond to the gospel and their compatibility with the existing community by race, socio-economic class, ethnic origin, generational status or position on liberal-conservative issues.

The gospel must be "culture-free" in the new diversity just as it was in the New Testament when there was "neither Jew nor Greek, slave nor free, male nor female" (Galations 3:28). These differences in ethnic origin, social status and gender in the first century are just as pronounced as the new diversity will be in the 21st century, but more than ingrained attitudes will have to be changed.

The greatest challenge of the new diversity will come down to resources. Will Free Methodists, known as tithing people, be willing to invest their resources in ministries of compassion with disadvantaged peoples? The loop that began with the doctrines of holiness and stewardship closes in the ministry of compassion for the poor. This was historic Free Methodism at its best, and it is future Free Methodism at it finest.

The third challenge for the Free Methodist Church of the 21st century comes from the decline of denominationalism. The first issue is denominational authority. Traditional differences upon which denominations were formed, traditional authority upon which denominations were dependent, and traditional functions upon which denominations were validated have all given way to changes in the religious culture and evangelical subculture. Hierarchical authority must now be shared with decentralized units of governance; clergy leadership must be shared with laity; and male control must be shared with women. To the credit of Free Methodism these issues are being addressed in the 1990s. Full resolution, however, will require persistent attention to this fundamental challenge.

Denominational symbolism is another challenge for the Free Methodist Church in the 21st century. Identity for a denomination depends upon symbols, beginning with the historic name of the church and logo of the church and ranging through publications and mode of worship to a national or international headquarters. Free Methodism in the 1990s has already been witness to the reduced level of importance for each of these symbols as identifiers for the church and its members. Yet a denomination cannot exist without symbols. Therefore, the challenge of the Free Methodist Church of the future will be to infuse the traditional symbols with new meaning and develop new symbols with which the contemporary generation will identify.

Closely related to the challenge of denominational symbolism will be the retention of denominational connectionalism. True to its Methodist birthright, the Free Methodist Church has found strength in its connectionalism, not just by structure but by confession of faith, experience, witness and spirit. Over the years, its connectional strength has been the bond for the development of a denominational "family" with all the celebratory events that hold a family together. Even general conferences, heavy with legislative duties, have been a time of reunion for the family.

Now with the lessened importance of denominational symbols and reduced emphasis upon family events, especially among the younger generation of Free Methodists and the new generation of converts coming from outside the tradition, a rising challenge is to retain the strength of connectionalism at the denominational level in a changing context. Just as there will always be the need for symbols to give Free Methodism its identity, there will also be the need for some form of connectionalism to give the church its sense of family. Connectionalism through spiritual and relational bonds is a prime and growing asset of the local church. The challenge is to recreate similar bonds at the denominational level.

Is the Free Methodist Church equal to these challenges to its message, ministry and model in the 21st century? We have already seen that the past is prologue. Now we will also see that the future is in the present.

CHAPTER 18

Readiness
to
Serve

Is the Free Methodist Church ready for the 21st century? Under the vision and goals of the "New Day Under God," the church has projected itself into the future. The "New Day," however, must be likened to the architectural dream for skyscrapers in the renaissance of a city.

The vision for the superstructure cannot be realized without the support of the infrastructure upon which the skyscrapers can be built. So with highest commendation for the vision and goals of the "New Day" strategy, the question of readiness still depends upon the continuing strength and contemporary vitality of the foundational principles upon which the church of the future will be built.

By combining the assessment of strengths and weaknesses in the mission and ministry of the church with the evidence of stability and change in support for its foundational principles, the groundwork can be laid for writing a working agenda for Free Methodism in the 21st century. Unanimous agreement is not expected on these results, but the process will be justified if it opens vigorous and constructive debate on the future of the church at all levels, in all sectors and among all people who are called Free Methodists.

An overview of the history of the Free Methodist Church from 1960-1995 leads to observations about established and emergent strengths as well as evident weaknesses and incipient threats. In combination these observations become a profile on the readiness of the church for the 21st century.

Established Strengths of the Free Methodist Church

The greatest strength of the Free Methodist Church in the last decade of the 20th century is its hope-filled vision of the future. Denominational self-esteem has risen on that vision, and the church is looking forward and outward once again. The prominent strengths undergirding that vision, however, come out of history. These strengths are foundational building blocks for the future.

1. THEOLOGICAL INTEGRITY — Free Methodism, along with other movements in the Wesleyan tradition, has frequently been accused of being theologically "soft" and susceptible to liberalizing influences. John Wesley himself was accused of being more interested in orthopraxy (practical theology) than in orthodoxy (systematic theology). In truth Wesley brought balance to the two dimensions of theology when other traditions swung from one extreme to the other.

Yet we cannot deny that Wesleyans walk theologically on a "razor's edge." Many denominations with Wesleyan roots have fallen prey to the wiles of modernity as defined by Thomas Oden.[1] The Free Methodist Church, however, can look back upon its history between 1960 and 1995 and conclude that it has remained true to its biblical, Arminian, Wesleyan, holiness and evangelical roots.

In fact, through its Study Commission on Doctrine (SCOD), the case can be made that Free Methodists regained a leadership role in relating biblical and Wesleyan theology to contemporary issues. In the 1970s Free Methodists and Wesleyans studied in depth their theological positions, especially the doctrine of entire sanctification, as they anticipated denominational merger. In the 1980s when a narrow definition of scriptural inerrancy rising out of Reformed Theology became a litmus test for evangelical credibility, Free Methodists reviewed their theological background and held firm to their Wesleyan position.

The 1990s brought a new challenge regarding membership requirements. What might have been called liberal and conservative factions could have caused a deep division in the church, but instead SCOD drove the issue back to biblical and Wesleyan theology.

As the Free Methodist Church moves toward the 21st century, theological issues will be compounded by the battle for the mind of the masses and the warfare over moral, spiritual and ethical issues. For the future, Free Methodism brings the strength of its faithfulness to biblical and Wesleyan doctrine throughout its history, its openness to the study of controversial issues, its willingness to communicate its theology in relevant terms and its spirit of reconciliation around a biblical position for the sake of the church. If the Free Methodist Church continues to define its mission and discipline its ministry on the search and discovery of biblical and Wesleyan theology as applied to contemporary issues, the church will enter the 21st century from a position of strength.

2. GLOBAL MISSION — Every projection for the viable organization of

the future, secular or religious, begins with a global perspective. Whether in communications, economics, education, politics or warfare, the world became an interlocking and interdependent ecological system in which everything is connected with everything else. At the same time the specter of nationalism, based upon tribal, ethnic and religious differences, will not go away. Globalization is a balance between independence and interdependence among the nations of the world.

To this challenge the Free Methodist Church brings the strength of its history in the growth of world missions under the indigenous principle. As the church approaches the 21st century, when globalization will become a test of denominational viability, the Free Methodist Church brings its record of spectacular growth in overseas churches leading to the formation of general conferences under national leadership.

The New Day goals for 500,000 members of overseas churches with 10 or more general conferences and a Free Methodist presence in 50 countries by A.D 2000 is a show of confidence in the momentum of world missions into the 21st century.

3. EVANGELISTIC PRIORITY — Free Methodism took more than three-quarters of a century to recover from decisions of the 1890s that blunted the initiative of aggressive evangelism that accounted for the spectacular growth of the church in its first 30 years. Evangelism remained high on the denominational agenda through its first century and into the decade of the 1970s. A Manifesto on Evangelism, initiated by the Board of Bishops in 1976, adopted by the Board of Administration in 1978 and confirmed by the General Conference of 1979, changed the focus and direction of the church. Aggressive evangelism, under the less offensive name of church growth, once again became the centerpiece for the mission of the church, occupying first position in its priorities and marshaling all its resources in the ministry of outreach.

The church has not backed away from its evangelistic mandate. Whether through the Bishops' School for Renewal, Superintendents' Convocations, New Day goals, church-planting projects or urban and ethnic ministries, the Free Methodist Church is intentionally evangelistic. The results are mixed.

Growth in total church membership in North America is minuscule, but vital signs of growth are evident along the coastlines, in some local churches and among ethnic groups in major cities. As the rising tide raises all ships, the rising tide of evangelism is raising all churches. Even small, rural and declining churches are beginning to believe in revitalization through the new mode of evangelism in church-growth principles and church-planting projects. If the focus of attention on evangelism and direction of outlook toward unreached people determine the readiness of the church for effective ministry in the 21st century, Free Methodism stands strong.

4. SHARED GOVERNANCE — To avoid the abuses that Free Methodist founders suffered at the hands of clergy-dominated conferences in the Methodist Episcopal Church in the 1860s, the Constitution of the Free Methodist Church required a balance of clergy and laity in the governance of the church. Although the scale was still tipped toward the clergy in key leadership positions throughout the first 120 years of the denomination's history, laity still played important roles in selected areas of governance, such as administration and finance.

Beginning in the 1960s the scales began to tip the other way. Under the influence of a culture in which leaders had to earn their authority and hierarchies had to justify their existence, power in the denominations shifted away from the clergy and toward the laity.

The Free Methodist Church was ahead of the cultural shift with a policy that went back to the writing of its original constitution. Out of the General Conferences of the 1980s and 1990s came actions which put laity into the leadership role of the Board of Administration and assured a clergy-laity balance at all levels of governance in the church.

The balance provides protection against the abuse of power by the clergy and the lack of theological sophistication by the laity. Although the test of the balance is yet ahead, the implementation of shared governance is a strength that readies the Free Methodist Church for a future in which clergy and laity must be complementary partners in the mission and ministry.

5. EDUCATIONAL RESOURCES — In the Age of Information, leadership belongs to the "knowledge industry." As noted earlier, whoever accumulates information may have wealth, and whoever controls information may have power, but whoever makes meaning out of information will be the leader. To this frightening future, the Free Methodist Church brings a strength that is yet to be recognized. Its system of institutions and affiliations in Christian higher education has outsized the church in the past, but as leaders in the knowledge industry of the future, the same system is an asset upon which the church must capitalize.

The Free Methodist Church and its educational institutions are mutually interdependent. The church counts upon the colleges to offer its youth the opportunity for Christian higher education, to prepare its clergy, to develop its lay leadership and to represent the church in its educational witness. In turn the colleges expect the church to provide the spiritual grounding for its future students, to encourage their attendance at Free Methodist schools, to provide current and long-term financial support and to serve as an alumni base for their graduates.

All these functions will continue in the future with the Age of Information opening new dimensions of ministry. The church will expect the colleges to lead in addressing the moral and ethical, theological and spiritual issues rising out of the communications revolution. Also, the church will expect the colleges to be developing students who are Spirit-guided, discerning consumers of mass information from the perspective of a Christian worldview, a biblically-based theological reference and a Wesleyan witness in holy living. In support of these expectations, the colleges will look to the church for support against the attitude of anti-intellectualism. Among the challenges for the Free Methodist Church in the 21st century none is greater in risk or potential.

Emergent Strengths of the Free Methodist Church.

Promise fills the future for the Free Methodist Church. Especially during recent years as the church has grappled with such crucial issues as mission, theology, organization, resources and diversity, new patterns of promise have emerged. They are still under test and will be further tested in the years ahead. Nevertheless, they qualify as emergent strengths upon which the future of the denomination can be built.

1. FREE METHODIST WORLD CONFERENCE — In support of its established strength in global missions, Free Methodist leaders have put the concept of globalization based upon the indigenous principle into a structure for governing a world church in the 21st century. Even as this history is being written, general conferences across the world are voting on the ratification of the Constitution for the Free Methodist World Conference. With ratification full franchise will be given for general conferences under national leadership and a scale of developing representation for mission districts, provisional conferences, annual conferences and provisional general conferences to move toward general conference status.

This new organization is a far cry from the original structure of the Free Methodist World Fellowship in 1960, which was convened by a North American panel with national delegates still in a secondary leadership position. The World Conference must be classified as an emergent strength for the future. If the organization comes to maturity in its informal dynamics as well as its formal provisions, it will quickly signal the readiness of the Free Methodist Church to move into position as a world church in the 21st century.

2. THE WORLD MINISTRIES CENTER — Denominations have a tendency to grow toward centralized authority, a hierarchical organization and bureaucratic procedures. They tend to lose touch with their constituencies but expect ever-expanding financial support. The symbol of these tendencies is to identify the executive offices of the denomination as "headquarters" with

nious subtitles as "The Vatican" of a Protestant church or "Mecca" ch its members bow.

The Free Methodist Church has been mercifully spared the worst of these evils. Nevertheless, in the development of the denomination, tendencies took over when the church was organized in 1931 on a corporate model and the move was made to Winona Lake, Indiana, where power came to focus in "Free Methodist World Headquarters." At the same time, the Free Methodist family looked to the gracious Christian conference setting in Winona Lake as "home" for the church.

In the 1970s, however, farsighted leaders of the church recognized that the world and the church were changing. Mission in the future would be global in context, and ministry in the future would follow the migration to the cities. As gracious and homey as Winona Lake had proved to be, its facilities were deteriorating, its location militated against cost- and time-effective travel, and its setting symbolized Free Methodism of the past, not of the future.

Two years of intensive study by a Committee on Relocation led to the recommendation to move denominational offices to Indianapolis. Heated debate preceded the decision of the 1989 General Conference to make the move to an urban site. Relocation required a long-term loan to amortize the capital debt and included the risk of moving before selling the Winona Lake property in a depressed real estate market. These issues, coupled with the financial crisis in denominational budgets, created another defining moment in the history of the church.

From the perspective of 1995, not only was relocation the right move for a church looking toward the future, but the move helped trigger a conceptual shift in the identity and function of denominational offices. The committee recommended that the name be changed from "Free Methodist World Headquarters" to "Free Methodist World Ministries Center." Symbolically, the name change was intended to signal the shift from the idea of headquarters as the locus of power to a hub whose purpose was service.

This shift paralleled the reorganization plan of 1990 in which the leadership, administration and staff of the World Ministries Center underwent change consistent with financial stringencies and the new model of service as a resource center for the denomination. Despite the strain of relocation, the storm of financial crisis and the stress of executive reorganization, the Free Methodist Church has moved from the prospect of crippling weakness to emergent strength in its preparation for the future through the symbol and service of the World Ministries Center.

3. PASTORAL LEADERSHIP — The history of the Free Methodist Church might well be written biographically through the lives of its denominational leaders, especially the bishops. In each generation, the church has

called leaders whose gifts matched the needs of the times. This same observation applies to the leadership of the church as it readies itself for ministry in the 21st century.

In 1960 Free Methodism flourished under a leadership pattern that tended to be "top-down" in organizational terminology. The locus of formal power rested in the Board of Bishops and the center of informal power in the hands of the designated senior bishop. The pattern matched the times and worked well. But by 1995 the church, as well as the culture, had gone through a social revolution. Power was no longer centralized at the top of denominational hierarchies but decentralized in the local church where the ministry meets the people. Right or wrong, the leadership revolution in Free Methodism has gone from top-down to bottom-up in the short span of 35 years.

The change in leadership has not been a knee-jerk reaction to social change. As early as the 1960s, bishops of the church asked for relief from administrative overload in order to give attention to their pastoral calling. In the 1970s they not only led Free Methodism to reestablish its priority on evangelism but followed personally with Bishops' Schools for Renewal throughout the church.

On the tide of these events, the bishops took another forward step in the mid-1980s when they cast a vision for A.D. 2000 under the theme of a "New Day Under God" and became leading advocates for church planting, church revitalization and urban and ethnic ministries. But the cloud of financial crisis soon cast a shadow over that vision. Reorganization not only reduced the number of bishops and increased their workload but also added to the role of the central area bishop the responsibility as overseer of the World Ministries Center.

These events have not been interpreted by the Board of Bishops as a loss of power or prestige. Rather, in a precedent-setting declaration at the 1995 New Day Mobilization Conference with all conference superintendents and denominational officers, they presented themselves as participants in the process of goal-setting for the future of the church with responsibility for co-creating a vision for the church, co-laboring with superintendents and pastors in seeing it through and joining with them in accountability for the goals that were set.

As an indication of their intentions, the agenda of the conference was revised at the request of the superintendents who felt that they needed to return home to engage their pastors and people in setting realistic goals for the local church. Goals would then be compiled into denominational goals in which all have participated. The superintendents vowed to follow the model of servant leadership that the bishops had demonstrated for them. Servant leadership is a biblical model that the future will demand. The Free Methodist Church may well have a head start into that future.

4. URBAN AND ETHNIC MINISTRIES — Despite its strong stand for freedom from slavery and compassion for the poor in its founding principles, Free Methodism in North America has continued to be a predominately small, rural and white church for the rising lower-middle class. Racial and ethnic diversity is synonymous with Free Methodist world missions, but in North America ventures in diversity have been highly selective and usually motivated by local leaders and churches rather than the denomination.

Examples range from the self-perpetuating churches of the Pacific Coast Japanese to the inner-city missions under the auspices of interracial evangelism in the early 1960s. These efforts, however, would hardly qualify the church to minister with strength among the rising numbers of diverse people and segmented groups predicted for the years ahead.

While the denomination may have been slow to address the changing demographics of North America during the tumultuous days of the 1960s, its conscience was kept by a small group of clergy and laity on the fringes of denominational authority. In 1974 Free Methodism went through a turning point when the first conference on Continental Urban Exchange (CUE) was held. The participants were primarily a younger set of Free Methodists with a keen social conscience, who might have left the church in another generation. Leaders of the church encouraged the movement and followed it through annual meetings until 1985.

That year social, urban and ethnic ministries gained recognition as an official division of the church under the aegis of the Department of Evangelism and Church Growth. Another decade passed before the division gained full status with the appointment of its first full-time director. But the mandate under which she will operate is a conscious commitment of the Free Methodist Church to be in the forefront of social issues, urban evangelism and ethnic ministries in the 21st century.

Meanwhile, church plants of the late 1980s and early 1990s in cities and among ethnic people are setting the pace for growth and putting out the challenge of diversity for all of Free Methodism. If a small, rural, white and middle-class denomination can catch this vision for change, it will be Pentecost!

5. MEMBERSHIP DEVELOPMENT — The action of the 1995 General Conference to revise the requirements for membership is too recent to warrant a judgment. One test will be to watch the numbers of conferences that exercise the "local option" to hold the traditional requirement for preparatory membership. A study comparing membership growth, maturity and loyalty in these conferences with those that enact the new requirements will be of interest in the future. For now, however, our observation of the action as an emerging strength or weakness must rest upon the biblical and Wesleyan basis that justified the revision.

To read the background documents for the Membership Covenant is to return to the roots of the church. The biblical theology and Wesleyan practice behind the revised requirements represent a landmark in Free Methodist history. Rather than assuming that theological precedent or traditional practice gave unquestioned validity to denominational policy, extensive research by theologians, historians and sociologists drove the church back to the point of its responsibility for discipling converts to Christian maturity. Such a position is consistent with the motivation of Free Methodists to "go on to Christian perfection."

Regrettably, the intensity of this drive has been diminished in recent generations, either because of the lack of clarity in communicating the doctrine of entire sanctification or because of the lack of understanding the experience in relationship to the wholeness of life. Also, the church suffered when external disciplines related to dress and lifestyle took priority over the internal disciplines of spirituality and service as evidence of holy living.

Now with the new membership requirements, Christian maturity is recast in a sound biblical and Wesleyan context as a process of spiritual development embracing both internal and external disciplines. To date, the Free Methodist Church does not have a good record on discipling its converts. Whether or not the new membership requirements will make a difference is an open question. If the local church becomes known for its discipling ministry, Free Methodism will grow strong. If not, the church will be seriously weakened by a generation of members stunted in their spiritual growth.

6. GROWING CHURCHES — To a statistician the Free Methodist Church is a conundrum. At the same time that a majority of its local churches report fewer than 50 members in the congregation, the number of churches with 200 or more members is the fastest growing segment in the denomination. In 1976 the Board of Bishops took the risk of criticism by giving special recognition to local churches with 200 or more members, and 50 churches qualified in that original number.

Since then there has been an annual meeting of pastors of growing churches with 200 or more members. By 1993 their ranks had increased, and the growth rate required a new category of churches with 400 or more members. Enriching those statistics were urban and ethnic churches, which were among the fastest growing congregations in Free Methodism.

The Board of Bishops in 1976 is to be commended for taking action to change the image of the Free Methodist Church from a denomination characterized by small, rural and declining congregations to one of large, urban and growing churches. This action was taken in confirmation of the priority for evangelism and with confidence in church-growth and church-planting principles as the primary method of evangelism. Undoubtedly, the proof that Free

Methodist churches can grow and be large is a stimulus for existing churches as well as new church plants.

At the same time, the profile of the church has been changed from a bell-shaped curve skewed to the left by a majority of small and struggling churches to the dromedary humps of small churches on the left and large churches on the right. As the church moves into the future, this division will be accentuated, and decisions will have to be made. Effective small churches will need to be recognized, struggling small churches will need to be revitalized, and if this fails, declining small churches will have to close. In any case, to assume that current demographic patterns will persist on a rising straight line of growth is fatal for the future.

Even before the 21st century has arrived, there is evidence that disenchanted urbanites are reversing the trends and returning to smaller communities and resort areas where they seek to reestablish hometown values. Yet they bring their urban values of bigness, change, diversity, conflict management and mobility with them.[2] While large and growing local churches represent an emergent strength in the Free Methodist Church, the greater strength of the denomination for the future may be in the diversity of its congregations and the effectiveness of various ministries.

Present Weaknesses of the Free Methodist Church

Even a strong church has weaknesses. The history of Free Methodism from 1960-1995 has revealed some present weaknesses and incipient threats that confront the church as challenges for the future. Some of these weaknesses and threats persist through the history of the denomination; others rise out of social change. Again, different observers would most likely make a different list with different priorities. The common goal, however, should be realistic optimism. By addressing the weaknesses and anticipating the threats, the Free Methodist Church can write an agenda for its future, rather than being either a passive victim of these trends as they develop or a reactive agent against these trends after they mature.

1. RETAINING THE YOUNG — It may come as a surprise to read that the retention of the young is first in the list of major weaknesses affecting the church. No resource is more valuable to the church than the next generation of its children and youth. This is more than the opinion of an author with a lifetime ministry in Christian higher education. George Gallup's polls and Dean Kelley's research mutually confirm the fact that strong and growing churches conserve their children and youth for active membership.

Free Methodism, despite its history of staunch family relationships and generations of leaders coming from within its ranks, shows signs of serious weakness at this point. Between 1960 and 1995 Sunday school enrollments in the United States churches declined from approximately 135,000 to 89,000 and Free Methodist Youth (FMY) enrollment dropped from approximately 12,000 to 8,200.

As early as 1961 the author of this history conducted a church-wide study on the retention of youth through the Sunday school and FMY to form a future pool of prospects for Free Methodist colleges. The timing for the study coincided with the denominational goal for the 1960s to "Double in a Decade." The results of the study revealed the fact that if the church conserved for future membership only 25 percent of the children and youth enrolled in its Sunday schools, the Free Methodist Church would double in the decade!

Membership statistics speak for themselves. The church is not growing by its inreach. Moreover, the priority given to evangelism by church growth and church planting puts emphasis upon unchurched people outside the denominational family. Goals for the New Day vision are also geared to external evangelism. Even the Christian education strategy to develop M.O.D.E.L. churches does not include numerical goals for increasing the retention of youth for membership in the church. Nor does either of these strategies sound an urgent note for making inreach to children and youth an intentional focus of the church at least equal to the mandate for outreach evangelism.

Advocates of the new strategy will contend that a holistic approach to families, both inside and outside the church, is a more healthful and more effective approach to church growth than the segmented plan of the past. They may well have a point that is yet to be proved. Until the results are in, the evidence that strong and growing churches give high priority to the retention of children and youth must stand as a fact that reveals a fundamental weakness in the Free Methodist Church as it readies itself for the future.

2. DISCIPLING CONVERTS — The most alarming statistic coming out of the Free Methodist Church in the 1990s was that more than 51,500 persons were converted in local churches between 1990 and 1995, while there was a net loss in total membership in the United States annual conferences for the same period of time, totaling 1,196 persons. More than 85,000 persons attended morning worship services during 1995 in comparison with a total membership of 74,735. The 1995 statistics also showed 9,191 persons converted through local church ministries. How can we also account for a loss of 1,184 total members, which translates into a 1.6 percent loss for the year? Assured that these statistics are accurate, we must conclude that Free Methodism is a church of lost opportunity.

Legislation enacted by the 1995 General Conference on membership requirements may have a positive effect upon these statistics. To assure permanent and long-term growth, however, the quality of discipling converts in the Free Methodist Church must be radically improved. The challenge for the church of tomorrow is to turn a major weakness into a prominent strength.

3. FINANCING MINISTRIES — The scarcity of financial resources is nothing new for the Free Methodist Church as it anticipates its ministry in the 21st century. Neither the church nor its members have been flush with wealth. Yet we cannot forget that Free Methodists have a standing reputation as a tithing people and that the Free Methodist Church always ranks near the top for per capita giving among all denominations in North America.

As the church made the turn into its second century in 1960, yellow flags of caution were already flying. In fact the beginning of the end of the "Light and Life Hour" can be seen in the financial pressure at that time. Free Methodists were not alone. Budgets across the spectrum of denominations were showing early signs of future deficits. And with other denominations, Free Methodists sought the remedy in a unified budget.

Although competition among departments decreased, the ever-increasing opportunities for denominational ministries led to ever-increasing budget goals. Denominational membership failed to keep pace with these goals for denominational ministries. And when the culture spun out of control in the 1960s, denominational loyalty was undercut along with the credibility of all centralized authority. These forces finally converged with full impact in the financial crisis of 1990, when resolution came by letting income set goals in the UMC budget and by downsizing the denominational organization and operations.

Free Methodism takes into the future a denominational economy based upon limited financial resources. The turnaround of the 1990s is a credit to tough discipline. The current financial organization that is managing debt, maintaining efficiency and maximizing services is a credit to sound stewardship. From this viewpoint a lean financial organization is a strength that readies the church for ministry in the 21st century.

But the threat is not over. Even with UMC goals set by feasible income projections, it is cause for celebration when the budget goals are achieved. Because the margins are so narrow, the relative strength of today can become a weakness of tomorrow. There is little room for resourcing the expansion of world missions or the inclusion of ministries for diversity or compassion, which need initiative at the denominational level.

Our survey of members shows that personal tithing still ranks high in importance among them as a spiritual discipline. It is the ever-expanding funding requirements of growing local churches and the attraction of parachurch ministries and trans-denominational networks that are competing with the denominational dollar. Without a significant increase in membership or a new commitment to denominational ministries, the limits of financial resources will continue to be a weakness for the church in the 21st century.

4. SPEAKING PROPHETICALLY — For a church founded upon its social witness, a strength becomes a weakness when the prophetic voice is lost. Currently the church has no instrument through which to speak out on social issues, except by resolutions at general conference. The result tends to be a voice that lags in time, speaks softly to political compromise and carries a small, conservative stick. A future filled with social, moral and spiritual conflict will test the strength of that voice.

The Free Methodist Church must decide whether or not it will have a prophetic voice to join with its evangelistic outreach and its pastoral ministry. Admittedly, the prophetic voice carries the highest risk. It will not always be the popular voice of conservative Christianity because the issues of justice as well as mercy and morality must be addressed. Here is where the recent precedent of thorough research into biblical theology and Wesleyan practice takes hold. If the prophetic voice of the church is timely and grounded in biblical and Wesleyan foundations, Free Methodism will find new strength in the future for its social witness.

Other weaknesses, of lesser impact, should be noted. One is the fact that a majority of Free Methodist churches have fewer than 50 members. It will become increasingly difficult to staff and support these churches with the denominational emphasis upon evangelism by church growth and church planting.

Another weakness is the lack of diversity in the leadership of the church, particularly with regard to women, minorities and youth. Progressive steps are being taken in each of these areas. The policy for change is in place, and apologies have been made for discrimination. But entrenched patterns and attitudes, often unconscious, must catch up with the formal action if diversity of leadership is to become a strength for the future.

Incipient Threats to the Future of the Church

While the weaknesses of the church tend to be internal, threats to the church tend to be external or created by circumstances or influences over which the church may have little control. Without elaborating on details, the Free Methodist Church should be alert to these incipient threats as its writes the agenda for its future.

1. CHURCH-STATE RELATIONS — Lyle Schaller sees deteriorating relationships between the church and the state as "the biggest cloud on the

horizon."[3] Specifically, he refers to the legal battles over tax exemptions and the use of land for religious purposes. This is not an idle threat. Even now the tax exemption for church property is considered a loop hole by many legislators and citizens. Abuses of the exemption by some religious groups have reinforced this viewpoint. Law suits are mounting over the varied use of land by churches for such purposes as day schools, counseling centers, gymnasiums and administrative offices.

In protest churches are claiming a violation of the First Amendment if the state should determine the nature of their mission and the definition of their ministries. If and when local restrictions that have already been imposed on churches, the pending lawsuits or the legislation arising out of state-wide referenda reach the Supreme Court of the United States, Schaller believes that the decision "on the use of land [will] move ahead of strategies for new-church development as the second most crucial variable in shaping American Protestantism in the twenty-first century."[4]

Free Methodist churches, whether small and struggling or large and growing, cannot afford the costs of either legal fees or annual taxes. Smaller churches might not survive, and larger churches could lose their growing edge.

2. CHRISTIAN HIGHER EDUCATION — Free Methodist higher education has been noted as a prominent strength of the church. At the same time it is subject to external forces that could jeopardize its integrity in Christian higher education and its relationship to the church. Because none of the schools has the luxury of sizable endowments, they are classified as enrollment-driven, tuition-supported and financial aid dependent. None of these factors is directly under college control.

Enrollments fluctuate according to the college-age population, tuition rises with the economy, and financial aid comes primarily from governmental sources. For most of the period between 1960 and 1995 the colleges have enjoyed growth in each of these areas. The margins of their operations are so thin, however, that a quick downturn in enrollments, tuition or financial aid could affect their educational and spiritual quality as they scramble for resources in the marketplace. As it is, the colleges are serving a shrinking pool of Free Methodist students who will become clergy and lay leaders for the next generation of the church. Further reduction in that pool because of declining enrollments, rising tuition or the lack of financial aid is an incipient threat with profound ramifications for the church.

3. GENERIC THEOLOGY — Warnings have already been posted about a future generation of evangelical Christians who are caught in a wave of theological heterodoxy as they interpret the Bible according to their own needs

and wishes. There is evidence that theological distinctions have been washed out into generic beliefs that characterize all evangelicals. For Free Methodists this means blunting their theological identity, especially with relationship to the Wesleyan doctrine of entire sanctification, the Wesleyan experience of spiritual crisis and the Wesleyan practice of holy living with social compassion.

Both secular and spiritual forces are moving toward a generic theology without labels. Although most evangelicals would be adamantly opposed to theological pluralism that has plagued mainline churches, they can become innocent victims of its influence under the guise of tolerance. Tolerance can mean an unwillingness to stand for the "scandal of particularity" in which salvation is found in Christ and Christ alone. Free Methodists are far from that position, but not immune to the forces that can threaten their theological integrity.

In the previous chapter we noted other threats against the future of Free Methodism in the form of global communications that can cause the reaction of cocooning in the security of the local church and the decline of denominational connectionalism in which Free Methodism has found strength. These, too, are incipient threats with which the church must deal.

Readiness for the 21st Century

Is the Free Methodist Church ready for the 21st century? Its evident and emergent strengths mean that the church is as well prepared for the challenges of the future as at any time in its history. Upon its established strengths it can build, and upon its emergent strengths it can grow. Free Methodism today has a vision that looks outward and forward with a new measure of denominational self-esteem. It also has the model of growth in the overseas church from which the North American church can learn.

All these advantages, however, stand in jeopardy unless the Free Methodist Church comes to grips with its evident weaknesses. An honest appraisal of those weaknesses along with decisions on their priorities will test the flexibility of the church in years just ahead. Meanwhile, the church must remain alert to the incipient threats to its ministry that will arise primarily from external forces. Paranoia and a defensive posture must be avoided, but an alert church is a ready church.

Anticipation, then, is the fulcrum of the future upon which the readiness of the Free Methodist Church depends. With the wisdom of the serpent and the harmlessness of the dove, Free Methodism of the future can remain firm in its founding principles without losing flexibility in its response to changing needs.

C H A P T E R 19

Agenda
for
Tomorrow

W hat will be the agenda of the Free Methodist Church for the 21st century? The recent history, current status and future readiness of the church converge in this question to create a strategy for its mission and ministry. By building upon its established strengths, developing its emerging strengths, addressing its evident weaknesses and staying alert to its incipient threats, a natural flow of goals and priorities will emerge as items on a working agenda for the 21st century.

With no intention of writing the official agenda for the Free Methodist Church of tomorrow, the following issues are put forward for serious discussion, in-depth study and careful planning. It is hoped that this agenda will provide a framework through which visionary leadership, effective ministry and stewardly accountability under the tutelage of the Holy Spirit will characterize the Free Methodist Church in the 21st century.

1. PROCLAIMING THE CENTRAL MESSAGE OF HOPE — A new generation of Free Methodists must not forget the larger motivation that led to the founding of the church and the meaning of the ministry in the 19th century. The founding fathers were driven and energized by the mandate for all Methodists "to spread scriptural holiness across the land and reform the nation." This motivation took them far beyond the reaction against liberal tendencies in the Methodist Episcopal Church or the protest against the evils of slavery in the society.

Both of these issues were resolved early in the history of the church. Yet the enthusiasm for aggressive evangelism, the discipline of experiential piety, the creativity of experimental religion, the commitment to preach the gospel to the poor and the conviction that the church had a mission in America persisted. Free Methodists believed that they were part of manifest destiny to spread the message of scriptural holiness, not just as a personal end for those fleeing from the wrath to come, but for the purpose of seeing a Christian America through spiritual revival and social reform. When Free Methodists lost this larger vision to preoccupation with denominational development or forfeited it to liberal Christians at the turn of the century, historically they opened a century-long chapter of groping for ways to become a dynamic movement once again.

Recent history gives Free Methodism hope. The church is rediscovering its self-esteem by looking forward through the vision of the New Day, the prospects of a world church and the anticipation of spiritual awakening in the new millennium. In the long run, this will not be enough. Doctrine and discipline must once again come together and be synergized by the power of the Holy Spirit. Free Methodists must joyously embrace scriptural holiness as the hope for a community of believers who will represent the counterculture of holy living in a selfish, secular society.

With equal conviction Free Methodists must believe that their witness of experiential piety, worked out through social compassion, is a redeeming influence that will be part of spiritual awakening and moral reform in that society. Skeptics who label this message of hope as "idealistic" forget that this is the legacy of Christians in every generation. Free Methodists have the message; they need the motivation. Holiness is hope.

2. CULTIVATING THE GLOBAL MISSION OF THE CHURCH — Free Methodism has a head start into the future with the strength of its world mission and the potential of its World Conference. Priority now needs to be given to the implementation of its global character formally in governance and informally in relationships.

The 1995 General Conference proved that the franchise for international delegates involved more than legal provisions for their representation. Barriers of cultural and language differences must be anticipated and overcome. Here the indigenous principle, which Free Methodists celebrate overseas, comes to its critical test. If full franchise is to be granted to delegates of diverse general conferences in a world church as an inalienable right guaranteed in the Constitution of the World Conference, it must mean shared power and mutual sensitivity for all participants.

Equally important, an understanding of the indigenous principle must be established throughout the global sphere of Free Methodism. A defensive attitude may be the first response to global connections. But Free Methodism in particular cannot crouch behind the fortress walls of an outmoded denominationalism with a siege mentality and remain viable as a church. An even greater threat will come if cocooning in the comfort of the local church becomes the prevailing mode of Free Methodism.

Now is the time to develop new lines of relationships for the global church. A beginning might be to create a network of sister churches with exchange programs for pastors and people. An advancement on that strategy would be to have international leaders become the teachers of church growth for North American pastors and Western resources fund missionaries from overseas churches to evangelize unreached peoples on this continent. Structure as well must change.

Very soon the World Ministries Center at Indianapolis may become one among many ministry centers strategically located in regions of the world or even a satellite to another world center located outside of North America. The ultimate would be to have all Free Methodists praying and working together for a great spiritual awakening that is global in scale.

3. NURTURING YOUTH FOR CHURCH LEADERSHIP — Not enough can be said about the importance of retaining the children and youth of today for the church of tomorrow. The Free Methodist Church cannot grow without an adjustment in its priorities. It must focus upon the trust that it has been given in the resources of the youth who are brought up in Free Methodist families, enrolled from non-Free Methodist homes in one or more ministries of the church or registered as students in Free Methodist higher education. Simple stewardship dictates this priority.

Evangelism among unreached and unchurched peoples may be more dramatic than nurturing the young but it is not so cost-effective. Money, time and energy multiply in aggressive evangelism. And the harvest is less productive when the Word is sown on a variety of soils. Not that Christian education should be done and evangelism left undone. Inreach and outreach are two sides of the same coin in the currency of the church. When Jesus presented the Great Commission in the strategy of concentric circles "beginning at Jerusalem," He left no doubt about the priority of the home base.

The Free Methodist Church has rare and valuable resources in Christian education for nurturing the next generation toward Christian maturity and church leadership. The strength of the Free Methodist family with its devotional schooling and parental modeling toward holy living and denominational loyalty is the fundamental resource. Building upon that foundation, the denomination has the components of a complete system of Christian education.

Beginning in the local church with the day school or similar ministries; advancing through Sunday school, CLC, Bible quizzing and FMY programs; offering higher education through Free Methodist colleges and universities and culminating again in the local church with opportunities for life-long learning, the Free Methodist Church has the makings of an educational system *par excellence*. The need is to integrate this system in progressive steps so that the nurturing of the young is a natural process that the elders demonstrate and the young anticipate.

Urgency attends this need. With the time-honored policy of balance between clergy and laity in the governance of the church, the leadership of the laity must be cultivated in each generation. Also, if the equipping of the laity for ministry is more than a buzz word for the local church, their effectiveness depends upon an educational system that assures their understanding of the history and theology of the church as well as the methods and techniques of evangelism and church planting.

In the past the nurturing of the young for leadership in the church has been a spontaneous process as generations of Free Methodists who were naturally identified with the church cycled through the educational system. Those generations are passing. Changes in the culture and diversity in the church now demand a more intentional and calculated process through which lay leadership is developed. An educational process cannot be guaranteed to produce the next generation of Free Methodist leaders. Until an integrated and progressive system of Christian nurture, based upon a sound theology of Christian education, becomes a priority of the church, the results will never be known.

4. REGAINING THE MOMENTUM OF AGGRESSIVE EVANGELISM — After a century of efforts to restart the evangelistic thrust that characterized Free Methodism in the first 30 years of its history, the church has regained a significant measure of momentum in the last two decades. Stimulated by church-growth methods and focused upon church-planting projects, the spirit of aggressive evangelism has been recaptured.

No apology should be made for "aggressive evangelism" because there can be no other kind. This does not mean using the wiles of proselytizing or the weapon of militarism. Aggressive evangelism is driven by biblical conviction, energized by self-giving, humbled by the spirit of Christ and dependent upon the Holy Spirit for results. Free Methodists should always be accused of enthusiasm for evangelism but never for the arrogance of aggression.

Can aggressive evangelism become a motivating force for the whole church? To date, the drive for evangelism has been most evident in pockets of the church. In the majority of local churches and among the majority of members, it is business as usual. Consequently, the losses outweigh the gains. The Free Methodist Church still needs a turnaround to be viable in the future. New churches must be planted, old churches must be restarted, converts must be discipled, and members must be increased.

Aggressive evangelism must be at the forefront of the turnaround but it cannot stand alone. In the eras of evangelism identified in this history between 1960 and 1995, none has yet made the difference for which every Free Methodist longs. Whether the problem is top-down goals, short-term fads, piecemeal efforts or promotion without accountability, the lessons of history must be heeded. Until the enthusiasm for aggressive evangelism permeates the whole church from leaders to members as it did in the first generation, there will be no difference. Methods can never be the substitute for motivation.

5. DISCIPLING CONVERTS FOR CHURCH MEMBERSHIP — Next to the need for retaining its youth, Free Methodism's greatest weakness is discipling its converts. The Free Methodist Church in North America stands tall among denominations for worship attendance that exceeds its membership and conversions through its ministries that are far above the norm. Despite these encouraging facts the membership of the Free Methodist Church of North America is almost stagnant, even in decline.

If the Free Methodist Church is to realize its untapped potential, the discipling of converts must become as important as winning people to Christ. The new membership requirements call for a discipline of discipling for which Free Methodism is not known. Heady evangelism is always more attractive than the hard work of making disciples. But with the action of the 1995 General Conference, the church has lost its excuse for the failure to grow. Denominational, conference and local church leaders must now give personal priority to the activation of a discipling system that will reverse the trend.

Recognition of large and growing churches must be matched by rewards for performance in discipling converts toward Christian maturity, into church membership and involvement in effective ministry. Again, the church has no track record for projecting the results. It is a fact, however, that the fastest growing churches are the ones that expect the most of their members.

Can the Free Methodist Church in North America grow again? It can and will if pastors and people come to grips with the twofold truth that the growth of the church depends upon the nurturing of its young and the discipling of its converts.

6. ASSURING A QUALITY CLERGY — Contrary to trends that mute the authority and influence of the ordained clergy, Free Methodists still esteem their pastors as men and women called of God. They expect them to be spiritually credible, professionally competent and personally confident in their appointed role.

As noted earlier, one of the major trends in the Free Methodist Church between 1960 and 1995 has been a shift away from the narrowing of the track for clergy preparation at the seminary level and toward the broader, three-track option for ministerial education. A companion shift has been away from the theories of systematic theology to the methods of practical theology. These trends carry with them the danger of lowering the professional standards for clergy at the same time that the oncoming generation of laity is better educated than ever before. Let the church be warned. If the qualifications of the laity are on the rise at the same time that the expectations for the clergy are on the decline, Free Methodism is creating the condition for future loss in the local church.

History also suggests that one of the key factors in the trend away from the expectation for seminary education has been the predominance of small and struggling churches that cannot support a full-time pastor. By A.D. 2000 it is predicted that a minimum of 150 members will be required to sustain a full-time pastor. If so the church may be caught in the vicious cycle of reduced expectations for clergy preparation in order to perpetuate a majority of Free Methodist churches with 50 or fewer members.

Another crisis could develop in the church if ambitious projections of growth require the recruitment of clergy from outside the denomination without adequate preparation. There are signs in some sectors that pastors with a limited understanding of historical Free Methodism or Wesleyan theology can shape churches that are neither Free Methodist nor Wesleyan. Yet many of these transfers bring with them the commitment and creativity for planting new churches and revitalizing old ones.

Lyle Schaller minced no words when he spoke of his hope for the future of the church. He stated, "Unquestionably the most influential single factor will be the quality, the commitment, the value, the traits, the goals, the character, the priorities, the competence, the productivity, and the theological stance of the next generation of parish pastors."[1] In response to this challenge, the history of the Free Methodist Church reveals an unswerving commitment to a qualified clergy. Strength for the future is still found in that commitment.

Clergy development is the key. At the same time that academic requirements for preparation of the clergy are being broadened on optional tracks, the expectation for the evaluation of pastoral performance is being raised and intensified. When the Free Methodist Church entered its second century in 1960, it had already broken from a rigid episcopal system of pastoral appointments by permitting a congregational vote of "Yes" or "No" on the return of the pastor. The procedure changed from a confidential vote known only to church authorities, to communication of the results to the local congregation, and then into a formal evaluation of pastoral performance on a regularized cycle.

Paralleling the formalization of pastoral evaluation has been the move toward continuing education as a process of life-long pastoral learning. It is no exaggeration to say that the developing plan of the 1990s for the personal and professional growth of the clergy will be the most advanced in the history of the Free Methodist Church. All the pieces are present. They need to be put together into a complete package that begins with early identification of prospects, advances through recruitment and education, continues in performance evaluation and proceeds through continuing education over a lifetime.

Free Methodists mean more than professionalism by their commitment to a well-trained clergy. At the core of clergy development must be the fundamentals of historic Christianity, requiring that ordained clergy be "blameless in character" and "true to the Word." Spiritual, theological and historical integrity take precedence over professional competence, but neither can stand alone for the clergy of tomorrow.

7. RESOURCING MINISTRIES OF COMPASSION AND DIVERSITY — To be true to its heritage, the Free Methodist Church must recapture its identity as a church with compassion for the poor and ministry among minorities. Behind this conviction is the "egalitarian piety" of historic Free Methodism, which shaped every element of its corporate life from the simplicity of its worship to the simplicity of its architecture.

Howard A. Snyder, one of Free Methodism's best-known scholars, sees missional self-understanding in the original commitment of the church "to preach the gospel to the poor." With loving criticism, he traces the erosion of this commitment in the mission statements adopted by the church, beginning in 1927 and confirmed in the latest statement of 1980. Snyder notes that the original statement of 1860, which emphasized the mission to the poor, is now consigned to a historical section in the back of the *Discipline.*

In a plea for the recovery of its missional self-understanding, Snyder offers the premise that preaching the gospel to the poor is the "charism" or gift of God that uniquely identifies and justifies the Free Methodist Church. He writes, "It remains to be seen whether this early charisma of Free Methodism will experience a substantial rediscovery in the late 1990s and beyond."[2]

The effectiveness of the church in urban areas among ethnic groups and with the poor has already been proven in the growth statistics of the 1990s. But can the church reignite the Wesleyan genius for personal and social holiness that saved England in the 18th century, unified the eastern and western states in the early 19th century, and motivated Free Methodists to march across America in the second half of the same century?

Reignition of the church as a redemptive force in society goes against the momentum of denominational development, which tends toward structural rigidity and cultural accommodation. Free Methodists are rising in class, gaining in affluence and locating in suburbs. The distance between the "haves" and "have nots" is increasing. Not that local churches have neglected ministries of compassion and diversity. The problem is that their work comes to our attention only in bits and pieces.

But denominational development at the expense of organizational vitality is not inevitable. If the Free Methodist Church of the future is to be characterized by its witness of personal and social holiness, the vision must be cast and risk ventures taken at the denominational level. Only a church-wide declaration of intent, followed by resources, will seal the commitment. A major step in that direction has been taken with the establishment and staffing for the Department of Social, Urban and Ethnic Ministries.

Now, the question is resources. With a denominational declaration of intent, budgetary funding to activate a church-wide thrust through the local church, and long-term support from the Free Methodist Foundation, the Free Methodist Church can once again be known for its witness of social holiness through its ministry of compassion, from advocating policies for social justice to planting churches among the poor.

As a denomination in search of an identity, the Free Methodist Church need look no further than its own history. If Free Methodism is to be known as the church that cares, the spirit of compassion must be activated at every level, not as a token of guilt or a low-risk venture into missions, but as the pervasive influence of a deep-seated biblical conviction.

B.T. Roberts' vision of a "free church" for the poor has not lost its meaning. To be accessible by location, simple in style and compassionate in spirit are functional equivalents of free seats for the poor in our generation. To demonstrate this conviction in the 21st century is to define the character of a Free Methodist.

8. LEADING THE RESURGENCE OF WESLEYAN THEOLOGY — The current status of the Free Methodist Church, coupled with its history, accentuates the need for advanced research into biblical and Wesleyan theology. This need applies especially in the areas of entire sanctification, ecclesiology, worship, evangelism, Christian education, stewardship and the Sabbath.

A theology of entire sanctification is needed to clarify the doctrine in contemporary terms; a theology of the church is needed to avoid the pitfalls of localized self-interest; a theology of worship is needed to balance the extremes between freedom and order; a theology of evangelism is needed to assure its biblical integrity; a theology of Christian education is needed to support the ministry of nurture and discipleship; a theology of stewardship is needed to resource the ministries of compassion and diversity; and a theology of the Sabbath is needed to restore the sacramental values that early Free Methodists found in the day of rest as a means of grace.

Whatever the future may hold for the Free Methodist Church, the integrity of its theology will be at the center of that future. Some predict that change is the only constant of the future. Their prediction is only half true. Change will require flexibility in the organization of the church and adjustment in its methods of operation. But these changes will demand firmness only at its theological center.

The history of the Free Methodist Church from 1960-1995 and forward has shown us a denomination adapting its organization and strategy to shifts in the secular and religious cultures. With a touch of irony, the church that has been identified in the past by the separation of its people from the world is an organization shaped by secular trends in its mode, evangelical trends in its methods and denominational trends in its management. This is not necessarily bad. If the theological stake remains firm, the tether of mode, method and management can play out with flexibility.

For this reason alone the future of the Free Methodist Church depends upon the clarity and vitality of its theological center. Even now, in the decline of mainline denominations, the divisive issues of abortion, homosexuality and feminism swirl around the central question of biblical authority. No one expects these issues to go away. They will be aggravated in the future by the add-ons of bioethics relating to human heredity and social ethics relating to human environment. The question, now and in the future, is, "How does the Word of God speak to these issues?" In the evangelical sphere, theological issues have migrated from classical concerns to the practical matters of evangelistic methods and worship modes.

The Free Methodist Church mirrors these concerns. Absorbed by the methods of church growth and church planting, a biblical theology of evangelism is a necessary check and balance upon a system heavily influenced by cultural anthropology, social psychology, management and marketing. Equally high on the theological agenda must be a theology of worship. Douglas R. Cullum, in a penetrating historical study of Free Methodist worship, concluded that the diversity of contemporary worship was defining a new kind of pluralism in the church. At the same time, he wrote, Free Methodists were revivalistic and liturgical, "Wesleyan and evangelical, holiness and anabaptist, neopentecostal and catholic."[3]

Perhaps it is the wisdom of the Spirit that leads the church to be all things to all people with the goal of winning some. But then again perhaps it is the crosswinds of religious culture that toss the mode of worship from one mode to another. In either case Free Methodists need to understand the theological implications of change in worship from what Cullum called simplicity to multiplicity.

Such a theological agenda would appear to be overwhelming except for the fact that the Free Methodist Church already has the precedent of its Study Commission on Doctrine researching delicate and controversial issues. The Free Methodist Church of the past has been strong in its practical theology. In a future of chaotic change, paradoxical problems and quixotic complexity,

Wesleyan theology will again be a truth whose time has come. Free Methodists can take the lead in that future.

9. CULTIVATING A FREE METHODIST PRESENCE IN COMMUNICATIONS TECHNOLOGY — Although some might disagree, Free Methodism stepped back a century when it lost the ministry of the "Light and Life Hour" and failed to find a successor in the ministry of communications. True, the radio broadcast was not cost-effective. True, its evangelistic impact for the growth of the church was minimal. True, Free Methodists in the grass roots did not adequately own the ministry. Still, the "Light and Life Hour" gave Free Methodists a national and international identity that positioned the church for a leadership role in the Information Age. With the loss of the radio broadcast, the church retreated back into more traditional functions of denominationalism that have been eroding one at a time.

Light and Life Communications (formerly Light and Life Press), for instance, has been one of the strongest symbols of denominationalism. Even so, it continues to fight an uphill battle to maintain Free Methodist imprints on publications against rising competition from trans-denominational sources. Certainly, there is room in the future for a denominational press but only as a part of the larger paradigm called "communications."

The argument will be made that local churches will not provide the resources for denominational media or that media transmission is more effective at the local-church level. Both programming and advertising in the communications industry counter these arguments. A creative 30-second spot of national advertising for the Free Methodist Church with a local-church "stringer," a home page on the worldwide web or a pilot series on a "free church" for the 21st century are examples of options that need to be explored.

Nathan Hatch, American historian, notes that the holiness and pentecostal movements took the lead in communications by print in the 19th century and by radio in the 20th century. The leadership has now been forfeited by scandal among televangelists and timidity among other evangelicals, especially holiness people. Billy Graham, even in his declining days, is proving that the media offers an outreach to the globe via satellite networks and an inreach to the youth culture via MTV that can be envisioned only through the eyes of the Holy Spirit. On a smaller scale, but with equal creativity, the Free Methodist Church needs to see the potential of expansion in the ministry of Light and Life Communications.

10. DEVELOPING A NEW DENOMINATIONALISM — As difficult as it may be, we must admit that old differences, such as theological particularities, experiential nuances, lifestyle expectations and ethnic backgrounds, out of which more than 200 denominations were spawned in America, are no

longer the distinctives for denominations in the future. Furthermore, the traditional functions from which denominations derived their authority have been taken over by the local church, parachurch movements and trans-denominational networks. The shift of power can neither be denied nor recaptured.

Even more precisely for Free Methodism, the dominant symbols of "headquarters" and "home" around which the denomination developed are all but dead. Lovers of our history are also appalled to see "Free Methodist" replaced in the name of local churches, because its meaning is presumably lost or irrelevant for this generation. Like the layers of an onion, the functions and symbols out of which the denomination was formed are being peeled away layer by layer until there seems to be little left.

A decline in the functions and symbols upon which denominations were built in the past may turn to advantage for the future. If the denomination is stripped to the essence of what it means to be a Christian church, a new and revitalized denominationalism may emerge. A global vision, a core of biblical convictions, a statement of unifying mission, a community of memory, a stewardship for outreach, a network of information, a system for nurture, a spirit of compassion, a ministry of diversity, a bond of relationships, a leadership of servanthood, a voice of Christian conscience, a responsibility for strategic goals and an accountability for effectiveness still validate the connectional life of a denomination.

Information will be a key component of the new denominationalism. Through communications technology, Free Methodists worldwide can be instantly informed of issues, events and needs that will bond them together. The updated history from 1960-1995 and forward has shown us that the Free Methodist Church is one of evangelical Christianity's best kept secrets.

Few members know all that the church is doing, and fewer outsiders know of its impact. The hundreds of Free Methodist martyrs in Africa or the dynamic growth of ethnic churches along the North American coastlines serve as unforgettable examples. A global system of timely information could give Free Methodists a personalized sense of their relationship to the global church and their bonding with sisters and brothers in the faith. In fact the Free Methodist Church may again become "home" for many sincere and earnest souls whom B.T. Roberts described as "dissatisfied with being outer-court worshippers, they are desirous of dwelling in the secret place of the Most High."[4] Connectionalism is not dead. It just needs to be communicated.

Somehow the values of Free Methodism must find expression in the name, slogan and logo for the church of the future. Building upon these symbols of identity, the Free Methodist Church can model a dynamic denominationalism for the 21st century.

11. FOSTERING A BIBLICAL COMMUNITY IN MULTICULTURAL MINISTRIES — Too many gaps will exist between diverse segments of people in the 21st century to bridge them just by discussion, compromise or conflict resolution. The only hope is in the creation of a genuinely biblical community characterized by Christian reconciliation, fellowship and service. Small cells of people who are more alike than different and clustered in local-church settings model these qualities of the Christian community on a limited basis.

A genuine biblical community must stand the test of diversity. In the future, diversity will be magnified by race, age, gender, ethnic origin, social class, economic status, educational achievement and family pattern to name a few of the multicultural variations with which the small-group ministry of local churches will have to contend.

How will the Free Methodist Church respond to the new diversity? On one extreme is the tolerance, connected with pluralism, that bleeds off into theological relativism in a live-and-let-live attitude. At the other extreme is the prejudice growing out of self-interest that justifies discrimination and rejection by quoting out of context Christ's words, "The poor you have with you always."

Free Methodists must remember their spiritual ancestry. Wesleyans come from a company of millers and miners, weavers and woolers, farmers and frontier people whom the Spirit of God welded into a powerful redemptive force. Following in the footsteps of that heritage, Free Methodism asserted the conviction from the first day of its founding that "the provisions of the gospel are for all."[5] The new diversity of the 21st century will put that conviction to test again. Even before the full impact of that diversity hits the church, a transformation of attitudes must open the doors into the upper room where the biblical community is found. Free Methodism is a family that will grow in strength as the circle is expanded and diversity is celebrated locally, nationally and globally.

12. HONORING THE DIVERSITY OF CHURCHES — Evangelicals have fallen prey to the secular mindset in evaluating churches. At the top of the scale are megachurches and metachurches characterized by multiple staffs, seven-day week ministries, contemporary worship styles, organizational independence, charismatic leadership, suburban, upwardly mobile congregations, market orientation and abundant resources. All other churches tend to be measured against these values but find themselves pursuing a phantom that is always above and beyond them. Smaller, traditional and stable churches develop an inferiority complex because they cannot keep up with the competition.

A biblical scale for evaluating a church is just the opposite. It is horizontal with a diversity of congregations recognized for the individualized values that they bring to enrich the body of Christ. An example is a small and traditional Free Methodist church in a rural area of the East with a record of producing leaders for the church on a per capita basis far beyond its size. The intensity of its spiritual impact upon young lives from generation to generation is a quality that gives that church a distinction not measured on the vertical scale.

The appeal for the future is not to justify stagnant or declining congregations, which characterize many Free Methodist churches. In the long run, decisions about these churches may have to be made on the *triage* principle in which these churches are placed in one of three categories — those that show signs of revitalization on their own; those that have the potential for revitalization by intervention; and those that show no signs of survival either on their own or with intervening resources. In the first case, self-regenerating churches should be commended for the signs of self-renewal. In the third case of dying churches, closure or merger might be merciful. But in the case of struggling churches with potential, the denomination and the annual conference should dedicate their limited resources to intervene with the strong hope of transformation.

Behind such an aggressive process must be an evaluation of the churches on the biblical scale, recognizing their diversity, honoring their strengths, confronting their weaknesses and prescribing the steps to effectiveness. As tough-minded as this process may seem, it is no tougher than the Son of Man's assessment of the seven churches in the book of Revelation. Through the angel assigned to each of these churches, a realistic assessment was written with the remedy for its weaknesses and the promise of grace to overcome them. But if the church failed to address its weaknesses and overcome its failures, there would be no hesitation to remove its candlestick. The Free Methodist Church of the future must be committed to a similar discipline.

13. INCREASING EFFECTIVENESS THROUGH COOPERATION — The Free Methodist Church was not alone in the financial crisis of 1990. Sooner or later all denominations come face-to-face with the reality of reduced resources. The future bodes no better. Even with belt-tightening and downsizing, a small denomination cannot keep pace and, with the need for expanding resources, function effectively, especially when the church is on the verge of a breakthrough into a new day.

As the Free Methodist Church moves into the 21st century, it is depending upon high per capita giving from a growing membership, coupled with distributions from the Free Methodist Foundation, for its expanding resources. Sound financial management will assure the efficiency in the application of these funds for ministry. Limited ventures, such as the consortium of holiness publishers, will continue. Interest in denominational merger, however, is almost nonexistent.

Two realities require another look at cooperative ventures and denominational merger. One reality is the escalating cost of technical services and information systems, which are indispensable to denominational effectiveness. The other reality is the struggle of the holiness movement to maintain its viability, not just in the secular culture but in the evangelical subculture as well. Regrettable though it may be, the holiness movement has been ignored by the secular culture and dismissed by the evangelical subculture because holiness churches have not combined their numbers, merged their resources, advanced their scholars and unified their voice on behalf of the movement.

It is not too late. A summit meeting of holiness church leaders and Wesleyan-oriented evangelicals in larger denominations, perhaps called at the initiative of Free Methodists and funded by a foundation grant, should be on the agenda for the future. The purpose of the summit would be to develop a strategy for the holiness movement in the 21st century, including the options for cooperation, federation and even merger. Otherwise, if holiness churches hold to differences that are now passé and depend upon local churches for expanded resources, they may well join the ranks of other denominational dinosaurs lumbering toward extinction on the religious landscape.

14. PURSUING THE NEW ECUMENISM OF NETWORKING — In 1960 the Free Methodist Church took leadership in cooperative relationships with evangelical, Methodist and holiness associations. At the same time parachurch ministries blossomed, especially among youth in such movements as Youth for Christ, Campus Crusade, Inter-Varsity and Navigators. Whether the fault lay with the independence of these groups or the inflexibility of denominations, competitive tension kept church and parachurch ministries suspiciously eyeing each other at a distance.

In 1995 parachurch ministries gave way to evangelical networks that were trans-denominational in scope, single-purposed in their nature and information-based in their communication. No study has been done to determine the influence of these networks upon local Free Methodist churches and membership, but both pastors and people talk enthusiastically about participating in them. Likewise, most of the new networks are "denomination-friendly" and intentionally try to avoid competition and conflict.

In cooperation with denominations and with each other, they hold promise for a powerful redemptive force at national and international levels. Free from institutional constraints, their potential for evangelism outstrips the denominational church. At all costs, however, they must avoid becoming captive of a political agenda, dominated by a cultic personality or swept into a theological stance for the sake of numbers. They must also resist the temptation to become quasi-denominations of their own making at the expense of their primary purpose.

Given these cautions, the new networks must be seen as a phenomenon motivated by the Spirit of God to serve needs neglected by the church, to address common needs across denominational lines or to respond in a new and timely fashion to needs produced by a changing culture. Rather than resisting their influence or denying their impact, the Free Methodist Church needs to learn from them, take leadership in them and complement their ministries wherever possible.

Trans-denominational networks will not go away because they are a product of the Information Age. They will continue to multiply across the evangelical landscape. Yet, to borrow a quip from the era of televangelism, trans-denominational networks "do not make house calls." The "hi-touch" ministry of the local church is needed more than ever.

15. SPEAKING WITH A PROPHETIC VOICE — Proclamation of the truth is a responsibility that the Free Methodist Church assumes by its commitment to the divine inspiration and final authority of the Word of God. The proclaiming voice must be heard from the pulpit of the local church and the platform of the denomination. Currently the prophetic voice of the church is strong from the pulpit but weak from the platform. Whether the issue is local poverty or global persecution, silence is consent. An instrument needs to be found from which the Free Methodist Church can once again become a goad for the social conscience of the church and the culture.

B.T. Roberts found that voice through his editorials in *The Earnest Christian*. He dared to speak as boldly of justice as he did of mercy. No one can doubt that he met opposition both within and without the church. Yet he spoke.

In the Information Age when discordant voices are causing confusion once again, the Free Methodist Church must speak. Otherwise, its people will be overwhelmed by the bombardment of secular values because no one speaks biblical truths or applies Wesleyan theology with clarity and precision. The Free Methodist Church must find this instrument and speak this voice if it is to fulfill its God-given mission as a prophetic church in the 21st century.

16. SEEING THE VISION OF THE YOUNG — The agenda for tomorrow culminates in the vision that young leaders under the age of 35, clergy and laity, men and women, see for the church in the future. Under the adage, "Everything that goes around comes around," they are recycling the vision of original Free Methodism. To them the mission of the church comes to focus in the experience of personal holiness. They are still motivated to "spread scrip-

tural holiness across the land, and reform the nation." They find meaning in the 1860 mission statement, "to maintain the Biblical standard of Christianity and to preach the Gospel to the poor."

Contrary to the current criticism that the younger generation has failed to read the minutes of the last meeting, future leaders of the Free Methodist Church have not only read those minutes; they have read their history. All Free Methodists, whether young or old, contemporary or traditional, can be confident that the future is in good hands.

One final word completes this updated history of the Free Methodist Church. Each generation that comes to a new millennium anticipates spiritual awakening. Our generation is no different as we look forward to the tick of the clock at midnight on January 1, A.D. 2001. Who knows? God may well use the motive of this millennial moment to visit us with His Spirit, call us to repentance, give us the promise of renewal in the church and challenge us to lead in the reformation of the global society.

Even now the early signs of spiritual awakening can be seen. Pessimists see these signs as proof of end times and hold little hope for the redemption of a corrupt culture. Optimists, however, see the same signs and claim the promise of the prophet Joel: "In the last days, God says, I will pour out my Spirit on all people. Your sons and daughters will prophesy, your young men will see visions, your old men will dream dreams" (Acts 2:17).

Free Methodism can claim that promise for the 21st century. In the dreams of the old, we see our past; in the ministry of today's sons and daughters, we see our present; and in the visions of the young, we see our future. With confidence in that promise, the Free Methodist Church has a future in its history.

Servant Leaders of Our Generation

1960-1995 and Forward

History is biography. The story of the Free Methodist Church can not be written without the recognition of clergy and laity who, in the spirit of Jesus Christ, are the servant leaders of the generation.

From its beginning, one of the affirming signals of God's anointing upon the church has been its clergy, who have inherited the leadership legacy of B.T. Roberts. Almost as one from bishops to local pastors, they have been faithful to model holy living, preach biblical truth, show compassion for the poor and serve sacrificially with humility and joy. Although this history can name only those who served in denominational leadership roles by the election of their peers, through them the ministry of conference and district superintendents, local church pastors and pastoral staffs is also honored. No one questions the fact that the front line of ministry for the Free Methodist Church is in the trenches of the local parish. So to all of the unnamed clergy who served faithfully during the era from 1960-1995, let the list of those whom they chose to lead be the tribute to their own servanthood.

Lay leaders, as well, walk hand in hand with clergy through the history of the Free Methodist Church in our generation. From the earliest beginnings of the church, the equality of laity in leadership has been recognized as fundamental. B.T. Roberts, who suffered injustice at the hands of an all-clergy conference in the Methodist Episcopal Church, stood firm on the principle of lay equality in the governance of the new church.

Special meaning is also attached to the fact that the genesis of the church came out of Laymen's Conventions where men and women gathered, not just to protest the injustice against clergy and laity who were expelled from the parent church, but more affirmatively, to take their stand for personal and social holiness. Thus, out of the organizing conference for the church came this report: "The deep interest and close scrutiny of the intelligent laymen who were present as delegates, must have convinced anyone that that church is a great loser which excludes them from her councils."[1]

Nor can we pass lightly over the contribution of national and international leaders from across the world, especially young adult members of the church who represent a rising generation of clergy and lay leadership. A distinct shift can be detected in the names of those who are elected to denominational office from the 1960s to the 1990s. As Free Methodism in the 1860s recognized the value of lay leadership, the church in the 1990s is now recognizing the invaluable contribution of its worldwide family in the governance of a diversified and enriched global church.

With this introduction, we recognize the clergy and laity, men and women, nationals and internationals who were elected, employed or honored by the Free Methodist Church as servant leaders for our generation.

Among these honored persons, two stand out. They may not be the best-known names; they may not have held the highest office; they may not be remembered for the most dramatic achievement. But they represent the spirit and life of Free Methodism that must be remembered. They are Ken Leech and Alan Ramm, respectively the clergy and lay leaders of the Free Methodist Church in the United Kingdom. On October 31, 1994, while returning home from the annual Board of Administration meetings at the World Ministries Center in Indianapolis, Indiana, they died tragically in the crash of American Eagle flight 4184. (The life story of Ken Leech is contained in *Dark Providence, Bright Promise*, published by Light and Life Press, Indianapolis, IN, 1995).

The life stories of Rev. Ken Leech and Alan Ramm will be told time and time again as part of the "community of memory" in the Free Methodist Church. To add to that memory bank, there is the recollection of the tape recorded interview that was held with Leech and Ramm in the week immediately preceding their death.

The two-hour session is now an essential part of the background research for the writing of this history. For the final question of the interview, they were asked, "What is your vision for the future of the Free Methodist Church in the United Kingdom?" They were as one in the burning desire to see local congregations grow and new churches planted in England and Ireland through the equipping ministry of pastors and the personal evangelism of the people.

Later in the day, word came that Leech and Ramm wanted to add a footnote to the interview. The fire in their eyes matched the urgency in their voices as they said, "You asked about the future of the Free Methodist Church in the U.K. We forgot the most important thing of all. *Preach holiness.* That is our future and our hope."

After the numbing news came about the death of Ken Leech and Alan

Ramm, the tape of their interview was played again. As each of them told the story of his own spiritual journey and then recalled with deference the leaders of the Free Methodist Church in the United Kingdom who preceded them, a common thread came through.

Leech, a member of the clergy and the newly elected superintendent of the two annual conferences of the church in the United Kingdom, and Ramm, a member of the laity and the long time executive assistant to the superintendent, shared the experience of life as they shared the experience of death. Ken Leech and Alan Ramm were:

    ... *Converted* to Christ through the witness of the church,

    ... *Won* to Free Methodism through the spirituality of the church,

    ... *Sanctified* by the Holy Spirit through the preaching of the church,

    ... *Discipled* in faith through the nurture of the church,

    ... *Called* into ministry through the agency of the church,

    ... *Prepared* for service through the avenues of the church,

    ... *Chosen* for leadership by the people of the church,

    ... *Inflamed* with vision for the growth of the church,

    ... *Convinced* that the message of holiness represented the future of the church, and they

    ... *Labored* faithfully through the struggle of the church and

    ... *Sacrificed* their lives while in the work of the church.

WHAT IS A FREE METHODIST? When the question is asked of our people today and tomorrow, one answer can be, "Let me tell you the story of Ken Leech and Alan Ramm." Their story is the story of our church.

Servant Leaders of Our Generation

Recognized Leaders

I. BISHOPS OF THE FREE METHODIST CHURCH — 1960-1995
North America General Conference:

Leslie R. Marston	1935-1964
Charles V. Fairbairn	1939-1961
J. Paul Taylor	1947-1964
Walter S. Kendall	1958-1969
Edward C. John	1961-1974
Myron F. Boyd	1964-1976
Paul N. Ellis	1964-1979
W. Dale Cryderman	1969-1984
Donald N. Bastian	1974-1990
Elmer E. Parsons	1974-1985
Clyde E. Van Valin	1976-1991
Robert F. Andrews	1979-1991
Gerald E. Bates	1985-
David M. Foster	1985-1997
Noah Nzeyimana	1985-

(Burundi Jurisdictional Conference)
Bya'ene Akulu Ilangyi   1989-
   (Zaire Provisional General Conference)
Daniel Ward   1989-
   (India Provisional General Conference)

Richard D. Snyder   1991-
Luis Uanela Nhaphale   1993-
    (Mozambique Provisional General Conference)
Jim Tuan   1994-
    (Philippines Provisional General Conference)
Kevin W. Mannoia   1997-

Japan General Conference:
Kaneo Oda   1961-1962
Takesaburo Uzaki   1962-1982
Motoi Hatano   1982-1992
Hachiroemon Naiki   1992-1996
Sukenari Iwamoto   1996-

Egypt General Conference:
Ayad Girgis   1962-1966
Habeeb Buctor   1966-1970
Nathan Gindi   1970-1996
Mounir H. Gindy   1996-

Rwanda General Conference:
Aaron Ruhumuriza   1985-

Canada General Conference:
Donald N. Bastian   1990-1993
Gary R. Walsh   1993-1997

II. BOARD OF ADMINISTRATION OFFICERS — 1960-1995

Presidents:
Bishop L.R. Marston   1947-1964
Bishop W.S. Kendall   1964-1969
Bishop Myron F. Boyd   1969-1976
Bishop Paul N. Ellis   1976-1979
Bishop W. Dale Cryderman 1979-1984
Bishop Clyde E. Van Valin 1985-1989

Chairs:
Rev. John E. Van Valin   1989-1990
Bernard Hansen   1990-1995
Hank Bode   1996-

Vice-Presidents:

Bishop Paul N. Ellis	1975-1976
Bishop W. Dale Cryderman	1976-1979
Bishop Clyde E. Van Valin	1979-1985
Bishop Donald N. Bastian	1985-1989

Vice-Chairs:

Bernard Hansen	1989-1990
Rev. Wayne Neeley	1990-

Secretaries:

Dr. Claude A. Watson	1951-1964
Rev. Cleo T. Denbo	1964-1985
Melvin J. Spencer	1985-1995
Carol Bartlett	1995-

III. BOARD OF ADMINISTRATION MEMBERS — 1960-1995

Ministers:

David V. Abbott	1974-1979
Donald J. Allgor	1974-1985
Merlin C. Baker	1989-1995
Douglas Bartlett	1995-
Donald N. Bastian	1964-1974 (elected bishop)
Donald E. Bateman	1964-1979
J. Wesley Bennett	1979-1985
Brian Bonney	1969-1989
G.H. Bonney	1974-1979, 1983-1990
Arthur Brown	1991-1994
Robert J. Buchanan	1985-1990
Earl S. Bull	1971-1979
Forest C. Bush	1969-1974
Ralph V. Cleveland	1979-1983
Herbert H. Coates	1979-1989
David G. Colgan	1989-
G.M. Cottrill	1964-1974
Robert A. Crandall	1985-1989
T.R. Crown	1979-1985
William L. Cryderman	1990-

E.A. Cutler	1964-1969
Elwyn E. Cutler	1969-1972
Jack Delamarter	1985-1992
C. Dorr Demaray	1964-1969
C.T. Denbo	1955-1985
Lloyd E. Ehmcke	1969-1971
J. Allan Ellershaw	1995-
Raymond Ellis	1985-1988
Jimmie Estrada	1979-1985, 1989-
Larry Evoy	1995-
David Foster	1979-1985 (elected bishop)
William Fox	1979-1986
Richard Gabriel	1974-1979
Dwight Gregory	1989-
Claude Griffith	1990-1995
Nelson Grimm	1994-
Glenn A. Hall	1951-1965
John Harrell	1989-
B.F. Hibbett	1955-1964
Darold L. Hill	1985-1989
Jon Honda	1995-
Claude A. Horton	1969-1971
Dwight N. Horton	1969-1983
Joseph James	1995-
E.C. John	1960-1961 (elected bishop)
Roger Johnson	1979-1985
Theodore S. Johnson	1985-1989
W.D. Kinney	1979-1985
C.D. Kirkpatrick	1960-1964
Eustice Kirkpatrick	1974-1979
Kenneth Leech	1994-1994
Paul Leitzke	1989-1995
Richard C. Leonard	1979-1989
Jack Logan	1974-1979
Robert J. Magee Sr.	1969-1974
Don Mank	1989-1995

Kevin Mannoia	1989-1996 (elected bishop)
James L. Mason	1974-1979
Richard Maurer	1992-
Wayne McCown	1985-1989
John M. Miyabe	1974-1979
R.G. Mumaw	1964-1969
Robert A. Neal	1985-1994
Wayne Neeley	1989-
Royal S. Nelson	1969-1974
C.F. Olson	1960-1969
H.D. Olver	1951-1964, 1969-1974
W.B. Orr	1966-1969
C.W. Oscarson Sr.	1974-1979
Ralph L. Page	1969-1985
W.J. Parmerter	1951-1964
Darrold Phillips	1988-1989
Virgil L. Raley	1969-1979
Carson Reber	1972-1974
L.A. Robart	1955-1974
J.A. Robb	1960-1964
Howard D. Rose	1964-1979
David A. Rupert	1989-
M. Orin Scandrett	1974-1979
Earl Schamehorn	1979-1985
David Shigekawa	1985-1989
Ward Sipes	1989-
H. Austin Smith	1955-1964
Richard Snyder	1979-1991 (elected bishop)
James D. States	1979-1985
Ronald Taylor	1989-1990 (honorary), 1990-1991
Larry Thomas	1995-
Samuel H. Tinsley	1994-
Frank Van Valin	1969-1979
John E. Van Valin	1983-1990
J.L. Walrath	1969-1974
J. Barrie Walton	1991-1994

Leslie H. Whitehead	1985-1991
Wesley R. Wilder	1964-1969
J.O. Wiles	1960-1964
Robert E. Williams	1986-1989
Erle Wirth	1991-1995
D.A. Woods	1964-1969, 1971-1989

Laypersons:

Gerald Atkinson	1969-1985
K. Ray Barnes	1980-1985
Carol Battleson	1995-
Robert Battleson	1985-1989
Roland Bentley	1969-1974
Selwyn Belsher	1979-1985
Hank Bode	1979-
Wayne Bovee	1989-1995
Calvin Burge	1974-1979
Charles Canon III	1989-
Adele Cisneros	1985-1989
Merlin Coates	1964-1969
John Conaway	1989-1995
Lee Cromwell	1979-1989
John Davis	1995-
Guy Delamarter	1969-1995
Paul Embree	1985-1989
Byron Forbes	1995-
Leslie A. Freeman	1969-1979
George Fuller	1951-1969
Richard Galbreath	1974-1979
Floyd Gallogly	1985-1989
Bernard Hansen	1985-1995
Robert Harnishfeger	1964-1969
Roy Harrington	1951-1969
Leon Hartzell	1989-1995
Forrest Hayden	1964-1974
James Heldreth	1969-1979
W.O. Hepker	1964-1974

Joe Higginbotham	1995-
E.A. Holtwick	1955-1964
Lawrence Houston	1985-
Eldon R. Johnson	1969-1980
Betty Ivers	1995-
Gene Keene	1995-
Eugene Keffer	1974-1985
James Keys	1985-1989
Lowell Kline	1955-1964
Davis Kobayashi	1979-1985, 1989-
William Langer	1964-1969
Ronald Long	1979-1985
Norman McCracken	1979-1989
Elmer McDowell	1955-1969
Pearson Miller	1979-1985, 1995
Gene Mogg	1989-1995
Weldon Munson	1960-1969
B.L. Murray	1964-1979
Ronald Nesbitt	1995-
Mark Orchard	1995-
John Orrantia	1974-1979
Hershal Paul	1995-
Raymond Picken	1969-1974
Alan Ramm	1989-1990 (honorary), 1990-1994
Ray Reed	1989-1995
Herbert Rice	1995-
John Rice	1969-1989, 1995
J.R. Roark	1969-1974
Larry Roberts	1995-
Richard Roggenbaum	1960-1964
Doris Scofield	1979-1989
Wesley Skinner	1960-1979
Charles Smout	1974-1985
Keith A. Snyder	1985-1995
Leon Spangler	1979-1985
Melvin J. Spencer	1969-

Lyle Stone	1979-1985
Craig Tidball	1989-1995
Carlos Twichell	1979-1985
Ian Van Norman	1985-1990
Paul Van Note	1989-1995
Merlyn W. Voller	1960-1964, 1969-1979
J.E. Wade	1939-1964
Paul T. Walls	1969-1979
Glenn E. White	1985-
Hugh A. White	1947-1985
Mark Whitlock	1989-1995
Art Wilkinson	1989-1995
Wayne Winnett	1979-1989
W.L. Woods	1955-1969

Overseas Representatives:

1969-1974:

Felix Canete	Julio Oyama

1974-1979:

Aaron Ruhumuriza	Celio Rodriguez de Almeida

1979-1985: (Four to serve each year)

Wilton Mdubeki	Israel Brito
Andrew Ndebele	Sebastian Rivera Pena
Karuba Macinda	Ismael Andaya
Daniel Ward	Aaron Ruhumuriza

1985-1989:

Makoto Ono	Nelson Shinga
Bya'ene Akulu Ilangyi	Pablo Ventura
Terence Ndihokubwayo	Ismael Andaya
Derek Ho	Elesinah Chauke

1989-1995:

Charite Noel	Robert Nxumalo
Jim Tuan	Makoto Ono
Kubatu Mndeumo	Ismael Chay
Hung-fai Leung	Pedro Vanderlinder
Nzigo Onesiphore	

1995- :

Vallante Encarnado	Jonathan Lu
Charité Noël	Donizetti Rosado
Osseias Jeremias	Alfred Kurubone
Onesiphore Nzigo	Lincoln Shembe

IV. DENOMINATIONAL EXECUTIVES — 1960-1995

General Church Secretary:
Cleo T. Denbo   1964-1967; part-time 1967-1985

General Headquarters Administrators:
Bishop W. Dale Cryderman 1981-1984 (interim)
Bishop Clyde E. Van Valin 1984-1985 (interim)
Earl R. Schamehorn   1985-1988
T. Dan Wollam   1988-1991

Treasurers, Directors of Finance:
Alfred S. Hill   1948-1967
William B. Bruce   1967-1972
Lloyd E. Ehmcke   1972-1978
Marvin Stevens (acting)   1978
M. Jack Crandell   1978-1983
Philip B. Nelson (acting) 1983
Philip B. Nelson   1984-1991

Comptroller:
Gary M. Kilgore   1991-1992

Director of Administration and Finance, and Treasurer:
Gary M. Kilgore   1992-

World Ministries Communication
Director:
Claude A. Horton   1971-1972

Information and Stewardship
Director:
George L. Ford   1973-1979

Communications
Director:
Donald E. Riggs   1979-1981

Christian Education
General Directors Free Methodist Youth:
C. Mervin Russell	1958-1964
Robert A. Crandall	1964-1967

General Director, Intermediate Youth:
Floyd M. Todd,	1953-1967

General Directors of Service Training:
C. Hoyt Watson	1962-1965
C.T. Denbo (acting)	1965-1966
A.D. Zahniser	1966-1967

General Sunday School Secretaries:
Royal S. Nelson	1955-1964
C.H. Barnett	1964-1967

General Directors of Christian Education:
Robert A. Crandall	1967-1981
Catherine Stonehouse	1981-1987
Daniel L. Riemenschneider	1987-

Higher Education and the Ministry
General Education Secretaries:
C. Hoyt Watson	1962-1965
C.T. Denbo (acting)	1965-66

General Secretaries of Higher Education:
A.D. Zahniser	1966-1973
L.R. Schoenhals (acting)	1973-1974
Timothy Beuthin	1995-

General Secretaries of Higher Education and the Ministry:
L.R. Schoenhals	1974-1981
Bruce L. Kline	1981-1994

John Wesley Seminary
Dean:
W. Curry Mavis	1947-1962

Director-Chaplain:
Clyde E. Van Valin	1962-1974

Directors:
Lawrence R. Schoenhals	1974-1981
Bruce L. Kline	1981-1994

Gerald E. Bates (interim)	1994-1995
Timothy Beuthin	1995-

Evangelism

General Secretary of Evangelism:

L.W. Northrup	1955-1967

General Directors of Evangelistic Outreach:

Dale A. Woods	1967-1970
Robert F. Andrews	1971-1978

Directors of Evangelism and Church Growth:

Forest C. Bush	1979-1988
Raymond W. Ellis	1988-

Light and Life Hour

Director-Speakers:

LeRoy M. Lowell	1944-1945
Myron F. Boyd	1945-1965
Robert F. Andrews	1965-1980

Missions

General Missionary Secretaries:

Byron S. Lamson	1944-1964
Charles D. Kirkpatrick	1964-1985

Directors of World Missions:

Elmore L. Clyde	1985-1990
M. Doane Bonney	1990-1996
Larry Houck	1997-

Publishers

General Publisher:

Lloyd H. Knox	1954-1979
Donald E. Chilcote	1979-1982

Directors of Light and Life Press:

Wilmer Bartel	1982-1988
T. Dan Wollam (acting)	1988-1990

Publisher:

John E. Van Valin	1990-

Executive Editor, Sunday-School Literature

Donald M. Joy	1960-1972

The Free Methodist / Light and Life
  Editors, *The Free Methodist*:
  James F. Gregory   1955-1964
  Byron S. Lamson   1964-1970
  Editorial Board, *Light and Life*
  Off-site Editors:
  Robert M. Fine,   Donald E. Demaray,
  U. Milo Kaufmann,   Frank Van Valin   1970-1975
  Associate Editors:
  Frank Van Valin, Donald Demaray, Forest C. Bush   1975
  Frank Van Valin, Donald Demaray, Gary Walsh   1976
  Donald Demaray, Forest C. Bush, Wayne McCown   1977
  Managing Eitors:
  Jay E. Benson   1970-1971
  G. Roger Schoenhals   1971-1977
  Editor:
  G. Roger Schoenhals   1977-1981
  Executive Editor and Managing Editor:
  Donald N. Bastian, Exec. Editor   1982-1986
  Lyn D. Cryderman, Managing Editor   1982-1986
  Editor:
  Robert B. Haslam   1986-1996
  Douglas Newton   1996-
Free Methodist Foundation/Planned Giving
  Directors of Planned Giving:
  Stanley B. Thompson   1975-1982
  David Samuelson   1982-1984
  Brad C. Brail   1985-1987
  David Samuelson (interim)   1987-1988
  President, Free Methodist Foundation:
  Stanley B. Thompson   1988-

V. AUXILIARY ORGANIZATION OFFICERS — 1960-1995
Women's Missionary Society, Women's Missionary Fellowship International, Women's Ministries International

Presidents:

Adine McDowell	1951-1964
Bessie R. Kresge	1964-1969
Viola L. Walton	1969-1974
Leona K. Fear	1974-1979
Evelyn L. Mottweiler	1979-1985
Elizabeth Cryderman	1985-1989
Carollyn Ellis	1989-

Editors, *The Missionary Tidings*

Bessie R. Kresge	1955-1964
Alice E. Fensome	1964-1975
Marian W. Groesbeck	1975-1990

Transferred 9-1-90 to Department of World Missions

Editor, Dan Runyon	1990-

1995 Renamed *World Mission People*

Light and Life Men's Fellowship, Light and Life Men International

Presidents:

W. Milburn Wills	1967-1971
Wesley Skinner	1971-1979
Tom Black	1979-1985
U. Milo Kaufmann	1985-1995
James Stetler	1995-

Executive Secretaries/Directors:

Charles Kingsley	1956-1967
Robert Andrews	1967-1971
Charles Kingsley (acting)	1971-1975
Howard A. Snyder	1975-1980
Henry G. Church, Jr.	1980-1981
T. Joe Culumber	1982-1984
Lucien Behar	1986-

Association of Free Methodist Educational Institutions:
  Presidents:

C. Dorr Demaray	1960-1962
Ellwood A. Voller	1962-1965
Glenn A. Richardson	1965-1968
David L. McKenna	1968-1970
Bruce L. Kline	1970-1972
Lawrence R. Schoenhals	1972-1974
Orley R. Herron	1974-1975
Ellwood A. Voller	1975-1976
Paul L. Adams	1976-1977
David L. McKenna	1977-1979
W. Richard Stephens	1979-1982
Kenneth H. Coffman	1982-1985
Dorsey Brause	1985-1987
William C. Crothers	1987-1989
David C. LeShana	1989-1991
W. Richard Stephens	1991-1993
John A. Martin	1993-1994
Robert Smith	1994-

Association of Social Service Agencies
  Presidents:

Harry Livermore	1971-1977
Kenneth M. Walton	1977-1979
Harold Schwab	1979-1982
Robert Hartley	1982-1986
Donald Cutler	1986-1992
David Samuelson	1992-1993
John P. Ellis	1993-1996
David Fairchild	1996-

Free Methodist Medical Fellowship (Founded 1960)
  Presidents:

Paul W. Yardy	1971-1975
Bruce N. Davenport	1975-1983
Lionel Hurd	1983-1988

Bruce N. Davenport	1988-1992
Merlin Coulter	1992-1994

FMC Ministries, Inc. (International Friendship House)

Directors:

Stanley Long	1970-1972
Arden L. Reed	1972-1973
William A. Coates	1973-1974
Al Lawrence	1974-1975
Jack H. Mottweiler	1975-1976

Department of Special Ministries, Director:

Jack H. Mottweiler	1976-1981

International Friendship House, Managers:

Ivanelle Kirkpatrick	1981-1988
Linda Pyle	1988-1990

Free Methodist Chaplains Association

Presidents:

Randall R. Tucker	1983-1985
Daniel Hummer	1986-1988
Myron B. Henry	1988-1990
E. Dean Cook	1990-1992
Harold C. Cranston	1992-1994
Harold Hannum	1994-

VI. FREE METHODIST WORLD FELLOWSHIP LEADERS — 1960-1995

Officers:

Presidents:

L.R. Marston	1962-1964
W.S. Kendall	1964-1969
Paul N. Ellis	1969-1974
Myron F. Boyd	1974-1978
W. Dale Cryderman	1976-1979 (acting), 1979-1985
Clyde E. Van Valin	1985-1989
Gerald E. Bates	1989-1995
David M.Foster	1995-

Vice-Presidents:

Kaneo Oda	1962-1964

Elijah Cele	1964-1969
Takesaburo Uzaki	1969-1974
Nathan Gindi	1974-1985
Motoi Hatano	1985-1989
Narendra John	1989-

Secretary-Treasurer:

Hugh A. White	1962-1985
Evelyn L. Mottweiler	1985-1989
Barbara Fox	1989-

Executive Secretary:

Harold Ryckman	1962-1965
V. James Mannoia	1971-1973

Executive Assistant:

Jack H. Mottweiler	1987-1989

Area Fellowships: (Representatives on World Fellowship Board)
Asia:

Jesse Nathar	1962-1964
Felix Canete	1964-1969
Ching-Shen Chen	1969-1974
V.B. Samudre	1974-1979
Ismael Andaya	1979-1989
Jim Tuan	1989-

Central Africa:

Simoni Ndikumazambo (Ruanda-Urundi)	1962-1964
Stefano Rutuna (Rwanda-Burundi)	1964-1969
Jason Mzuri	1969-1974
Aluba Macinda Elyanga	1974-1979
Matayo Myiruko	1979-1989
Noah Nzeyimana	1989-

Latin America:

Joao Mizuki	1962-1964
Teofilo Garcia	1964-1969
Rosario Moreno	1969-1970
Julio Oyama	1972-1974

Expedito Calixto	1974-1979
Yoshikazu Takiya	1979-1989
Valdir Ruiz	1989-

Southern Africa:

Isaac Shembe	1962-1964
Elijah Cele	1964-1974
Naison Chauke	1974-1979
Moses Phiri	1979-1982
Seth Msweli	1989-

North America:

Leslie R. Marston	1962-1964
Hugh A. White	1962-1985
George Fuller	1962-1969
Edward C. John	1962-1969
Walter S. Kendall	1962-1969
W.J. Stonehouse	1964-1974
Paul N. Ellis	1969-1979
Myron F. Boyd	1969-1978
Wesley Skinner	1969-1989
W. Dale Cryderman	1974-1985
Donald N. Bastian	1974-1989
Robert F. Andrews	1979-1989
Elmer E. Parsons	1979-1985
Clyde E. Van Valin	1979-1989
Selwyn Belsher	1979-1989
Richard Ewing	1979-1989
Evelyn Mottweiler	1985-1989
Gerald E. Bates	1985-1989
David M. Foster	1985-1989

North Atlantic:

Gerald E. Bates	1989-
David M. Foster	1989-
Donald N. Bastian	1990-1993
Gary R. Walsh	1993-
Gerald Merrill	1990-
Keith Snyder	1990-1995

M. Doane Bonney	1990-
Richard D. Snyder	1991-
J. Allan Ellershaw	1995-
Ian Van Norman	1995-
Norman Edwards	1995-
Stephanie Crothers	1995-
Ronnie Nesbitt	1995-
Glenn White	1995-
Joe Higginbotham	1995-

VII. LEADERS OF NEW FULL ANNUAL CONFERENCES FORMED — 1960-1995
(Founding Superintendents)
International:
India
Conference Superintendent:

Jesse S. Nathar	1961-1964

District Superintendents:

Moses David	1964-1973
S.R. Bhonsle	1964-1966
S.D. Macasare	1964-1967
Gordon Bell	1964-1968

India Provisional General Conference
President (Bishop):

Daniel T. Ward	1989-1997

Rwanda-Burundi (Ruanda-Urundi)
Co-Superintendents:

Yosefu Rudagaza	1961-1963
Gerald E. Bates	1961-1963

Rwanda
District Superintendents:

Epayineto Rwamunyana	1965-1967, 1968-1976
Paul Orcutt	1965-1967, 1969-1971

Conference Superintendent:

Epayineto Rwamunyana	1967-1968, 1976-1982

Rwanda General Conference
President (Bishop):

Aaron Ruhumuriza	1985-

Burundi
District Superintendents:
Gerald Bates	1964-1967, 1968-1969, 1982-1985
Rumoka M.	1964-1971
Yosefu Rudagaza	1964-1965, 1966-1974
Ronald Collett	1964-1965

Burundi Jurisdictional Conference
President (Bishop):
Noah Nzeyimana	1985-

Philippine
Conference Superintendent:
Felix P. Canete	1963-1972, 1977-1980

District Superintendents:
Enriquita Monencillo	1987-1990
Felipe Paniamogan	1987-1990
Felix P. Canete	1987-1990
Jeremias Palero Sr.	1987-1991

Eastern Mindanao (Philippines)
Conference Superintendent:
Rosendo Campus	1991-

Northern Mindanao (Philippines)
Conference Superintendent:
Victor T. Amandoron	1991-

Southern Mindanao (Philippines)
District Superintendents:
James Paniamogan	1991-1993
Ephraim Agupita	1991-
Jeremias Palero Sr.	1991-

Northern Philippine
Conference Superintendent:
Fernando Frias	1991-

Philippine Provisional General Conference
President (Bishop):
Jim Tuan	1994-

Taiwan (Formosa)
Conference Superintendent:
Wang Yang-Wu	1963-1964

District Superintendents:

Huang P'ei-Min	1978-1979
Lo Cheng-Chi	1978-1979
Hsieh Chin-Yu	1978-1979

Mexican

District Superintendents:

Meliton Moncivaiz	1965-1968
Amado Alvarez	1965-1967, 1972-1975
David Alvarez	1965-1967
Leopoldo A. Padilla	1965-1967

Conference Superintendent:

Jose Gonzalez N.	1968-1970

Mozambique and Transvaal

District Superintendents:

T. Nhachowo	1965-1968
F. Ziuku	1965-1972
J. Gudwani	1965-1970
J.M. Dickinson	1965-1970, 1973-1980
M. Nyachengo	1965-1968
Clifford O. Guyer	1965-1971, 1974-1975
S. Nheve	1965-1970

Central Mozambique

District Superintendents:

Tomas J. Malemane	1992-
Elias M. Matsinhe	1992-
Francisco J. Mahwaye	1992-
Lucas G. Covane	1992-

Southern Mozambique-South Africa Mines

District Superintendents:

Franisse S. Muvile	1992-
Luis Q. Guambe	1992-
Aramando J. Cambule	1992-
Titos S. Mundlovu	1992-

Mozambique Provisional General Conference

President (Bishop):

Luis Uanela Nhaphale	1993-

Transvaal

District Superintendents:

Wesley Crist	1984-1985, 1986-1990
Fillemon Chau	1984-1992

Conference Superintendent:

Trygvar M. Brauteseth	1986-1987
Board of Administration	1992-

Zimbabwe (Rhodesia)

Conference Superintendent:

Tillman Houser	1965-1967

District Superintendents:

Joram Shumba	1967-1969, 1971-1973
	1974-1977, 1981-1982
	1987-1988, 1990-1991
Simon Dziva	1967-1969, 1977-1981
	1982-1984, 1988-1990
Simon Chauke	1967-1969, 1987-1988
Samson Maluleke	1967-1969
Jackson Chauke	1967-1969, 1971-1978
	1982-1984, 1987-1991

Nikkei

Conference Superintendent:

Seiiti Simizu	1966-1970

Brazilian (Paulista)

Conference Superintendent:

Clancy J. Thompson	1966-1970

Zaire

President, Church Council:

Bya'ene Akulu Ilangyi	1975-1989

District Superintendents:

Luhangela Byam'nobe	1975-1985
Bitondo 'Yangya	1975-1984
Wacwamwilelo Mkane	1975-1976, 1977-1984
Mlondami Mwenebunde	1975-1982
Bisengeta Basengelele	1975-1977
Misabeo A'umba	1975-1978

Zaire Northeast
District Superintendents:

Efunga Mbele'elo	1985-
'Yanga Icibangyela	1985-
Bichingini Elema	1985-
Mahota Nduwayo	1985-1987
Mwichwa Asende	1985-1987
Ngini Ababele	1985-
Emedi Luochi Mwenebenga	1985-1988

Zaire Southeast
District Superintendents:

Luhangela Byam'nobe	1985-
Mlanda Dunia	1985-
W'elongo Luhe'ya	1985-1987
M'mumbelwa Lumona	1985-
Bitebetebe Rusingizwa	1985-
Byondo Ngendahayo	1985-
Wilondja Mwenalongwe	1985-
Mahirwe Kaparasi	1985-
Mboko Mkongwa	1985-

Zaire Provisional General Conference
President (Bishop):

Bya'ene Akulu Ilangyi	1989-

Haiti Inland
District Superintendents:

Adrien Oscar	1979-1980, 1981-1983
Jacques Jean-Gilles	1979-1981
Clovis Momplaisir	1979-1989, 1991-

Hong Kong
Conference Superintendent:

Derek Ho	1986-1987

United Kingdom-Great Britain
United Kingdom-Northern Ireland
Conference Superintendent:

Victor Trinder	1982-1988

Canada Jurisdictional Conference: (became General Conference, 1990)
   President:
      Bishop Donald N. Bastian   1974-1990
   Executive Secretaries:
      Claude A. Horton   1977-1985
      Paul G. Johnston   1985-1990

United States:

Arizona
   Conference Superintendent:
      Gilbert C. Ablard   1991-

Centenary
   Conference Superintendent:
      Harold S. Schwab   1960-1963

Pacific Coast Japanese
   Conference Superintendent:
      John M. Miyabe   1964-1985

Pacific Coast Latin American
   District Superintendents:
      Sixto Tarin   1967-1977
      Eleazar Padilla   1967-1970
   Conference Superintendent:
      Victor Rodriguez   1979-1981
      (merged with Southern California 1994)

West Virginia
   Conference Superintendent:
      Roger L. Yeager, Sr.   1992-1995

VIII. PRESIDENTS OF FREE METHODIST COLLEGES — 1960-1995
Aldersgate College/Moose Jaw Bible College
Moose Jaw, Saskatchewan

   J. Wesley Stewart   1958-1967
   Paul H. Buffam   1967-1969
   George E. Leasor   1969-1979
   J. Leon Winslow   1979-1982
   David A. Scott   1983-1985
   Gerald Merrill (acting)   1985-1986

Norman Swanson (interim)	1986-1987
Robert J. Shoaff	1987-1989
Joseph F. James	1989-1995 (closed 1995)

Central College
McPherson, Kansas

Elmer E. Parsons	1955-1964
Bruce L. Kline	1964-1980
Dorsey Brause	1981-1987
Harvey L. Ludwick	1987-1990
John A. Martin	1990-1996
Donald Mason	1996-

Greenville College
Greenville, Illinois

Wilson T. Hogue	1892-1904
Augustin L. Whitcomb	1904-1908
Eldon G. Burritt	1908-1927
Leslie R. Marston	1927-1936
Henry J. Long	1936-1962
Glenn A. Richardson	1962-1970
Orley R. Herron, Jr.	1970-1977
W. Richard Stephens	1977-1993
Robert E. Smith	1993-

Lorne Park College/Foundation
Port Credit, Ontario

Byron Withenshaw	1959-1965
Claude A. Horton	1965-1967

(closed 1967, Foundation established)

Directors:

Claude A. Horton	1967-1971
David Gyertson	1971-1974
Gary Walsh	1974-1977
Claude A. Horton	1977-1985
Paul G. Johnston	1985-

Los Angeles Pacific College
Los Angeles, California

Robert J. Cox   1954-1965
(merged with Azusa Pacific College)

Roberts Wesleyan College
Rochester, New York
Ellwood A. Voller   1957-1968
Lawrence R. Schoenhals   1968-1974
Donald D. Kerlee   1973-1974 (Acting President)
Paul L. Adams   1974-1981
William C. Crothers   1981-

Seattle Pacific Seminary/College/University
Seattle, Washington
C. Dorr Demaray   1959-1968
David L. McKenna   1968-1982
David C. LeShana   1982-1991
Curtis A. Martin
   Provost/Chief Ex. Officer   1991-1992
   President   1992-1994
E. Arthur Self   1994-1995
Philip Eaton
   Provost/Chief Ex. Officer   1995-1996
   President   1996-

Spring Arbor College
Spring Arbor, Michigan
Roderick J. Smith   1958-1961
David L. McKenna   1961-1968
Ellwood A. Voller   1968-1979
Kenneth H. Coffman   1979-1987
Dorsey W. Brause   1987-1991
Allen Carden   1991-1996
James L. Chapman   1997-

Wessington Springs College
Wessington Springs, South Dakota
Robert F. Andrews   1960-1965
Merle S. Olson   1965-1967
D. Robert Short   1967-1968

(Merged with Central College)

John Wesley Seminary Foundation
Directors:

Lawrence R. Schoenhals	1974-1981
Bruce L. Kline	1981-1994
Gerald E. Bates (interim)	1994-1995
Timothy Beuthin	1995-

Cooperating Institutions

Azusa Pacific College/University
Azusa, California

Cornelius P. Haggard	1966-1976
Paul E. Sago	1976-1990
Richard Felix	1990-

Oakdale Christian High School
Jackson, Kentucky

Douglas Newton	1991-1996
Dale Bidwell	1996-

X. RECIPIENTS OF DENOMINATIONAL AWARDS — 1960-1995

Earnest Christian Award

Presented by the Council on Social Action to recognize Free Methodists active in social ministry.

1992	David and Nellie Fenwick
1993	Olive Hodson
1994	Celeste Langer
1995	Rick Clyde

Layperson/Churchman of the Year

Presented at the annual Board of Administration meetings by the Board of Bishops.

1971	Hugh A. White
1972	Roy Harrington
1973	Leslie A. Freeman
1974	Burton L. Murray
1975	Ellwood Voller
1976	Paul T. Walls

1977   Gerald Atkinson
1978   Wesley R. Skinner
1980   Eldon R. Johnson (posthumously)
1981   Paul Lynch
1983   Lyle Stone
1984   Melvin J. Spencer
1985   Wendell Beckwith
1986   Alan Ramm
1987   Nicki Stansberry
1988   Dick Mack
1990   David L. McKenna
1992   Norman L. McCracken
1993   Philip and Sharon Cullison
1994   John W. Rice
1995   Gerald and Berta Merrill

Christian Education Hall of Fame

Presented by the Department of Christian Education at the General Conference for distinguished service in Free Methodist Christian education.

1979   Lloyd H. Knox
1979   Royal S. Nelson
1979   Ben H. Pearson
1979   Floyd M. Todd
1979   Pauline H. Todd
1985   Ernest L. Keasling
1985   Esther Roberts Lyon
1985   Mona McKeown
1989   Robert A. Crandall
1989   Jack H. Mottweiler

XI. MISSIONARIES COMPLETING 25 OR MORE YEARS OF SERVICE — 1920-1995

ADAMSON, Frank	South Africa	1929-1936
and Hazel	Rwanda-Burundi	1937-1964
ADAMSON, Myra	Rwanda	1955-1971
	Zaire	1974-1990

ANDERSON, Myrtle	Kentucky Mountain	
	Mission and School	1926-1947;
		1949-1950
	Japan	1951-1968
BATES, Gerald	Burundi	1958-1971;
and Marlene		1981-1985
	Zaire	1971-1981
BICKSLER, William	Taiwan	1958-1969;
and Marith		1973-1977
		1983-
BONNEY, M. Doane	Dominican Republic	1957-1989
	DWM Home Office	1990-1997
BONNEY, Ruth	Dominican Republic	1957-1989
BRAUTESETH, Trygvar	Transkei and Transvaal	1956-1994
and Anne	(South Africa)	
CANNON, Elizabeth	Paraguay	1949-1966
(Reynolds)	Dominican Republic	1966-1986
CAPP, Phil	Zimbabwe	1958-1976
and Carmena	South Africa	1981-1994
CARTER, Florence	Portuguese East Africa	1949-1979
	(Mozambique)	
CLEMENS, Edwin	Mozambique	1950-1975
and Esther	Haiti	1978-1986
COLLETT, Ronald	Congo-Nile (Burundi)	1936-1967
and Margaret	Haiti	1968-1970
COX, Elizabeth	Burundi	1944-1979
	Rwanda	1980-1986
CRANSTON, Robert	Florida Spanish Mission	1957-1963
and Carolyn	Philippines	1963-1978
	Indonesia	1978-1980
	India	1980
	Philippines	1982-1995
CURRENT, Mary	Natal-Transkei	1945-1958;
	(South Africa)	1962-1979
DAVIS, Roland	India	1919-1964

DAVIS, Melba	India	1919-1937
DAVIS, Muriel	India	1943-1964
DeMILLE, Clarke and Ellen	Southern Rhodesia (Zimbabwe)	1958-1977
	Transvaal (South Africa)	1977-1990
DeMILLE, Wesley and Lela	Portuguese East Africa (Mozambique)	1937-1949
	South Africa	1949-1978; 1979-1980
DeSHAZER, Jacob and Florence	Japan	1948-1978
DICKINSON, Merrill and Edna Mae	Portuguese East Africa (Mozambique)	1938-1970
FENWICK, David and Nellie	Pacific Coast Latin American Mission	1954-1967; 1969-1981
GUYER, Clifford and Myrtle	South Africa	1948-1988
HAIGHT, Gertrude	Natal-Transkei (South Africa)	1945-1963
	Zimbabwe	1971-1977
HARPER, Harry and Mildred	Pacific Coast Latin American Mission	1936-1944; 1946-1967
HAWLEY, Earle and Doreen	Egypt	1959-1967
	Haiti	1967-1968
	Egypt	1969-1986
HEATH, Evelyn (Rupert)	Burundi	1951-1978
	Rwanda	1979-1980; 1984-1985
HESSLER, Ruth	Dominican Republic	1942-1978
HOUSER, Tillman and Gwen	Southern Rhodesia (Zimbabwe)	1948-1961
	South Africa	1963-1964
	Southern Rhodesia (Zimbabwe)	1965-1982

365

HUSTON, Ernest and Lucy	Paraguay	1957-1983
JACOBS, Ila	South Africa	1929-1935;
	Congo-Nile (Burundi)	1937-1946;
	Rwanda	1949-1965
JOHNSON, Warren and Jean	Natal-Transkei (South Africa)	1951-1971; 1975-1980
	Malawi	1980-1983
LAND, Warren and Della	Burundi	1970-1979
	Haiti	1980-
KASTEN, Wilma	Kentucky Mountain Mission & School	1947-1958
	Taiwan	1964-1993
KING, J. Wesley and Mary	Brazil	1955-1972; 1976; 1977-1989
KING, Lily (Horwood)	Mozambique	1946-1977
	South Africa	1979-1980
KIRKPATRICK, Virgil and Martha	Burundi	1964-1978
	Rwanda	1978-1994
	Equatorial Africa	1994-
KLINE, Frank and Betty	India	1936-1964
LINDSAY, Naomi	Egypt	1950-1967
	Haiti	1967-1968
	Egypt	1969-1986
MACY, Victor and Susan	Mozambique	1936-1962; 1971-1973
	South Africa	1963-1967
	Zaire	1969-1971; 1974-1976
	Brazil	1980

MEREDITH, Doris	Burundi	1955-1985
(Moore)	Rwanda	1975-1976
MEREDITH, Lois	Burundi	1969-1982
	Rwanda	1983-1993
	Equatorial Africa	1993-
MORRIS, Ruth	Southern Rhodesia (Zimbabwe)	1952-1976
	Burundi	1977-1984
PERKINS, Nahum	Dominican Republic	1936-1960
and Ruth	Mexico	1961-1963
	Haiti	1964-1965
	Florida Spanish Mission	1965-1966
RABER, Dorothy	Taiwan	1960-1995
REID, Pearl	China	1934-1950
	Japan	1950-1970
RICE, J. Lowell	Natal-Transkei	1938-1963
and Marjorie	(South Africa)	
RIDDLE, Maxine	Haiti	1964-1994
ROOT, Elmer	India	1922-1970
and Loretta		
RYFF, Frederic	Transvaal (South Africa)	1939-1947
	Natal (South Africa)	1947-1953
	Transvaal (South Africa)	1954-1971
	Mozambique	1971-1975
	Southern Rhodesia (Zimbabwe)	1974-1976
	Transvaal (South Africa)	1976-1983
RYFF, Georgia	Portuguese East Africa (Mozambique)	1950-1975
	Southern Rhodesia (Zimbabwe)	1975-1976
	Transvaal (South Africa)	1976-1987
SAYRE, Eldon	Portuguese East Africa	1945-1977
and Florence	(Mozambique)	

SCHLOSSER, John	China	1946-1949
and Ruby	Philippines	1949-1968;
		1977-1981
	Hong Kong	1969-1974
SMIDDERKS, Dean	Transvaal (South Africa)	1963-1968
and Faith	South Africa Mines	1969-
SMILEY, Rachel	Dominican Republic	1929-1947;
		1950-1964
SNIDER, K. Lavern	Japan	1957-1964;
and Lois		1968-1992
SNYDER, C. Albert	Burundi	1955-1961
and Louise	Natal-Transkei	1962-1963
	(South Africa)	
	Rwanda	1968-1991
STILLMAN, James	Zaire	1970-1990
and Barbara	Burundi	1991-1994
	Equatorial Africa	1994-
STRAIT, Virginia	Southern Rhodesia	1948-1977
	(Zimbabwe)	
	Rwanda	1979-1980
STREUTKER, Raymond	Philippines	1952-1971;
and Loraine		1974-1986
TAYLOR, James Hudson	China	1926-1946
and Alice	Taiwan	1953-1967
TAYLOR, James H. III	Taiwan	1954-1980
and Leone		
TITE, Verna	Mozambique	1946-1977
WILLARD, Burleigh	Dominican Republic	1945-1959
and Alma	Mexico	1959-1985
WINSLOW, Harry	Hong Kong	1963-1966;
and Ruth	Taiwan	1966-1982
	Hong Kong	1983-

Endnotes

Prologue

1. Robert Bellah, *Habits of the Heart: Individualism and Commitment in American Life* (New York: Harper and Row, 1985), 152.
2. Bellah, Ibid., 134.
3. Bellah, Ibid., 333.
4. Bellah, Ibid.
5. Bellah, Ibid., 282.
6. William Bridges, *Transitions: Making Sense of Life's Changes* (Reading, MA: Addison-Wesley, 1980), 550.

Chapter 1

1. Ichak Adizes, *Corporate Lifecycles* (Englewood Cliffs, NJ: Prentice Hall, 1988), Part I, Chapters 1-4.
2. Charles E. White, "Grandmother of Free Methodism," *Light and Life* (June 1985): 14.
3. Richard R. Blews, *Master Workmen: Biographies of the Late Bishops of the Free Methodist Church During Her First Century, 1860-1960* (Winona Lake: Light and Life Press, 1960), 22-23.
4. Elton O. Smith, "B.T. Roberts - Speaking Out for Freedom," *Light and Life* (February 1993): 11.
5. B.T. Roberts, "New School Methodism," *The Northern Independent* (1857).
6. Blews, *Master Workmen*, 36-37.
7. "Notice for Camp Meeting and Conventions," *The Earnest Christian* (September 1860): 260.
8. Benson H. Roberts, *Benjamin Titus Roberts* (North Chili, NY: Earnest Christian Office, 1900), 235.
9. From the preface to *Hymns and Sacred Poems* (1739), para. 5, p. viii.
10. Leslie R. Marston, *From Age to Age A Living Witness* (Indianapolis: Light and Life Press, 1960), 274.
11. Benson H. Roberts, *Holiness Teachings* (North Chili, NY: Earnest Christian Publishing House, 1893).
12. Benson, H. Roberts, *Benjamin Titus Roberts* (North Chili, NY: Earnest Christian Office, 1900), 321 ff.
13. B.T. Roberts, "Editorial," *The Earnest Christian* (July 1861): 226-27.
14. Marston, *From Age to Age*, 427.

15. *Book of Discipline*, 1891, para. 201, p. 81.
16. Marston, *From Age to Age*, 434.
17. Marston, Ibid., 360.
18. Marston, Ibid., 499.
19. Nathan Hatch, *The Democratization of American Christianity* (New Haven and London: Yale University Press, 1989), 217.
20. B.T. Roberts, "Mission Field," *The Earnest Christian* (June 1862), 187.
21. *Book of Discipline*, 1989, para. B1030, p. 194.

Chapter 2

1. Benson H. Roberts, *Benjamin Titus Roberts: A Biography* (North Chili, NY: The Earnest Christian Office, 1900), 550.
2. Leslie R. Marston, *From Age to Age A Living Witness* (Indianapolis: Light and Life Press, 1960), 436.
3. Marston, Ibid., 436.
4. Marston, Ibid., 437.
5. Marston, Ibid., 439.
6. *Book of Discipline*, 1915, para. 119, p. 56.
7. Marston, *From Age to Age*, 500.
8. Marston, Ibid., 501.
9. Marston, Ibid., 442.
10. Marston, Ibid., 422.
11. Marston, Ibid.
12. Marston, Ibid., 447.
13. Marston, Ibid., 441.
14. Marston, Ibid., 379.
15. Marston, Ibid., 469.

Chapter 3

1. Leslie R. Marston, *From Age to Age A Living Witness* (Indianapolis: Light and Life Press, 1960), 252.
2. Marston, Ibid., 572.
3. *Book of Discipline of the Free Methodist Church in Canada*, 1993, 10.
4. *Book of Discipline*, 1995, para. A119, p. 13.
5. *Book of Discipline*, 1923, para. 248a:6(1), p. 149.
6. Marston, *From Age to Age*, 187.
7. Marston, Ibid.
8. Marston, Ibid.
9. Marston, Ibid., 576.
10. Marston, Ibid., 331.
11. B.T. Roberts, "Fanaticism," *The Earnest Christian* 2 (February 1892): 40.
12. Marston, *From Age to Age*, 359.

13. Marston, Ibid., 407.
14. Marston, Ibid., 507.
15. Marston, Ibid., 385.
16. *Book of Discipline*, 1995, para. A336, p. 49.
17. Marston, *From Age to Age*, 466.
18. Marston, Ibid., 466.
19. *Book of Discipline*, 1882, para. 151-53, p. 67.
20. Marston, *From Age to Age*, 562.

Chapter 4

1. David L. McKenna, *The Coming Great Awakening* (Downers Grove, IL.: InterVarsity Press), 20.
2. Wade Clark Roof, *A Generation of Seekers* (San Francisco: HarperCollins, 1993), Chapter II.
3. Robert E. Coleman, *One Divine Moment* (Old Tappan, NF: Fleming H. Revell Company, 1970).
4. Daniel Yankelovich, *New Rules: Searching for Self-fulfillment in a World Turned Upside Down* (New York: Random House, 1981), 4-5.
5. Studs Terkel, *The Great Divide: Second Thoughts on the American Dream* (New York: Pantheon Press, 1988), 11-12.
6. Yankelovich, *New Rules*, 244-64.
7. Walbert Buhlmann, *The Coming of the Third Church* (Maryknoll, NY: Orbis Books, 1972), 11-12.
8. Buhlmann, Ibid.
9. Joel Barker, *Future Edge* (New York: Wm. Morrow and Company, 1992), 32.
10. Robert Bruce Mullin and Russell E. Richey, eds., *Reimagining Denominationalism* (Oxford: Oxford Univ. Press, 1994), 87.
11. Mullin and Richey, LOC.CIT.
12. Mullin and Richey, Ibid., 90.
13. Leith Anderson, *Dying for Change* (Minneapolis, MN: Bethany House Publishers, 1990), 137.
14. Keith Drury, "The Holiness Movement Is Dead," *Holiness Digest* (Winter 1994): 13-15.
15. Kenneth Boulding, *The Meaning of the Twentieth Century: The Great Transition* (New York: Harper Colophon Books, 1965).
16. Roof, *A Generation of Seekers*, Chapter II.

Chapter 5

1. Leslie R. Marston, *From Age to Age A Living Witness* (Indianapolis: Light and Life Press, 1960), 299.
2. "Our Centenary Trust," Pastoral Address, 1960.
3. Pastoral Address, 1960.

4. *Book of Discipline*, 1995, Para. A/119, p. 13.
5. Marston, *From Age to Age*, 379.
6. Robert Walter Wall, "The Embourgeoisement of the Free Methodist Ethos: A Content-Analysis of The Free Methodist's Disciplines' Idea of the Christian Life, *Wesleyan Theological Journal* no. 25 (1990): 117-29.

Chapter 6

1. Leslie R. Marston, *From Age to Age A Living Witness* (Indianapolis: Light and Life Press, 1960), 421.
2. *Executive Handbook*, World Ministries Center (January 1994), 4.
3. *Executive Handbook*, Ibid., 8.
4. World Conference Constitution, Para. A/253, Item 1.
5. Robert J. Buchanan, "The Development of Ecclesiastical Autonomy for the Free Methodist Church in Canada." D. Min. Dissertation., Asbury Theological, 1990.
6. Buchanan, Ibid., 50.
7. Buchanan, Ibid., 62.
8. Buchanan, Ibid., 63.
9. Buchanan, Ibid., 90.
10. Buchanan, Ibid., 133-134.
11. The 1990 Canadian Report, The Free Methodist Church in Canada, Donald N. Bastian, Bishop.
12. Keith Elford, "Changes at Canadian General Conference," *Light and Life* (March 1995): 18.
13. *Free Methodist Herald*, no. 1 (January/February, 1996): 4.
14. Gary Walsh, Vision Paper, 1994 Canadian General Conference.
15. Wayne Kleinsteuber, "A Rich Heritage," *Light and Life* (August 1990): 9.
16. Leslie R. Marston, "It is Now Your Turn," *The Free Methodist* (November 3, 1953): 3.
17. The Constitution of the Free Methodist World Fellowship, Article II — Purpose.
18. The Constitution of the Free Methodist World Fellowship, Article VII — Area Fellowships.
19. Agenda Paper — Asia Fellowship, April 1960.
20. Africa Area Fellowship, 1962.
21. Report of the Committee on the Church, Asia Area Fellowship Conference, 1962.
22. Report by Byron S. Lamson, March 1962.
23. Lamson, Ibid.
24. Adopted by The Free Methodist World Fellowship, June 30, 1995.

Chapter 7

1. "The Forward Movement and Free Methodism's New Century Advance," A paper presented by the Bishops of the Free Methodist Church, December 7, 1960.
2. "Our Centenary Trust," Pastoral Address, 1960.
3. An open letter to all church leaders from Walter S. Kendall, Coordinator, The Forward Movement, March 16, 1961.
4. Joel Arthur Barker, *Future Edge* (New York: William Morrow, 1992), 32.
5. Max DePree, *Leadership Is An Art* (New York: Bantum-Doubleday, 1990), 60.

Chapter 8

1. Leslie R. Marston, *From Age to Age A Living Witness* (Indianapolis: Light and Life Press, 1960), 273.
2. John Wesley, *The Nature, Design, and General Rules of the United Societies*, Par. 5.
3. Myron F. Boyd, World Mission Brochure #1, The Committee on Promotion and Coordination, *The Free Methodist* (April 27, 1965): 13.
4. B.H. Gaddis, "Historical Sketch," *The Free Methodist* (November 6, 1936): 3.
5. Marston, *From Age to Age*, 482-83.
6. Marston, Ibid., 483.
7. Lloyd H. Knox, "Light and Life: A New Name," *Light and Life* (July 1970): 2.
8. Board of Administration *Minutes*, October 1986, 123-24.
9. Executive Reports, 1995, Robert B. Haslam, Editor, *Light and Life* magazine.

Chapter 9

1. "A Call to Action," Addressed to Free Methodists. St. Petersburg, Florida, December 11, 1995.
2. Leslie R. Marston, *From Age to Age A Living Witness* (Indianapolis: Light and Life Press, 1960), 420.

Chapter 10

1. *Book of Discipline*. 1860, p. 4.
2. Special Report. Department of Evangelism and Church Growth, Ray W. Ellis, Director, July 20, 1994.
3. Leslie R. Marston, *From Age to Age A Living Witness* (Indianapolis: Light and Life Press, 1960), 436.
4. 1969 Quinquennial Report. Department of Evangelism and Outreach, Dale A. Woods, Director.
5. 1969 General Conference *Minutes*, pp. 322-23.
6. Report of the Director of Evangelism and Church Growth to the 1985 General Conference, quoting Peter Wagner at the Church Growth Conference in Hous-

ton, 1985.
7. Executive Report to the 1989 General Conference. Department of Evangelism and Church Growth, Ray W. Ellis, Director.
8. "Effective Evangelism: Training and Equipping for Lifestyle Evangelism, Resource Packet." Department of Evangelism and Church Growth.
9. 1964 Quadrennial Report. Light and Life Hour Director, Myron F. Boyd.
10. Ibid.

Chapter 11
1. "Missions at the Cutting Edge." Missions Quinquennial Report, 1974 General Conference.

Chapter 12
1. Paraphrase from Frank Gaebelein, *Christian Education in a Democracy;* cited by Leslie R. Marston, *From Age to Age A Living Witness* (Indianapolis: Light and Life Press, 1960), 497.
2. Quinquennial Report of the General Sunday School Secretary, 1960.
3. Executive Reports. Department of Christian Education, 1995 General Conference.

Chapter 13
1. Report of the Secretary of the Department of Higher Education and the Ministry, 1985.

Chapter 14
1. *1995 Book of Discipline,* Para. A/332.2.
2. Report of the 1969 General Conference Committee on Christian Social Action.
3. Leslie R. Marston, *From Age to Age A Living Witness* (Indianapolis: Light and Life Press, 1960), 418.
4. B.T. Roberts, *Ordaining Women: Biblical and Historical Insights* (Indianapolis: Light and Life Press, 1992), 104.
5. *Minutes,* 1911 General Conference; cited by Marston, *From Age to Age,* Ibid., 419.

Chapter 15
1. Leslie R. Marston, *From Age to Age A Living Witness* (Indianapolis: Light and Life Press, 1960), 564.
2. Marston, Ibid., 562.
3. Marston, Ibid., 466.

Chapter 17

1. John Naisbitt, *Megatrends* (New York: Warner Books, 1982).
2. Jacques Ellul, *The Technological Bluff* (Grand Rapids: William Beerdmans, September 1990).
3. Robert N. Bellah, *Habits of the Heart: Individualism and Commitment in American Life* (New York: 1985), 28.
4. Russell Chandler, *Racing Toward 2001* (Grand Rapids: Zondervan, 1992), 28.
5. Ibid., 19.
6. Leith Anderson, *A Church for the 21st Century* (Minneapolis: Bethany House Publishers, 1992).
7. Lyle E. Schaller, *Strategies for Change* (Nashville: Abingdon, 1993), 66-67.
8. Robert Bruce Mullin and Russell E. Richey, eds., *Reimagining Denominationalism* (New York: Oxford University Press, 1994), 89.
9. Ibid.
10. Ibid., 90.
11. Schaller, *Strategies for Change*, 142.

Chapter 18

1. Thomas C. Oden, *After Modernity ... What?* (Grand Rapids: Zondervan, 1990).
2. Russell Chandler, *Racing Toward 2001* (Grand Rapids: Zondervan, 1992), 20.
3. Lyle E. Schaller, *21 Bridges to the 21st Century* (Nashville: Abingdon, 1994), Chapter 15.
4. Ibid., 144.

Chapter 19

1. Lyle E. Schaller, *Bridges to the 21st Century* (Abingdon Press: Nashville, 1994), 143.
2. Howard A. Snyder, "To Preach the Gospel to the Poor: Missional Self-Understanding in Early Free Methodism 1860-90." *Wesleyan Theological Journal*, vol. 31, no. 1 (Spring, 1996): 7-39.
3. Douglas R. Cullum, "From Simplicity to Multiplicity: Sunday Worship in the Free Methodist Tradition." A chapter in the book *20th Century Worship in the Methodist Tradition*, ed., Karen Westerfield Tucker (Nashville: Abingdon/Kingswood, 1995-1996).
4. B.T. Roberts, "Object and Scope of this Magazine," *The Earnest Christian*, vol. 1, no. 1 (January 1860): 5.
5. B.T. Roberts, *The Earnest Christian*, vol. 1, no. 1 (March 1860): 69-74.

Epilogue

1. B.T. Roberts, "Convention at Pekin," *The Earnest Christian*, vol. 1, no. 9 (September 1860), 291.

I N D E X

Biographical

Subject